Reading Poulantzas

READING POULANTZAS

Edited by
Alexander Gallas, Lars Bretthauer
John Kannankulam & Ingo Stützle

MERLIN PRESS

First published in Germany in 2006 by VSA: Verlag as:
Poulantzas lesen
This English translation first published 2011
by The Merlin Press
6 Crane Street Chambers
Crane Street
Pontypool
NP4 6ND
Wales

www.merlinpress.co.uk

© the contributors, 2011

ISBN. 978-0-85036-647-1

British Library Cataloguing in Publication Data is available from the British Library

Cover photo courtesy VSA Verlag

CONTENTS

Notes on the Editors 7

Notes on the Contributors 7

Introduction 9

Clyde W. Barrow
(Re)reading Poulantzas:
state theory and the epistemologies of structuralism 27

Bob Jessop
Poulantzas's *State, Power, Socialism* as a modern classic 41

Joachim Hirsch and John Kannankulam
Poulantzas and form analysis: on the relation between
two approaches to historical-materialist state theory 56

Lars Bretthauer
Materiality and condensation in the work of Nicos Poulantzas ... 72

Alexander Gallas
Reading 'Capital' with Poulantzas: 'form' and 'struggle'
in the critique of political economy 89

Max Koch
Poulantzas's class analysis 107

Jörg Nowak
Poulantzas, gender relations and feminist state theory 122

Urs T. Lindner
State, domination and politics: on the relationship
between Poulantzas and Foucault 138

Sonja Buckel
The juridical condensation of relations of forces:
Nicos Poulantzas and law 154

Ingo Stützle
The order of knowledge: the state as a knowledge apparatus ... 170

Markus Wissen
Territory and historicity: space and time in Nicos Poulantzas's *State, Power, Socialism* — 186

Hans-Jürgen Bieling
European statehood — 201

Jens Wissel
The transnationalization of the bourgeoisie and the new networks of power — 216

Thomas Sablowski
Crisis and statehood in the work of Nicos Poulantzas — 231

Ulrich Brand and Miriam Heigl
'Inside' and 'outside': the state, movements and 'radical transformation' in the work of Nicos Poulantzas — 246

Alex Demirovi
Rule of the people? Democracy and the capitalist state in the work of Nicos Poulantzas — 261

Peter Thomas
Conjuncture of the integral state? Poulantzas's reading of Gramsci — 277

Abbreviated References — 293

Name Index — 295

Subject Index — 297

Notes on the Editors

Dr. Alexander Gallas teaches at the Department of Asian and African Studies, Humboldt University of Berlin. He works on Karl Marx and Nicos Poulantzas; the political economies of Great Britain and Germany; and class, crisis, and the state.

Lars Bretthauer is a PhD candidate at the Department of Political Science (OSI), Free University of Berlin. He works on materialist state theory, the politics of surveillance and intellectual property rights.

Dr. John Kannankulam is Junior Professor for Political Economy and European Integration at the Institute for Political Science, Marburg University, Germany. He works on the political economies of Great Britain and Germany; European integration and migration; and (Marxist) state theory.

Ingo Stützle is an editor at the monthly ak - analyse & kritik and a PhD candidate at the Department of Political Science, Marburg University. He works on the Critique of Political Economy; materialist state theory; and European Integration.

Notes on the Contributors

Clyde W. Barrow is Chancellor Professor of Public Policy and Director of the Center for Policy Analysis at the University of Massachusetts, Dartmouth. He specializes in political economy and political theory with an emphasis on state theory and higher education policy.

Ulrich Brand is Professor of International Politics, at the Institute of Political Science, University of Vienna.

Hans-Jürgen Bieling is Professor of Politics and the Organization of Civil Society at Bremen University of Applied Science. He works on International Political Economy, European Integration, and state, political and social theory.

Sonja Buckel works at the Institute for Social Research (IfS), Goethe University Frankfurt. She is the head of a research project on the transnationalization of the state and European migration control policy.

Alex Demirović teaches political theory at the Berlin Institute of Technology (TU Berlin) and works on critical social theory in the areas of nature, economic development, the state, and culture.

Joachim Hirsch is Professor Emeritus, Faculty of the Social Sciences, Goethe University Frankfurt. He works on state theory, the theory of capitalism, and international political economy.

Miriam Heigl is head of the specialist department for tackling right-wing extremism at Munich City Council. Her main research topics are privatization processes, landgrabbing, Latin America, political theory in general and state theory in particular.

Bob Jessop is Distinguished Professor for Sociology and Co-Director of the Cultural Political Economy Research Centre at Lancaster University. He works on the changes in contemporary capitalism and the dynamics of 'variegated capitalism'; changes in the state's form, scale, and functions; governance; cultural political economy; and the strategic-relational approach.

Max Koch is an associate professor in sociology and social policy at the School of Social Work and Social Welfare, Lund University. His research interests include political economy, social theory, industrial relations and the analysis of social structures, labour markets and welfare regulation, particularly in comparative perspective.

Urs Lindner, currently living in Berlin, has written a PhD thesis on 'Marx and Philosophy: Critique of Metaphysics, Scientific Realism and Moral Perfectionism'.

Jörg Nowak is a political scientist living in Berlin who works on Marxist and feminist state theory. He actively participates in workplace struggles in the service industries and in struggles around social welfare.

Thomas Sablowski is teaching Political Science and lives in Frankfurt, Germany.

Peter Thomas, Lecturer in the History of Political Thought, Department of Politics and History, Brunel University. He is currently working on critical study of recent debates on the notion of the political.

Jens Wissel works at the Institute for Social Research (IfS), Goethe University Frankfurt. He is currently part of a research project on the transnationalisation of the state and European migration control policy.

Markus Wissen is assistant professor at the University of Vienna, Institute of Political Science. His research focuses on the spatial dimensions of the transformation of the state, on societal relationships with nature and on international environmental politics.

INTRODUCTION

We first published this volume in German in 2006.[1] Back then, we observed a rise of left-wing movements and parties in Germany and beyond that were in one way or another contesting neoliberal capitalism. In this situation, we proposed to revisit Nicos Poulantzas's works. In our view, left-wing activists and politicians were facing, once more, a question that had bothered Poulantzas throughout his life and time as a socialist scholar: considering there is a capitalist state, what are the political conditions for a socialist transformation? In our view, Poulantzas offered important insights into the workings of the capitalist state and politics under capitalist conditions, which had been buried when the edifice of post-war Marxist social theory had been brought down by the global advance of neoliberalism and the downfall of authoritarian socialism in Eastern Europe. We inferred that it was time to recover these insights from the rubble.

Today, the issue of the relationship between left politics and the capitalist state remains as valid as ever. And yet, we have entered a new conjuncture, in which the advance of left-wing political forces appears to have stalled. In other words, our political observations from 2006 seem overly optimistic. Nonetheless, we contend that Poulantzas is more relevant than ever. The near-collapse of the global financial system poses a serious challenge to the neo-classical, institutionalist, and pluralist accounts of contemporary statehood and contemporary capitalism that have been dominant in the last three decades. In contrast to the scholars associated with these traditions, Poulantzas was grappling with systematic links between the three issues that define the current conjuncture: crisis, the state, and class. Moreover, he concerned himself with the authoritarian ways in which capitalist crises are managed.

Our decision to make our book available in English was not solely motivated by the fact that Poulantzas's interventions are highly topical. It also represents a modest yet serious attempt to break down some of the linguistic barriers that still blight Marxist and broader left-wing debates.

1   Bretthauer, Lars/Gallas, Alexander/Kannankulam/Stützle, Ingo (eds.) (2006) *Poulantzas lesen: Zur Aktualität marxistischer Staatstheorie* (Hamburg: VSA-Verlag).

Whereas political leaders, top-level bureaucrats and key representatives of capital are part of more or less closely integrated transnational networks, the same does not hold for left-wing activists committed to contesting and transforming the global capitalist order – at least not to the same degree. Consequently, we see it as our responsibility to work towards redressing this imbalance. Obviously, our book is as provincial as any other. It captures debates that more often than not remain ignorant of how certain concerns and ideas are specific to the language area they have arisen in. By translating the book, we certainly want to encourage criticism from outside our linguistic comfort zone. But we also would like to highlight issues that we believe deserve more attention in English-language debates. Both may be necessary in order to establish truly internationalized Marxist debates, which are sensitive to regional specificities as well as global tendencies.

1. Why Marxist state theory?

Poulantzas develops a 'theory of the capitalist type of state' (Hirsch et al. 2002: 7; translated). In so doing, he aligns himself with the Marxist tradition in state theory. Obviously, this tradition is fairly marginal in the social sciences today, especially compared to the 1970s. So why have we chosen to revisit it? In our view, Marxist approaches are better equipped than mainstream ones in terms of capturing the fact that contemporary societies and states are pervaded by relations of domination. We see three instances of this:

    i. Marxist approaches analyze the state and the political in conjunction with the capitalist character of the economy. Marx's analysis of the capitalist relations of production in the *Critique of Political Economy* raises the question of how they constitute, stabilize and destabilize state structures. Along these lines, Poulantzas emphasizes the "constitutive presence" of the state in the relations of production (SPS: 17f.). Marxist state theories do not view statehood as an 'innocent' institutional arrangement. They stress the key role of state institutions in the reproduction of capitalist relations of exploitation. The contributors to the West German state derivation debate in the 1970s[2] may have struggled with analyzing real-concrete states (cf. Jessop 1982: 78ff.)[3], but they were still able to show that under capitalist conditions there are systematic limits to state interventionism. They successfully criticized the 'welfare state illusion', which guided mainstream politics in Western Europe at the time.

    ii. Marxist state theories go against conceptions of the state that portray it

---

2   See the overview provided in Holloway/Picciotto (1978).

3   See also Hirsch/Kannankulam in this volume.

as an expression of 'professionalized reason'. Contrary to commonplace perceptions, the state does not constitute a shell protecting any kind of political project, but is in fact the political form in which the hegemony of the bourgeoisie is organized. Nonetheless, it can only be grasped if the specificities of the projects inscribed in it are also taken into account. Following Poulantzas, the processes by which hegemony is organized can be understood as a 'material condensation of relationships of forces' (SPS: 128f.), i.e., as the integration of very different political forces and interests into state politics by way of institutional mediation, obstruction and amplification. Accordingly, Poulantzasian conceptions of the state go against assumptions of 'unitary statehood'. They focus on analysing the selective representation of societal interests and the social relations of forces within state apparatuses, which tend to benefit specific fractions of capital.

iii. Marxist state theory is characterized by its explicit references to left-wing political strategies. In so doing, it is not so much analyzing facts, but potentials for the transformation of specific state configurations. Such references can be found in Antonio Gramsci's reflections on Italian Fascism in the *Prison Notebooks*; in the debate about the welfare state following on from an article by Wolfgang Müller and Christel Neusüß (1970); in Poulantzas's engagement with Eurocommunism and his reflections on the conditions for a transition to a democratic socialism, which were inspired by Rosa Luxemburg (SPS: 251, 265); and in contemporary approaches that base their strategies of overcoming different relations of domination simultaneously on a materialist conception of the state (Demirović/Pühl 1998). Obviously, addressing strategic questions always also involves discussing how post-capitalist societies could and should be organized politically.

2. Why Poulantzas?

Poulantzas occupies a unique position within 20th century Marxism. His biography shows this: born just before World War II, he was too young to be considered one of the 'greats' of the immediate post-war era, who came to be regarded as the intellectual forebears of the revolt of 1968.[4] Since he committed suicide in 1979, he also did not witness the massive

---

[4] This is not to suggest that Poulantzas was ignored at that time: 'At the beginning of the 1970s, his work was being so unusually widely read in the very important field of Sociopolitics that in René Lourau and George Lapassade's textbook *Clés pour la sociologie* [...] he became the single most represented sociologist: "Everywhere they accused us of having granted Poulantzas an enormous amount of space in our book, but back then, that seemed only natural to us"' (Dosse 1999: 216).

loss of influence suffered by Marxist scholars from his own generation as a result of the neoliberal offensive of the 1980s and the rupture of 1989. This makes Poulantzas particularly interesting. For example, he discussed the dissolution of the Fordist mode of development well *before* the rupture of 1989 produced tectonic shifts within leftist discourses. In our view, this has not necessarily had a negative impact on his work. He reflected on the transformations in capitalism and the challenges posed by the petrification of Marxist theory without having to make concessions to the post- or even anti-Marxist *Zeitgeist* that became hegemonic in the period following the collapse of authoritarian socialism.[5] Unsurprisingly, many of Poulantzas's themes and insights became obscured in the course of this epochal transformation. Yet we contend that they are still useful for analyzing capitalist societalization in general, the authoritarian implementation of neoliberalism and its current dominance, as well as the conditions for a renewal of socialist politics.

Poulantzas's insights into the character of the capitalist state are the result of a lifetime's work. His intellectual biography is shaped by the dominant theoretical developments of the respective phases of his life, but also – and this is crucial – by the contemporary politico-historical context that shaped them.

Just before the events of May 1968 in Paris, Poulantzas completed his first major book, *Political Power and Social Classes* (PPSC). In it, he sketches a 'regional' theory of the state. This is inspired by Louis Althusser's assumption that capitalist societies constitute 'articulations' of 'relatively autonomous' regions, namely the economy, politics/the state and ideology.

Poulantzas became more widely known thanks to his debate with Ralph Miliband that started in 1969.[6] This debate was largely an epistemological one. Whereas Miliband wanted to grasp and criticize the capitalist state by way of empirical research, Poulantzas's aim was to create the conceptual and theoretical prerequisites for such an empirical engagement. Although this debate did bring certain fundamental questions to the fore, its dominance in the reception of Poulantzas's work prevented an open engagement with the latter's complexity.

Poulantzas's second main work is his 1970 book *Fascism and Dictatorship* (FD). He provides a primarily class-based analysis of the rise of fascism in Italy and Germany, in which he highlights the differences between exceptional regimes. In so doing, he rejected blanket denunciations of the Greek coup d'état or Charles de Gaulle's Vth Republic as 'fascist'.

5 Note Poulantzas's critique of the French 'new philosophers' in SPS (45, 112, 149, 203).
6 See Clyde Barrow's contribution to this volume and his account of the debate from 2002.

Poulantzas repeats his call in *The Crisis of the Dictatorships* (CD), published in 1975. Here he applies his state-theoretical concepts to the imploding military dictatorships of Greece, Portugal and Spain, and spells out its implications for a political strategy of the left. Poulantzas emphasizes that the regimes in question had perished not due to a frontal outside attack by insurgents, but because of internal contradictions that resulted from the incoherence of state apparatuses in military dictatorships.

This work is also evidence of Poulantzas's increasing doubts about the formalist structuralism of the Althusser-school, which had already become apparent in his 1974 book *Classes in Contemporary Capitalism* (CCC). This text dealt with questions of class theory, in particular with the effects of supervisory tasks in production on the constitution of classes, and with question of political strategy. It also focused on (US-) imperialism and the looming crisis of Fordism.

Poulantzas's final book, *State, Power, Socialism* (SPS), represents at once the 'culmination' of his theoretical development and a departure towards new theoretical and political horizons. Poulantzas contends that the state is characterized by its co-constitutive presence in the capitalist relations of production. In so doing, he rejects dichotomous interpretations of the relationship between state and economy, which either portray the state as an instrument of the ruling class or as a subject capable of neutralizing the inequalities resulting from capitalist production. Poulantzas develops a relational conception of the capitalist state, which is summarized in his famous statement that it constitutes the 'material condensation of a relationship of forces' (128f.). Finally, Poulantzas emphasizes that 'democratic socialism' remains on the agenda, thereby responding to the rise of a new form of capitalist state that emerged as a result of the 1970s crisis in the capitalist metropolises: authoritarian statism (cf. Kannankulam 2008).

3. Poulantzas's heritage

Poulantzas was all but forgotten soon after his death. This was probably also due to the fact that he had remained faithful to the Marxist project. When anti-Marxist stances became dominant in the social sciences in the 1980s, his work no longer received much attention. And yet, he left some traces even in debates that had no obvious connection to Marxism. Accordingly, it makes sense to examine how Poulantzas's heritage was taken up.[7]

---

7   Obviously, mapping out the influence of an author who had an impact on the social sciences for more than three decades is a mammoth task. We do not claim this overview to be exhaustive. Rather it should be seen as demarcating the intellectual context out of

3.1. Poulantzas and the social sciences

Soon after Poulantzas's death, a number of scholars began to adopt themes found in Poulantzas's works, and integrated them into their own research agendas. The engagement with Poulantzas is an ongoing process. This is not only demonstrated by the existence of this volume, but also by the release of a slightly revamped English-language edition of SPS in 2000, and the recent publication of a *Poulantzas Reader* (Martin 2008).

By far the most comprehensive appraisals of Poulantzas's writings can be found in two monographs, one written in English (Jessop 1985), the other in German (Demirović 1987).[8] Both books reconstruct his theoretical and political development as a state theorist and political intellectual, and draw on his ideas in order to further develop Marxist state theory. In particular, Bob Jessop's work (1990; 2002; 2008) can be seen as an attempt to continue the theoretical project begun by Poulantzas. Jessop stresses the relational character of Poulantzas's conception of the state (1985: 114ff., 336ff.), while at the same time criticizing his ultimate failure to explain the relative autonomy of the state (131ff.). He suggests adopting the concept of strategy in order to close this gap, and integrating form-analytical theory and historic-concrete analyses of capitalist statehood and of its contested nature (340ff.). Jessop terms his own theoretical approach to state theory and political analysis the "strategic-relational approach" (2002: 36).

Alex Demirović makes Poulantzas's sometimes cumbersome theory (and language) accessible, and explains it with reference to theories of hegemony in the Gramscian vein. He chooses to proceed in a systematic, not an historical fashion, and he does so by explaining Poulantzas's stance on different epistemological 'objects' such as the social formation, the mode of production, class, the state and the state form. In the second edition of the book, Demirović also discusses the concept of condensation in the light of psycho-analytical approaches in the Lacanian vein, and reiterates Poulantzas's claim that there is an internationalization of the state by introducing the concept of the 'transnational network state'.

Stuart Hall is another author who has drawn upon Poulantzas's state theory. In 1978, he, Chas Critcher, Tony Jefferson, John N. Clarke, and Brian Roberts authored a study of British post-war capitalism, and argued that there was a crisis of hegemony (319), which resulted in the emergence of an exceptional state (272). This echoed the analyses provided by Poulantzas

---

which *Reading Poulantzas* emerged.

8 Poulantzas's work also received critical acclaim in three edited collections: Buci-Glucksmann (1983); an issue of the *Journal of the Hellenic Diaspora* from 1999, and Aronowitz/Bratsis (2002).

in FD and CD. Moreover, Poulantzas had argued in SPS that the capitalist type of state was being remodelled into an 'authoritarian statist' entity supplementing its normal form with exceptional elements (203ff.). Similarly, Hall et al. stated: 'One of the deep structural shifts underway throughout the whole of our period, which is masked by the more immediate, phenomenal forms of the "crisis", is indeed the massive reconstruction of the position, role and character of the capitalist state in general. This involved the progressive intervention of the state into spheres – the economic mechanisms of capital itself on the one hand, the whole sphere of ideological relations and social reproduction on the other – hitherto formally regarded as belonging to the independent spheres of "civil society"' (1978: 303). Against this backdrop, Hall and Martin Jacques later identified Thatcherism as 'authoritarian populism' (1983: 10).

Bob Jessop, Kevin Bonnett, Simon Bromley, and Tom Ling in turn criticized this term for being unspecific and contradictory (1988: 71f.). Drawing on Poulantzas's method in FD,[9] they supplied their own analysis of Thatcherism according to which the latter was based on an authoritarian strategy that divided Britain into two 'nations' and was ultimately incapable of becoming hegemonic (88f.).

Poulantzas's inquiries into authoritarian state forms, especially FD, influenced debates on theories of fascism. David Abraham (1981) applied them to the breakdown of the Weimar Republic and the rise of German fascism. However, Poulantzas is also criticized heavily in this field. Ernesto Laclau (1977) accuses him of jumping too quickly from a class place to a purported corresponding ideology, and of thus having paid too little attention to the successful 'interpellation' of subaltern classes by fascism.[10]

A related field of inquiry is that of imperialism. For Poulantzas, a follower of many of Lenin's (but not Marxist-Leninist) positions, this formed a central aspect of his analysis. Every one of his major works contains thoughts on this subject. But it was his central text on the subject, *Internationalisation of Capitalist Relations and the Nation-State* (INT)[11] that became better known.[12] This essay has shaped concrete analyses as well as theoretical concepts in multiple ways. Most noteworthy is the work of Leo Panitch, a student of

---

9   See Jessop's remarks in the Notes on the Contributors in the German edition of this book.
10 For a rejoinder, see Thomas Sablowski's chapter in this volume.
11 Initially, INT was a standalone article in Economy & Society. It later became a chapter of CCC in a slightly amended form.
12 Cf. Jessop (2001) and Panitch (2000). Note that there is a French text on imperialism from the early 1970s that had already taken on board Poulantzas's PPSC (Amin/Palloix 1971).

Miliband (Panitch 1994, 2000; Panitch/Gindin 2004, 2005).

Poulantzas's assumption that the state represents the political formation of geographical space has been taken up by critical geographers.[13] His remarks on the space-time-matrix coincided with the emergence of materialist geography, which criticised the "spatial blindness" of Marxist social theory (cf. Soja 1989; Läpple 1991). Some proponents of the regulation approach have also appropriated Poulantzas, albeit largely as an 'ancillary' scholar brought in whenever they were being criticized for failing to account for the state. In particular, Joachim Hirsch (1994: 157ff.; 1995: 51ff.) has referred to Poulantzas in this context, and Alain Lipietz (1992) awards an important role to him in facilitating the development of regulation approach out of the Althusser school (cf. Wolf 1994). Moreover, Poulantzas's state theory plays a central role in Thomas Sablowski's regulationist account of Italy after Fordism (1998).

Next to his state theory, Poulantzas's work on class is also influential.[14] Erik O. Wright, one of the most influential Marxist class theorists, explicitly draws on Poulantzas in his 1978 book *Class, Crisis and the State*. He remarks about CCC that 'this work is [...] the most systematic and thorough attempt to understand precisely the Marxist criteria for classes in capitalist society' (31). Just like Poulantzas, Wright links classes to places within the capitalist division of labour, but he criticizes him for overlooking the occasionally contradictory character of such places in terms of class constitution (cf. 61ff.).

Frequent accusations of class-reductionism notwithstanding, feminist scholars draw on Poulantzas – either explicitly (Hartsock 1983; Sauer 2001: 76ff.) or implicitly (e.g., Haney 1996). Along these lines, Jessop expands Poulantzas's conception of the state. Jessop states that 'the exercise and effectivity of state power are the contingently necessary material condensations of the changing balance of forces in political struggle' (2004: 218). He implies that these forces include a multiplicity of relations of domination, including gender relations.

3.2. The 'Neo-Poulantzasian' Discourse in the German-speaking Countries

If the international debates around capitalism, class, domination and the state in the critical social sciences constitute the wider intellectual context out of which *Reading Poulantzas* emerged, there is also a more specific discourse

---

13 See Markus Wissen's chapter in this volume.
14 In the field of class theory, Poulantzas is treated as a seminal author. This is evidenced by the inclusion of his work in textbooks on the subject (Jaeggi 1976; Giddens/Held 1982).

in the German-speaking countries that involves many of the contributors to this volume. This discourse goes further in the re-appropriation of Poulantzas than most earlier discussions on his work: quite a few of the participants are not just concerned with recovering specific insights of Poulantzas, but also with attempting to rebuild his intellectual project. Accordingly, some of them call their approaches "neo-Poulantzasian" (Brand et al. 2007; Gallas 2008, 2009).

The pre-history of this 'neo-Poulantzasian' discourse started with Joachim Hirsch's critique of the state derivation debate in the mid-1970s. Hirsch established the limitations of "derivationism" (1977: 161; translated) by pointing out the missing link between the 'abstract-categorical derivation' of the state form and 'empirical analyses of concrete political processes' (1976: 99; translated). As a remedy, he proposed taking on board Gramsci's, Althusser's, and Poulantzas's contributions to state theory. In the 1980s, Demirović took up the baton by writing his monograph on Poulantzas.

The 'neo-Poulantzasian' discourse was started properly by the re-issue of two seminal texts by Poulantzas in German that had been out of print for a long time. Hirsch and Jessop acted as editors of INT, which they made available again in 2001 (Hirsch/Jessop/Poulantzas 2001); and in 2002, Demirović, Hirsch and Jessop oversaw a new edition of SPS and wrote a new introduction (Poulantzas 2002). INT connected to the debates among left-wing German scholars on 'globalization', while the renewed interest in SPS reflected that the rise of left-wing social movements and parties (see above) had put the state back onto the agenda of political debate.

The scholars participating in the discourse in question share a concern for two key themes to be found in Poulantzas: (1) the fact that the state constitutes a contested terrain and is invested in relations of domination; and (2) the intertwined yet separated mode of existence of the economic and the political in capitalism. However, they use different entry points and hence diverge in terms of where their respective foci lie.

Ulrich Brand, Christoph Görg and Markus Wissen sketch a neo-Poulantzasian research agenda in International Political Economy that departs from the institutionalism of many left-leaning approaches in the field and strongly focuses on social movements. They start from Poulantzas's assumption that there is an internationalization of the state, but also reflect on his work as a socialist organic intellectual (Brand 2005). In a nutshell, they assert that Poulantzas's conception of the state as a condensation of relations of forces can be applied to supranational forms of statehood. In this context, they speak of "second-order condensations" (Brand/Görg/Wissen 2010; cf. Brand/Görg/Hirsch/Wissen 2008). They use Poulantzas in order to analyse the role of NGOs (Brand 2000; Brand et al. 2001) in international relations and the relationship of social movements and actors based in civil society to state apparatuses. In so doing, they also criticize global governance approaches. In a similar move, Lars Bretthauer and Ingo Stützle propose to employ Poulantzas in order to analyse the G8 (Bretthauer/Stützle 2007).[15]

Scholars working in critical EU studies, many of them with links to the Philipps University of Marburg, are drawing upon the debate between Poulantzas and Ernest Mandel in the 1970s about the role of the EU (cf. Beckmann 2005).[16] Wissel (2010) portrays the EU as a specific condensation of relations of forces, which also reflects the relations of forces within the European national states. In so doing, he stresses the multiple dimensions and the diversification of relations of domination in contemporary capitalism. In addition, John Kannankulam, Fabian Georgi and Nikolai Huke (2010) develop an operationalization of the concept of relations of forces with reference to the Europeanization of migration policies, drawing upon the notion of a 'project' as developed by Jessop and others.

A number of authors are using similar approaches in order to capture political projects formed at the national level. Lars Bretthauer (2009) examines the state management of digital property rights with reference to the German feature film industry. He argues that the German copyright laws regulating feature film production reflect processes of condensation insofar as these laws create a stable framework for the exploitation of labour power in this branch of industry. Moreover, Jörg Nowak (2009) transfers Poulantzas's terminology into the area of gender relations. He refers to the gender regime of condensation, highlighting the dominant strategies formulated within the state that contribute to gender divisions of labour.[17]

John Kannankulam also analyzes the national level, but he is concerned with the transition of Western European states to what Poulantzas called 'authoritarian statism'. He argues that the neoliberal restructuring of the British and German states triggered, respectively, by the Thatcher and Kohl governments exemplify this trend (2008).[18] Alexander Gallas draws upon Poulantzas's concept of the power bloc in order to establish the internal configuration of the ruling class in 19th century England (2008). In

---

15   See also Wissel in this volume and Wissel (2007).
16   See also Bieling in this volume.
17   Nowak borrows the concept "regime of condensation" from Alexander Gallas (2009: 85).
18   Note that Christos Boukalas (2008), who is not directly involved in the German debate, engages in analogous line of argument in relation to the US. He contends that the 'anti-terror' legislation of the Bush administration amounts to the onset of a third phase of authoritarian statism after Keynesian crisis management and neoliberal hegemony.

a separate piece (2010), he argues that Poulantzas's account of a strategy towards democratic socialism based on the articulation of forces within and outside the state is still relevant today, because it establishes the political-institutional prerequisites of a successful transformation of capitalist social formations.

Years before there was a renewed interest in Poulantzas, Alex Demirović, Katharina Pühl and Birgit Sauer had already drawn on Poulantzas's work in order to capture how gender relations and the state each play a key role in the constitution of the other (Demirović/Pühl 1998; Sauer 2001). Today, there is a number of feminist authors who share this perspective. They criticize Poulantzas's narrow focus on class domination, but still appropriate his insights to feminist state theory. Poulantzas rejected Marxist conceptions of the state that portrayed it either as an instrument of class domination or as a subject neutralizing it. Similarly, the authors in question go against feminist conceptions of the state that either portray it as an instrument in the hands of a male bond or as a subject neutralizing gender discrimination. For example, Stefanie Wöhl (2007) engages in a critical analysis of gender mainstreaming in the EU by pointing out the connection between masculine hegemony and the state. Anita Fischer (2008) discusses the relation between capitalist statehood and the gender division of labour, arguing that the state reflects not just class, but also gender struggles, which tie in with heterosexual and binary gender identities. Similarly, Gundula Ludwig and Sauer (2010; cf. Ludwig et al. 2009) refer to Poulantzas's relational conception of the state in order to argue that gender relations should be seen as distinct power relations existing alongside class relations.

In early 2010, Demirović, Stephan Adolphs and Serhat Karakayali completed an edited volume on Poulantzas that forms part of a renowned books series on conceptions of the state (*Staatsverständnisse*, Nomos-Verlag). This is a sign that Poulantzas is starting to reach a broader audience in German academia. We may finally be moving beyond a situation where mainstream perceptions of Marxist state theory are characterized by nothing but 'ignorance, arrogance and parochialism' (Esser 2008: 255; translated).

4. Overview of the Chapters

Poulantzas's status as a classic author in the area of Marxist state theory is visible in the wide range of readings of his works represented in this volume. Each section builds on a particular theme. Accordingly, the book maps controversies around these themes, which also reflect different views on how to continue Poulantzas's work, and where to go beyond him.

The contributions in the first section all deal with ontological and epistemological questions. They are located at the level of the mode of production, which constitutes an ensemble of forms or structures. The key question in this section is how capitalist societality and the relationship between the economy and politics/the state can be conceptualized on the basis of Poulantzas's work. Following Clyde W. Barrow, Poulantzas is a "historical structuralist", who portrays the structure of the capitalist mode of production as contradictory and shaped by class conflicts that pose a threat to its existence. Bob Jessop argues that Poulantzas developed a theory of the 'capitalist type of state'. The capitalist type of state is formally adequate to purely capitalist social formations and is being modified according to their transformations. Following Poulantzas, the current 'normal form' of the capitalist type of state is "authoritarian statism". Next, Joachim Hirsch and John Kannankulam discuss the question of how Poulantzas explains the existence of the capitalist state. They find that his line of argument is compatible with the form-analytical approaches developed in the state derivation debate. They suggest that this is particularly obvious when Poulantzas explains the separation of economic and political domination with reference to the separation of the workers from the means of production in capitalism. Subsequent to this, Lars Bretthauer reconstructs Poulantzas's concepts of 'materiality' and 'condensation', elaborating on his conception of the state as the material condensation of relations of forces. He argues that Poulantzas's state theory provides points of departure for analyzing the historical-concrete reproduction of capitalist forms of intercourse by stressing the importance of studying specific conjunctures of relations of forces. Finally, Alexander Gallas engages with Marx's Critique of Political Economy by drawing upon Poulantzas's later works. According to him, Marx's line of argument implies that the capitalist mode of production under-determines the behaviour of actors, which provides these actors with the opportunity to challenge its existence.

The second section addresses two key questions: Can we draw on Poulantzas to conceptualize power and domination in capitalism in its multiple configurations? And which role does the state play in the process? Max Koch reconstructs Poulantzas's class theory in conjunction with his state theory. He objects to Poulantzas explaining classes with reference to a substantialist version of the 'productive/unproductive labour' distinction, and contends that there remain ambivalences as regards identifying the instance of society that ultimately constitutes classes. He also criticizes Poulantzas for not providing a convincing account of the articulation of different relations of domination in capitalism. In contrast, Jörg Nowak asserts that Poulantzas did indeed link gender relations, class relations and political power, but failed to develop this connection systematically. Nowak shows how much feminist state theory draws on Poulantzas's ideas without necessarily highlighting this. More critically, Urs T. Lindner charges Poulantzas with 'class reductionism'. Nevertheless, he takes up themes from Poulantzas's account of capitalist statehood in order to demonstrate that Foucault employs an 'equivocal concept of power' and equates domination with politics. Lindner argues that Foucault's analytics of power should be separated from his concept of power. This may render Foucault's ideas useful for establishing a version of materialist social theory that is capable of theorizing the reproduction of life. Sonja Buckel also engages with Foucault, but with regard to Poulantzas's concept of law. She argues that combining Foucault's conception of governmentality with Poulantzas's state theory will enable us to grasp the connection of law and the state in their 'relational autonomy', without falling into Poulantzas's 'politicist' exaggeration of the importance of the state. The section concludes with Ingo Stützle's contribution. Following Poulantzas in PPSC, Stützle contends that the state – understood as the societal instance of generating cohesion – functions as a knowledge apparatus necessary for the reproduction of the capitalist mode of production. In so doing, it plays a key role in organizing the hegemony of the ruling classes. Foucault is important in this context: Stützle argues that he helps us to overcome 'state-centric' aspects of Poulantzas's conception of knowledge.

The third section demonstrates that capitalist statehood is not 'unidimensional', but can only be understood with reference to the social formation of space and time. Markus Wissen discusses time, space and nationhood in SPS. He sees Poulantzas's ideas as 'groundbreaking' insofar as they address the relation between the national state and the capitalist mode of production. And yet, he observes a tendency in Poulantzas to portray characteristics of Fordism as aspects of capitalism in general. Similarly, Hans-Jürgen Bieling deals with the question of how statehood beyond the national level can be grasped with Poulantzas. According to him, Poulantzas's thoughts on internationalization are a 'heuristic source of inspiration' for theories of European integration. More broadly, Jens Wissel draws on Poulantzas's concept of the 'interior bourgeoisie' as well as on his account of internationalization in order to analyse the transnationalization of the relations of production, which is visible in the neoliberal 'political project'. This is said to have led, in the last decades, to the emergence of a new global power bloc.

The last section of this volume deals with the effect of the relation between the state and mode of production in capitalism on the formation of political forces and their strategies. Thomas Sablowski discusses Poulantzas's concept of crisis and shows how he analyses fascism as a crisis reaction that takes the form of an exceptional state being imposed. Sablowski praises Poulantzas's ability to distinguish between different state forms and regime changes within capitalism. On the other hand, he criticizes Poulantzas for neglecting the economic component of crises. Ulrich Brand and Miriam Heigl discuss potentials for a 'radical transformation' of capitalist societies. They spell out what Poulantzas's strategy of a 'path towards democratic socialism' means, and discuss his plea for a link-up of political forces 'within' and 'outside' the state by using the example of anti-privatization struggles. Brand and Heigl criticize Poulantzas for being 'state-centric' and argue that this caused him to neglect transformations in non-state areas. Alex Demirović addresses these questions on the grounds of a theory of democracy. He lauds Poulantzas for proposing to transform representative democracy rather than smash it in a Marxist-Leninist fashion, because it guarantees political freedoms. At the same time, he stresses that Poulantzas also called for grass-roots struggles 'at a distance' from the state. Against this backdrop, Demirović points out that the establishment of connections between the different movements and fields of conflict remains an unresolved problem. The book concludes with a piece by Peter Thomas, who also addresses the question of transformation. Thomas examines Poulantzas's critique of Gramscian concepts such as 'integral state' and 'dual power'. He argues that Poulantzas's interpretation of Gramsci does not do justice to Gramsci's distinction between 'wars of movement' and 'wars of position'. Thomas proposes an alternative reading of Gramsci that combines the political strategies of both theorists. All contributions in the last section share the conviction that Poulantzas's political impulses are not obsolete; in fact, they are more topical than ever. The publication of this volume can be seen as an attempt to highlight a political need present in all of Poulantzas's writings – the need to abolish exploitation and domination.

To conclude, we would like to thank all the people without whose help and support there would have never been an English-language edition of this book. Julian Müller and Tadzio Müller translated most of the chapters. Bob Jessop translated Kannankulam and Hirsch's chapter into English. Peter Bratsis, Ian Bruff, Emma Dowling, Stuart Shields, Fiona Summers, Ben Trott, Myfanwy Williams, Sean Wilson and Luke Yates proof-read chapters and helped us deal with the vagaries of the English language. Clyde W. Barrow and the University of Massachussetts-Dartmouth contributed a substantial sum towards covering the costs of the translation. All the other contributors made funds available, too. Leo Panitch established the connection to Merlin Press. Anthony Zurbrugg at Merlin Press oversaw the completion of the English edition. Christoph Lieber and VSA-Verlag published the German edition and removed all legal obstacles to releasing the book in English. Peter Thomas and the editorial committee of *Historical Materialism* invited us twice to present the project at the journal's annual conferences. The enthusiasm our project was greeted with in this context motivated us to embark on the project of translating this book, as did the foreign-language reviews of the German edition. For more information as well as updates on Poulantzas and on activities connected to the book see www.poulantzas-lesen.de.

References

Abraham, D. (1981) *The Collapse of the Weimar Republic* (Princeton: Princeton Univ. Press).
Amin, S. / Palloix, C. (1971) *Neuere Beiträge zur Imperialismustheorie*, vol.1 (München: Trikont-Verlag).
Aronowitz, S. / Bratsis, P. (eds.) (2002) *Paradigm lost. State Theory reconsidered* (Minneapolis: Univ. of Minnesota Press).
Barrow, C.W. (2002) 'The Miliband-Poulantzas Debate: An Intellectual History', in Aronowitz, S. / Bratsis, P. (eds.) *Paradigm lost. State Theory reconsidered* (Minneapolis: Univ. of Minnesota Press) 3-52.
Beckmann, M. (2005) 'Marxistische Politische Ökonomie', in Bieling, H.J. / Lerch, M. (eds.) *Theorien der europäischen Integration* (Wiesbaden: VS-Verlag) 117-144.
Boukalas, C. (2008) 'Counterterrorism Legislation and the US State Form: Authoritarian Statism, Phase 3', *Radical Philosophy*, no. 151, 31-41.
Brand, U. (2000) *Nichtregierungsorganisationen, Staat und ökologische Krise* (Münster: Westfälisches Dampfboot).
Brand, U. / Demirović, A. / Görg, C. / Hirsch, J. (eds.) (2001) *Nichtregierungsorganisationen in der Transformation des Staates* (Münster: Westfälisches Dampfboot).
Brand, U. (2005) 'Den Staat als Verhältnis denken. Nicos Poulantzas und die Reformulierung kritischer Internationaler Politischer Ökonomie', in Brand, U. *Gegen-Hegemonie. Perspektiven globalisierungskritischer Strategien* (Hamburg: VSA-Verlag) 45-59.
Brand, U. / Görg, C. / Wissen, M. (2007) 'Verdichtungen zweiter Ordnung: Die Internationalisierung des Staates aus einer neo-poulantzianischen Perspektive', *Prokla*, vol. 37, no. 2, 217-234.
Brand, U. / Görg, C. / Hirsch, J. / Wissen, M. (2008) *Conflicts in Environmental Regulation and the Internationalization of the State. Contested Terrains* (London: Routledge).
Brand, U. / Görg, C. / Wissen, M. (2010) 'Second-order Condensations of Societal Power Relations. Environmental Politics and the Internationalization of the State from a Neo-Poulantzian Perspective', *Antipode. A Radical Journal of Geography*, vol. 42, no. 5 (forthcoming).

Bretthauer, L. (2009) *Geistiges Eigentum im Digitalen Zeitalter* (Münster: Westfälisches Dampfboot).
Bretthauer, L. / Stützle, I. (2007) 'Mit Poulantzas die G8 verstehen. Das Gipfeltreffen der Industriestaaten als staatstheoretisches Problem', *ak – Zeitung für linke Debatte und Praxis*, no. 518, 22.6.2007, 20.
Buci-Glucksmann, C. (ed.) (1983) *La gauche, le pouvoir, le socialisme. Hommage à Nicos Poulantzas* (Paris: Presse Univ. de France).
Demirović, A. (1987) *Nicos Poulantzas. Eine kritische Auseinandersetzung* (Hamburg: Argument-Verlag).
Demirović, A. / Pühl, K. (1998) 'Identitätspolitik und die Transformation von Staatlichkeit: Geschlechterverhältnisse und Staat als komplexe materielle Relation', in Kreisky, E. / Sauer, B. (eds.) *Geschlechterverhältnisse im Kontext politischer Transformation* (Opladen: Westdeutscher Verlag) 220-242.
Demirović, A. / Adolphs, S. / Karakayali, S. (eds.) (2010) *Das Staatsverständnis von Nicos Poulantzas. Der Staat als gesellschaftliches Verhältnis* (Baden-Baden: Nomos Verlag).
Dosse, F. (1999) *Geschichte des Strukturalismus* (Frankfurt am Main: Fischer Taschenbuch Verlag).
Esser, J. (2008) 'Reflexionen über ein gestörtes Verhältnis: Materialistische Staatstheorie und deutsche Politikwissenschaft', in Hirsch, J. (ed.) *Der Staat der Bürgerlichen Gesellschaft. Zum Staatsverständnis von Karl Marx* (Baden-Baden: Nomos Verlag) 203-219.
Fischer, A. (2008) 'Von geschlechtlicher Arbeitsteilung über Geschlecht zum Staat. Eine geschlechtertheoretische Auseinandersetzung mit dem Staat bei Nicos Poulantzas', in Wissel, J. / Wöhl, S. (eds.) *Staatstheorie vor neuen Herausforderungen. Analyse und Kritik* (Münster: Westfälisches Dampfboot).
Gallas, A. (2008) 'Kapitalismus ohne Bourgeoisie. Die ›Gentlemanly Association‹ und der englische Block an der Macht', in Lindner, U. / Nowak, J. / Paust-Lassen, P. (eds.) *Philosophieren unter anderen. Beiträge zum Palaver der Menschheit* (Münster: Westfälisches Dampfboot) 263-287.
Gallas, A. (2009) *Offensive Completed: A neo-Poulantzasian Analysis of the Thatcherite Era, 1977-1999* (Ph.D. thesis, Department of Sociology, Lancaster: Lancaster University).
Gallas, A. (2010) 'We may not like it, but we have to be part of it'. Poulantzas, die Linke und der Staat', *Arranca*, vol. 17, no. 41, 22-26.
Giddens, A. / Held, D. (eds.) (1982) *Classes, Power and Conflict. Classical and contemporary debates* (Basingstoke: Macmillan).
Hall, S. / Critcher, C. / Jefferson, T. / Clarke, J. / Roberts, B. (1978) *Policing the Crisis. Mugging the state, and law and order* (London/Basingstoke: Macmillan).
Hall, S. / Jacques, M. (1983) 'Introduction', in Hall, S. / Jacques, M. (eds.) *The politics of Thatcherism* (London: Lawrence and Wishart) 9-16.
Haney, L. (1996) 'Homeboys, Babies, Men in Suits. The State and the Reproduction of Male Dominance', *American Sociological Review*, vol. 61, no. 5, 759-778.
Hartsock, N.C.M. (1983) *Money, sex, and power: toward a feminist historical materialism* (New York: Longman).
Hirsch, J. (1976) 'Bemerkungen zum theoretischen Ansatz einer Analyse des

bürgerlichen Staates', *Gesellschaft: Beiträge zur Marxschen Theorie*, vol. 8/9, 99-149.
Hirsch, J. (1977) 'Kapitalreproduktion, Klassenauseinandersetzungen und Widersprüche im Staatsapparat', in Brandes, V. (ed.) *Handbücher zur Kritik der politischen Ökonomie, Band 5 – Staat* (Frankfurt am Main: Europäische Verlagsanstalt) 161-181.
Hirsch, J. (1994) 'Politische Form, politische Institutionen und Staat', in Esser, J. / Görg, C. / Hirsch, J. (eds.) *Politik, Institutionen und Staat. Zur Kritik der Regulationstheorie* (Hamburg: VSA-Verlag) 157-212.
Hirsch, J. (1995) *Der nationale Wettbewerbsstaat. Staat, Demokratie und Politik im globalen Kapitalismus* (Berlin: Ed. ID-Archiv).
Hirsch, J. / Jessop, B. / Poulantzas, N. (2001) *Die Zukunft des Staates. Denationalisierung, Internationalisierung, Renationalisierung* (Hamburg: VSA-Verlag).
Hirsch, J. / Demirović, A. / Jessop, B. (2002) 'Einleitung der Herausgeber', in Poulantzas, N. (ed.) *Staatstheorie. Politischer Überbau, Ideologie, Autoritärer Etatismus* (Hamburg: VSA-Verlag) 7-34.
Holloway, J. / Picciotto, S. (eds.) (1978) *State and Capital: A Marxist Debate* (London: Arnold).
Jaeggi, U. (ed.) (1976) *Sozialstruktur und politische Systeme* (Köln: Kiepenheuer & Witsch).
Jessop, B. (1982) *The Capitalist State: Marxist Theories and Methods* (Oxford: Robertson).
Jessop, B. (1985) *Nicos Poulantzas. Marxist theory and political strategy* (Basingstoke: Macmillan).
Jessop, B. (1990) *State Theory: Putting capitalist states in their place* (Cambridge: Polity Press).
Jessop, B. (2001) 'Globalisierung und Nationalstaat. Imperialismus und Staat bei Nicos Poulantzas – 25 Jahre später', in Hirsch, J. / Jessop, B. / Poulantzas, N. (eds.) *Die Zukunft des Staates. Denationalisierung, Internationalisierung, Renationalisierung* (Hamburg: VSA-Verlag) 71-100.
Jessop, B. (2002) *The Future of the Capitalist State* (Cambridge: Polity Press).
Jessop, B. (2004) 'The Gender Selectivities Of The State: A Critical Realist Analysis', *Journal of Critical Realism*, vol. 3, no. 2, 207-237.
Jessop, B. (2008) *State Power: a strategic-relational approach* (Cambridge: Polity Press).
Jessop, B. / Bonnet, K. / Bromley, S. / Ling, T. (1988) *Thatcherism: A Tale of Two Nations* (Cambridge: Polity Press).
Journal of the Hellenic Diaspora (1999) *JHD back issue*, vol. 25, 1-2 (New York: Pella Publishing, Hellenic American Society).
Kannankulam, J. (2008) *Autoritärer Etatismus im Neoliberalismus. Zur Staatstheorie von Nicos Poulantzas* (Hamburg: VSA-Verlag).
Kannankulam, J. / Georgi, F. / Huke, N. (2010) 'EU-Citizenship and the Social Relationship of Forces. On historical materialist policy analysis' (forthcoming paper).
Laclau, E. (1977) *Politics and Ideology in Marxist Theory: Capitalism – Fascism –*

Populism (London: New Left Books).
Läpple, D. (1991) 'Essay über den Raum. Für ein gesellschaftswissenschaftliches Raumkonzept', in Häußermann, H. (ed.) *Stadt und Raum. Soziologische Analysen* (Pfaffenweiler: Centaurus-Verlag) 157-207.
Lipietz, A. (1992) 'Vom Althusserismus zur ›Theorie der Regulation‹', in Demirović, A. / Krebs, H.-P. / Sablowski, T. (eds.) *Hegemonie und Staat. Kapitalistische Regulation als Projekt und Prozess* (Münster: Westfälisches Dampfboot) 9-54.
Ludwig, G. / Sauer, B. / Wöhl, S. (eds.) (2009) *Staat und Geschlecht. Grundlagen und aktuelle Herausforderungen feministischer Staatstheorie* (Baden-Baden: Nomos Verlag).
Ludwig, G. / Sauer, B. (2010) 'Engendering Poulantzas oder: Sinn und Zweck feministischer Anrufung materialistischer Staatstheorie', in Demirović, A. / Adolphs, S. / Karakayali, S. (eds.) (2010) *Das Staatsverständnis von Nicos Poulantzas. Der Staat als gesellschaftliches Verhältnis* (Baden-Baden: Nomos Verlag) 173-188.
Martin, J. (ed.) (2008) *The Poulantzas Reader. Marxism, law, and the state* (London: Verso).
Müller, W. / Neusüß, C. (1970) 'Die Sozialstaatsillusion und der Widerspruch von Lohnarbeit und Kapital', *Sozialistische Politik*, vol. 2, no. 6/7, 4-67.
Nowak, J. (2009) *Geschlechterpolitik und Klassenherrschaft. Eine Integration marxistischer und feministischer Staatstheorien* (Münster: Westfälisches Dampfboot).
Panitch, L. (1994) 'Globalisation and the State', *Socialist Register*, vol. 30, 60-93.
Panitch, L. (2000) 'The New Imperial State', *New Left Review*, vol. 1, no. II.2, 5-21.
Panitch, L. / Gindin, S. (2004) 'American Imperialism and Euro-Capitalism: The Making of Neoliberal Globalization', *Studies in Political Economy*, no. 71/72, 7-38.
Panitch, L. / Gindin, S. (2005) 'Superintending Global Capital', *New Left Review*, no. 35, 101-123.
Poulantzas, N. (2002) *Staatstheorie. Politischer Überbau, Ideologie, autoritärer Etatismus* (Hamburg: VSA-Verlag).
Sablowski, T. (1998) *Italien nach dem Fordismus. Regulation und organische Krise einer kapitalistischen Gesellschaftsformation* (Münster: Westfälisches Dampfboot).
Sauer, B. (2001) *Die Asche des Souveräns. Staat und Demokratie in der Geschlechterdebatte* (Frankfurt am Main: Campus Verlag).
Soja, E.W. (1989) *Postmodern Geographies. The Reassertion of Space in Critical Social Theory* (London: Verso).
Wissel, J. (2007) *Die Transnationalisierung von Herrschaftsverhältnissen. Zur Aktualität von Nicos Poulantzas' Staatstheorie* (Baden-Baden: Nomos).
Wissel, J. (2010) 'Kräfteverhältnis', in Haug, W.F. (ed.) *Historisch-Kritisches Wörterbuch des Marxismus*, vol. 7/II (Hamburg: Argument-Verlag) 1941-1955.
Wöhl, S. (2007) *Mainstreaming Gender? Widersprüche europäischer und nationalstaatlicher Geschlechterpolitik* (Königstein/Taunus: Helmer).
Wolf, F.O. (1994) 'Althusser-Schule', in Haug, W.F. (ed.) *Historisch-kritisches Wörterbuch des Marxismus*, vol. 1 (Hamburg: Argument-Verlag) 184-191.
Wright, E. O. (1978) *Class, Crisis, and the State* (London: New Left Books).

(RE)READING POULANTZAS: STATE THEORY AND THE EPISTEMOLOGIES OF STRUCTURALISM

CLYDE W. BARROW

1. The legacy of structuralist abstractionism

Nicos Poulantzas's reputation as a state theorist was secured in Europe by the publication of *Political Power and Social Classes* (cf. Jessop 1985: 9ff.; Touraine 1968; Singer 1970). However, his work captured worldwide attention following his review of Ralph Miliband's *The State in Capitalist Society* (Poulantzas 1969), which set off what is now known as the Poulantzas-Miliband debate (1969-1976).[1] Soon, Poulantzas's book was influencing left-wing academics and political activists everywhere, leading Bob Jessop to suggest that 'it is no exaggeration to claim that Poulantzas remains the single most important and influential Marxist theorist of the state and politics in the postwar period'. (1985: 5).

Most observers agree that the Poulantzasian structuralists tended to prevail in the debate until state theory itself receded into the intellectual background of the 1980s and 1990s (cf. Piven 1994: 24). Yet, despite Poulantzas's apparent triumph in the early state debate, renewed discussion about his thinking among state theorists today should recognize that there is considerable disagreement about how to understand Poulantzas's political theory and particularly its relation to Althusserian structuralism. Nicholas Abercrombie, Bryan Turner, and John Urry (1976: 510ff.) have praised Poulantzas's political theory as one of 'the most sophisticated and developed products of the Althusserian revolution in the reading of Marx'. On the other hand, Ralph Miliband criticised PPSC for being '*obscurely*

---

1 The core of the Poulantzas-Miliband Debate consisted of three written exchanges or interventions, which were published in 1969/70 (Poulantzas-Miliband), 1973 (Miliband) and 1976 (Poulantzas) in the *New Left Review*. From the beginning, Poulantzas's focus was on the 'problem of method' in Marxist political theory. For an overview, see Barrow (2002: 3ff.).

written for any reader who has not become familiar through painful initiation with the particular linguistic code and mode of exposition of the Althusserian school to which Poulantzas relates'. (Miliband 1973: 83f.). Miliband (36) initially criticized Poulantzas's theory of the state for its 'structural superdeterminism', because the latter seemed to claim that state officials and institutions automatically respond to the functional imperatives of the capitalist system (King 1986: 77).

Moreover, in a subsequent critique, Miliband condemns the 'structuralist abstractionism' of Poulantzas's analytical method, which seemed to favour the elaboration of abstract concepts over empirical, historical, and institutional analyses of actually existing states. There is no question that Poulantzas eschewed what he calls 'the demagogy of the "palpitating fact", of "common sense", and the "illusions of the evident"'. However, in the debate's final exchanges, Poulantzas conceded that he used 'sometimes needlessly difficult language' and that in PPSC he had shared 'an overrigid epistemological position' with Althusser. Nevertheless, he continued to defend his position as one necessitated at the time by the requirements of a concentrated 'attack against empiricism and neo-positivism, whose condensates, in the Marxist tradition, are economism and historicism'. (Poulantzas 1976: 66ff.).

While Poulantzas seemed to shift his position toward the end of the Poulantzas-Miliband debate, his theory has consistently been read by proponents, and similarly dismissed by critics, as being dependent on Althusserian structuralism. Sympathetic commentators have attempted to supersede the legacy of structuralist abstractionism either by exaggerating Poulantzas's shift of position or by dismissing Miliband's epithets as a mere caricature of his real position. Paul Thomas, for example, argues that shortly after the initial rounds of the Poulantzas-Miliband debate, Poulantzas 'quickly, adroitly, and in principle moved beyond this hidebound *point d'appui*' (i.e., Althusserian structuralism) toward a class struggle approach that first appears in *Fascism and Dictatorship* (1970), but is only fully developed in *State, Power, Socialism* (1978). Thomas attributes this transition to an 'epiphany' (i.e., an epistemological break) that resulted from the events of May 1968 (Thomas 2002: 74; see also Thomas 1994).

In a similar vein, Bob Jessop (1985: 24) describes PPSC as a 'hybrid Althusserian and Gramscian approach', which can be distinguished as a particular phase in Poulantzas's theoretical development and isolated from the rest of his theoretical production. Both of these readings isolate PPSC as a short-lived theoretical episode, thereby dismissing the entire Poulantzas-Miliband debate as a distraction from Poulantzas's mature political theory.

And indeed, Jessop (ibid.) has described the debate as 'misguided and insignificant for his later development'.

A second approach to the problems of structural superdeterminism and structural abstractionism is offered by Stanley Aronowitz and Peter Bratsis. They argue that the Poulantzas-Miliband debate generated caricatures of both theorists' 'true positions, offering no substantive insight into a theory of the state'. They claim that 'state theory was never the object of a rigorous and sustained critique'. Instead, each theorist's caricature of the other was perpetuated by subsequent authors, who eventually dismissed Poulantzas, Miliband, and other state theorists with 'a couple of paragraphs and footnotes'. (Aronowitz/Bratsis 2002: xii).

The (re)reading of Poulantzas elaborated below documents that he was neither a 'structural superdeterminist' nor a 'structural abstractionist', but that attaching these labels to his early work during the Poulantzas-Miliband debate obscured the fact that structuralism was not a monolithic methodological or theoretical perspective even within the narrow confines of state theory. It is my contention that a close reading of the leading 1970s structuralists would have revealed significant theoretical differences between them, which divided this school of thought into 1. structural determinist; 2. technological determinist; and 3. historical structuralist (or class struggle) approaches from the outset (Balibar 1970: 199ff.; Therborn 1976; Amin 1976: 13ff.; Hindess/Hirst 1975: 1ff.; Hindess/Hirst 1975; Wright 1978).

Poulantzas never embraced the metaphysical structural determinism of Louis Althusser and Étienne Balibar, nor the technological determinism of Göran Therborn, but he did not articulate those differences explicitly (i.e., in a polemical form) until political events in the 1970s brought them into sharp relief. This also implies that the positions developed in Poulantzas's mature works build on concepts and ideas that he had already developed in PPSC.

Thus, while correcting the caricature of Poulantzas inherited from the Poulantzas-Miliband debate requires a more sophisticated analysis of his position *within* structuralism, it is not necessary to allude to epiphanies or to rescue a 'mature Poulantzas' from an 'early Poulantzas'. Instead, I suggest that because the Poulantzas-Miliband debate was always about epistemology, rather than state theory, that if we re-read Poulantzas outside this legacy and thereby shift the focus of analysis from the methodological to the conceptual level, one finds a remarkable continuity in Poulantzas's thinking about *the capitalist state*.[2]

---

2   In Barrow (1993: 9ff. and ch. 6) I argue that political theories have an analytic and a methodological dimension. The analytic dimension of a political theory consists of the

2. Poulantzas's theory of the state

In PPSC, Poulantzas claims that every mode of production can be understood theoretically in terms of the functional interrelations between its economic, political, and ideological levels (PPSC: 1ff.; Clarke 1977: 1ff.).

Each level in a mode of production consists of *structures* which contribute to the reproduction of the mode of production and *class practices* which generate conflicts and contradictions within the mode of production (PPSC: 37, 86). A structure consists of one or more institutions that fulfill specific economic, political, or ideological functions necessary to reproduce a particular mode of production. For instance, the economic structures of the capitalist mode of production (CMP) are constituted primarily by the social relations of production and the forces of production. A stable mode of production is one in which the structures at each level function together as an integrated system to maintain and extend the conditions that allow a dominant class to appropriate surplus value from a subordinate labouring class.

However, Poulantzas also emphasises that the normal functioning of structures within a capitalist mode of production generate contradictory *class practices* that simultaneously destabilize the conditions of ruling-class domination. Poulantzas defines class practices as the effects of: 1. structural dislocations generated by class struggle and 2. the uneven development of structures *between* and *within* the levels of a social formation (PPSC: 41; also see, respectively, Wright 1978 and Amin 1976).

Importantly, Poulantzas views specific class practices as synonymous with the concept of 'contradiction', because 'class practices can be analysed only as conflicting practices in the field of class struggle [...] for example, the contradiction between those practices which aim at the realisation of profit and those which aim at the increase of wages'. (PPSC: 86).

2.1. The general function of the state

The contradictory effects of class practices on the structural equilibrium

> key concepts that select, name, and logically interrelate a specified range of phenomena; in this instance, a range of phenomena identified as 'the state'. The central problem at the analytic level of state theory is to define what range of phenomena are encompassed by a concept of the state. However, in selecting and interrelating phenomena, political theories simultaneously put forward specific claims about how various events and phenomena are related to one another. Hence, political theories must also advance a methodological position that enables scholars to specify what kinds of research and evidence are necessary to test those hypothetical claims and to provide rules about what counts as an adequate explanation of the state. Competing theoretical approaches to the state emerge from the various ways in which these two dimensions – analytic and methodological – are linked together by different theorists.

of the CMP means that potential crisis tendencies are always disrupting its functional integration. It is this persistent disruption of the CMP's functional integration that necessitates a separate structure – the State – the general function of which is to serve as *'the regulating factor of its global equilibrium as a system'*. (PPSC: 45; Poulantzas insists that 'a good deal of guidance on these questions is found in the Marxist classics', but in practice he cites Easton, Deutsch, Apter, Almond and Coleman; 48).

In particular, Poulantzas identifies three ensembles of class practices that require regulation by the state. First, Poulantzas argues that the economic level of the CMP has never 'formed a hermetically sealed level, capable of self-production and possessing its own "laws" of internal functioning'. Rather, the economic level of the CMP is only *relatively* autonomous from the political and ideological levels. Because of this relative autonomy among the levels, structural 'equilibrium is never *given* by the economic as such, but is maintained by the State'. (45). To this extent, the state fulfils a general maintenance function *'by constituting the factor of cohesion between the levels of a social formation'*. (ibid.).

Consequently, Poulantzas identifies a second ensemble of class practices, determined by the fact that *'the political field of the State* (as well as the sphere of ideology) *has always, in different forms, been present in the constitution and reproduction of the relations of production'*. (SPS: 17). Capitalist relations of production do not appear *ex nihilo* in history, nor do they reproduce themselves on a day-to-day basis without struggle and resistance. Hence, in maintaining the cohesion of the levels of a social formation, Poulantzas observes that 'the function of the state primarily concerns the economic level, and particularly the labour process, the productivity of labour'. (PPSC: 52). The state thus establishes and enforces the rules which organise capitalist exchanges (property and contract law, enforcement, punishment). Finally, Poulantzas calls attention to an ensemble of class practices which occur 'at the strictly political level' of the capitalist mode of production. Poulantzas identifies the strictly political function of the state with 'the maintenance of political order in political class conflict'. (53). By maintaining political order, by punishing disobedience, and by monitoring political 'subversion', the state represses revolution and, thereby, maintains conditions of class exploitation under the neutral guise of law and order. Regardless of the level at which the state function is effected, Poulantzas contends that the general function of the state is always oriented 'with particular reference to the productivity of labour'. (50, 53). These modalities of the state function are always implemented through three functional subsystems of the state: the judicial apparatus, the ideological apparatus, and the political-administrative apparatus.

It should be emphasized as a point of considerable theoretical significance that *structures* are not reducible to economic, political, or ideological *institutions*.[3] On this point, David Gold, Clarence Lo, and Erik Olin Wright observe that for Poulantzas the concept of 'structure does *not* refer to the concrete social institutions that make up a society, but rather to the *systematic functional interrelationships among these institutions*'. Hence, Poulantzas's structural analysis emphasized 'the *functional relationship* of various institutions to the process of surplus-value production and appropriation' (Gold, Lo and Wright 1975: 36, fn.; italics by C.W.B.), whereas Miliband ostensibly emphasized only the formal organization and control of particular institutions by networks of corporate and political elites.

2.2. State power

Poulantzas and Miliband also articulate different concepts of state power that are linked to their methodological differences. Whereas Miliband articulates an institutionalist conception of power, anchored by the methodological (Weberian) assumptions of power structure research, Poulantzas articulates a functionalist conception of power anchored by the methodological (Parsonian) assumptions of structural functionalism. Notably, and in direct contrast to Miliband, Poulantzas draws a sharp *analytic* distinction between the concepts of state power and the state apparatus (Therborn 1978: 148).

Poulantzas defines *state power* as the capacity of a social class to realize its objective interests through the state apparatus (PPSC: 104). Bob Jessop observes that within this framework 'state power is capitalist to the extent that it creates, maintains, or restores the conditions required for capital accumulation in a given situation and it is non-capitalist to the extent these conditions are not realised'. (Jessop 1982: 221). In this respect, the objective *effects* of state policies on capital accumulation and the class structure are the objective indicators of state power (and not who occupies the positions of formal political authority) (PPSC: 99).[4] In direct contrast to Miliband, Poulantzas insists that 'the institutions of the state, do not, strictly speaking,

3   PPSC: 115, fn. 24, defines an institution as 'a system of norms or rules which is socially sanctioned [...] On the other hand, the concept of structure covers the *organising matrix* of institutions'. However, on this point, Poulantzas also notes 'that structure *is not* the simple principle of organisation which is *exterior to* the institution: the structure is present in an allusive and inverted form in the institution itself'.

4   This assumes that the important conditions of capitalist accumulation are the productivity of labour, the security of private property, an efficient system of exchange and contract, etc. as identified by Poulantzas.

have any power. Institutions, considered from the point of view of power, can be related only to *social classes which hold power.*' (115). State institutions are political arenas for the exercise of class power and exist as such only by virtue of their functional role in the CMP.

3. The Poulantzas-Althusser-debate

The differences between Poulantzas and the other structuralists manifest themselves more explicitly after 1968, mainly because Poulantzas shifts the focus of his epistemological critique to what he called formalism and economism. In PPSC, Poulantzas's epistemological criticisms are directed mainly against the major variants of Marxist 'historicism', i.e., Georg Lukács, Karl Korsch, Antonio Labriola, and Antonio Gramsci (PPSC: 11, 37ff.). Poulantzas immediately identified Miliband as a contemporary exemplar of Marxist historicism. Significantly, the critique of historicism is a philosophical project that Poulantzas shared with Althusser and the other structuralists until about 1970, when he published FD. In *Pour Marx*, Althusser argued that Marx had 'established a new *science*: the science of the history of "social formations"' (FM: 13), but this science was threatened by the emergence of historicist and humanist (e.g., Sartre) strains of Marxism.

However, the merely *political* unity between Althusser and Poulantzas began to disintegrate after May 1968, when despite a series of major upheavals around the world, capital began to re-establish and reconstitute the basis of its political and economic power; first, in individual nations, and then on a global scale. In response to the Greek and Latin American coups d'etat, Poulantzas turned his attention to the analysis of the 'exceptional states' of Nazi Germany and fascist Italy, because as the 'sharpness of class struggle' intensified inside the imperialist heartlands (i.e., the USA and Europe), it was putting the question of fascism back on the political agenda as a possible response by the capitalist class (FD: 11). Moreover, the State's response to popular upheavals in the United States, Germany, Japan, and elsewhere was growing increasingly violent. Thus, in FD, Poulantzas began more explicitly to differentiate his position from Althusser's on two points that he would elaborate in subsequent works in much greater detail. First, Poulantzas argues that Althusser's widely acclaimed essay on ideological state apparatuses (IISA) 'suffers to some extent from both abstractedness and formalism: it does not give the class struggle the place it deserves'. (FD: 300f., fn. 2). Second, Poulantzas claims that Althusser badly underestimates 'the economic role of the State apparatuses, to the extent of completely neglecting it theoretically' in his famous formula: The State = Repression +

Ideology (303, fn. 5).[5]

While both critiques are muted as mere footnotes deep inside the text, it is notable that several years prior to being labelled a structural abstractionist by Miliband, Poulantzas was actually criticising Althusser for his abstractedness and formalism! For Poulantzas, Althusser's failure to conceptualize this function was a major theoretical flaw. Furthermore, Poulantzas's locates the State's presence *inside* the economic instance as an element necessary to *constituting and reproducing* the social relations of production. This concept of the State was not a new departure in FD, but a central feature of his analysis in PPSC.

Unlike FD, Poulantzas explicitly begins CCC with an explicit criticism of the Althusser/Balibar school. Indeed, Poulantzas apologizes for the 'critical and sometimes even polemical character' of this book, but he states that 'instead of suppressing differences and thus inevitably choosing to brush fundamental problems under the carpet, I have preferred to dwell on them, in so far as criticism alone can advance Marxist theory'. (CCC: 11).

In a passage that would seem to contravene Jessop's and Thomas's references to an epistemological break or an epiphany, Poulantzas insists that the arguments advanced in CCC 'are based on those of *Political Power and Social Classes*', but they 'are in some respects rectified, a process already begun in *Fascism and Dictatorship*'. Nevertheless, Poulantzas emphasizes that 'both the theoretical framework and the essence of the earlier arguments are maintained'. (13, fn. 1). Poulantzas not only calls attention to his differences with the Althusser/Balibar school of structuralism, but points out that such differences had always existed: 'In the domain of historical materialism, for instance, fundamental differences already existed between, on the one hand, my *Political Power and Social Classes* [...] and on the other hand Balibar's 'The Basic Concepts of Historical Materialism' (1966), which is marked by both economism and structuralism." (ibid.).

In the wake of the first two rounds of the Poulantzas-Miliband debate, it is more than ironic to find Poulantzas criticizing Balibar for economism and *structuralism*. In *State, Power, Socialism* (1978), Poulantzas continues this critique with the observation that 'today more than ever it is necessary to distance ourselves from the formalist-economist position', which he identified with the works of Althusser, Balibar, and Therborn, among others (SPS: 15). His earlier references can leave no doubt that his goal is to emphasize the 'fundamental differences' between himself and the other structuralists.

5 Poulantzas was shocked by Althusser's formula: 'Taking this to its logical conclusion, the State would have only a repressive and an ideological role!'

Poulantzas identifies the main limitation of the formalist-economist position with its assumption that 'the economy is composed of elements that remain unchanged through the various modes of production – elements possessing an almost Aristotelian *nature* or *essence* and able to reproduce and regulate themselves by a kind of internal combinatory'. (ibid.) It views the economic instance, as well as the state-political instance, as a fixed set of structural relations between essentially immutable forms. The theoretical (as opposed to epistemological) problem with this type of structuralist abstractionism is that it represented the relation between the economic and the political as one 'of "base" and "superstructure"; namely, a conception of the State as a mere appendage or reflection of the economic sphere, devoid of its own space and reducible to the economy'. (ibid.) What disturbs Poulantzas about this formulation is that 'the essential autonomy of the superstructural instances [the State, ideology; C.W.B.] would then serve to legitimise the autonomy, self-sufficiency and self-reproduction of the economy'. (16). This is not to say that formalists did not recognise the existence of structural 'interventions' by one instance into another, but that such interventions occurred from 'relations of exteriority' as a *deus ex machina*. He insists that this conception of state 'interventions' in the economy are theoretically incorrect, because they suggest that the state is something external to the economic that only periodically intrudes into its otherwise autonomous functioning and development.

A second major flaw with this theoretical position, as Poulantzas notes, is that it 'obscures the role of struggles lodged in the very heart of the relations of production and exploitation'. (15). He reiterates a point he had made with equal vigour in PPSC: 'In this perspective, the differences presented by the object (the economy) from one mode of production to another are to be explained purely in terms of a self-regulating and rigidly demarcated economic space, whose *internal* metamorphoses and transformations are unravelled by the general theory of the economy ("economic science").' (16).

Poulantzas is adamant about reiterating two additional points in SPS. First, he again rejects Althusser and Balibar's claim that it is possible to deduce an *a priori* science, or general theory, of the modes of production. This claim has two bases in Poulantzas's *historical* structuralist epistemology. For Poulantzas, theoretical analysis begins with the concept of the mode of production itself, rather than its elements, because it is the totality of these economic, political, and ideological determinations that fixes the boundaries of these elemental spaces in each mode of production.[6] Consequently, these

---

6 See, Balibar (RC: 201) for his discussion of 'The Elements of the Structure and Their

concepts will have different meanings, extensions, and boundaries in each mode of production.

Poulantzas had actually made the same point in PPSC, although he articulated it in such abstruse structuralist language that it was probably not recognized by most readers: 'We are concerned with a combination (*combinaison*) and not with a combinatory (*combinatoire*), because the relations of the elements determine *their very nature*, which is modified according to the combination'. (PPSC: 25f. fn. 9).[7]

Furthermore, Poulantzas observes that at the superstructural levels, the formalist-economist position diverges into two distinct structuralisms that he considers equally flawed. The formalist variant – what is properly called structuralist abstractionism – argues that the general theory of the economy 'has to be duplicated by analogy in a *general theory* of every superstructural field – in this case, the political field of the State'. The economist variant – what is generally called technological determinism – conceptualizes the superstructural instances 'as mechanical reflections of the economic base'. (SPS: 16).[8] Poulantzas adds in his conclusion that: '[...] just as there can be no general theory of the economy (no "economic science") having a theoretical object that remains unchanged through the various modes of production, so can there be no 'general theory' of the state-political (in the sense of a political "science" or "sociology") having a similarly constant object [...] What is perfectly legitimate, however, is a *theory of the capitalist State.*' (19).

Second, Poulantzas carries this critique a step further by emphasising that he retains the distinction between *mode of production* as an abstract-formal object and concrete *social formations* as articulations of several modes of production at a given historical moment.[9] One cannot deduce the characteristics of a social formation 'as merely heaped up concretisations of abstractly reproduced modes of production; nor, therefore, should a concrete

> History'. Balibar argues that the basic concepts of historical materialism are 'the "mode of production" and the concepts immediately related to it'. The elements in this 'system of forms' are the means of production, the labourer, the non-labourer, the property relation, and the relation of real appropriation. For Althusser and Balibar, the basic concepts of historical materialism are not historical generalizations or empirical inductions, but 'abstract concepts whose validity is not as such limited to a given period or type of society'.

7 SPS: 51ff., draws on these same arguments to dismiss the *Ableitung* or derivationist approach to state theory.
8 See Therborn (1976: 353ff.) as an example of technological determinism.
9 Poulantzas never clarifies the epistemological status of an abstract-formal object. On the one hand, he rejects structuralist abstractionism (i.e., formalism) which seems to assign an objective reality to these concepts, but he is equally vehement in rejecting Max Weber's heuristic notion of an ideal-type. See PPSC: 145ff..

State be considered as a simple realisation of the-State-of-the-capitalist-mode-of-production'(25). Quite the contrary: Poulantzas emphasizes that '[s]ocial formations are the actual sites of the existence and reproduction of modes of production. They are thus also the sites of the various forms of State, none of which can simply be deduced from the capitalist type of State understood as denoting an abstract-formal object [...]. A theory of the capitalist State can be elaborated only if it is brought into relation with the history of political struggles under capitalism.' (ibid.).

An additional theoretical basis for this conclusion is found in Poulantzas's understanding of the relative autonomy of the economic instance. In SPS, Poulantzas restates his earlier observation that the economy has never been 'a hermetically sealed level, capable of self-reproduction and possessing its own "laws" of internal functioning' in any mode of production. Instead, 'the political field of the State (as well as the sphere of ideology) has always, in different forms, been present in the constitution and reproduction of the relations of production'. However, Poulantzas now acknowledges that 'the position of the State vis-à-vis the economy has changed not only with the mode of production, but also with the stage and phase of capitalism itself'. (17).

In SPS, Poulantzas argues that in the stage of competitive capitalism, and even in the early phases of monopoly capitalism, 'the State's strictly economic functions were *subordinated*, though not reduced, especially to its repressive and ideological functions'. The state was mainly involved in 'organising the socio-political space of capital accumulation', i.e., in creating nations. However, while others were bemoaning an emerging crisis of the welfare states in the 1970s, Poulantzas was already theorizing the causes of this development. According to Poulantzas, 'the State's present role in the economy alters the political space as a whole, economic functions henceforth occupy the *dominant place* within the State [...]. *The totality of operations of the State are currently being reorganised in relation to its economic role.*' (167). The state was now actively responding to the sharpening of domestic class struggle, and to the crisis of imperialism, by managing these contradictions with new strategies and policies designed to reconstitute the relations of production, the division of labour, the reproduction of labour-power, and the extraction of surplus value.

Poulantzas observed that the state's economic functions were increasing to such an extent that one could now theoretically identify a specialized *state economic apparatus* in addition to the repressive and ideological state apparatuses (e.g., the strengthening of central banks, finance and trade ministries, state labour exchanges, workforce retraining, etc.).

Against this background, the Althusserian view of autonomous instances and independently functioning apparatuses was completely incapable of theorizing this restructuring of the state form. Thus, Poulantzas insisted that 'unless we break with the analogical image according to which the state apparatuses are divided into watertight fields, we cannot grasp the reorganisation, extension, and consolidation of the state economic apparatus as the restructuring principle of state space'. (170).

In a period of historical transition, Poulantzas focused his attention, first, on Althusser's formalism, and, second, on economism, which would see post-Fordist globalization as an autonomous, inexorable economic development determined by new technological innovations that circumvented the state.[10] But far from being powerless, the capitalist state was actively reconstituting the relations of production on a new basis, while the abstract and immutable concepts employed by most structuralists were incapable of comprehending this (or any) process of *transition* to a new state form.

4. From structuralist abstractionism to historical structuralism

The stated objective of PPSC was to produce a concept of the capitalist state and to produce 'more concrete concepts dealing with politics in capitalist social formations'. (SPS: 16). For Poulantzas, this constellation of concepts, including the general function of the state, constitutes a *regional* theory of the capitalist state. However, the purpose of a regional theory is to organize and facilitate the development of particular theories of actually existing states in capitalist social formations.

The transition from a Fordist to a Post-Fordist state form required Poulantzas to sharpen the distinction between his type of historical structuralism and the structuralist abstractionism (i.e., formalist-economism) of Althusser, Balibar, and Therborn. But there were other theorists who reinforced Poulantzas's conception by identifying mechanisms of functional constraint (e.g., investment strikes and public debt) without relying on any form of abstractionism or functionalist metaphysics (Mandel 1971; Bridges 1974: 161ff.; Offe 1975: 125ff.; Block 1977: 6ff.; see Barrow 1993: 58ff. for a summary).

Poulantzas left us with an unfinished research agenda starting with the need to describe, conceptualize, and theorize the emergence of a state economic apparatus. Moreover, he presciently diagnosed the expansion of this apparatus, as the newly dominant state apparatus, as the basis

---

10   Manuel Castells (1997: 243) claims that '[s]tate control over space and time is increasingly bypassed by global flows of capital, goods, services, technology, communication, and information'.

for creating the political and ideological conditions for a new American imperialism *within* the territories of nation-states (see, also, Barrow 2005).

There is on-going work that reconceptualizes this new capitalist State form at a regional level (e.g., post-Fordism, regulation theory), but there is even more work to be done at the level of particular theories that describe and analyse this process theoretically within individual nation-states or geographic areas. Finally, Poulantzas offers a timely reminder that the revolutionary objective of socialism is not 'only a shift in *State power*, but it must equally *"break"*, that is to say radically change, the State apparatus'. (1969: 68). The objective is not to capture the capitalist state, or to merely change its personnel, but to alter its structural configuration as an apparatus and its class relation to the mode of production.

References

Abercrombie, N. / Turner, B. / Urry, J. (1976) 'Class, State and Fascism. The Work of Nicos Poulantzas', *Political Studies*, vol. 24, no. 4, 510-519.
Amin, S. (1976) *Unequal Development* (New York: Monthly Review Press).
Aronowitz, S. / Bratsis, P. (2002) 'State Power, Global Power', in Aronowitz, S. / Bratsis, P. (eds.) *Paradigm Lost. State Theory Reconsidered* (Minneapolis: Univ. of Minnesota Press) xi-xxvii.
Balibar, E. (1970) 'The Basic Concepts of Historical Materialism', in Althusser, L. / Balibar, E. *Reading Capital* (London: New Left Books).
Barrow, C. W. (1993) *Critical Theories of the State. Marxist, Neo-Marxist, Post-Marxist* (Madison: Univ. of Wisconsin Press).
Barrow, C. W. (2002) 'The Miliband-Poulantzas Debate. An Intellectual History', in Aronowitz, S. / Bratsis, P. (eds.) (2002) *Paradigm Lost. State Theory Reconsidered* (Minneapolis: Univ. of Minnesota Press) 3-52.
Barrow, C. W. (2005) 'The Return of the State: Globalisation, State Theory, and the New Imperialism', *New Political Science*, vol. 27, no. 2, 123-145.
Block, F. L. (1977) 'The Ruling-Class Does Not Rule. Notes on the Marxist Theory of the State', *Socialist Revolution*, vol. 7, no. 3, 6-28.
Bridges, A. B. (1974) 'Nicos Poulantzas and the Marxist Theory of the State', *Politics and Society*, vol. 4, no. 2, 161-190.
Castells, M. (1997) *The Information Age: Economy, Society, and Culture*, vol. 2 (Oxford: Oxford Univ. Press).
Clarke, S. (1977) 'Marxism, Sociology, and Poulantzas's Theory of the State', *Capital and Class*, vol. 1, no. 2, 1-31.
Piven, F. F. (1994) 'Reflections on Ralph Miliband', *New Left Review*, vol. 35, no. I.206, 23-26.
Gold, D. A. / Lo, C. Y. H. / Wright, E. O. (1975) 'Recent Developments in Marxist Theories of the Capitalist State. Part I', *Monthly Review*, vol. 27, no. 27, 29-43.
Hindess, B. / Hirst, P. Q. (1975) *Pre-Capitalist Modes of Production* (London: Routledge).

Jessop, B. (1982) *The Capitalist State. Marxist Theories and Methods* (New York: New York Univ. Press).
Jessop, B. (1985) *Nicos Poulantzas. Marxist Theory and Political Strategy* (New York: St. Martin's Press).
King, R. (1986) *The State in Modern Society* (Chatham: Chatham House Publications).
Mandel, E. (1971) *The Marxist Theory of the State* (New York: Pathfinder Press)
Miliband, R. (1970) 'The Capitalist State. Reply to Poulantzas', *New Left Review*, vol. 11, no. I.59, 53-60.
Miliband, R. (1973) 'Poulantzas and the Capitalist State', *New Left Review*, vol 14, no. 82, 83-92.
Offe, C. (1975) 'The Theory of the Capitalist State and the Problem of Policy Formation', Lindberg, L. (ed.) *Stress and Contradiction in Modern Capitalism* (Lexington: Lexington Books) 125-144.
Poulantzas, N. (1969) 'The Problem of the Capitalist State', *New Left Review*, vol. 10, no. I.58, 67-78.
Poulantzas, N. (1976) 'The Capitalist State. A Reply to Miliband and Laclau', *New Left Review*, vol. 17, no. I.95, 63-83.
Singer, D. (1970) *Prelude to Revolution. France in May 1968* (London: Cape).
Therborn, G. (1976) *Science, Class, and Society* (London: Cape).
Therborn, G. (1978) *What Does the Ruling Class Do When It Rules?* (London: New Left Books).
Thomas, P. (2002) 'Bringing Poulantzas Back In', in Aronowitz, S. / Bratsis, P. (eds.) *Paradigm Lost. State Theory Reconsidered* (Minneapolis: Univ. of Minnesota Press) 73-88.
Thomas, P. (2002) *Alien Politics* (New York: Routledge).
Touraine, A. (1968) *Le mouvement de mai, ou le communisme utopique* (Paris: Edition du Seuil).
Wright, E. O. (1978) *Class, Crisis, and the State* (London: New Left Books).

POULANTZAS'S *STATE, POWER, SOCIALISM* AS A MODERN CLASSIC

BOB JESSOP

I would like to advance three theses on Poulantzas's *State, Power, Socialism* (SPS). First, Poulantzas formulated a contribution to the theory of the *capitalist type of state* that goes well beyond conventional Marxist analyses of the *state in capitalist society*. Second, he conceived the state as a social relation, a concept that holds for the capitalist type of state, diverse states in capitalist social formations, and statehood more generally. Third, his analysis of the current form of the capitalist type of state was highly prescient, with 'authoritarian statism' far more evident now than when he noted this emerging trend in the 1970s. Despite some basic limitations, SPS should be regarded as a modern classic.

The capitalist type of state

In *Political Power and Social Classes* (PPSC) as well as in SPS, Poulantzas aimed to develop a form-analytical theory of the capitalist type of state. Both texts seek to answer a question initially posed by Pashukanis: 'why in order to assert its political domination, does the bourgeoisie dispose of the quite specific state apparatus which is the capitalist state – the modern representative State, the national-popular class state' (SPS: 49; cf. PPSC: 123). In both cases, Poulantzas argued that, whereas direct class rule would be regarded as illegitimate, the modern representative state offers a flexible framework to unify the long-term political interests of an otherwise fissiparous power bloc, disorganize the subaltern classes, and secure the consent of the popular masses.

In PPSC, Poulantzas proceeded in three steps. First, he argued with Althusser that the institutional separation between economics and politics typical of the capitalist mode of production (hereafter CMP) required an autonomous theory of the political region. Second, he drew on concepts of juridico-political theory to describe the institutional matrix of the capitalist type of state: a hierarchically organized, centrally-coordinated, sovereign territorial state based on the rule of law and, in its ideal-typical 'normal' form, combined with bourgeois democracy. This form addresses political subjects as individuated citizens rather than as members of opposed classes and thereby disguises exploitation and class power. Third, referring to Gramsci, he argued that political domination depends on the capacity of the dominant class to promote a hegemonic project linking individual interests to a national-popular interest that also served the long-term interests of the capitalist class and its allies in the power bloc.

SPS also has a tripartite structure. Poulantzas's argument moves from general *propositions about the state* through *a theory of the capitalist type of state* to a more concrete-complex *theory of this type of state in the current phase of capitalism*. The steps in the argument are articulated respectively to general propositions on production in general, on the capitalist social division of labour, and on the current stage of capitalism. Here Poulantzas described the state not only as an integral element in political class domination but also as a central instance for securing important economic and extra-economic conditions for accumulation. He also stressed the centrality of class powers and struggles to the labour process, social relations of production, and the state.

Poulantzas combined two types of analysis: an account of the capitalist type of state and the state in capitalist societies (PPSC: chs. 2-4). The former begins with an *abstract-simple* analysis of the *formal adequacy* of a given type of state in a pure capitalist social formation, argues that its form typically problematizes its functionality, and examines how and to what extent political practices may overcome such problems in specific periods and conjunctures (Jessop 1982, 1990). In contrast, the latter focuses in relatively concrete-complex terms on '*actually existing states*' in capitalist societies. It examines whether their activities are *functionally adequate* for capital accumulation and political class domination and how this functional adequacy is achieved (or not) in specific conjunctures through specific strategies and policies promoted by particular social forces.

In his theoretical studies, Poulantzas used form analysis to identify the historical specificity of the capitalist type of state. This is exemplified by PPSC, *Classes in Contemporary Capitalism* (CCC), and SPS. His historical work prioritized the analysis of the changing balance of forces. He showed how political class struggles and their outcomes are mediated and condensed through specific institutional forms in particular periods, stages, and conjunctures regardless of whether these forms corresponded to the capitalist type of state. This approach is illustrated by the concrete analyses in PSSC, by his periodized analyses of exceptional regimes in *Fascism and*

Dictatorship (FD) and *Crisis of the Dictatorships* (CD).

While both approaches proved productive for their specific purposes, it is not clear whether Poulantzas wanted to combine them to produce a coherent relational account of the capitalist state or whether they simply reflect different approaches to different analytical objects without being fully reconcilable. While both approaches are clearly compatible with his claim that the state is a social relation, the former prioritizes form-analysis and the latter privileges social forces. Moreover, missing in his work are more detailed studies of the mediating role of the institutional and organizational forms of politics and their strategic-relational implications for the balance of forces. If he had delivered these it would be easier to assess whether the two approaches can, as I suspect, be adequately reconciled.

The state as a social relation

Poulantzas's studies are based on his claim that *the state is a social relation*. He explicitly rejected the view that the state is an entity – whether a docile instrument or rational subject. Instead, *'like "capital", it is [...] a relationship of forces, or more precisely the material condensation of such a relationship among classes and class fractions, such as this is expressed within the State in a necessarily specific form'* (SPS, 128f.). By analogy with Marx's analysis of capital as a social relation, this claim can be reformulated as follows: the state is not a thing but a social relation between people mediated through their relation to things (cf. CI: ch. 23); or, again, the state is not a subject but a social relation between subjects mediated through their relation to state capacities. More precisely, *state power* (not the state apparatus) can be seen as a *form-determined* condensation of the changing balance of forces in political and politically-relevant struggle.

To translate this account into concrete-complex analyses of specific political conjunctures requires the study of three interrelated moments: (1) the state's historical and/or formal constitution[1] as a complex institutional ensemble with a spatio-temporally specific pattern of structurally-inscribed 'strategic selectivity';[2] (2) the historical and substantive organization and configuration of political forces in specific conjunctures and their strategies, including their capacity to reflect on and respond to the strategic selectivities inscribed in the state apparatus as a whole; and (3) the interaction of these forces on this strategically-selective terrain and/or at a distance therefrom. With this approach to state power, Poulantzas implicitly rejected a general

---

1   Poulantzas discussed both the historical formation and functioning of the capitalist state as a hybrid form (PPSC: 144ff., 154f., 161ff., 168ff.) and its formal constitution as a capitalist type of state (148ff., 189, chs. 3-5).
2   On strategic selectivity, see Jessop (1982, 1985, 1990 and 2007)

theory of the state in favour of form-analytical historical analyses of the agency-mediated expanded reproduction (or transformation) of the capital relation. He recognized that the state's historical and formal constitution is not pregiven but results from past struggles and is also reproduced (or transformed) through struggle. He also refused to treat the balance of forces as fixed and explores how it is modified through shifts in the strategic-relational terrain of the state, economy, and wider social formation as well as by changes in organization, strategy, and tactics.

The contribution of *State, Power, Socialism*

Poulantzas developed the strategic-relational character of the state in SPS. Part One deals with the institutional materiality of the capitalist type of state and its impact on class struggle. Poulantzas first showed that *all* of the state apparatuses (including the economic and repressive apparatuses and not just the ideological apparatuses) are the expression of the separation of mental from manual labour. He then traced the consequences of this for political struggle. Next he explored the significance of individualization for the forms of political struggle and, drawing on Gramsci, noted how the modern democratic state, grounded in individual citizenship and a national sovereign state, encouraged normal politics to take the form of a struggle for national-popular hegemony. He also developed powerful arguments on the roles of force and law in shaping the strategic terrain of the capitalist type of state and on how resort to them is shaped in turn by class struggles. After this sketch of the institutional materiality of the state, Poulantzas showed how it operates to modify and condense the balance of forces in political struggles. He continued to argue that this state serves to organize the dominant classes and to disorganize the dominated classes but argued, in this context, that the state is fractured and disunified and how this poses problems for the exercise of state power. This is particularly important as he now recognized that the dominated classes and their struggles are present in the state system itself as well as at a distance from it. Thus he could show how state power was grounded in the social relations of production and the institutional materiality of the state – thereby rejecting a generalized theory of power and resistance in favour of a revolutionary materialist account of class power and its overdetermination.

In a third analytical step, moving towards the concrete-complex in a particular period, Poulantzas analysed the changing relationship between the economic and extra-economic conditions of capital accumulation in the contemporary phase of capitalism. Here he built on arguments from *Classes in Contemporary Capitalism* to develop four themes: first, the state's economic functions are growing more important, which is reflected in the structure and organization of the state; second, the boundaries between the economic and the extra-economic have been redrawn, with previously extra-economic elements now being seen as directly relevant to valorization; third, the state's economic interventions are increasingly focused on the social relations of production themselves and on the attempt to increase relative surplus-value; and, fourth, even those policies most directly concerned with economic reproduction nonetheless have an essentially political character and must be carried through in relation to social cohesion in a class-divided society. This extension in state intervention intensifies tensions among different fractions of capital and also accentuates inequalities and disparities between the subordinate and dominant classes. The state is therefore assuming some of the features of an exceptional state but on a continuing basis. In this sense, it must be seen as the new 'democratic' form of the bourgeois republic in contemporary capitalism.

Exceptional regimes

Before I come to the particular forms of the exceptional state, I want to look briefly at Poulantzas's early work. This largely ignored two issues that would become important in his later work: the periodization of the capitalist state and the distinction between normal and exceptional regimes. PPSC focused on the capitalist type of state in its generic normal form (liberal bourgeois democracy). Later studies investigated exceptional forms of the capitalist state, particularly fascism and military dictatorships, and the interventionist state. SPS combined these concerns in the claim that the capitalist type of state is now '*permanently and structurally characterized by a peculiar sharpening of the generic elements of political crisis and state crisis*' rather than showing intermittent signs of short-term, conjunctural crisis. The basis of this claim was elaborated in an essay on 'The Crisis of the State' (1976). Poulantzas argued that, while the generic elements of crisis are constantly reproduced in capitalist societies, crises only emerge when these elements condense into a distinct conjuncture and develop according to specific rhythms (1976: 21f., 28). They must therefore be related first to the field of political class relations and only secondarily to specific political institutions (PPSC: 63; 1976: 23, 28).

Only one type of political crisis produces an exceptional form of state, namely, a crisis of hegemony within the power bloc. This occurs when no class or fraction can impose its 'leadership' on other members of the power bloc, whether by its own political organizations or through the 'parliamentary democratic' state (72, 100f., 124f.). Symptoms include: a crisis of party representation, that is, a split between different classes or fractions and their parties (73, 102, 126); attempts by various social forces to by-pass political parties and influence the state directly; and efforts by different state apparatuses to impose political order independently of decisions coming through formal channels of power (74, 102f.; 1976: 28). Even when the state can continue functioning, such phenomena can undermine the institutional and class unity of the state (334). The state may also lose its monopoly of violence (335).

The outcome of political crises always depends on class strategies and struggles. Fascism emerged because a political crisis coincided with an offensive step by the bourgeoisie and a defensive step by the working class (78ff., 107f., 130f., 139ff.). Class struggles not only contribute to the genesis of political crises but also determine whether they are resolved by restoring democracy or resorting to an exceptional state. Economic crises do not directly cause political and state crises but they do shape the conjuncture in which such crises emerge (53; 1976: 25, 34). When crises affect all social relations rather than one particular field of relations they become 'organic' or 'structural' crises (Poulantzas 1976: 26).

Poulantzas's analysis of the exceptional state derives from his view that the definitive features of the normal form of the capitalist type of state are democratic institutions and hegemonic class leadership. Normal states correspond to conjunctures in which bourgeois hegemony is stable and secure; and exceptional states are responses to a crisis of hegemony (FD: 293; PPSC: 11, 57ff., 72, 298, 313; CD: 92f.). Thus, while consent predominates over constitutionalized violence in normal states, exceptional states intensify physical repression and conduct an 'open war' against dominated classes (FD: 226; PPSC: 152, 316ff., 330; CD: 9, 92, 129). This basic contrast is reflected in four sets of institutional and operational differences between the two forms of state.

- Whereas the normal state has representative democratic institutions with universal suffrage and competing political parties, exceptional states suspend the electoral principle (apart from plebiscites and/or referenda closely controlled from above) and end the plural party system (FD: 123, 230; PPSC: 324ff.; CD: 42, 91, 114).
- The transfer of power in normal states follows constitutional and legal rules and occurs in stable and predictable ways. Exceptional states suspend the rule of law, however, to facilitate constitutional and administrative changes allegedly required to help solve the hegemonic crisis (FD: 226f., 311; PPSC: 320ff.; SPS: 87ff.).

- Ideological state apparatuses (ISA) in normal states typically have 'private' legal status and enjoy significant autonomy from official government control. In contrast, ISA in exceptional states are generally subordinated to the repressive state apparatus and lack real independence. This subordination serves to legitimate the increased resort to coercion and helps overcome the ideological crisis that accompanies a crisis of hegemony (PPSC: 314ff.; CD: 113f.).
- The formal separation of powers within the repressive state apparatus (RSA) is also reduced through the infiltration of subordinate branches and power centres by the dominant branch and/or through the expansion of parallel power networks and transmission belts cutting across and linking different branches and centres. This produces greater centralization of political control and multiplies its points of application in the state. This serves to reorganize hegemony, to counteract internal divisions and short-circuit internal resistances, and to secure flexibility in the face of bureaucratic inertia (PPSC: 315f., 327ff.; CD: 50, 92, 100f.; SPS: 87ff.).

Poulantzas argued that representative democratic institutions facilitate the organic circulation and reorganization of hegemony and thereby inhibit major ruptures or breaks in social cohesion. However, if political and ideological crises cannot be resolved through the normal, democratic play of class forces, democratic institutions must be suspended and the crises resolved through an open 'war of manoeuvre'. But the act of abolishing democratic institutions tends to congeal the balance of forces prevailing when the exceptional state is stabilized. This makes it harder to resolve new crises and contradictions through routine and gradual policy adjustments and to establish a new equilibrium of compromise. Thus Poulantzas concluded that the alleged strength of the exceptional state actually hides its real brittleness. These make exceptional states vulnerable to sudden collapse as contradictions accumulate. Conversely, apparently weak democratic states bend under the strain and therefore provide more flexible means to organize political class domination (CD: 30, 38, 48ff., 90ff., 106, 124).

The opposite holds for exceptional regimes. They lack any specialized politico-ideological apparatuses to channel and control mass support and are thereby isolated from the masses. They display a rigid apportionment of state power among various distinct political 'clans' entrenched in each apparatus. And they lack an ideology that can forge the necessary state unity and can establish an effective national-popular cohesion. This produces a muddle of inconsistent policies toward the masses as the exceptional regime attempts to neutralize their opposition. It also leads to purely mechanical compromises, tactical alliances and settling of accounts among 'economic-corporate' interests among the dominant classes and fractions. In turn this intensifies the internal contradictions of the state apparatus and reduces its flexibility in the face of economic and/or political crises (49f., 55ff., 79f., 83f., 91ff., 112f., 120f., 124ff.).

Poulantzas saw important differences among exceptional forms of state. He seemed particularly struck by fascism's flexibility and manoeuvrability. In contrast, military dictatorship is the least flexible type; and Bonapartism is located halfway between these extremes (Jessop 1985). Poulantzas nonetheless insisted that no exceptional regime can secure the sort of flexible, organic regulation of social forces and the smooth circulation of hegemony that occurs under bourgeois democracies (124). Accordingly, just as the movement from a normal to an exceptional state involves political crises and ruptures rather than taking a continuous, linear path, so the transition from an exceptional to a normal form will also involve a series of crises rather than a simple process of self-transformation. This places a premium on the political class struggle to achieve hegemony over the democratization process. Indeed Poulantzas insisted that the class character of the normal state will vary significantly with the outcome of this struggle (90ff., 124 and *passim*).

Authoritarian statism

These reflections are developed in Poulantzas's account of the new 'normal' form of the capitalist type of state, i.e., 'authoritarian statism'. Its basic developmental tendency is described as 'intensified state control over every sphere of socio-economic life combined with radical decline of the institutions of political democracy and with draconian and multiform curtailment of so-called "formal" liberties' (SPS: 203f.). More precisely, the main elements of 'authoritarian statism' and its implications for representative democracy are: first, a transfer of power from the legislature to the executive and the concentration of power in the latter; second, an accelerated fusion between the legislature, executive, and judiciary, along with a decline in the rule of law; third, the functional decline of political parties as the leading channels for political dialogue with the administration and as the major forces in organizing hegemony; and finally, the growth of parallel power networks cross-cutting the formal organization of the state and holding a decisive share in its various activities (FD: 303ff., 310ff.; CCC: 173; 1976: 55ff.; SPS: 217ff.; 1979: 30).

These changes are a permanent, structural feature of the modern state. They correspond to a sharpening of the generic elements of political and state crisis accompanying the long-term economic crisis that is supposedly besetting the entire current phase of the CMP. Among the most important crisis-tendencies in this phase are: the politicization of working-class resistance to capital's attempt to resolve the economic crisis; the politicization of the new petty bourgeoisie because of the deepening of the social division of labour within the ranks of intellectual labour itself; the decomposition of the traditional alliance between the bourgeoisie and the old and new petty bourgeoisie; the ideological crisis accompanying the growth of new social movements on erstwhile 'secondary' fronts; and the sharpening of the contradictions within the power bloc because of the tendential division of labour between the comprador and interior fractions of capital (SPS: 210ff., 219, 221).

Moreover, whether the state disengages or intervenes to moderate a given crisis-tendency in one area, it aggravates other crisis-tendencies in other areas. Thus the postwar state's ability to moderate the 'wilder' aspects of capitalist crises (as evident in the 1930s) requires it to assume direct responsibility for the purgative effects of crisis. This can threaten its legitimacy and stability. This occurs because it has become much harder for the dominant fraction to sacrifice its short-term economic-corporate interests in order to promote its long-term political hegemony. Yet failure to act against economic crisis-tendencies will undermine capital accumulation. Likewise, the state's growing involvement politicizes the popular masses – especially as postwar social policy commitments exclude spending cuts, austerity, and recommodification. The resulting legitimation crisis leads the masses to confront the state directly and threaten its stability. But any failure to intervene in these areas would undermine the social reproduction of labour power. The state's growing role in promoting the internationalization of capital also provokes problems for national unity. This is especially clear in its impact on less developed regions and national minorities (141f., 154f., 210ff., 219, 221, and 245f.).

Poulantzas used to argue that exceptional regimes are always temporary and occur in response to specific conjunctures. Thus, because these crisis-tendencies are permanent features of contemporary capitalism, authoritarian statism must be seen as normal. For significant 'exceptional' features co-exist with and modify 'normal' features of the capitalist type of state. This involves a constant symbiosis and functional intersection of normal and exceptional structures under the control of the commanding heights of the state apparatus and the dominant party (SPS: 208, 210, 245; cf. 1979: 30). Real power is concentrated and centralized at the summits of the governmental and administrative system, which seals itself off from the representational role of parties and parliaments. The latter are now simple electoral 'registration chambers' (Harold Laski). The state administration has become the main site for developing state policy, guided by the political executive. This massively politicizes the administration and risks its fragmentation behind a formal façade of bureaucratic hierarchy and unity (SPS: 236). Indeed, politics is increasingly focused in the staff office of a president or prime minister. Standing at the apex of the administrative structures, this office appears as a purely personalistic presidential-prime-ministerial system. The pressure of many contradictory forces is condensed here so that the fragile configuration of forces becomes evident in contradictions inside the administration (SPS: 221ff., 226ff., 233, 236ff.; cf. FD: 311ff.).

Poulantzas related this 'irresistible rise of the state administration' mainly to the state's growing economic role. For state intervention means that law can no longer be confined to general, formal, and universal norms whose enactment is the preserve of parliament as the embodiment of the general will of the people-nation. The rule of law is weakened because legal norms are increasingly modified and elaborated by the administration (SPS: 218f.; cf. Scheuerman 2005). This change is the product of the permanent instability of monopoly hegemony within the power bloc and over the people as well as of changing economic imperatives. Indeed, the decline of the rule of law also affects the political sphere. One sign of this is that pre-emptive policing grows at the expense of judicial punishment (SPS: 219f.). More generally, the crisis of monopoly hegemony means that the state administration becomes the *central* site at which the unstable equilibrium of compromise between the power bloc and the popular masses is elaborated, and that is located within the power bloc itself. It also transforms the parties of power (or 'natural parties of government' in contrast to those parties destined for a permanent oppositional role) into a single (or duopolistic) authoritarian mass party whose task is more to mobilize mass support for state policies in a plebiscitary fashion than it is to directly articulate and represent popular interests and demands to the state. This is also related to an increasingly dense network of crosscutting ties between big business and the central administrative apparatuses of the state (especially the economic apparatuses) and to a general increase in political and administrative centralism. A further aspect here is the increased personalism of power at the top of the executive. This does not involve a genuine Bonapartist dictator who concentrates despotic powers in his hands but rather involves the search for a charismatic frontman who can give a sense of strategic direction to the complexities of politics both for the dominant classes and in more plebiscitary fashion for the popular masses (cf. Grande 2000).

Despite this centralization of administrative power, Poulantzas emphasized the relative weakness of the authoritarian state. This is faced, according to Poulantzas, with the growing incompressibility of economic contradictions and new forms of popular struggle. There are also changes among the parties in power (220). Their ties of representation to the power bloc loosen because monopoly capital finds it harder to organize its hegemony through parliamentary parties. It therefore concentrates its lobbying on the administration (PPSC: 171; FD: 313f. fn., 320; SPS: 221ff.). Thus the parties no longer fulfil their traditional functions in policy-making and in political legitimation through elections. They are now little more than transmission belts for official decisions and merely differ in the aspects of official policy that they choose to popularize (SPS: 229f., 237). In turn, political legitimation is redirected through channels based on plebiscitary and manipulative techniques that are dominated by the executive and channelled through mass media (229).

Nonetheless the activities of the state administration continually run up against limits inherent in its own structure. This is particularly clear in the internal divisions between different administrative coteries, clans, and factions and in the reproduction inside the state system of class conflicts and contradictions. Thus we must ask how the administration overcomes these tensions so as to act effectively on behalf of monopoly capital. Exceptional states achieve this through a political apparatus (such as the fascist party, the army, or the political police) that is distinct from the administration. In the 'normal' form of representative democracy, it is achieved through the organic functioning of a plural party system located at a certain distance from the central administrative apparatus (SPS: 231, 232f.; cf. PPSC: 316f., 332, 340f., 353; FD: 318ff., 335ff., 345f., 348, 353ff.; CD: 33, 104ff.). But how does this occur under authoritarian statism?

Poulantzas suggested that the dominant mass party functions as a parallel network and acts as a political commissar at the heart of the administration, developing a material and ideological community of interest with key civil servants. It must also transmit the state ideology to the popular masses and organize the legitimation of authoritarian statism in a plebiscitary manner (SPS: 236f.). Hence the dominant *mass* party actually functions as the dominant *state* party in so far as it represents the state to the masses rather than vice versa. Such a mass party is most likely to develop during a long period without alternation among the governing parties. But similar functions can be performed by a single inter-party 'centre' that dominates the alternating parties of power (232, 235f.).

The irresistible rise of the state administration cannot prevent a further sharpening of the generic elements of political and state crisis. Examples include: (a) the politicization of the bureaucracy, especially among its lower ranks, in opposition to the dominant 'state party'; (b) the greater difficulties facing the administration than a flexible plural party system in organizing hegemony and managing the unstable equilibrium of class compromise; and (c) the growth and impact of mass struggles precipitated by new forms of state intervention with potentially major dislocating effects within the state itself (240ff.). Thus the rise of 'authoritarian statism' involves a paradox. While it clearly strengthens state power at the expense of liberal representative democracy, it also weakens its capacities to secure bourgeois hegemony (241, 263ff.).

Authoritarian statism today

Poulantzas's analysis of authoritarian statism was remarkably prescient. The various trends that he identified in SPS have become even clearer. They are reactions to the growing political crisis in the power bloc, the representational crisis in the political system, the legitimacy and state crises associated with the twin failures of the postwar interventionist state and the neoliberal turn, and the growing challenge to the primacy of the national territorial state in the face of globalization. We should particularly note the continued decline of parliament and the rule of law, the growing autonomy of the executive, the increased importance of presidential or prime ministerial powers, the consolidation of authoritarian, plebiscitary parties that largely represent the state to the popular masses, and, something neglected by Poulantzas, the mediatization of politics as the mass media play an increasing role in shaping political imaginaries, programmes, and debates. An increased emphasis on issues of national security and pre-emptive policing associated with the so-called war on terror at home and abroad has also reinforced the attack on human rights and civil liberties. New Labour is a particularly compelling illustration of these tendencies but the same trends are also starkly evident other metropolitan societies.

Poulantzas's success in this regard can be explained in terms of his commitment to combining theoretical and historical analyses rather than engaging in crude *Staatsableiterei* or reducing every form of capitalist state to a simple dictatorship of the bourgeoisie.[3] For Poulantzas, an adequate periodization of the capitalist type of state should consider the changing forms of articulation of its economic, political, and ideological functions linked to the different stages of capitalism. Combined with his more sophisticated

---

[3] On the importance of this approach, see section 5 of his introduction to PPSC.

analysis in SPS of the economic, political, and ideological moments of social relations of production and the changing spatio-temporal matrices of capital accumulation, this enabled him to theorize the 'transformed form' of the economic functions of the 'strong state' in its latest phase (SPS: chs. 1-2). In addition he made careful generalizations from the case of fascism as the most flexible form of exceptional regime, updated from the interwar period to the current stage of capitalism and suitably modified to allow for the 'normality' of authoritarian statism. Poulantzas also seems to have extrapolated key features of authoritarian statism from French experience, with its strong étatist tradition and postwar history of Gaullism. He was probably also influenced by the character of the CDU-Staat in Germany and its subsequent transformation into a *Sicherheitsstaat* (Hirsch 1980). What distinguishes Poulantzas's analysis from contemporary libertarian, liberal, and leftist critiques of creeping authoritarianism is his ability to locate these tendencies in a form analysis of the capitalist type of state combined with a distinctive interpretation of contemporary imperialism and a neo-Gramscian analysis of the political crisis of the power bloc. Thereby he showed that the intensification of generic features of exceptional regimes involved both a strengthening and a weakening of the capitalist type of state. This illustrates well the heuristic and explanatory power of his key thesis that the state is a social relation.

This said, Poulantzas's account of authoritarian statism is problematic. First, relative to the weight allotted to it in explaining the genesis of authoritarian statism, Poulantzas hardly discussed the nature of hegemony and its crisis in contemporary capitalism. Second, he did not show how the exceptional features of authoritarian statism are articulated under the dominance of the normal elements. This would be crucial for his claim that this new form of the capitalist state is a normal democratic state. Third, while he argued that the rise of 'authoritarian statism' entails a *break* or *rupture* in the political process (since it involves a transition to a new state form), he admitted that it results from the gradual *accentuation of tendencies* coeval with monopoly capitalism and thus typical of interventionist states. He could extrapolate some of these tendencies into the most recent period of state monopoly capitalism but failed to predict the dominance of the neoliberal turn in the transition to a globalizing, post-fordist accumulation regime. In particular, he seems not to have anticipated the success of monopoly capital's offensive step and the weakening of organized labour in response to the crisis of Atlantic Fordism and its Keynesian welfare national states. Fourth, despite his recognition in SPS that the spatio-temporal matrices of capital accumulation were being radically reorganized, his analysis of authoritarian statism was still heavily imprinted by the assumption that the national state would remain the dominant scale for organizing political class domination. In short, even if we accept Poulantzas's basically descriptive account of 'authoritarian statism' as a normal form of capitalist state, he is less convincing in explaining its emergence and future development.

Moreover, despite his amazing theoretical acuity and astonishing prescience in some respects, he missed three other important trends in contemporary capitalism. First, in focusing on the changing forms of state economic intervention and highlighting its role in redrawing the boundaries between the economic and extra-economic, he missed the changes in the overall dynamic of capital accumulation that are associated with the transition from Atlantic Fordism to a globalizing knowledge-based economy. Second, in focusing on the role of national states in contemporary imperialism, he failed to note how far the growing multi-scalar interpenetration of economic spaces that he identified in *Classes in Contemporary Capitalism* also implied a major re-scaling of state apparatuses and state power. Although he correctly insisted on the continued importance of the national state in securing social cohesion, he did not anticipate how the reallocation of other functions would weaken its capacities to fulfil this crucial general function. And, third, although he recognized the vital role of networks in the state's operations, he did not realize how far this would shift the exercise of state power away from top-down planning and hierarchical rule towards decentralized context-steering and other forms of governance in the shadow of hierarchy.

Notwithstanding these closing criticisms, Poulantzas remains a crucial figure in the development of a materialist theory of the state. His insight that the state is a social relation not only invigorated his more abstract-simple form-analytical account of the capitalist type of state but also provided a powerful approach for dealing with the concrete-complex features of actually existing states in capitalist societies. He can be acknowledged for his role in providing subsequent theorists and militants with a rich and sophisticated theoretical and conceptual framework with which to analyse the contradictory and conflictual process of expanded reproduction from the viewpoint of the key strategic-relational contribution of the state (and interstate system) in organizing a power bloc and disorganizing subaltern classes. In short, Poulantzas's texts can be considered as modern classics in the sense that they pose important questions and provide answers that, even if they are no longer regarded as fully adequate, nonetheless point us in the right direction.

Continued recognition as a 'classic' text is not guaranteed. Indeed, 'in order for a text to achieve the accolade of a classic, it must typically overcome a variety of cultural hurdles; while to survive as one, it must be subjected to continual critical engagement, its concepts reformulated to meet new problems and trials' (Baehr and O'Brien 1994: 127f.). As the current volume shows, this fits Poulantzas well. His work is critically discussed, and there can be no doubt that its concepts can be redeployed and reformulated to enable us to meet new problems and trials in the contemporary period.

References

Baehr, P. / O'Brien, M. (1994) 'Founders, classics and the concept of a canon', *Current Sociology*, vol. 42, no. 1, 1-151.
Grande, E. (2000) 'Charisma und Komplexität. Verhandlungsdemokratie, Mediendemokratie und der Funktionswandel politischer Eliten', *Leviathan*, vol. 28, no. 1, 122-141.
Hirsch, J. (1980) *Der Sicherheitsstaat. Das ›Modell Deutschland‹, seine Krise und die neuen sozialen Bewegungen* (Frankfurt am Main: VSA-Verlag).
Jessop, B. (1982) *The Capitalist State* (Oxford: Martin Robertson).
Jessop, B. (1985) *Nicos Poulantzas: Marxist Theory and Political Strategy* (Basingstoke: Macmillan).
Jessop, B. (1990) *State Theory* (Cambridge: Polity Press).
Jessop, B. (2007) *State Power: a Strategic-Relational Approach* (Cambridge: Polity Press).
Poulantzas, N. (1976) 'Les transformations actuelles de l'État, la crise politique et la crise de l'État', in Poulantzas, N. (ed.) *La Crise de l'État* (Paris: Presses Univ. de France) 19-58.
Poulantzas, N. (1979) 'El Etatismo Autoritario recorre Europa. Entrevista con Nicos Poulantzas', *El Viejo Topo*, no. 35, 28-32.
Scheuerman, W.E. (2005) *Liberal Democracy and the Social Acceleration of Time* (Baltimore: Johns Hopkins Univ. Press).

POULANTZAS AND FORM ANALYSIS: ON THE RELATION BETWEEN TWO APPROACHES TO HISTORICAL-MATERIALIST STATE THEORY

JOACHIM HIRSCH AND JOHN KANNANKULAM

There is still no coherent historical-materialist account of the state. Marx did not leave a theory of the state, and later approaches were either instrumentalized for political purposes – a good example is the Marxist-Leninist theory of state monopoly capitalism – or they remained incomplete. The most important contributions to state theory in the interwar period were Antonio Gramsci's fragmentary remarks in the *Prison Notebooks*; and the work of the Soviet theorist Evgeny Pashukanis in the area of legal theory. In the wake of the student movement at the end of the 1960s, debates on the state experienced a noticeable upswing. At the time, the aim was to develop a critical analysis of the Fordist-Keynesian type of state, which had emerged in the capitalist metropolises after World War II. In this context, two approaches were of special significance, which had developed in very different political and theoretical contexts: the contributions to the West German debate on 'state derivation'; and the state theory of Nicos Poulantzas.

Poulantzas's theoretical background was both the 'structural' Marxism of the Althusser School and Weberian sociology. At the political level, his work dealt with the role of the French communist party (PCF), its commitment to the theory of state monopoly capitalism, and its theoretical judgment of the collapse of the Fourth Republic and the restructuring of the state and political system after Charles de Gaulle's coup d'état.

In contrast, the Communist Party in West Germany was insignificant both at the political and the theoretical level. Politically, the state debate in the country was motivated by the attempt to undertake an *Ideologiekritik* of the prevailing illusion in the reform capacities of the welfare state (*Sozialstaatsillusion*), which had been reinforced by the SPD's entry into government in the 1960s.[1] At the level of theory, the debate was embedded

---

1   See the programmatic and polemical contribution of Müller and Neusüß (1970).

in the re-appropriation of Marx's critique of political economy by left-wing intellectuals.

These contrasting political-theoretical conjunctures have shaped both approaches. The West German debate is characterized by a relatively abstract concern with the political form of capitalism and its contribution to making the state appear neutral in class terms. This involved attempts to extend Marx's analysis of the value-form and move it towards a theory of the political. Indeed, form analysis became an important foundation for historical-materialist theories of the state. However, the accounts in question were not capable of investigating political institutions, political struggles, and state transformation.

Poulantzas's approach was better equipped for this purpose: it was grounded in class theory and aimed at developing an analysis of real-concrete states. Nonetheless his approach also had certain flaws. He did not engage much with the West German debate. His mistrust of 'Hegelian' Marxism led him to ignore the fact that the proponents of state derivation were capable of deciphering the contradictions inherent in the capitalist mode of production (hereafter CMP) and their implications for the autonomous dynamic of the political process. This exposed him to the charge of class reductionism and functionalism, which was not entirely unjustified. The shortcomings of the two approaches give rise to the question whether their critical confrontation will enable us to refine our understanding of the state.

1. The problem

A particular flaw in Poulantzas's state theory was his failure to ground the 'relative autonomy' of the state at the theoretical level (PPSC: 29ff., 123ff., 188ff., 228, 253ff.; SPS: 25ff., 127ff., 140ff.). He simply posited, rather than 'derived', this constitutive feature of the bourgeois state. His attempt to trace the relative autonomy of the state back to the separation of manual and mental labour could possibly serve as an explanation (SPS: 54ff.). However, this separation also occurs in other historical formations, which suggests that it does not account for the specificity of the capitalist state.

In this chapter, we will remedy this shortcoming – admittedly in a preliminary fashion. In particular, we will pay attention to the question whether Poulantzas's approach can be reconciled with a form analysis of the state based on Marx's critique of political economy. We will proceed as follows: first, we will demonstrate that Poulantzas's middle-period writings are grounded in Althusserian epistemology; above all, we are interested in Louis Althusser's critique of approaches that describe capitalist society as an 'expressive totality'. This critique in turn explains why Poulantzas rejects economism and dismisses Pashukanis. Given Pashukanis's influence on form-analytical approaches to the state, it is worth considering whether Poulantzas's critique was appropriate, and how Pashukanis explains the existence of the state. In this context, the key question is whether Poulantzas's work contains, at least implicitly, a line of argument that resembles the most elaborate variants of the state derivation approach. To address this question, we will first reconstruct the form-analytical determination of the state developed in West Germany in the 1970s. After that, we will examine Poulantzas's elaboration of Gramsci's theory of hegemony because this aspect of his work marks a step forward from the West German debate.

2. Poulantzas in the context of Althusserian epistemology

Especially in *Political Power and Social Classes* (PPSC), Poulantzas discussed the state in the context of Althusserian epistemology. He remarked: 'A mode of production, as Engels stated schematically, is composed of different levels of instances, the economic, political, ideological and theoretical [...]. The type of unity which characterizes a mode of production is that of a *complex whole* dominated, in the last instance, by the economic. The term *determination* will be reserved for this dominance in the last instance. This type of relation between the instances can be distinguished from the one which is proposed in certain interpretations of Marxism. It is not, for example, a circular and expressive totality, founded on a central-subject instance which is the foundation category of the origins and the principle of genesis, and of which the other instances, "total parts" (*partes totales*), constitute only the phenomenal expression. [...] It is a type of relation inside which the structure in dominance governs the very constitution (the nature) of the regional structures, by assigning them their place and by distributing functions to them. The relations which thus constitute each level are never simple, but overdetermined by the relations of the other levels' (PPSC: 13f.; cf. Poulantzas 1967: 188ff.).

This is how Poulantzas explained his rejection of conceptions that portray capitalist society as an 'expressive totality', tracing all phenomena in the social world back to a single, basic social relation. His critique was directed against 'economistic' understandings of Marxism, which conceived the political superstructure as a 'phenomenal expression' or 'appearance' of the economy without any effects of its own. He argued, citing Friedrich Engels and following Althusser, that a mode of production should rather be seen as an articulation of three differentiated structural levels, namely the economy, ideology and politics. These structural levels 'are not already constituted essences, which then enter into external relations with each other, according to the schema of base and superstructure – a schema which, if taken literally, is ambiguous' (PPSC: 15). Instead, the configuration of the regional instances results from the total structure of a mode of production, i.e., from their distinctive articulation within a complex whole. According to Poulantzas, the structure of these regional instances in the CMP is characterized by their separation, which gives rise to the need for regional theories. Following this line of argument, Marx provided a systematic theoretical treatment of the economic region of the CMP, above all in *Capital* (20f.). Poulantzas argues that he did so not because 'nothing important happens in the other regions and because examination of them is a secondary task, but rather because [...] this mode of production is specified by a characteristic autonomy of its instances, which can be subjected to a particular scientific treatment, and, secondly, because the economic holds the dominant role in this mode, a role over and above determination in the last instance. Thus the other instances (the political and the ideological) are very definitely *present* in *Capital*, which is not, in this sense, an "exclusively" economic work, but they are present *implicitly*, that is through their effects in the economic region' (21).

Poulantzas achieved three things with this line of argument: first, he rejected a simple schema of 'essence' and 'appearance' that portrays the 'superstructure' as an epiphenomenon; second, he dismissed the idea that the structural levels of a social formation represent a 'combinatory', which suggests that they are always already there and articulated in a pre-given matrix; and, third, he justified the need for an autonomous regional theory of the political within the CMP.

3. Poulantzas's explanation of the separation between politics and the economy

The key question in this context is *how* Poulantzas *explained* the separation of the political from the economic as a distinctive feature of the CMP. His starting point is the capitalist *relations of production*. Their basic elements display a *homology*: the workers are separated from the means of production – both in terms of possession and ownership[2] (PPSC: 27, 32). Along these lines, Poulantzas remarked: 'The character of the economic in this mode of production, as a process of producing surplus value, results especially from this separation, which converts the labourer himself into an element of capital and his labour into a commodity. This combination determines a specific autonomy of the political and the economic' (32).

---

2   On this distinction, see also Poulantzas (1967: 194ff.).

The particular structure of the capitalist relations of production transforms labour power into a commodity, which *presupposes* that political domination is separated from these relations. It is characterized by the *relative autonomy*[3] of the political from the economic instance. In this context, Poulantzas stated: 'Because of the specific autonomy of instances characteristic of the CMP, the juridico-political and ideological instances are not analysed there on the same grounds as the economic instance, which is at the centre of the investigation. Yet there is an indication of the immanent presence of these instances in the capitalist relations of production: the effect of the juridico-political or ideological structure on the supports, in their distribution into capitalists and wage-earning labourers, is sketched in but only implicitly' (71).

Poulantzas discussed this point only briefly in PPSC. He developed it further in *State, Power, Socialism* (SPS). In his later book, just as in PPSC, he compared the capitalist with the feudal relations of production, arguing that under feudal conditions, the immediate producers are separated from the means of production at level of property, but not at the level of possession. The feudal configuration produced 'what Marx had called the close "overlapping" or "mixedness" of the State and the economy' (SPS: 18). According to Poulantzas, the exercise of legitimate violence is an organic moment of all hitherto existing relations of production. He wrote that in pre-capitalist modes of production the 'exercise of legitimate violence is [...] implicit in the relations of production, since surplus labour has to be extracted from direct producers who possess the object and the means of their labour. Because of these clear-cut [précis] relations between the state and the economy, their contour, scope and significance are quite other than in the capitalist mode of production' (ibid.). Within capitalist relations of production matters are organized in a different way. The immediate producers neither have property in the means of production, nor possession of them: 'We witness here the emergence of "free labourers" possessing nothing but

---

3   This expression does not mean 'just a little autonomy'. Rather, it is based on the epistemological claim that it is impossible to describe one structural level within a given mode of production without reference to the others (cf. Charim 2002: 38f.). Poulantzas specifies this claim for the CMP in his later work. At first sight, it appears to be contradictory, but it is in fact very precise: 'What is involved here is not a real externality [...]. *The separation is nothing other than the capitalist form of the presence of the political in the constitution and reproduction of the relation of production.* This separation of State and economy and the presence-action of the former in the latter – in effect two expressions of a single pattern of relations between State and economy under capitalism – traverse all the historical stages and phases of the mode of production; albeit in changing forms, they are rooted in the hard core of capitalist relations of production' (SPS: 18f.).

their labour power and unable to set the labour process in motion without the owner, whose involvement is juridically represented by the contractual buying and selling of labour power' (ibid.).

3.1. Poulantzas's relation to Pashukanis

Poulantzas's line of argument points to Pashukanis, who posed the classical question: 'why does [class rule] assume the form of official state rule, or – which is the same thing – why does the machinery of state coercion not come into being as the private machinery of the ruling class; why does it detach itself from the ruling class and take on the *form* of an *impersonal* apparatus of public power separate from society?' (1924: 139; italics by J.H./J.K.). Pashukanis answered this question with reference to the legal form, i.e., the juridical contract structure, which is tied closely to and grounded in the commodity form – the elementary social form of capitalist societies. According to Pashukanis, the legal form is 'a specific set of relations, which men enter into, not by conscious choice, but because the *relations of production* compel them to do so. Man becomes a legal subject by virtue of the same necessity which transforms products of nature into a commodity complete with the enigmatic property of value' (68; italics by J.H./J.K.). In other words, the contract for the purchase and sale of labour power presupposes the freedom of contract and the legal capacity of the subjects concerned. In this sense, the worker is actually 'free' to offer labour power on the market, which was not the case in feudalism. This freedom is rooted in the exchange of equivalents in the market, which in turn presupposes the legal *equality* of the subjects. It presupposes that the instance guaranteeing and enforcing formal freedom and equality is separate from the contracting parties. In other words, this separation is a formal requirement for the reproduction of the CMP.

Pashukanis's explanation for the existence of the legal form was a central reference point for the *form-analytical determination* of the state in the state derivation debate. And the Pashukanis question can even be found in Poulantzas's work, albeit in a modified version: 'why in general, does the bourgeoisie seek to maintain its domination by having recourse precisely to the national-popular State – to the modern representative State with all its characteristic institutions? For it is far from self-evident that the bourgeoisie would have chosen this particular form if it had been able to tailor a State to its requirements' (SPS: 12, cf. 50, fn.).

3.2. Poulantzas's critique of Pashukanis

Nevertheless, Poulantzas distanced himself from Pashukanis in both PPSC and SPS, and ascribed to him and his followers an economistic-historicist perspective.[4] He wrote: 'The principles of explanation of the capitalist state have posed numerous problems for the Marxist science of the state. The central theme of these problems is the following: what are the real characteristics of the economic which imply this capitalist state? [...] The invariant theme of these replies is the following: the emergence in the economic level of the CMP, i.e., in capitalist relations of production, of agents of production as *individuals*. [...] This individualization of the agents of production, *grasped precisely as a real characteristic of capitalist relations of* production, is seen as constituting the substratum of modern state structures; and the ensemble of these individuals-agents as constituting civil society, that is the way in which the economic is somehow present in social relations. Thus, on this theory, separation of civil society and the state indicates the role of a strictly political superstructure relative to these economic individuals, subjects of a society of exchange and competition' (PPSC: 124).

According to Poulantzas, the existence of 'economic individuals' should not be misconceived as the *ultimate reason* [Grund] for the existence of the state. Rather, they are, as legal subjects, an *effect* of the capitalist relations of production. The separation of the immediate producers from the means of production results in their constitution as 'juridical and political [...] subjects' (SPS: 66), which in turn impresses a 'determinate structure' (64) on the labour process. This configuration is associated with a specific division of labour, as Marx showed in his analyses of the commodity and the law of value: 'only such products can become commodities with regard to each other, as result from different kinds of labour, each kind being carried on independently and for the account of private individuals' (CI: 42; cited in PPSC: 129). This suggests that humans experience the utility of their work only in so far as they relate their products to one another, turning them into commodities. The CMP is a mode of production in which 'the real dependence of the producers [...] is concealed [...]. These labours are, within certain objective limits, carried out independently from another (private labours), *that is, without the producers having to organize their co-operation to begin with*. It is then that the law of value dominates' (PPSC: 129). In addition, Poulantzas emphasized that the economistic-historical conception 'prevents us from understanding the relation of the state to the class struggle: (i) since agents of production are conceived as originating individuals-subjects and not as supports of structures, it is impossible to

4   Poulantzas wrote: 'economism has tried to evade this problem by considering formal juridical relations of property: this can be seen clearly in Pashukanis, *General Theory of Law and Marxism*, 1924, 1927 [...]. This renders the cardinal distinction between real appropriation (i.e. economic property) and formal juridical property in the "pure" mode of production theoretically impossible' (PPSC: 72, fn. 20; cf. 1967: 181).

constitute social classes from them and (ii) since the state is at the origin related to these economic individuals-agents, it is impossible to relate it to classes and class struggle' (125).

However, Sonja Buckel (2005: 91, translated) has shown that Poulantzas did not take the trouble 'to recognize the ambivalences in Pashukanis's approach' and did not get to the heart of the argument. Poulantzas's critique is certainly directed against Pashukanis but may be more fitting for his epigones. The same holds for Poulantzas's critique of the attempt to derive the state '*in the domain of the circulation of capital and "generalized" commodity exchange*' (SPS: 50). Ironically, there is a meeting of minds at this point between the protagonists of the state derivation debate, who wanted to explain the state, in an 'idealist' manner,[5] with reference to the *interests* of commodity owners, and their critics like Poulantzas. Both sides overlook the fact that the spheres of circulation and production cannot be conceived as strictly separate instances. Money, for example, acts as an expression of the value form when it mediates transactions in the sphere of circulation. But it simply does not follow that this suffices to explain the value form, which can only be deciphered in *connection* with the sphere of production; and circulation can only be given its 'proper' place when this connection is taken seriously. Marx's statement that the creation of surplus value does not occur in circulation but cannot take place apart from circulation (CI: 179ff.) shows precisely how both moments form a contradictory and mutually conditioned unity, which rules out any 'one-sided' reference to circulation.[6]

The limits of Poulantzas's critique of Pashukanis give rise to the question whether there remains a common ground between the two. Poulantzas rejects the form-analytical determination of the state in a polemical fashion, charging it with 'historicism', by which he means Hegelianism. Does this mean that his own approach is incompatible with form analysis? We do not think so. For Poulantzas's explains the *separation* of 'politics' and 'economics', 'the state' and 'society', with reference to the capitalist relations of production, which is similar, in its substance, to the points made by the more sophisticated approaches to state derivation. And one could say that this explanation informs most of Poulantzas's thinking about the state – even if his explicit remarks on the issue are very brief and interlarded with polemic.

---

5   It would be wrong to charge Pashukanis, without further ado, with subscribing to this 'idealist' approach. In fact, he explicitly rejected it (cf. 1924: 52f., 67f.). In the West German debate, Sibylle von Flatow and Freek Huisken (1973) can be said to have adopted it; see also Kannankulam (2000: 37ff.).
6   It is important to see that this critique was also voiced in the state derivation debate – a point that Poulantzas recognized (cf. SPS: 50).

4. Form analysis and the state

Against this backdrop, a new question arises: what exactly is form analysis, and how can the state be derived in a form-analytical fashion? Before providing an answer, we will identify some of the limitations of the form-analytical determination of the state, which were also criticized by Poulantzas.

4.1. The limitations of form analysis

One of the key problems discussed by participants of the West German debate[7] was the identification of the 'correct' starting point for a derivation of the state. Should the state be derived from production or circulation? Despite all the criticisms, the majority of people involved in the debate opted for circulation. But why was this so?

As might be suspected, the reason was Marx himself. In the chapter in *Capital* on exchange, he wrote: 'It is plain that commodities cannot go to market and make exchanges of their own accord. We must, therefore, have recourse to their guardians, who are also their owners. Commodities are things, and therefore without power of resistance against man. [...] In order that these objects may enter into relation with each other as commodities, their guardians must place themselves in relation to one another, as persons whose will resides in those objects, and must behave in such a way that each does not appropriate the commodity of the other, and part with his own, except by means of an act done by mutual consent. They must therefore recognise in each other the rights of private proprietors. This juridical relation, which thus expresses itself in a contract, whether such contract be part of a developed legal system or not, is a relation between two wills, and is but the reflex of the real economic relation between the two. It is this economic relation that determines the subject-matter comprised in each such juridical act' (CI: 88).

This so-called commodity guardian theorem was also important for Pashukanis, who used it in order to determine the legal form within the CMP (see above). He argued that one of the logical presuppositions of the CMP is a relation of recognition between commodity owners, who must recognize each other as formally free and equal legal subjects. This state of affairs requires the existence of an instance for adjudication that is separated from the relations of recognition. Law as a form separated from other societal relations thus can be explained with reference to the *structural* conditions of commodity exchange.

Drawing upon Pashukanis, we have discussed the structural determina-

---

7   For overviews, see Holloway and Picciotto (1978), Jessop (1982), Kostede (1976) and Kannankulam (2000).

tions of the commodity form. The passage from Marx suggests that these determinations involve a *relation of wills* between the relevant actors. In other words, the legal form is created and reproduced through conscious decisions of commodity owners. However, it at the same time 'covers up' the relations of domination and exploitation inherent in capitalist production: legally speaking, the owners of the means of production are equal to those who can only bring to the market their labour power. Both sides, the argument continues, encounter each other, on the level of circulation (the market), as commodity owners. And both sides are confronted with the legal form. The sphere of circulation thus creates a system of illusions [*Verblendungszusammenhang*], which serves as a condition for the reproduction of these relations of production. The one-sided derivation of the legal form from the sphere of circulation leaves this system of illusions more or less intact.

Poulantzas rightly criticized this line of argument for portraying the relation of the state and class struggle as a purely external relation. Furthermore, classes are absent on the level of law and the state. All that we find here are individualized commodity-owners who are also legal subjects, and who constantly create and reproduce the state and law through the pursuit of *their interests* (PPSC: 126f.).

Along the lines of this critique, Marx contended that 'individuals *seem* independent (this is an independence which is at bottom merely an illusion and it is more correctly called indifference), free to collide with one another and to engage in exchange within this freedom; but they appear thus only for someone who abstracts from the *conditions*, the *conditions of existence* within which these individuals enter into contact (and these conditions, in turn, are independent of the individuals and, although created by society, appear as if they were *natural conditions*, not controllable by individuals)' (1973: 163f.). In other words, the one-sided derivation of the state from the relations of commodity owners in the sphere of circulation ignores the constitutive role of the relations of production in the emergence of subjects as citizens. More generally, it overlooks the class dimension of law and the state in capitalism.

4.2. The form-analytical determination of the state

It remains an open question how the modern state, which has emerged with the development of capitalism, can be reconstructed with the help of form analysis. What is obvious is that we have to discuss it in relation to the relations of production, more precisely to the capitalist way of producing and appropriating the surplus product. Capitalist society is characterized by private ownership of the means of production, private production, wage labour and competition. The production and appropriation of the surplus product does not occur on the basis of personal dependency and the immediate use of force, but is mediated through the sale and purchase of commodities, including labour power, on the market. The peculiarity of capitalist class relations consists in the fact that the owners of capital competing with one another are faced with a formally free group of wage earners who are also competing. These distinctive features of class and exploitation in capitalism suggest that the stability, reproduction and development of capitalist society are only guaranteed when physical coercion is centralized in a special apparatus that is formally separated from the social classes. A fundamental condition for economic reproduction regulated through the law of value is that economic and political domination must be detached from each other. This characterizes the form of the political in capitalism. It does not simply result from the circulation of commodities but from the overall ensemble of exploitation and appropriation. Social individuals always belong to a class and are, at the same time, free and equal market subjects. The political form is sustained by a relation of class domination and coercion, which combines the 'dull compulsion of economic relations' and the state monopoly of violence. The 'political' form and the 'economic' form (the form of value) are connected through a tight relation of mediation. Poulantzas captured this well when he wrote: 'It is in this sense that we should understand Marx's analysis of the CMP, in particular the "absence of *violence*" in the economic level of this mode, and not, as is often believed, in the sense of the non-intervention of state repression in this mode's *social relations of production.* Such repression is in fact constantly present: it should not be confused with the state's intervention or non-intervention in the *structure of the relations of production*' (PPSC: 227f.).

We have now sketched the essence of the line of argument informing state derivation (or the form analysis of the political), and it becomes clear that this line of argument is compatible with Poulantzas's approach. Instead of 'relative autonomy', we suggest speaking of 'particularization' – a concept that may capture better the relation of unity and contradiction between the economy and politics.

The political is indeed *neither* a 'superstructure' of the economic *nor* an instance simply separate from it. It was a misconception of certain participants in the state derivation debate to think that they had produced a finished state theory. Establishing the particularization of the political from the economic in capitalism is only a *first* yet fundamental step in the formulation of such a theory. It is not possible to say anything meaningful about the institutional structure and the functioning of the state by just looking at the political form at a high level of abstraction. Moreover, it still needs to be clarified what all of this implies for real-concrete class configurations. The political form can take on different modalities, reflecting different relations of forces in the prevailing patterns of capital accumulation.[8] This is of key importance for analysing the transformation of state systems and the differences in capitalist states over space and time. In this context, three points need to be considered:

1. It is crucial to avoid a functionalist reading of the derivation of the political form. Under capitalist conditions, the economy does not automatically produce the political form, whose existence, however, is necessary for its reproduction. Rather, the capitalist economy and the modern state, understood as a centralized apparatus of coercion, are constituted in an historical process involving the actions and strategies of a multiplicity of actors, and both sides depend on each other. In line with Poulantzas (PPSC: 228), the political and the state do not constitute a 'superstructure'. They are integral *elements* of the relations of productions.
2. The political form is neither always already there, nor does it come into existence due to the functional requirements of the economy. Rather, it results from the actions of antagonistic actors. As a result, its 'relative autonomy' remains contested.
3. The form determination of the political is the foundation and starting point for analysing the state, class relations, and the historical transformations that support statehood and class domination. This is exactly where we can link Poulantzas's approach with form analysis.

Against this backdrop, we are now able to decipher Poulantzas's conception of the state as a material condensation of class relations. Again, there are three key points:

1. Poulantzas refers to the fact that, under capitalist conditions, repression takes a particular form: it is institutionalized in the form of a distinct apparatus that is separated from the social classes, follows its own rules, and displays its own dynamic (cf. Weber 1922: 822). The attribute 'material' indicates that this apparatus requires its own resources and is managed by special personnel with its own interests and conditions of reproduction.
2. Poulantzas suggests that the relations between the classes and their various fractions are mediated through this apparatus, which thus has a specific character and a specific dynamic. He says that the dominant class, which is

---

8   On the relation of forms and institutions, see Hirsch (1994; 2005).

internally divided through competition, can only exercise political power and constitute itself as a power bloc with the help of the state apparatus, which is not under its direct control; and he adds that this apparatus also serves to disorganize the dominated classes by creating divisive modes of organization (SPS: 127ff., 140ff.). The form of the political turns populations into individualized, free and equal citizens, with the result that class places are not immediately present in the political system but are reflected in the form of party political or associational ties.

3. By linking the organization of class relations to the state, Poulantzas emphasizes that the social relations of forces characteristic of capitalism are not reflected directly in political processes, but in the internal processes and dynamics of the state. They are *form-determined* – not just in this regard.

All in all, the relation of the state and classes is characterized by the fact that all the different parts of the state mediate relations between classes and between class fractions. According to Poulantzas, these parts represent instances of support for the dominant class or its individual fractions, and they create specific relations to the exploited and dominated classes. As a result, the state appears as a system of heterogeneous and often mutually conflicting components. It is not a closed entity but a *field of struggle*. At the same time, its relative unity is a precondition for the coherence of political processes and, thus, for the stable reproduction of society as a whole. This unity, however, is far from guaranteed. It is possible that concrete institutional configurations turn out to be detrimental to maintaining the political form, in which case they lead to a crisis of the state. In sum, the particularization or relative autonomy of the state is always a result of conflicts and struggles mediated and shaped through its materiality.

If we want to explain that the relative unity of the state administration persists, we need to return to Antonio Gramsci's concept of hegemony. 'Hegemony' involves the ability of the dominant class(es) to formulate a concept of social order and development that binds together different fractions and, at the same time, offers certain material concessions to the subordinate classes. As a result, a relatively stable capitalist formation emerges – an historical bloc, which is characterized by the unity of coercion and consent (SPN: 158ff.; FS: 403f.). Hegemonic configurations have several dimensions: an *ideological* one – the assumption that the given social order is just and right is rooted in the collective consciousness of the masses; an *institutional* one – a system of institutions exists that creates legitimate decisions, participation and access rights; and a *political* one – political leaders are capable of producing loyalty among the masses with the help of 'national-popular' programmes (Jessop 1990: 207ff.). The relative unity of the state at all these levels is created through achieving a hegemonic configuration: there is (a) a dominant ideological consensus; (b) a system of procedures of inter-bureaucratic control, coordination, and steering; and (c) a political leadership that coordinates activities in different parts of the state with the help of comprehensive political guidelines. This suggests that hegemony always has a material basis, which not only consists in social practices but also in a specific configuration of political institutions. It is therefore inscribed in the institutional structure of the state apparatuses and their relation to one another.

5. Conclusion

Our initial question concerning the potential for state theory of confronting Poulantzas's approach with form analysis can now be answered with more clarity. By returning to form analysis, we are able to address the lack of an explanation for the *relative autonomy* of the state in Poulantzas's line of argument.

Even if Poulantzas criticized, at times in a very polemical fashion, attempts by Pashukanis to 'derive' the state from the structure of capitalist relations of production, we contend that this critique was mainly directed at Pashukanis's followers, many of whom were fixated on the sphere of circulation and on the link between the interests of commodity owners and their status as legal subjects. They can indeed be charged with covering up the class dimension of law and the state in capitalism. We have shown that Poulantzas did address the Pashukanis question, and that his brief answer referring to the capitalist relations of production is compatible with attempts to provide a form-analytical explanation for the existence of the state, which derives it from the configuration of exploitation and appropriation specific to capitalism.

Finally, we have demonstrated that the political struggles, the system of political institutions and the ongoing transformations of the state and the state system can be analysed in an exact and differentiated manner if we consider Poulantzas's conception of the state as a material condensation, as well as Gramsci's notion of hegemony. This type of analysis would be impossible solely on the basis of the fundamental, yet abstract contribution of form analysis.

In conclusion, we suggest that the critical confrontation of the two approaches looks promising in terms of providing a historical-materialist explanation for the existence of the state. If we wanted to take things even further, we would have to address the central challenge materialist state theory is faced with today, namely, to grasp the transformations in the state and the state system triggered by the restructuring of global capitalism since the 1980s, which are commonly referred to as 'globalization' (Hirsch/Kannankulam 2011). Poulantzas himself performed important preparatory work in this regard in the 1970s – especially in his study of the internationalization of the capital relation (INT), where he developed the concept of the 'interior bourgeoisie' as a new class fraction with a marked impact on politics (cf. Kannankulam/Wissel 2004).

References

Buckel, S. (2005) *Subjektivierung & Kohäsion. Zur Rekonstruktion einer materialistischer Theorie des Rechts*, PhD thesis, Faculty of the Social Sciences, Goethe University (Frankfurt am Main).
Charim, I. (2002) *Der Althusser-Effekt. Entwurf einer Ideologietheorie* (Wien: Passagen Verlag).
Flatow, S. v. / Huisken, F. (1973) 'Zum Problem der Ableitung des bürgerlichen Staates. Die Oberfläche der bürgerlichen Gesellschaft, der Staat und die allgemeinen Rahmenbedingungen der Produktion', *Prokla*, vol. 3, no. 7, 83-156.
Hirsch, J. (1994) 'Politische Form, Politische Institutionen und Staat', in Esser, J. / Görg, C. / Hirsch, J. (eds.) *Politik, Institutionen und Staat. Zur Kritik der Regulationstheorie* (Hamburg: VSA-Verlag) 157-212.
Hirsch, J. (2005) *Materialistische Staatstheorie: Transformationsprozesse des kapitalistischen Staatensystems* (Hamburg: VSA-Verlag).
Hirsch, J. / Kannankulam, J. (2011) 'The Spaces of Capital: The Political Form of Capitalism and the Internationalization of the State', *Antipode*, vol. 43, no. 1, 12-37.
Holloway, J. / Picciotto, S. (eds.) (1978) *State and Capital: A Marxist Debate* (London: Arnold).
Jessop, B. (1982) *The Capitalist State: Marxist Theories and Methods* (Oxford: Robertson).
Jessop, B. (1990) *State Theory: Putting capitalist states in their place* (Cambridge: Polity Press).
Kannankulam, J. (2000) *Zwischen Staatsableitung und strukturalem Marxismus. Zur Rekonstruktion der staatsheoretischen Debatten der siebziger Jahr*, MA dissertation, Faculty of he Social Sciences, Goethe University (Frankfurt am Main).
Kannankulam, J. / Wissel, J. (2004) 'Innere Bourgeoisie', in Haug, W. F. (ed.) *Historisch-Kritisches Wörterbuch des Marxisimus*, vol. 6/II (Hamburg: Argument-Verlag) 1136-1141.
Kostede, N. (1976) 'Die neuere marxistische Diskussion über den bürgerlichen Staat. Einführung – Kritik – Resultate', *Gesellschaft. Beiträge zur Marxschen Theorie*, vol. 8/9 (Frankfurt am Main: Suhrkamp) 150-197.
Marx, K. (1973) *Grundrisse. Foundations of the critique of political economy* (Harmondsworth: Penguin Books).
Müller, W. / Neusüß, C. (1970) 'Die Sozialstaatsillusion und der Widerspruch von Lohnarbeit und Kapital', *Sozialistische Politik*, vol. 2, no. 6/7, 4-67.

Pashukanis, E. B. (1924) *Law and Marxism: A General Theory* (London: Pluto Press, 1989).
Poulantzas, N. (1967) 'Aus Anlass der marxistischen Rechtstheorie', in Reich, N. (ed.) *Marxistische und sozialistische Rechtstheorie* (Frankfurt am Main: Athenäum Fischer Taschenbuch Verlag, 1972) 181-200.
Weber, M. (1922) *Wirtschaft und Gesellschaft. Grundriss der verstehenden Soziologie* (Tübingen: Mohr, 1985).

MATERIALITY AND CONDENSATION IN THE WORK OF NICOS POULANTZAS

LARS BRETTHAUER

> In locating the State as the material condensation of a relationship of forces, we must also grasp it as a *strategic field and process*.
>
> (SPS: 136)

Introduction

The notion that capitalist statehood represents a 'material condensation of relationships of forces' plays a key role in state theoretical debates referring to Poulantzas (cf. Demirović 1987: 79ff.; Jessop 1985). Thus, I will examine the two main concepts of Poulantzas's state theory: 'materiality' and 'condensation'. I am aiming to respond to the questions: how should we design materialist state theory if we want to apply it to historically concrete state configurations, and how far does it reach?

1. The concept of 'materiality'

In *State, Power, Socialism,* Poulantzas defines the materiality of capitalist statehood as the distinct 'functioning' (SPS: 54) of political relations of domination in capitalist societies. However, he struggles to theoretically determine it, because in doing so, he moves between addressing three different topics: (1) the relationship between political subjects and state apparatuses, in particular the specific relation of repression and ideology in the constitution of state subjects that obtains in states governed by the rule of law; (2) the specific mode of organization of capitalist statehood in relation to the capitalist economy; and (3) the capacity of state institutions to 'resist' the strategies and interests of political actors. In this section, I will primarily look at the first two aspects. I will discuss the 'density' of state institutions vis-à-vis the interests of political forces later.

1.1 The mode of operation of materiality

In defining the materiality of capitalist statehood, Poulantzas draws on Louis Althusser's theory of ideology (IISA). When Althusser analysed the 'reproduction of the relations of production', he emphasized the importance of ideological state apparatuses (148). Accordingly, he referred to the 'materiality of ideology' in order to criticize approaches that treat ideology and the 'ideas' held by subjects as mere 'thoughts' (cf. Charim 2002: 69). These approaches ignore the fact that ideas 'have material existence' in so far as the ideas of an individual subject 'are *his material actions inserted into material practices governed by material rituals*' (IISA: 169). The latter, however, are not shaped by the individual decisions of subjects, but by ideological state apparatuses separate from them – in modern states particularly by schools. In other words, subjects are designed, 'taught' and controlled in such apparatuses. Departing from arguments based on the concept of alienation, Althusser stresses the positive role of meaning in the constitution of subjectivity. The latter results from the ideological interpellation of the subjects: they act 'in all consciousness according to [their] belief[s]' (170).

Poulantzas takes up Althusser's ideas in his account of the conditions that political subjects face in situations of state domination. He emphasizes the constitutive presence of state-determined ideological relations within the relations of production. These ideological relations do 'not consist merely in a system of ideas or representations', e.g., the state as 'representative of the common good', but rather involve 'a series of *material practices*, embracing the customs and life-style[s]' (SPS: 28).

And yet, Poulantzas also rephrases Althusser's concept of ideology. For him, the latter's concept of materiality negates the contested nature of ideological state apparatuses and focuses solely on the constitution of subjects within relations of domination. Poulantzas insists that ideological relations should not be construed as reflecting a 'unified discourse' (32). Rather, they are formed in class-specific ways: there are 'several discourses that are adapted to the various classes and differentially incarnated in its [the state's; L.B.] apparatuses according to their class destination' (ibid.). Accordingly, Poulantzas's definition of materiality starts from the pluralistic and contested nature of 'world views'. Drawing on Antonio Gramsci (SPN: 161), he explains the consensual integration of subaltern class fractions with reference to the construction of class compromises. These compromises are more than just symbolic concessions or monetary bribes. They also affect the fields of possibility of material practices: 'the relation of the masses to power and the State – in what is termed among other things a *consensus* –

always possesses a material substratum' (SPS: 30f.). This implies that state apparatuses are actively creating forms of subjectivation that transform the social terrain of capitalist relations of production. In other words, the state to some extent acts 'in a positive fashion, *creating, transforming and making reality*' (30).

Moreover, Poulantzas criticizes Althusser's distinction between repressive state apparatuses and ideological state apparatuses. Althusser sees the former as controlling the instruments of direct physical coercion, and the latter as producing meaning and realizing it in material practices and rituals. Yet for Poulantzas, first, it is impossible to determine, in a 'nominalist or essentialist' manner, which state apparatuses belong to which group, because this is the result of historically and locally specific constellations of forces (33). Second, Althusser's distinction obscures the growing relevance of economic state functions. Third, state repression is always a constituent part of the material practices and meanings of political subjects and must be integrated into the concept of materiality (cf. Demirović 1987: 90f.).

Poulantzas expands the concept of repression beyond 'institutions which actualize bodily constraint and the permanent threat of mutilation (prison, army, police, and so on)' (SPS: 29). In states where state domination is primarily enforced through the law and juridical relations, repression also means that 'a *bodily order*' is enforced 'which both institutes and manages bodies by bending and moulding them into shape and inserting them in the various institutions and apparatuses' (ibid.). These mechanisms are constitutive for the concept of violence. For Poulantzas, they represent 'repression [...] in the most material sense of the term: *violence to the body*' (ibid.).

According to Poulantzas, the relation between repression and ideology constitutes the mode of operation of the capitalist state's materiality. It cannot be grasped, however, without referring to the specific effectiveness of the monopoly over the means of physical coercion. This is because the possibility of coercion is always already present in the disciplinary techniques of the state, legally established norms, and hegemonic policies: '*State-monopolized physical violence permanently underlies the techniques of power and mechanisms of consent: it is inscribed in the web of disciplinary and ideological devices; and even when not directly exercised, it shapes the materiality of the social body upon which domination is brought to bear.*' (81).[1]

---

1   Poulantzas is well aware that, with regard to this question, he is generalizing from a locally and historically specific phase of Western statehood in the 20th century. In this phase, the state's monopoly on the legitimate use of force had been implemented, but

1.2 Attributes of materiality

Poulantzas not only deals with the *modus operandi* of the materiality of the state. He also addresses the questions as to how this materiality is organized as a relation of domination, and how social theory should describe the relationship between materiality and the capitalist economy. In *State, Power, Socialism* he accounts for materiality by focusing on four aspects of state domination: (1) the monopolization of knowledge in the state bureaucracy; (2) the state's role in individualization and homogenization; (3) the legal form; and (4) the nation (SPS: 54). These aspects are relevant to his state theory in three different ways: (1) they provide information about the internal organization of state apparatuses; (2) they describe the form in which the state is present in non-state social relations; and (3) they are characterized by social interdependence, that is they are shaped by other relations, especially the relations of production, and must be explained. I will demonstrate that Poulantzas is strongest whenever he talks about the internal organization of state apparatuses and the state's co-constitutive presence, and weakest whenever he attempts to relate the materiality of the state to the relations of production.

Poulantzas declares the first main component of the materiality of capitalist statehood to be the monopolization of intellectual labour by the state bureaucracy. He shows how the monopolization of political and administrative knowledge by state apparatuses – as opposed to 'manual labour [that] tends to be concentrated in the popular masses' (56) – contributes to stabilizing relations of domination. Accordingly, state theory has to analyse bureaucracy as a social relation, and should refrain from covering up its relational character by focusing on 'rationalization' or 'good governance'. After all, the subaltern 'are separated and excluded from these organizational functions' (ibid.). According to Poulantzas, the monopolization of intellectual labour is based on the separation of intellectual and manual labour in the relations of production as described by Karl Marx in *Capital* (cf. CI: 420ff.). He does not, however, provide reasons *why* relations of state domination, which are based on bureaucratic procedures, develop out of relations of domination in the realm of production organized around intellectual labour, and why they do not constitute a type of domination *sui generis* instead.

> force was only deployed to a degree, and policies were formulated on the basis of laws emerging out of legal procedures. Hence, he criticizes the 'short memories' and the 'Eurocentric light-mindedness' (SPS: 80) of approaches that take the pacified phase in the development of Western states in the late 20th century as their point of departure for a comprehensive theory of capitalist statehood.

Something similar applies to the functions of individualization and homogenization that the state apparatuses fulfil. According to Poulantzas, these functions correspond to the tendency towards individualization inherent in the relations of production, which in turn results from the capitalist division of labour. He demonstrates that this tendency is not only constituted and reproduced by juridical individualism and the disciplinary institutions of the state, but is also subject to homogenization. State apparatuses produce homogenization with the help of 'the representation of the unity (national representative State) and organization-regulation [...] of the constitutive fracturings'. Poulantzas explains the presence of compatible processes of individualization and homogenization in both state and economy by arguing that the state apparatuses reproduce 'the very material frame of reference or space-time matrix that is implied by the relations of production' (SPS: 65). He does not, however, explain why the materiality of capitalist statehood adapts in this particular way to the spatio-temporal matrices of the capitalist mode of production.

The third attribute of the materiality of the state – the law – is defined by Poulantzas as an '*axiomatic system*, comprising a set of *abstract, general, formal and strictly regulated norms*' (86) and representing a '*code of organized public violence*' (77). Here, again, Poulantzas's strength lies in establishing the presence of modern law in the capitalist relations of production. The modern law 'institutes individuals as juridico-political subjects-persons' (86f.), thus constituting stable relations of exploitation between doubly free wage labourers and capitalists. At the same time, the law also pacifies subjects by re-combining their 'individual interests' and turning them into members of a people-nation distanced from the relations of production. It also shapes the internal organization of the state apparatuses: the legal form defines their 'centralizing-bureaucratic-hierarchic framework' (88), as well as their respective scopes. State apparatuses operate by virtue of the insulation of the political administration, which is effected by the '*state secret*' (90), and the social legitimation of the procedures in question that result from their rationalist form of truth. In spite of producing these insights, Poulantzas remains vague when he argues that the law is 'inextricably bound up with the real fracturing of the social body in the social division of labour' and 'with the individualization of agents that takes place in the capitalist labour process' (86). After all, he fails to provide criteria for this qualitative coherence.

The fourth attribute of the materiality of the capitalist state, according to Poulantzas, is the modern nation with its spatial and temporal matrices. He reconstructs the nation by linking it with the space-time-matrix of the capitalist division of labour, which consists of a *'serial, fractured, parcelled, cellular and irreversible* space' (103) and 'a *segmented, serial, equally divided, cumulative and irreversible time that is oriented towards the product*' (110). On the one hand, modern national statehood constitutes this matrix through the individualizing effects of civil law and its disciplinary institutions. On the other hand, it also creates a unified national territory by way of the domestic market. Moreover, it mediates the varying temporal dynamics of development in different social spheres in capitalist societies with the help of traditional nationalist narratives. It does so by creating a 'historicity without a fixed limit' (113).

As a result, capitalist statehood homogenizes the individuality of legal subjects into and through the notion of the people-nation: 'The national State realizes the unity of the individuals of the people-nation in the very movement by which it forges their individualization' (105f.). However, just as was the case with the first three attributes of materiality, Poulantzas leaves a key question unanswered: how is it possible to explain the relatively stable connection between nationalist narratives disseminated by state apparatuses and the economic space-time-matrix of the capitalist division of labour?

1.3 From derivation to the analysis of historically concrete forms of bourgeois rule

The inadequacy of Poulantzas's explanation of the relationship between the state and the economy could be seen as resulting from him paying insufficient attention to the form-analytical arguments of the West German state-derivation approach (Holloway/Piccioto 1978)[2]. The latter tried to derive capitalist statehood from different aspects of the forms of the capitalist mode of production. Departing from this view, I contend that Poulantzas did indeed explain the separation of economy and politics by referring to the structure of the capitalist mode of production, but that he consciously refrained from *deriving* the state from it[3]. This reading draws on passages in *State, Power, Socialism* where Poulantzas advocates a state theory that does not start from assumptions of stability and coherence, but sees the latter as possible *historical results*. This raises the question how state theory can account for (a) the historically concrete reproduction of the capitalist relations of production and modern statehood, and (b) their relative congruence within conjunctures based on specific configurations of relations of forces?

---

2   See Kostede (1976) for an overview.
3   Regarding the different status of *explanations of the state*, such as functionalist derivation or retroductive inference, see Gallas in this volume.

Accordingly, Poulantzas criticizes established modes of presentation in Marxist state theory: 'To situate the capitalist State first and foremost with reference to the relations of production is not the same as to construct on that basis the theoretical object of that State; it does not give rise, that is, to an ideo-typical object susceptible of being particularized or concretized in various ways according to the course of the class struggle in given social formations. A theory of the capitalist State can be elaborated only if it is brought into relation with the history of political struggles under capitalism' (SPS: 25). In line with this, Poulantzas proposes a new mode of presentation in Marxist state theory. Hitherto, it had been presupposed that there existed a stable relationship between the abstract forms of capitalist production and the state and their historically concrete configurations. This was usually illustrated by referring to historical processes of the reproduction of states in a second step. In contrast, Poulantzas argues that 'abstract' state theory has to take into account the conditions of possibility for the reproduction of capitalist rule and the fact that the latter is grounded in historically concrete struggles. For him, state theory will only be viable 'if it manages to grasp the reproduction and historical mutations of its object at the very place where they occur – that is to say, in the various social formations that are the sites of the class struggle' (24).[4]

This revision of state theory not only suggests that relations of forces are constitutive of its subject matter. Above all, it highlights that concepts are needed which are useful for analysing historically concrete configurations of the state. This is what Poulantzas has in mind whenever he focuses on the *historically concrete materiality of capitalist states* rather than *the* materiality of capitalist statehood as such. In its historically concrete form, materiality consists in the specific arrangement of state apparatuses and their relation to one another, which is not fixed *a priori*: 'Depending on the form of State and regime and on the phase of reproduction of capitalism, a number of apparatuses can slide from one sphere to the other and assume new functions either as additions to, or in exchange for, old ones' (33). In other words, individual state apparatuses seem to possess diverging historically concrete materialities. This in turn implies that their structure contains a specific combination of bureaucratic procedures, individualizing and

---

4   At this point, Poulantzas tries to link the reproduction of capitalist relations of production and statehood back to struggles, because reproduction remains 'under-determined' at the level of theory. 'Over-determining' state theories posit a stable nexus between state and economy in terms of their reproduction at the level of form; in contrast, 'under-determining' state theories emphasize that such a nexus is only established within historically specific conjunctures of struggles, resistance and strategic shifts (cf. Jessop 1982: 134 and Gallas in this volume).

homogenizing functions, legal procedures, and nationalist narratives. This also suggests that materialities and practices of state control can change over time, as is demonstrated by the emergence of authoritarian statism (238f.).

Poulantzas spends considerable time developing concepts theorizing the conditions of existence of stable state forms. However, he barely even attempts to develop equivalent concepts concerning the possible coherence between the capitalist state and economy. Instead, he merely asserts that state apparatuses influence the constitution of the relations of production, and that the latter's structural features are reproduced and processed in a contradictory manner within the organization of the state. Nevertheless, he makes a genuine contribution to state theory by refraining from conceiving of the relations between state and economy either in terms of a simple causal relation (base/superstructure), or in terms of an abstract functional link ('What would statehood have to be like in order for capitalist societies to be reproduced in a stable fashion?').

Accordingly, Poulantzas conceptualizes state apparatuses as a '*strategic field and process*' (136). This allows him to conceive of relatively coherent relationships between the state and the economy as a result of the relations of forces in historically concrete conjunctures.[5] It follows that the position of individual state apparatuses is 'the outcome of the clash between various tactics expressing themselves within the State and the circuits, networks and apparatuses that incarnate them' (32f.). If there is a relative coherence between the state and the economy, this results from the "conflictual co-ordination of explicit and divergent micro-policies and tactics, and [...] the rational formulation of a coherent global project" (136; translation amended).[6] This insight gives rise to a new problematic for state theory – at least if it is discussed in combination with the assumption that the political is present in the economic: How should the relationship between the economy and the state be portrayed if the latter is seen as contested and strategic terrain which is always in need of re-stabilization?

2. The concept of 'condensation'

2.1 Condensation as a displacement of regional contradictions

The concept of 'condensation' had already been crucial for Poulantzas's understanding of capitalist statehood in *Political Power and Social Classes*. He argues that the political should be understood 'as a crucial level in which

---

5   Bob Jessop's strategic-relational approach (cf. 1982; 1990), among others, took up this idea.
6   Translators' note: Poulantzas speaks of the 'formulation *rationelle* d'un projet global et coherent' in the original text, which is turned into the '*national* formulation of a coherent global project' in the English translation.

the contradictions of a formation are reflected and condensed' (PPSC: 40). Following Althusser, these contradictions spring from the contradictions of the different regions of society, i.e., the economy, politics, and ideology (cf. Jessop 1985: 59ff.).

Since Poulantzas portrays these regions as being separate from one another, the concentration of their contradictions in the state presupposes a process of *displacement*, i.e., the diversion of contradictions towards political structures that function as a 'nodal point' (PPSC: 42) of a given social formation.[7] As a result, state institutions are over-determined by these contradictions. Thanks to the existence of the state, the contradictions are transformed into functional requirements specific to its regions; in other words, the state apparatuses process them with a view to overall social cohesion. The functional requirements encompass the economic functions of stabilizing wage labour and exchange relations through the legal system and the pacification of class conflict, as well as the ideological functions of educating and instructing the citizens. The political functions consist, above all, of the maintenance of the bourgeoisie's political class domination and the disorganization of the proletariat under conditions of constant political class conflict (cf. 55). Poulantzas assumes that state institutions can perform these functions precisely because they possess relative autonomy from the field of class struggle. They are able to act against the short-term interests of the bourgeoisie and secure bourgeois class domination in the long term (256). Accordingly, the state as a nodal point of condensation maintains 'the unity of a formation inside which the contradictions between the different levels condense into a political class domination' (54).

Poulantzas's first intensive engagement with the concept of condensation rests on three basic assumptions: (1) he takes the regions of society to be external to one another, and pervaded by constitutive contradictions; (2) he defines the state as the privileged *locus* of *condensation of the contradictions* inherent in capitalist social formations; and (3) he presumes that the result of the process of condensation is the stabilization of bourgeois political class domination.

2.2 Condensation and materiality

In *State, Power, Socialism*, Poulantzas still insists that the state constitutes 'the bourgeoisie as the politically dominant class' (125f.) and disorganizes the subaltern classes. However, he modifies his conception of how

---

7 In all likelihood, Poulantzas inherited the concept of condensation from Sigmund Freud and Jacques Lacan via Althusser (on condensation and displacement, see Laplanche/Pontalis 1972: 580, 604).

condensation is institutionally organized in and through the capitalist state. In his opinion, the 'State should not be regarded as an intrinsic entity; like "capital", *it is rather a relationship of forces, or more precisely the material condensation of such a relationship among classes and class fractions, such as this is expressed within the State in a necessarily specific form*' (127f.).

This new definition reflects three fundamental shifts in Poulantzas's state theory:

(1) He no longer sees the state as a regional instance separate from the economy, but as constitutively present in the latter. This goes against his earlier arguments in *Political Power and Social Classes*: state apparatuses are not charged with processing contradictions external to them; instead these contradictions result in the emergence of arrangements already co-constituted by the state, e.g., labour contracts, property rights, or the right to strike.

(2) Poulantzas no longer speaks of the 'condensation of social contradictions', but, following Antonio Gramsci (PN 2: 177), of the '*condensation of (class) relationships of forces*'. He contextualizes the condensation effects of the capitalist state in historically and locally specific processes of the reproduction of economic and political class domination on the terrain of the state. With this programmatic shift, he tries to 'construct a theory of the capitalist State which, starting from the relations of production, will explain *in terms of the very structure of its object* the State's differential reproduction as a function of the class struggle' (SPS: 124).

(3) The assumption that the capitalist state has to be understood as an institution that is functional to bourgeois class domination is now complemented by the attempt to conceptualize statehood as a strategic terrain of conflict with relative autonomy. For Poulantzas, this terrain is shaped by the materiality of the capitalist state. In other words, the bureaucratic procedures, laws, nationalist narratives, as well as the individualizing and homogenizing functions of state apparatuses constitute both a regulating instance rooted in the state and a strategic '*stake*' (115) in the social relations of forces. This, however, does not mean that materiality is a tool in the hands of a single social force. It results both from the specific state practices and rituals embodied in the state, as well as the political forces supporting it. Thus, it enjoys relative autonomy vis-à-vis the immediate interests of any individual group of actors: 'The State is not reducible to the relationship of forces; it exhibits an opacity and resistance of its own. To be sure, change in the class relationship of forces [...] adapts itself exactly to the materiality of the various state apparatuses, only becoming crystallized in the State in a refracted form that varies according to the apparatus.' (130f.). In sum,

Poulantzas highlights the modifications political forces have to make if they want to (a) transform their projects into state policies, (b) be present within 'state policies', and (c) inscribe themselves and their projects into the materiality of state apparatuses.

The changes in Poulantzas's understanding of condensation reflect the fact that he was grappling with the relationship between relations of forces and state apparatuses. Drawing on Claus Offe (1972: 74ff.), he started using the term 'structural selectivity' to describe these effects.[8] The term denotes the '"non-decisions" taken by branches and apparatuses of the State' (SPS: 134) that were already described by Peter Bachrach and Morton Baratz (1963), i.e., the state's 'determination of priorities and counter-priorities' (SPS: 134): the filtering of political interests as well as the measures taken by the state against oppositional forces.[9] Poulantzas again emphasizes the relevance of the materiality of specific state apparatuses for understanding the structural condensations effected by them. The selectivities of individual state apparatuses need to be seen as historical results of previous condensations and their current position 'in the configuration in the relationship of forces' (ibid.) in state and society. Therefore, individual apparatuses (ministries, agencies) possess different and at times contradictory selectivities with regard to political forces.

2.3 The relation between state apparatuses and relations of forces

Poulantzas's theoretical modifications emphasize two aspects of condensation:

(1) The materiality of capitalist states shapes social relations of forces through procedures of structural selection; and (2) these relations of forces retroact on state apparatuses because statehood is constitutively present in relations of forces. In other words, the materiality of state apparatuses 'carries the traces of [...] muted and multiform struggles' (SPS: 144).

Based on these two premises, one can identify five different types of condensation effects in *State, Power, Socialism*: (1) Condensation denotes the *constitution and stabilization of economic class relations* through the constitutive presence of the political in the economic. This aspect of condensation affects capitalists just like wage labourers, causing Poulantzas to repeatedly emphasize the 'specific presence' that the 'dominated classes and their particular struggles' (141) have within state apparatuses. For him,

---

[8] For Offe, selectivity refers to 'the non-contingent (i.e. systematic) restriction of a space of possibilities' (1972: 78; translated).

[9] These are directed against the 'popular masses' as well as against individual fractions of the bourgeoisie that confront the apparatuses (cf. SPS: 135).

the condensation of economic class relations is structurally selective because the appropriation of the means of production or products by workers is prohibited by the state, and because economic conflicts are met with arbitration (e.g., in the case of conflicts over wages) or with open repression (e.g., in the case of theft).

(2) Condensation also refers to the *political unification or disorganization of different class fractions through their transfer onto the terrain of the state*. Poulantzas's take on the subaltern classes is contradictory: On the one hand, he sticks to his assertion in *Political Power and Social Classes* that the state apparatuses are 'permanently disorganizing-dividing' (SPS: 140) subaltern forces, and that the only way in which subaltern interests are represented on the terrain of the state is through compromises offered by the power bloc. On the other hand, he rejects the assumption that subaltern forces remain external to the terrain of the state by referring to the 'State's complex articulation with the totality of power mechanisms' (141). For him, the state's institutional entanglement with other social spheres causes subaltern struggles to feed back into state apparatuses. However, there are diverging structural selectivities in different parts of the state, which is why, historically speaking, it had been easier for subaltern forces to access some apparatuses (schools, the army, electoral institutions) than others (such as the police, the judiciary, and the administration). Usually, the latter were organized more bureaucratically and employed mechanisms of 'physical exclusion' (152).

Contrary to his rather nuanced discussion of how subaltern interests get to be represented on the terrain of the state, Poulantzas presumes that particular capital fractions are already operating on it. The assumption – already developed in *Political Power and Social Classes* – was that the state unifies the 'power bloc' (SPS: 140). This seems problematic because, following Poulantzas, the state's openness to fractions of the bourgeoisie can only be explained with reference to the class contradictions inscribed in its institutional structure: '*The establishment of the State's policy must be seen as the result of the class contradictions inscribed in the very structure of the State* (the State as a relationship)' (132). In other words, Poulantzas starts from the class contradictions in the relations of production and the state's co-constitutive presence within them and then jumps to the condensation effects triggered by them in the state apparatuses. In doing so, he dodges the question as to how far this is possible, given his emphasis on the materiality of individual state apparatuses, their position within the state's overall structure, and the relations of forces present within them.

In sum, the concept of condensation in Poulantzas's later works exhibits a tension: whereas he tries hard to grasp the complexity, autonomy, and contradictory nature of state apparatuses vis-à-vis the strategic interests of social forces, he ultimately still claims that bourgeois class rule is successfully reproduced. Bob Jessop has already demonstrated (1982: 134ff.) that, in the context of analysing the conditions for the reproduction of class domination, this constitutes an unfounded assertion. A theory of the capitalist state cannot simply assume the successful reproduction of economic class domination by virtue of legal norms. The same applies to political class domination in and through the state. Poulantzas's arguments reach their limits – and he clearly names them when it comes to materiality – whenever they are used to determine the conditions for the reproduction of bourgeois class domination – let alone its elimination. Materialist state theories should *anticipate* the conditions of the reproduction of bourgeois class rule by using concepts like 'structural selectivity', but they should not assume reproduction as a given. Conversely, they need to be able to also name the conditions of the unsuccessful reproduction of political class rule.

(3) Another condensation effect identified by Poulantzas is the *arrangement and potential stabilization of political class relations on the terrain of the state*. He notes that different fractions of capital attach themselves to different apparatuses so that the relationship between state apparatuses can be understood in terms of the relationships between individual fractions of capital (SPS: 132f.). This periodically renders certain state apparatuses hegemonic. They dominate others and unify the terrain of the state. In this context, Poulantzas again refers to the materiality of state apparatuses. According to him, a general 'lack of malleability' (138) is the reason why state institutions do not follow the immediate interests of social forces if hegemonic constellation changes.

(4) In *State, Power, Socialism*, Poulantzas develops a novel understanding of policy formulation and 'political governance'. The specific materiality of state apparatuses and the practices inscribed in them pose a challenge to *linear modes of governance based on operating 'through the apparatuses'*. Poulantzas criticizes conceptions of the state that view it as 'a completely unified mechanism, founded on a homogeneous and hierarchical distribution of the centres of power' (133). Policy formulation and its implementation in and through state apparatuses are subject to processes of condensation, and they are confronted with alternative projects formulated by other political forces. Accordingly, the terrain of the state has to be understood as a '*strategic field and process* of intersecting power networks, which both articulate and

exhibit mutual contradictions and displacements' (136).

(5) With the term 'condensation', Poulantzas also tries to capture what initially seems a paradox: the fact that *state policies determine the institutional boundaries and gradations of state power*. A good example is the separation between the public and the private. Poulantzas rejects models that see the state as an embodiment of reason and interpret these processes as 'rational self-realization' of state institutions. In turn, he sees the historically specific boundaries of state apparatuses, such as the 'individual-private', as the result of the relations of forces and their 'condensation in the state' (73). Instead of conceiving of state and society as strictly separate, he highlights the distinctions between state and non-state sectors that are often separated only by different forms of private and public law. These distinctions also reflect the form of condensation of class relations that is specific to states governed by the rule of law. If relations of production are regulated by civil law, class relations rely on the mutual recognition of legal subjects (employer, wage-labourer). Conflicts between them are transferred onto the terrain of state apparatuses such as penal authorities, courts, and the police. Similarly, political arguments about the state's organization are shifted onto the terrain of institutions with a representative role, such as parties (cf. Bretthauer 2009).

3. The integral state as material condensation of class relations

Poulantzas's state theory is as interesting as it is contradictory. Accordingly, there is considerable potential for developing and updating it. It has been criticised, justifiably, for being class-centred. As a consequence, people drawing upon Poulantzas have tended to ignore his assertion that the relationships of forces being condensed are, indeed, *class relations* (cf. SPS: 117; cf. also, among others, Brand 2001). After all, state apparatuses also constitute and condense other important relations of forces, such as gender relations, race relations, or even the relations between political forces and social movements in civil society (cf. Demirović/Pühl 1998: 234).

Accordingly, re-entering a dialogue with Gramsci and his theory of hegemony provides us with an opportunity to analyse those areas of civil society that are commonly seen as 'private'. Here, struggles are being fought over the hegemony of world-views (FS: 290ff.). In Poulantzas's work, civil society is covered up by the concept of 'popular struggles' (SPS: 140). This concept neither captures how hegemonic forms of thought are stabilized in and through the institutions of civil society such as the press, schools, and think tanks, nor how subaltern groups attempt to organize themselves in liberal democratic societies. Moreover, Poulantzas's focus on the state lead him to neglect political power relations that are *not* constituted as relations of state domination thanks to the law. Differentiating between the state and politics along the lines of Gramsci allows us to look at these relations and at civil society, and reveals their contested nature.[10.]

Yet Poulantzas also has something to offer for Gramscian theories of the state. Gramsci's notion of the integral state assumes that hegemony is first formed in civil society, and then inscribed into state apparatuses. Poulantzas's state theory departs from this position. After all, it accounts for the relationship between state apparatuses and economically relevant sections of civil society by highlighting the constitutive presence of the political in the economic.

However, Poulantzas does not provide a clear distinction between the relations of production and the political public. It is important to stress that the state is present in civil society – just like the political is present in the economic. In states under the rule of law, relations of forces are being constituted and condensed in civil society in a structurally selective manner by way of forms of representation, too – for example by the party systems, freedom of speech, and the right to demonstrate (cf. Jessop 1990: 207ff.). This privileges political forces that accept bourgeois legal subjectivity and political-bureaucratic domination, and that approve of the state's mediating and sanctioning role in cases of conflict (cf. Bretthauer 2004: 73ff.). Accordingly, Poulantzas points out that the strategic aims of political forces – even of those hegemonic in civil society – may be amplified, refracted, redirected, or even repelled by the institutional materiality of the state as well as by the forces supporting it.

4. The prospects for state theory and state analyses

Poulantzas's state theory is an attempt to understand capitalist statehood as a structurally selective relation of condensation that is subject to social change – a position that departs from the rationalistic, instrumentalist, abstract-logical, and uncritical approaches that continue to shape public understandings of the state. It is to his lasting merit that he grasped the state as an instance of domination. He demonstrated this by examining everyday practices that refer to the state and which most textbooks describe as its defining features: the monopolization of intellectual labour, the techniques of individualization and homogenization, the transformation of wage labourers into legal subjects, and the dissemination of nationalist narratives, which portray the state as the expression of an homogeneous

---

10 These comprise labour relations, mafia-type networks, corruption, but also areas not directly constituted by the state such as relationships and family structures.

'national will'. The task ahead for a state theory in Poulantzas's footsteps could be to explore further his analysis of the materiality of capitalist states, and capture its effect on historically concrete processes of the condensation of polycentric relations of forces.

This, however, would also mean moving beyond some aspects of Poulantzas's theory of the capitalist state by stressing others. Following Poulantzas, the capitalist nature of the state is only constituted *ex post* as a consequence of the material condensation of relations of forces. This suggests that we should refrain from postulating the existence of functional correlations between state and economy in the abstract, and should instead analyse how historically concrete state apparatuses secure the conditions of the reproduction of relations of domination in capitalist societies. This requires identifying political and state projects, struggles, and resistances that allow for establishing the capitalist nature of the state in retrospect. Poulantzas has provided some important hints in that direction that are well worth pursuing.

References

Bachrach, P. / Baratz, M. (1963) 'Decisions and non-decisions. An analytical framework', *American Political Science Review*, vol. 57, no. 3, 632-642.
Brand, U. (2001) 'Nichtregierungsorganisationen und postfordistische Politik. Aspekte eines kritischen NGO-Begriffs', in Walk, H. / Klein, A. / Brunnengräber, A. (eds.) *NGOs als Legitimationsressource. Zivilgesellschaftliche Partizipations- und Handlungsformen im Globalisierungsprozess* (Opladen: Leske + Budrich) 73-94.
Bretthauer, L. (2004) *Realist accounts of the relation between state forms and the relation of forces*, M.A. thesis (Lancaster University).
Bretthauer, L. (2009) *Geistiges Eigentum im digitalen Zeitalter. Staatliche Regulierung und alltägliche Kämpfe in der Spielfilmindustrie* (Münster: Westfälisches Dampfboot).
Charim, I. (2002) *Der Althusser-Effekt. Entwurf einer Ideologietheorie* (Wien: Passagenverlag).
Demirović, A. (1987) *Nicos Poulantzas. Eine kritische Auseinandersetzung* (Hamburg-Berlin: Argument-Verlag).
Demirović, A. / Pühl, K. (1998) 'Identitätspolitik und die Transformation von Staatlichkeit. Geschlechterverhältnisse und Staat als komplexe materielle Relation', in Kreisky, E. / Sauer, B. (eds.) *Geschlechterverhältnisse im Kontext politischer Transformation, Politische Vierteljahresschrift*, vol. 29, no. 28 (Opladen: Westdeutscher Verlag) 220-240.
Holloway, J. / Piccioto, S. (eds.) (1978) *State and Capital: A Marxist Debate* (London: Arnold).
Kostede, N. (1976) 'Die neuere marxistische Diskussion über den bürgerlichen Staat. Einführung – Kritik – Resultate', *Gesellschaft. Beiträge zur Marxschen Theorie*, vol. 8/9 (Frankfurt am Main: Suhrkamp) 150-197.

Laplanche, J. / Pontalis, J.-B. (1972) *Das Vokabular der Psychoanalyse* (Frankfurt am Main: Suhrkamp).
Jessop, B. (1982) *The capitalist state: Marxist theories and methods* (Oxford: Robertson).
Jessop, B. (1985) *Nicos Poulantzas. Marxist theory and political strategy* (Basingstoke: Macmillan).
Jessop, B. (1990) *State theory. Putting capitalist states in their place* (Cambridge: Polity Press).
Offe, C. (1972) 'Klassenherrschaft und politisches System. Die Selektivität politischer Institutionen', in idem, *Strukturprobleme des kapitalistischen Staates. Aufsätze zur Politischen Soziologie* (Frankfurt am Main: Suhrkamp) 65-105.

READING 'CAPITAL' WITH POULANTZAS: 'FORM' AND 'STRUGGLE' IN THE CRITIQUE OF POLITICAL ECONOMY

ALEXANDER GALLAS

Marxists have interpreted the world in different ways – especially when they have reflected on how to change it. Presently, there appear to be two dominant positions: on one side are those who criticize *illusions of mutability* [Veränderungsillusionen]. They question both the notion that capitalism can be tamed by reforms and the idea of the historical mission of the working class. Currently, one of the most high-profile representatives of this position is Moishe Postone. On the other side, there are those who criticize *illusions of immutability* [Unveränderbarkeitsillusionen]. They aim to demonstrate that there are potentials for transformation which remain invisible if looked at from the dominant perspectives. John Holloway is probably the most well-known contemporary scholar to take this position.[1]

I employ a topology of 'form' and 'struggle' in order to examine an issue frequently touched upon by these thinkers, that is, capitalism's fragility/durability.[2] Marx's project of a Critique of Political Economy (CPE) is at the centre of my inquiry, since it constitutes the entry point for most Marxist debates about capitalist societalization. I also draw on the later works of Nicos Poulantzas. This may seem unusual, since Poulantzas is not necessarily a renowned theorist of the 'core structure' of capitalism. His theoretical grammar, however, is based on a distinctive reading of Marx. This is relevant for my topic because Poulantzas does not assume that the relationship between form and struggle is characterized by *unidirectional* causation. Rather, he sees both as having equal weight, at least in principle, and I therefore want to show how Marx can be read with Poulantzas. In the first part, I highlight the advances Poulantzas has made on other Marxist

---

1   This opposition is not new. See Anderson (1976).
2   My inspiration for doing so stems from a conversation with Urs Lindner. Of course, I still take full responsibility for the line of argument presented here.

theorists with respect to my topic. In the second part, I discuss how far his assertions are supported by the CPE.

1. Form and struggle in Marxism

In this section, with the help of my topology of 'form' and 'struggle', I will establish the relationship between potentials for stabilization and destabilization in capitalism. I will begin by giving preliminary, fairly open definitions of the two terms. This will allow me to link the terms with a variety of diverging positions within Marxism, and to criticize Postone and Holloway without presupposing a theoretical position outside their respective conceptual frameworks. I will end the section by demonstrating that Poulantzas's work provides us with a solid foundation for an alternative conception of 'form' and 'struggle'.

1.1. Preliminary definitions

Marx uses the concept of 'form' in order to determine the *historically specific* aspects of the organization of societies. The capitalist '*form* of society' (CI: 46; my italics) as a configuration of social relations differs from earlier forms by virtue of its dominant mode of production, i.e., the historically specific form in which the production of the population's means of survival takes place. In turn, the capitalist mode of production is a systemic configuration [Zusammenhang] of social relations, that is, of more specific social forms such as the commodity, money or capital. These forms have a structuring effect on activities in production. In other words, they affect actors by becoming *solidified conditions of action*. Accordingly, Marx described his method as an 'analysis of economic forms' (8). Today, it is common to simply refer to it as 'form analysis'.

In contrast, Marx invokes 'struggle' to describe specific *courses of action*. He emphasizes that the capitalist mode of production constitutes a conflict-ridden social configuration, giving rise to 'violent' confrontations between actors who pursue diverging goals and employ means of coercion to achieve them.[3] Therefore, Marx suggests that social relations in capitalism exist in and through *violent action*.[4] In this context, he usually refers to the 'class struggles' between the capitalist and working class, but sometimes also to interactions induced by competition between members of a single class.[5]

[3] In my understanding, 'violence' does not just refer to physical coercion, but also to the coercive effects of discursive interventions.

[4] The distinction between 'structure' and 'agency', which is prominent in mainstream sociology (cf. Giddens 1979), resembles 'form/struggle' to a degree. After all, it addresses the relationship between the conditions and the courses of actions, too. Yet in certain respects, both distinctions also diverge from each other: some Marxists question whether social relations can in fact be understood as structures (cf. Bonefeld 1995), and the term 'struggle' is far more specific than 'agency'.

[5] See for example CIII: 251f.

1.2. Reductionism in Postone and Holloway

This raises the question of how Marx sees the relationship between 'form' and 'struggle'. As pointed out in the introduction to this volume, it is impossible to enter an 'innocent' relationship with any author's work. I therefore approach my topic by discussing two divergent readings of the CPE. I have chosen Postone's as well as Holloway's interpretation because the connection between 'form/struggle' and 'durability/fragility' can be established easily by engaging critically with their work.

Postone describes the relationship between 'form' and 'struggle' as follows: 'Class conflict in capitalism, according to the critique of political economy, is structured by, and embedded within, the social forms of the commodity and capital' (1993: 314). 'Embeddedness' does not only suggest that forms constitute the conditions within which struggles take place, but also that they place clearly defined limits on the development and results of struggles. Accordingly, Postone describes class conflicts as conflicts between workers as sellers and capitalists as buyers of the commodity 'labour power', who argue over the contractual conditions of its sale. The fact that they see themselves as commodity owners and buyers is an effect of the forms within which they interact (317f.). This configuration leads to conflicts that are fought out collectively. Due to the systemic imbalance of power between capitalists and workers, the latter only become real commodity owners with bargaining power if they form a collective (318). In other words, class struggle transforms workers into real commodity owners. This suggests that it does not pose a threat to the capitalist configuration of forms, but in fact completes and stabilizes it. For Postone, 'embeddedness' means that struggles are fully subordinate to forms, and therefore he portrays capitalism as being free of tensions in the last instance – despite its class dimension: 'Class conflict and a system structured by commodity exchange [...] are not based on opposed principles; such conflict does not represent a disturbance in an otherwise harmonious system' (317). This implies that it is possible to describe the course of struggles fully by describing the configuration of forms in which they are grounded. In keeping with Marx's preface to the first edition of *Capital*, Postone sees actors as 'supports' of the configuration of forms (CI: 10; translation amended), who execute the logic internal to the latter.

So why is this perspective flawed? Marx shows in *Capital* that the dynamic of accumulation entailed by the reproduction of the capitalist mode of production leads to constant 'revolutionizing' in production. Strategies to increase productivity continue to modify the physical and technical base of production (320), and potentials for crisis are being actualized time and again (627). This renders long-term developments unpredictable. If the future is uncertain, however, it is impossible to simply read off from the capitalist configuration of forms how actors will behave.

Therefore, wage-dependent people in principle have two options for dealing with their situation: they can either enter the labour market, or they can try to withdraw from it. If labour power is in demand, there is a strong incentive to sell it in order to ensure individual reproduction. However, certain constellations potentially make it more attractive to claim benefits, or venture into crime. This suggests that the capitalist configuration of forms leaves the choices of actors under-determined. At most, it is possible to identify a strong *tendency* towards people selling their labour power, but this tendency may be weakened or even neutralized by *counter-tendencies* that emerge in specific constellations.

Thus, I contend that Marx's conception of actors as supports is a 'holding' construction (see below) that abstracts from the existence of multiple options for action. It is only possible for Marx to describe the configuration of forms as systemic in character and to demonstrate how it affects the behaviour of actors because he provisionally presumes that actors behave in accordance with the forms. Further into his presentation, however, it becomes apparent that this should not be seen as a general assumption about the 'conformity' of actors. He emphasizes, for example, that it is impossible to deduce the trajectory of struggles around the length of the working day at the level of forms. Accordingly, when Postone makes general statements about class struggles on the grounds of Marx's conception of actors as supports, he fails to see that the latter is a heuristic. Ultimately, his line of argument results in the *determination of the under-determined*.

Holloway, in contrast, suggests that the capitalist configuration of forms constitutes a function fully dependent on class struggles: 'Class struggle does not take place within the constituted forms of capitalist social relations: rather the constitution of those forms is itself class struggle' (2002: 143). The existence of forms is attributed to their usefulness for crushing the counter-power of the oppressed, and for the rulers' ability to organize society in their favour. For Holloway, struggle and anti-capitalist resistance always precede form: 'My starting point is that we want to destroy capitalism' (2003: 220; translated).

This position is problematic in two respects. First, it rests on a circular argument. Holloway makes sweeping statements about antagonisms that traverse the capitalist mode of production before he has even started to analyse its organization systematically. He does not explain why struggles exist in the first place, and why 'our' opposition to capitalism is so fundamental that 'we' want to smash it. Second, Holloway attributes to 'us', the 'oppressed', just one way of reacting to 'our' situation – the will to resist. This suggests that the latter is part of human nature, which is an arbitrary assumption. It would be just as well to claim that human beings are conformists. Following Holloway, the capitalist configuration of forms dissolves into struggles, which in turn accord to a voluntaristic pattern. This also means that forms do not have an independent structuring effect on the practices of actors (cf. Jessop 1991: 147). Thus, Holloway can be said to leave the *determined under-determined*.

To summarize: as a critic of illusions of mutability, Postone rejects the idea that forms can be ruptured by struggles. Thus, his approach can be said to be centred on form. Holloway, in contrast, is a critic of illusions of immutability. He claims that struggles in fact generate forms. Accordingly, his line of argument can be said to be centred on struggle. In other words, Postone and Holloway take positions which are exact opposites. Each author assumes one of the two poles of the relation between form and struggle to be the cause or independent variable, and its respective counterpart to be the effect or dependent variable. Thus, both can be accused of *reductionism* – Postone of '*form reductionism*', and Holloway of '*struggle reductionism*'.

1.3. Overcoming reductionism with Poulantzas

Poulantzas makes few explicit references to the questions discussed here.[6] However, several points of connection appear if we read *State, Power, Socialism* (SPS) as a contribution to materialist social theory. Poulantzas's line of argument is based on a reading of the CPE that includes a distinctive conception of the relationship between form and struggle. He asserts that the relations of production 'do not constitute an economic structure outside (before) social classes, *so they do not belong to a field external to power and class struggle*. There are no social classes prior to their opposition in struggle' (27).[7] This statement entails a rejection of 'form reductionism'. There is no socio-economic configuration that is prior to struggles and which determines them in their entirety. They repeatedly 'submerge' the forms within which they take place (141). Conjunctures like May 1968 in

6 There is an essay by Poulantzas about *Capital* that is largely shaped by the interpretation of Louis Althusser in his middle period (cf. RC). In it, Poulantzas takes a 'form reductionist' line: 'In production, "human beings" are only present as the *supports of structures*' (1968: 67). [Translators' note: This quotation has been translated into English based on the German translation used by the author of this chapter. The French original can be found here: Poulantzas, N. (1968) 'Brèves remarques sur l'objet du Capital', in Fay, V. (ed.) *En Partant du 'Capital'* (Paris: Anthropos) 235-247ff.]

7 This assertion implies that subjects are not mere 'supports' of 'structures'. Accordingly, it can be read as an implicit self-critique (see fn. 6).

France or the 2001-2 Argentine crisis are events which reveal that actors in principle can pose a threat to the continued reproduction of the capitalist configuration of forms.

On the other hand, Poulantzas undoubtedly presumed that forms are not just reflections of struggles, but that they have an independent effect on actors. He conceives of the 'relations of production' as a 'field of struggles' (39). The metaphor 'field' implies a structuring effect exerted by those relations that constitute the conditions under which acts of struggle take place. It is not a historical coincidence that the working class and the capitalist class face each other in class struggle; rather, it is a reflection of the capitalist configuration of forms. This suggests that struggles always take place in the context of forms which affect their trajectory. Struggles are not entirely determined by forms, but forms influence the direction of struggles.

In sum, for Poulantzas, struggles neither entirely govern forms, nor is it the other way round. Struggles and forms are *equal in importance* for the constitution of capitalism as a reproducible social system, *but not equal in kind*. The long-term stability of capitalist societies not only depends on the existence of a capitalist configuration of forms, but also on whether or not struggles threaten its reproduction.

Furthermore, Poulantzas implies that struggle and form are different aspects of one and the same set of social relations. If the relations of production are contained 'within' the struggles while at the same time governing them, it becomes impossible to assign form and struggle to two separate fields. This is confirmed by Poulantzas's take on the concept of capital. He describes capital as a 'relationship' (128), which is a reference to Marx, who conceives of it as 'a social relation between persons' (CI: 753). We can thus specify the concept and assert that it refers to a relation of production between workers and capitalists, mediated by the means of production.

But what does that imply for form and struggle? On the one hand, Marx argues that actors encounter capital as a stabilized condition of their actions. Capital entails 'dull compulsion' (726; cf. SPS: 168f.) because it tends to prompt actors to engage in activities that reproduce it. Wage dependent people, for example, usually agree to sell their labour power in order to secure their individual reproduction – at least as long as there is no plausible alternative (see above). Similarly, the capitalists find themselves in a competitive struggle, which forces them, 'under penalty of ruin' (CIII: 243), to ensure that their capital accumulates. The accumulation of capital, on the other hand, necessarily entails class struggles between the working and the capitalist class (CI: 243; cf. SPS: 106f.). If we take Poulantzas's reference to 'submersion' seriously, these struggles should not be taken as being conducive to the reproduction of the capital relation by default. There are constellations of rupture (see above; cf. SPS: 246f.) where the compulsion springing from the capital form does not develop its full strength because it is pushed back or even neutralized by class struggles. Thus, this compulsion exists only under the additional condition that the 'relationship of forces between classes in struggle' (84) is weighted towards capital, and workers do not perceive the option of permanently refusing wage labour as realistic. This suggests in turn that the concept of capital as a relation entails elements of both form and struggle, and neither of the two aspects is necessarily subordinate to the other. With reference to a point made by Poulantzas in SPS (17ff.), I contend that struggles are *constitutively present* in forms, and vice-versa. Accordingly, the composition and location of forms and struggles can shift, and they differ according to specific situations.

Following Poulantzas, we can distinguish three types of constellations of the relationship between the state as form and the struggles traversing it:

1. struggles within the state (184f.), for example around legal limits to the working day;
2. struggles at a distance from the state, which are nonetheless predicated on it and in turn affect it (195f.), for example around working conditions in a private company; and,
3. struggles around the state form (259) such as the insurrections in France and Argentina.

Against this backdrop, it is possible to develop an analogous typology for the capital relation:

1. struggles within the capital form, for example around contracted working hours;
2. struggles at a distance to the capital form which nonetheless affect it, e.g., civil war; and
3. struggles around the capital form, that is, around the commodification of labour power and the societal role of capital accumulation, as in the case of a general strike.

In sum, there are three basic configurations of the relationship between form and struggle if we build on Poulantzas: *struggles within forms, struggles at a distance from forms, and struggles around forms.*[8]

This typology is anti-reductionist because it includes both actions

---

8 In actual processes of struggle, these are of course bound to overlap.

conforming to social forms and acts of revolt going against them. The key point is that the capitalist mode of production as a configuration of forms entails a tendency towards its own reproduction, but this tendency is only actualized if the relations of forces and the trajectories of struggle permit. In capitalism, in other words, moments of stability and instability exist alongside one another.

2. With Poulantzas towards Marx

I have established where the deficits in Postone's and Holloway's arguments lie, and to what extent Poulantzas helps us overcome them. So far, however, I have avoided doing one thing: my statements on form and struggle have merely been *declarative*, that is, I have not grounded them in a theoretical reconstruction of capitalist society. The CPE is a comprehensive attempt at such a theorization. I will therefore close the gap in my argument by briefly reconstructing Marx's approach in *Capital* and sketching what a theoretical grounding of the conception of the relationship between form and struggle developed here could look like.

2.1. Presentation as explanation

Marx's goal is to portray the capitalist mode of production. Doing so requires addressing one fundamental question: in what order should the forms constituting this mode of production be described? The fundamental problem of every analysis of the social world is that the latter is characterized by synchronous, mutually interdependent causal relations, which the human mind can only grasp in the diachronic-linear mode of language. Thus, form analysis encounters problems such as the following: the commodity form and money seem to presuppose each other. In order words, it appears impossible to analyse one without understanding the other. What is to be done?

Marx distinguishes between method 'of inquiry' and 'method of presentation' (CI: 19). In the process of inquiry, the internal articulation of the 'material' (ibid.) is examined. The organization of the presentation in turn reflects this articulation. What does that mean? If we look at the different forms and their interconnections, we find that we can capture certain relationships in abstraction from others. It is possible, for example, to make statements about the commodity form of the product of labour without talking about money. On the other hand, there are relations that can be understood only against the background of prior analyses. To understand money we need to know the secrets of the commodity. This results in a hierarchy of levels of abstraction, which in turn provides the foundation for the order of presentation.

At the beginning of the presentation in *Capital*, we encounter the commodity as the 'primary form' (45; translation amended), i.e., the one form that can be analyzed in abstraction from all the others. The order of forms altogether constitutes an 'explanatory relationship' [Begründungszusammenhang] (Heinrich 1999: 173; translated)[9]: every form analysed is discussed against the background of knowledge gained by previously having analysed others, and the overall arrangement of forms renders their interrelations intelligible within the diachrony of language. Accordingly, Marx's presentation becomes more concrete and complex with every added determination. In the end, ideally, the capitalist mode of production will have been captured in its entirety, i.e., the complete configuration of forms constituting it will have been depicted.[10]

Thus, Marx's presentation results in the production of an 'object of knowledge' (RC: 41). The organization of this object reveals that forms in their systematic interrelationship represent a social 'whole' (CIII: 343) in so far as they only exist if they coexist. Money, for example, does not exist without commodity production, but commodity production can only become the socially dominant form of production if there is money. Since the translation of these synchronic relationships of co-constitution into the diachrony of language presupposes that the 'inquirer' actively organizes the forms in some way, presentation is always also an act of construction. Poulantzas infers that modes of production are 'abstract-formal object[s] which do [...] not exist in the strong sense in reality'. He distinguishes them from 'real-concrete' social formations, which are governed by dominant tendencies that belong to a particular mode of production, for example, 'France under Louis Bonaparte' and 'England during the Industrial Revolution' (PPSC: 15; cf. SPS: 25). Obviously, social analysis generally aims to unlock social reality, but following Marx and Poulantzas, this cannot be done without looking at modes of production. According to Poulantzas, analysing the latter constitutes the 'condition of knowledge of real-concrete objects' (13) because in so doing, the fundamental tendencies shared by all social formations dominated by a certain mode of production are established.

Marx establishes these tendencies by *initially* starting from forms. This is

9   This term accurately describes Marx's mode of presentation. However, my perspective differs fundamentally from Heinrich's as regards the question of what 'explanation' actually means.
10 Marx did not achieve this goal because he was unable to complete his work. The second and third volume of *Capital* were edited and published by Friedrich Engels, and Marx never wrote the planned volumes on 'landed property, wage labour; the State, foreign trade, world market' (MECW 29: 261).

plausible in so far as struggles do not take place in a non-societal space, but against the background of an environment of forms that structure them. This, however, gives rise to the question of whether Marx is not also guilty of form reductionism, and whether it is possible at all to justify Poulantzas's insights with the help of the CPE.

2.2. Dissection and retroduction

The problems raised can only be resolved by engaging with Marx's mode of presentation in a detailed fashion. The latter is guided by 'diagnoses concerning reality' (Althusser 1983: 141; translated; cf. Sayer 1979: 185, fn. 10) made during the process of inquiry. Hence, *Capital* opens with an observation from everyday life, i.e., the appearance of all social wealth in capitalism as an 'immense accumulation of commodities' (CI: 45). This observation is by no means arbitrary. It can be made in any capitalist setting and is therefore hard to dispute. Nonetheless, it still has the status of a 'postulation' (Althusser 1983: 130; translated). It is only proved correct once the entire capitalist mode of production has been reconstructed on this foundation. The purpose of Marx's postulation is to ground the mode of presentation in social reality and fend off idealist readings (cf. CI: 19). Moreover, it demarcates an area of analysis (cf. Althusser 1983: 130). This happens when Marx, through presenting his initial diagnosis, extracts the commodity. The latter constitutes the 'primary form', i.e., the first target of his analysis. Upon further examination, he adduces another everyday observation, which again constitutes a 'postulation'. At the end of the analysis of the commodity in *Capital*, 'we find' capital by looking at the circulation of commodities (CI: 158). This observation demarcates a second area of analysis. Marx remains within its confines until the end of the third volume. In sum, the presentation in *Capital* rests on two 'orders' (Wolf 1983: 127; translated) that build on each other – the 'production of commodities' (CI: 52) and the 'production for capital' (CIII: 249).

When Marx is exploring these orders with the help of form analysis, he employs a variety of theoretical procedures. The two most important ones are *dissection*, i.e., analysis in a narrow sense, and *retroduction*. The former consists of determining the characteristics of an *analysandum* that differentiate it from other analysanda. Marx uses this procedure at the beginning of his analysis of the commodity. He demonstrates that its characteristics are use value, exchange value, value and the double character of the labour necessary to produce it (CI: 45ff.). *Retroduction*,[11] in contrast,

---

11 The term was coined by Charles Sanders Pierce: 'Retroduction [...] depends on our hope [...] to guess at the conditions under which a given kind of phenomenon will

relies on establishing the *conditions of possibility of the existence* of *analysanda*. The analysis of the value form, which follows on from the dissection of the commodity, is a paradigmatic case (49ff.). Marx looks at exchange value once more by relating it to the scenario captured in his initial diagnosis. First, he discovers that exchange value constitutes a simple expression of value that involves two commodities, and that is incompatible with the conditions of existence of this scenario. Then, he modifies it without adding additional forms, that is, by simply repositioning the relations between the two commodities until both sides are compatible. In so doing, Marx does not add any new postulations, but maintains the relationship to the initial observation as a guiding thread that enables him to activate potentials for modification already contained in the commodity form. By this means, he manages to demonstrate that the appearance of social wealth as an immense accumulation of commodities not only entails the existence of exchange value, but that it also presupposes the existence of money. In other words, Marx shows that in capitalism money and commodities cannot but coexist, and does so with the help of *retroductive form development*. Overall, he constructs the capitalist configuration of forms as a systematic configuration by starting from everyday observations and making analytical and retroductive inferences.

2.3. The working day and the limits of form analysis

My sketch of Marx's mode of presentation at the beginning of *Capital* allows me to specify the questions posed at the end of section 2.1: where, within a configuration of forms constructed by way of dissection and retroduction, is there space for struggles that submerge it?

In order to address this problem, it appears useful to look at a chapter in *Capital* where Marx explicitly deals with the relationship between form and struggle. This is the chapter on the working day, in which Marx describes a stabilizing and a destabilizing tendency in capitalism and how they clash: the circulation of capital involves the realization of the commodity in the market. Accordingly, it is characterized by the competition between individual capitalists who seek to push their counterparts out of the market in order to secure their own position. Among other factors, competition takes place via work hours. By extending them, individual capitalists can potentially increase the number of products produced and turn an extra profit. As a result, there is a tendency for the constant extension of the working day, or, in Marx's words, for the 'increase of absolute surplus value' (CIII: 80).

present itself' (1913: 385ff.). Derek Sayer gives a detailed account of how Marx's mode of presentation relies on retroductive inferences (1979: 115ff.).

In the long run, this results in the deterioration of workers' health. If this tendency goes unchecked, it will undermine the source of surplus value, thus calling into question the viability of capitalist production.

Conversely, however, the capital form also relies on the existence of a class of wage labourers who secure their reproduction by selling their labour power. Given that reproduction is the motivation behind entering contracts of employment, the workers will resist work hours that endanger their health and survival – at least in the longer run. This also means that the long-term existence of capital is guaranteed only when the tendency towards the expansion of absolute surplus value is checked by the tendency towards active struggle of workers against it.

At the level of actors, this relationship appears as follows: "We see then, that, apart from extremely elastic bounds, the nature of the exchange of commodities itself imposes no limit to the working day, no limit to surplus labour. The capitalist maintains his rights as a purchaser when he tries to make the working day as long as possible, and to make, whenever possible, two working days out of one. On the other hand, the peculiar nature of the commodity sold implies a limit to its consumption by the purchaser, and the labourer maintains his right as seller when he wishes to reduce the working day to one of definite normal duration. There is here, therefore, an antinomy, right against right, both equally bearing the seal of the law of exchanges. Between equal rights force decides. Hence is it that in the history of capitalist production, the determination of what is a working day, presents itself as the result of a struggle, a struggle between collective capital, i.e., the class of capitalists, and collective labour, i.e., the working class" (CI: 243).

Here Marx identifies a systemic problem of capitalism: the commodity form and the conditions of exchange it entails leave the length of the working day '*per se* indeterminate' (240). The 'antinomy' mentioned refers to the fact that the rules of commodity exchange make it possible for both buyer and seller to insist on rights that contradict each other. The capitalists argue that they are free to dispose of the purchased good as they see fit – just like any other buyers of a commodity (241). The workers, however, claim that they must be able to dispose freely and fully of their labour power upon termination of a contract of employment, and that its continued reproduction therefore forms part of the conditions of sale (242). In order to enforce their rights, both sides enter into a struggle, which in turn leads to their constitution as collective class actors and antagonists.

Initially, this struggle appears as a struggle within the capital form. After all, the conditions of one specific transaction within the circuit of capital are at stake, that is, the transformation of variable capital into labour power to be expended in the process of production. However, the mere existence of a capitalist configuration of forms does not mean that the length of the working day is regulated in a way that guarantees the continued existence of capital. Otherwise, Marx would not view it as undetermined. This suggests that capital alone is not capable of reproducing its own preconditions and securing its continued existence. Rather, it is dependent on processes that it does not entirely determine. Thus, Bob Jessop speaks of the "constitutive incompleteness of the capital relation" (2002: 51).

This reveals a methodological problem concerning Marx's mode of presentation. He is not able to make statements about the length of the working day by reverting to his usual procedures, that is, dissection and retroduction. Capital is not endowed with a differentiating characteristic from which the length of the working day could be derived, and the latter do not form part of capital's conditions of existence. Capital can exist, after all, not just under conditions of a short- to medium-length working day, but also under conditions of an extremely long one – at least for rather short periods of time (cf. CI: 289). This in turn implies that the *conditions of existence* of capital are distinct from its *conditions of reproduction*: the mere existence of capital by no means entails its long-term *reproducibility* [Reproduktionsfähigkeit]. The latter cannot be derived from the former with the help of Marx's standard form-analytical toolkit.

This is a problem in so far as it is only justified to speak of a 'capitalist mode of production' constituting an object of knowledge if this is a reference to a configuration of forms that gets reproduced over time. Otherwise it would be possible to claim that we are dealing with a short-term, accidental conjuncture, whose observation has few implications for gaining a more general understanding of the contemporary social world. Thus, the reproducibility of the mode of production forms part of the CPE's explanandum. Accordingly, Marx's construction of his object of inquiry and the project of a CPE in general both hinge on his ability to deal with this difficulty.

Obviously, Marx has to expand his theoretical arsenal in order to do so. Faced with theoretical challenges of this kind, some Marxists take to employing *functionalist derivations*. They infer from the requirements for the reproduction of an existing social configuration that specific social relations must exist that ensure it. One example is Wolfgang Fritz Haug's interpretation of the analysis of the value form. He argues that the function or purpose of the value form is to express value, and concludes: 'Elements of the form that prevent it from fulfilling or realizing its purpose, that disturb its function, can [...] be understood as flaws in the form. The disturbance of function by form makes it impossible for the function to remain with this flawed form, causing it to move on' (1974: 144; translated). In other words, a flawed form cannot possibly remain in existence, because it is dysfunctional for the social configuration within which it emerges. In its place, a functional form emerges, which in this case is the money form (146).

It is noteworthy that functionalist derivation differs fundamentally from retroduction. In the case of the former, the existence of a form is derived from its functionality for a given social setting; in the case of the latter, the existence of a form is derived from the existence of a setting. In addition, functionalist derivation, in contrast to retroduction, relies on an *implicit assumption of stability*, for forms can only be assumed to be 'forced' to adapt the functional requirements of a given social setting if we also assume the stable reproduction of social relations. Yet the mere fact that something exists by no means implies that it works. Consequently, I have not included functionalist derivation in what I call form analysis. There are good reasons for this: assumptions of stability are undermined by the uncountable number of social crises in the history of humankind. In other words, they constitute arbitrary postulations which obscure the fundamental instability of the social world. Thus, functionalist derivations are in general of no use for the theorization of societality.

In line with this, Marx introduces a different type of theoretical tool in order to address the problem of reproduction. He resorts to producing a historical narrative and describes how the struggles between the working class and the capitalist class in 19th century England led state apparatuses to introduce a legal limit to the working day. The character of this description is that of a generalizable example – another historical configuration could have stood in its place – but it is no mere illustration. Marx does not refer to a real-concrete historical process in order to illustrate a socio-economic mechanism already derived elsewhere. Rather, he wants to show that it is possible for impediments to reproduction to be overcome, however precarious this overcoming may be, and that there is historical evidence for this. He draws on history as an 'ancillary science' which helps him overcome limitations of his primary method of analysis. The limits of form analysis[12] thus revealed are not external limitations of Marx's object of inquiry, but

12 My way of putting this is analogous to Marx's own. In 'The Original Text of the Second and the Beginning of the Third Chapter of *A Contribution to the Critique of Political Economy*' of 1858/59, he writes that 'the dialectical form of presentation is right only when it knows its own limits' (MECW 29: 505). In this context, he refers to the existence of the 'free worker' (ibid.) as a historical, non-derivable precondition of the capitalist mode of production.

internal to it. They mark shifts from form analysis to alternative modes of presentation that also contribute to its construction.[13] In turn, overcoming these limitations means moving to a different level within the object. Accordingly, Marx resorts to describing an institutional setting located in a real-concrete social formation when he establishes the reproducibility of the capitalist mode of production.

But is Marx's decision to shift levels compatible with his claim that he is supplying an internally consistent system of explanations? The analysis of the working day reveals that at the point where Marx cannot take form analysis any further, he employs a holding construction.[14] This is necessary because at the level of concretion reached with form-analytical tools, a central aspect of the reproducibility of the capitalist mode of production (the length of the working day) remains undetermined. Since Marx cannot simply presuppose the existence of the mode of production in the sense of a configuration of forms that gets reproduced, he is forced to 'jump ahead' of his argument and analyse conjunctural settings located at the level of the social formation. Consequently, Poulantzas points out that these social formations should not be regarded "as merely heaped up concretizations of abstractly reproduced modes of production [...]. Social formations are the actual sites of the existence and reproduction of modes of production" (SPS: 25).

This also means that Marx's line of argument is circular. He refers to forms that have not yet been developed systematically, but which will be derived later on the grounds of the references made in anticipation. Accordingly, the place of classes in the systematic order of presentation is not the chapter on the working day, but the (unfinished) final chapter of the third volume. Similarly, the state and state regulation were supposed to be dealt with in an altogether separate volume. Marx appears to be struggling with the fundamental problem of social theory discussed earlier: analysing society means dealing with synchronic interrelations. Marx's solution to this problem – the decision to include a historical narrative in his presentation – is by no means illegitimate, as long as we are aware of its declarative and preliminary status. Accordingly, shifting in anticipation to the level of a conjuncture in a specific social formation is a heuristic tool. Further into the presentation, it can be replaced by a more theoretically elaborate analysis.

13 We also encounter this kind of limit in chapter two of the first volume of *Capital*, where Marx deals with the social procedures for establishing a universal equivalent, and in the third section of the second volume, where he demonstrates that the balanced reproduction of capital is an 'accident' (CII: 494), thus implying a role for the state in the development of strategies of accumulation.
14 See also Jessop (2004: 7) on 'holding concepts'.

Against this backdrop, it becomes possible to give a more precise account of the relationship between form and struggle. The commodity form of wage labour leaves some aspects of the conditions of its sale undetermined. At the same time, the commodity 'labour power' cannot be detached fully from its sellers, so that the conflicting interests of buyers and sellers extend into the period of its use. This suggests that its 'incompleteness' as a form results in the emergence of a field where the initially merely contractual relationship between the two groups is transformed into a relationship of struggle. In other words, workers and capitalists attempt to prevail against each other by resorting to coercion.

Marx's reference to the decisive role of force underscores that the result of the conflict remains under-determined by the field of struggle. Although the latter constitutes a set of conditions of action, the result of the struggle is ultimately determined by the course of the struggle itself. If this was not the case, Marx would not have referred to a specific social formation, but would have declared in the abstract how normal working hours are determined.

The incompleteness of the form also suggests that workers and capitalists are both being positioned vis-à-vis each other in a particular way and set free at the same time. In other words, its effect is both limiting and enabling. This implies that actors possess freedom (cf. Laclau 1990: 44) – not in the sense of voluntaristic decision-making, but in the sense of a freedom to choose under conditions beyond one's control (cf. MECW 11: 103).

Overall, Marx's presentation suggests that the conception of actors as 'supports' is provisional in character and revised in due course, and that the potential 'submerging' of forms through actors becomes a real possibility. Therefore, precise statements about their activities can only be made on the grounds of concrete-complex ex-post analyses at the level of the social formation (cf. Jessop 2002: 269). Conversely, it turns out to be impossible to fully determine the conditions for the use of labour power by just resorting to form analysis. These conditions are also the result of struggles and of the resulting relations of forces. This means that real-concrete historical processes as well as a 'historical and moral element' (CI: 181) become part of the object of the CPE. Moreover, the reproduction of the mode of production remains uncertain as long as there is no equilibrium of forces between the working class and the capitalist class that forces the latter into making concessions which do not pose a challenge to their authority. This also means that reproducibility cannot be established once and for all. The indeterminate character of the length of the working day remains a systemic gap because any agreement reached will come under fire once the relations of forces start changing.

Consequently, Marx's mode of presentation renders Postone's form reductionism untenable and confirms Poulantzas's position. Form and struggle exist in and through each other, and one cannot be reduced to the other. In Marx's presentation, forms may precede struggles, but this does not imply that they are more important. In this respect, the order of Marx's line of argument reflects no more than the 'translation' of the synchrony of social reality into the diachrony of language and the necessity of explaining actions against the backdrop of their conditions. Thus, Marx shows in *Grundrisse* how the 'discovery' of struggle retroacts on how the forms introduced at the beginning of his presentation should be understood: 'the antagonism of wages and capital, etc., is already latent in the simple determination of exchange value and money' (MECW 28: 179f.). He adds that neglecting this amounts to 'a refusal to advance beyond the simplest economic relationships' and to overlooking the fact that they 'are mediated by means of the most profound contradictions' (180).

3. Fragility and durability

My initial question was whether capitalism is characterized by fragility or by durability. I would like to conclude by making a few remarks on this issue: first, both self-destructive and self-stabilizing tendencies are inherent in the capitalist mode of production. Second, social formations based on the capitalist mode of production can exist only if the configuration of forms is complemented by contingent factors, i.e., factors not entirely determined by it. Third, the relation of forces between workers and capitalists is the key issue. In sum, for capitalist social formations, stability is a state that requires a multiplicity of preconditions to be fulfilled. It relies on actors actively removing potential points of rupture, and is therefore subject to political negotiations, contestations and conflict.

Regarding the question of anti-capitalist strategy, I contend that struggles do not necessarily either transcend the system or reproduce it. Thus, on this very abstract level, there is no justification for refusing to intervene or participate in such struggles. If the question of the survival and shape of capitalism is decided at the level of the social formation, struggles over the institutional embedding of the mode of production play a key role in triggering processes of transformation. Reading Marx with Poulantzas leads me to conclude that the radical transformation of the dominant social order is not easily achieved, but is by no means impossible.

References

Althusser, L. (1983) 'Marx' Denken im Kapital', *Prokla*, Vol. 13, no. 50, 130-147.
Anderson, P. (1976) *Considerations on Western Marxism* (London: New Left Books).
Bonefeld, W. (1995) 'Capital as Subject and the Existence of Labour', in Bonefeld et al. (eds.) *Open Marxism*, vol. III, (London: Pluto Press) 182-212.
Giddens, A. (1979) *Central Problems in Social Theory* (London: Macmillan).
Haug, W. F. (1974) *Vorlesungen zur Einführung ins 'Kapital'* (Köln: Pahl-Rugenstein).
Heinrich, M. (1999) *Die Wissenschaft vom Wert. Die marxsche Kritik der politischen Ökonomie zwischen wissenschaftlicher Revolution und klassischer Tradition*, 2nd ed. (Münster: Westfälisches Dampfboot).
Holloway, J. (2002) *Change the world without taking power: the meaning of revolution today* (London: Pluto Press).
Holloway, J. (2003) 'Die Druckerei der Hölle. Eine Anmerkung in Antwort auf Joachim Hirsch', *Das Argument*, vol. 45, no. 250, 219-227.
Jessop, B. (1991) 'Polar Bears and Class Struggle. Much less than a self-criticism', in Bonefeld, W. / Holloway, J. (eds.) *Post-Fordism and Social Form. A Marxist debate on the post-Fordist state* (Basingstoke: Macmillan) 145-169.
Jessop, B. (2002) *The Future of the Capitalist State* (Cambridge: Polity Press).
Jessop, B. (2004) 'On the Limits of Limits of Capital', Web: http://www.lancs.ac.uk/fass/sociology/papers/jessop-limits-to-capital.pdf [26-07-2006].
Laclau, E. (1990) *New Reflections on the Revolution of Our Time* (London: Verso).
Pierce, C. S. (1913) 'A Letter to F. A. Woods', *Collected Papers*, Vol. 8, (Cambridge/MA: Belknap Press of Harvard Univ. Press, 1931-1958) 385-388.
Postone, M. (1993) *Time, labor, and social domination. A reinterpretation of Marx's critical theory* (Cambridge: Cambridge Univ. Press).
Poulantzas, N. (1968) 'Theorie und Geschichte. Kurze Bemerkungen über den Gegenstand des "Kapitals"', in Euchner, W. / Schmidt, A. (eds.) *Kritik der politischen Ökonomie heute. 100 Jahre 'Kapital'* (Frankfurt am Main: Europäische Verlagsanstalt), 58-69.
Sayer, D. (1979) *Marx's Method. Ideology, Science & Critique in 'Capital'* (Hassocks, Sussex: Harvester Press).
Wolf, F. O. (1983) 'Am Kapital arbeiten! Einführende Notizen zu Althussers Marx-Text', *Prokla*, vol. 13, no. 50, 127-129.

POULANTZAS'S CLASS ANALYSIS

MAX KOCH

In West German academia, analyses of social inequality and social structure were not usually carried out in terms of class. In the 1950s and 1960s, the period of the 'economic miracle', it was *en vogue* to assume that there was a 'levelled' or 'evened-out' middle-class society.[1] After a rather short-lived renaissance of class analysis in the 1970s, themes such as 'individualization' and 'new social inequalities' (Beck 1983) emerged and began to dominate debates. In the 1980s especially, German sociology of social inequality took as its starting point that the importance of class was diminishing or even that class was dissolving. Consequently, the fall of the Berlin Wall was seen as a sure sign that the capitalist market economy had finally succeeded and proved its historical superiority, and that the idea of a 'class society' should be abandoned for good. And yet, the farewell to class theory was a provincial development specific to West Germany. Debates in other countries, especially in France, the UK and the US, were hardly considered. Throughout the 1980s and 1990s, Nicos Poulantzas's class analysis shared the same fate as the theories of Pierre Bourdieu and Erik Olin Wright, among many others: it was largely ignored.[2] This was particularly unfortunate in the 1990s and 2000s. State welfare was gradually withdrawn and social exclusion was becoming more acute, so that people's social location became closer to 'market positions' (Max Weber) and, consequently, to class positions again.

Class analysis in the Marxian tradition takes the inherent tensions and contradictions of the capitalist mode of production as a starting point. On this basis, it proposes verifiable (and falsifiable!) hypotheses in relation to long-term developments of the social structure, thereby (re-)uniting empirical social inquiry with social theory. Just as in Poulantzas's days, the key issue is whether it is possible to prove that theoretically constructed classes are 'social classes', i.e., that there is a structural homology between

1   Helmut Schelsky (1965) referred to German post-war society as *equitable middle-class society*.
2   For more details, see Koch (1998).

such theoretical constructs and social actors with the same or equivalent living conditions that can be identified at the empirical level.

Nicos Poulantzas played an important role in reviving class analysis in the Marxian tradition. In West Germany he was only influential in the 1970s. In the English-speaking world his influence was more profound and long-lasting. Poulantzas outlined his first concept of class in *Political Power and Social Classes* (PPSC), albeit at a high level of abstraction.[3] He reflected critically upon this approach and developed it further in *Classes in Contemporary Capitalism* (CCC). Here, he provides concrete suggestions regarding the question of where to place boundaries between social classes. CCC was presented on a sufficiently 'concrete' level of abstraction that it became possible to discuss and test its main hypotheses empirically. The book played an important role in English-language debates on the theoretical and empirical reconstruction of Marxian class analysis. For example, it served as the point of departure for Erik Olin Wright's *Class, Crisis and the State* (1978). In *State, Power, Socialism* (SPS), Poulantzas elaborated the arguments of CCC and related them to the interdependency between classes and the state. However, in his last book he did not modify or revise his concept of social class. As a consequence, CCC remains the first and foremost point of reference for theoretical and empirical debates on class analysis.

1. Levels of abstraction in social theory and class analysis

In PPSC, Poulantzas introduces a distinction fundamental to his approach. It is the distinction between *mode of production* and *social formation*, which builds on Marxist structuralism and Louis Althusser in particular. The mode of production is a 'complex whole', i.e., a specific articulation of economic, political and ideological levels. Following Engels, it is 'dominated, in the last instance, by the economic' (PPSC: 14). Modes of productions can be distinguished through understanding the particular combination of these three levels. They constitute abstractions from real societies and do not exist as such. Only social formations can be identified empirically, e.g., France under Louis Bonaparte or Germany under Helmut Kohl. Social formations combine different modes of production. On the one hand, pre-capitalist social relations are not simply extinct in social formations dominated by the capitalist mode of production; on the other hand, it is at least conceivable that there are structures and social relations within these formations that

---

3   This book resonated with the social science community. Members of the *International Sociological Association* recently voted it into the Top 100 most important books of the 20th century (see http://www.ucm.es/info/isa/books).

reach beyond capitalism.

Consequently, emphasizing the combination of different modes of production in a given social formation means breaking with attempts to 'deduce' social classes simply and directly from abstract economic categories referring to one mode of production only:[4] 'the classes of a social formation' and their day-to-day struggles and practices 'cannot be deduced [...] from an abstract analysis of the modes and forms of production which are present in it, for this is not how they are found in the social formation' (CCC: 23).

Since social formations are complex combinations of different modes of production, the number of classes in a particular social formation depends not only on the class structure of the dominant mode of production, but also on the class structures of non-dominant modes of production. The overlap of different modes of production in a given social formation results in a plurality of class relations. Among these, two 'basic classes' stand out, which in turn reflect the dominance of a particular mode of production in the social formation: 'in capitalist societies there are the bourgeoisie and the proletariat' (ibid.). Further distinctions include *fractions* and *strata*, which Poulantzas uses interchangeably. Moreover, there are also *social categories*, which are defined primarily in terms of their positions within the political and ideological levels (ibid.). Poulantzas emphasizes that such 'social groups' are not located 'external to, alongside, or above classes'. Rather, they are fractions and strata marked by 'class membership', and 'their agents generally [belong...] to several different social classes' (CCC: 24). Finally, Poulantzas builds on Antonio Gramsci and elaborates on his term of the 'power-bloc'. In so doing, Poulantzas emphasizes the notion of particular political and economic conjunctures and their corresponding relations of domination (see, for example, SPS: 91). Power blocs are defined through alliances of dominant classes and class fractions. Political and economic conjunctures can be distinguished historically and empirically by observing and comparing the changing social compositions of such blocs.

2. Classes in contemporary capitalism

For Poulantzas, there were two basic classes in the capitalist social formations of Western Europe in the 1970s: the capitalist class and the working class. Moreover, he distinguished between several additional classes, groups and categories – above all, managers, state employees and the 'old' and 'new' petty bourgeoisie. The post-war era was characterized (a) by the fact that

---

4   'Projekt Klassenanalyse' (1973/1974), a West German team of authors, was most consequent in terms of deducing class positions and boundaries from categories of Marx's critique of political economy and his analysis of the capitalist mode of production.

the percentage of the old petty bourgeoisie (self-employed craftspeople, shopkeepers etc.) within the economically active population diminished, and (b) by the fact that the share of the new petty bourgeoisie (above all, white-collar employees, technicians, supervisory staff, civil servants) increased. For Poulantzas, whose academic interest in the class structure was secondary to his political goal of overthrowing the existing structures of capitalist exploitation and domination, the boundaries between the working class and the new petty bourgeoisie were of crucial importance. In his view, the Left could attain hegemony only through an alliance of the two classes. In his analysis, he tried to prove that the working class and the new petty bourgeoisie were distinct entities, and that the old and new petty bourgeoisie belonged to the same class. He drew on arguments that referred to the economic, political and ideological level to prove both.

Poulantzas refers to Marx's distinction between productive and unproductive work both in relation to the economic level, and in order to differentiate between workers and members of the new petty bourgeoisie. According to Poulantzas, wage labourers who are exploited but do not produce surplus value belong to the petty bourgeoisie. His subsequent discussion of the levels of politics and ideology further reduces the range of occupational groups from which the working class is recruited. Poulantzas argues that the work of supervisory staff, technicians and engineers should be considered as forming part of the political domination of capital over labour despite the fact that it normally produces surplus value in the Marxian sense: 'The work of management and supervision, under capitalism, is the direct reproduction, within the process of production itself, of the political relations between the capitalist class and the working class' (CCC: 227f.). Accordingly, Poulantzas assumes that the 'social division of labour', which relates to forms of political domination, dominates over the 'technical division' (227). As a consequence, he argues that supervisory staff, technicians and engineers do not belong to the working class. However, they are not part of capital either, because they are politically dominated by the capitalist class – just as the working class. Following Poulantzas, this sandwich position characterizes the contradictory class position of the new petty bourgeoisie: it is defined by the experience of dominating the working class and being dominated by the capitalist class.

Poulantzas portrays the working class not only as being exploited economically, but also as being dominated politically and ideologically. He refers to the division of mental and manual labour in order to make the division between the working class and the new petty bourgeoisie clearer. According to him, this division 'assumes specific forms in the capitalist mode of production, which is characterised by a quite particular "separation" of the two' (234). Following Poulantzas, the work of engineers, technicians and 'experts' helps to legitimize the subordination of labour under capital: the 'separation of the direct producers from their means of labour' appears to be a mere technical or natural necessity. As a consequence, mental work takes the 'form of a knowledge from which the direct producers are excluded' – either because they 'actually do know how to perform this work but do not do so' or because 'they in fact do not know how to perform it (since they are systematically kept away from it)' (238). Although mental workers might well carry out productive labour, their ideological function within the 'social division of labour' outweighs their role in the 'technical division'. Accordingly, Poulantzas subsumes them under the 'new petty bourgeoisie'. The same goes for the majority of white-collar jobs, secretaries and sales personnel.

It is more complicated to prove Poulantzas's second assumption, i.e., that the old and new petty bourgeoisie belong to the same social class. The difficulties arise from the fact that the old 'petty bourgeoisie does not belong to the capitalist mode of production, but to the simple commodity form which was historically the form of transition from the feudal to the capitalist mode' (285f.).[5] The decisive argument for Poulantzas for uniting them in one class is that both partake in the 'basic' class antagonism of capital and labour in the same way: 'If the traditional and the new petty bourgeoisie can be considered as belonging to one and the same class, this is because [...] these groupings are precisely both polarized in relation to the bourgeoisie and the proletariat' (294). According to Poulantzas, this equivalence in locations in the class structure is also expressed in 'certain analogous features' (ibid.) in the ideological positions of these fractions of the middle class. Both share an anti-capitalist sentiment, which cannot, however, damage their belief in individual advancement through achievement: 'Afraid of proletarianization below, attracted to the bourgeoisie above, the new petty bourgeoisie often aspires to "promotion", to a "career", to "upward social mobility", i.e., to becoming bourgeois (the ideological aspects of bourgeois imitation) by way of the "individual" transfer to the "best" and "most capable"' (292).

It is remarkable that Poulantzas does not give much attention to the bearer of his political hopes – the working class. He may discuss its boundaries with other classes, but his analysis of the capitalist class is much more detailed. Whereas he separates the working class from the new petty bourgeoisie by

5   In *Capital*, Marx discusses 'simple commodity production' as a logical step in his progression from the analysis of commodities to that of the production of capital. It is contentious, however, whether this form of production ever existed historically.

referring to the levels of politics and ideology, he defines the capitalist class by largely focusing on economic parameters. Generally, he distinguishes between industrial capitalists, banking and commercial capitalists, and large landowners. Moreover, he introduces a temporal dimension by considering different phases of capitalist development and establishing the corresponding dominant fractions within the capitalist class. In hindsight, Poulantzas's differentiation between competition and monopoly capital and his emphasis on their struggles within the power bloc appear to be dated. And yet, the general gist of his argument remains significant. Poulantzas deals with the contradictions between big and medium-sized capital, and between national and transnational capital. Furthermore, he focuses on the concrete combination of different developmental stages and capital fractions in one social formation (90ff.).

The point of departure of Poulantzas's analysis of the capitalist class is the separation of economic ownership and possession. The former is defined as 'real economic control of the means of production, i.e., the power to assign the means of production to given uses and so to dispose of the products obtained'. While the law 'generally ratifies economic ownership', it is possible 'for the forms of legal ownership not to coincide with the real economic ownership'. In this case, Poulantzas contends, it is the latter that is determining class boundaries. 'Possession', in turn, constitutes the 'capacity to put the means of production into operation' (18). This category is above all relevant for distinguishing between the capitalist and feudal mode of production. Even though feudal lords were both the legal and economic owners of the land, the serfs normally possessed it. They were protected by custom and 'could not be purely and simply dispossessed by the lord' (19). Indeed, as Marx showed with reference to the Scottish Highland Clearances in the chapter on the primitive accumulation of capital in *Capital*, violence was necessary to invalidate this customary law. There is a "decisive modification" in advanced capitalism, which lies in the separation of producers from the means of production: they have no alternative to selling their labour power, which has become a commodity (ibid.).

According to Poulantzas, managers and senior state employees are also part of the capitalist class.[6] In relation to the former group, he again refers to the differentiation of ownership and possession. In so doing, he largely follows Marx's observation that in the capitalist mode of production, the 'labour of superintendence, entirely separated from the ownership of

---

6   Poulantzas reserves the category 'manager' for what is normally known as 'senior management', while he regards middle and junior managers as parts of the supervisory personnel, i.e., of the new petty bourgeoisie.

capital, walks the streets'. Just as an 'orchestra conductor need not own the instruments of his orchestra' (MECW 37: 385) certain 'functions' of capital are 'not necessarily fulfilled by the owner-agents themselves'. In modern capitalism, senior managers or, in Poulantzas's words, 'directing agents' carry out these functions, 'occupy the places of capital, and thus belong to the bourgeois class even if they do not hold formal legal ownership' (CCC: 180). In contrast, he derives the class position of the 'heads of the state apparatus' from the relationship between the state and the capitalist class.[7] In Poulantzas's terminology, state officials form a 'social category'. And yet, he assumes that they 'generally belong to the bourgeois class, [...] because, in a capitalist state, they manage the state functions in the service of capital' (187).

The internationalization of capital has advanced considerably since Poulantzas's death. Against this background, his distinction between a 'comprador' and an 'internal' bourgeoisie, which refers to the international division of labour, is of particular interest. The comprador bourgeoisie 'is that fraction of a class whose interests are constitutively linked to foreign imperialist capital' (Poulantzas 1973: 200). It does not possess an independent foundation for capital accumulation and thus is subordinated to foreign capital. Poulantzas stresses that, due to US capital imports to Western Europe, it is not possible anymore to simply talk of 'national' capital. Increasing foreign direct investment and capital amalgamation have resulted in the emergence of a new fraction of capital, which he calls 'internal bourgeoisie'. He points to the fact that capital is 'implicated by multiple ties of dependence in the international division of labour and the international concentration of capital' (CCC: 72). This is the case even when it disposes of a national basis for accumulation that allows for a certain autonomy vis-à-vis the world market. However, the internal bourgeoisie maintains its own national base, which exists alongside manifold transnational ties and dependencies – especially with US capital. It constitutes a new kind of fraction of capital, whose economic independence and political and ideological autonomy is under threat, but not lost altogether.[8]

In contrast to Poulantzas's analysis, recent discourses on 'globalization' tend to exaggerate and simplify the transnational character of firms. Against this backdrop, it needs to be emphasized that enterprises remain tied spatially, and that a relevant number even retain their national roots.

7   See below.
8   Some of Poulantzas's arguments were taken up in the more recent debate on the existence of a 'transnational capitalist class' (for an overview, see Koch 2009).

3. Social class and the state

After discussing the boundaries between social classes, I shall now move to Poulantzas's take on the constitution and reproduction of class domination. Following him, this necessitates considering the role of the state: 'Wherever there is class division and thus class struggle and power, the state already exists as institutionalized political power'. Accordingly, relations of production and class are only intelligible in their interplay with the state. After all, the state 'organizes the market and property relations; [...] and it stamps and codifies all forms of the social division of labour' (SPS: 39). This is a historically new situation: in contrast to feudalism or the ancient world, social classes in capitalism are no longer closed social relationships into which people are locked from birth. Rather, it is the task of the state to allocate people to social positions, class position in particular. State apparatuses have 'to shape and condition, train and subordinate [...] agents in such a way that they are able to occupy class positions [...]. This role falls especially to the schools, but is also fulfilled by the army, prisons and the state administration' (75).

According to Poulantzas, the state itself should neither be conceived of as a 'thing', nor as a 'subject'. Whereas instrumentalist conceptions grasp the state as a 'passive, or even neutral, tool' in the hands of one class or fraction, those who see it as a subject overestimate its autonomy (129). Both conceptions converge in presenting the state as an extrinsic entity separate from the classes. In contrast, Poulantzas sees the state in a manner analogous to 'capital', that is, as a 'relationship of forces or, more precisely, the material condensation of such a relationship among classes and class fractions' (128). Following Poulantzas, the relationship between class and the state can be grasped as an articulation of two force fields, which are interwoven in practice but must be kept apart analytically. Accordingly, class relations are expressed in the institutional structure of the state, and the state plays an active role in allocating actors to social classes. Metamorphoses in the division of labour lead to shifts in the class structure, but also influence arrangements internal to the state; conversely, changes internal to state apparatus affect the relations of production and the social structure. Addressing the question of 'the mode' in which the class structure is 'inscribed' in the institutional structure of the state thus broadens our understanding of its 'differential forms and precise historical transformations' (125).

As a consequence, Poulantzas's concept of 'power bloc' does not presuppose that state policies are the simple expression of the interest of one specific class or class fraction. Rather, they reflect the way in which different 'bourgeois fractions' are combined (128). The state undertakes the task of organizing and harmonizing their alliance, but does so without giving up its relative autonomy vis-à-vis the particular interests of stakeholders. However, this organizing function has structural and temporal limits and is subject to transitions. On the one hand, the state cannot dispose of the crisis tendencies inherent in capitalist development; on the other, the interests of the classes and fractions of the power bloc vary with structural changes in the international division of labour so that the organizational challenges faced by the state also change. In short, the state is bound to reproduce the contractions of the power-bloc within the material structure of its branches and apparatuses.

Even though Poulantzas's analysis of the interdependency between classes and the state focuses primarily on understanding the organization of the power-bloc, he emphasizes that concrete policies are also always influenced by the dominated classes and groups. The state makes sure that exploitation and exclusion of dominated classes and groups remain within certain limits. This reflects the extent to which the dominated classes manage to use the state for their interests and to transform it into a *welfare* state. As such, it forms an indispensable corrective to the socio-economic dynamics of capital accumulation. By guaranteeing a minimum of social cohesion, the state constitutes the principal actor in the process of legitimizing the existing social order. In the words of David Lockwood (1992), it plays a leading part in the provision of social and system integration.

Gramsci showed that the creation of coherence within a power bloc is always problematic. Poulantzas elaborates on this by referring to the internationalization and transnationalization of capitalism. Remarkably, he saw more than 30 years ago that power blocs 'can scarcely be located any more on a purely national level'. It is not only that the interests of the 'domestic bourgeoisie' are represented within any such bloc, but also the 'interests of the dominant imperialist capital and those of the imperialist capitals, as these are articulated within the process of internationalization' (CCC: 75). The latter makes the problem of constructing and reproducing consensus and cohesion within the dominant class even more complicated and complex. Not only divisions at the national level, but also those that correspond to different degrees of integration into the international division of labour need to be addressed. Contemporary states must accommodate for these changes when carrying out tasks that aim at producing social and system integration.

Against the backdrop of simplifying discourses on 'globalization', Poulantzas's ideas regarding the extended role of the state are of special interest. It is a commonly held assumption that national states are losing power and influence in the area of socio-economic regulation. In contrast, Poulantzas contends that the role of the nation state within the regulation of the international division of labour is not weakened, but transformed.[9] The inter- and transnationalization and globalization of socio-economic relations does not lead to national states being abolished. Rather, the latter 'themselves take charge of the interests of the dominant imperialist capital in its development within the "national" social formation' (73). According to Poulantzas, national states are not passive objects of external practical constraints but active organizers of the evolving international division of labour. At the economic level, the state tends to enhance the competitiveness of the nationally dominant fraction of capital by supplying 'public subventions, tax concessions' and 'industrial policies' (ibid.). And when performing its role as the 'organizer of hegemony', it intervenes in a 'domestic field already structured by inter-imperialist contradictions' (74f.).

If it is true that national states orchestrate the 'internationalization of public functions on capital's behalf' (81), claims that the national state is substituted by international institutions and transnational corporations should be handled with care. National states remain indispensable for the time being: in an outward direction because they organize and regulate the international division of labour (partly through international bodies such as the IMF, the World Bank, the OECD, the ILO etc.), and in an inward direction because they guarantee a minimum of social cohesion in societies characterized by contradictions and tensions.

4. Critical discussion

When establishing the boundary between the working class and the new middle class, Poulantzas distinguishes between productive and unproductive labour. In so doing, he excludes unproductive workers from the working class. This class boundary cannot be operationalized easily for empirical purposes. After all, Marx employs a definition of productive work that abstracts from the concrete content of work. In the fifth chapter of *Capital*, Marx provides an original yet preliminary definition of productive work, which largely reduces it to the material modification of the object of labour. However, he boths narrows and extends this original definition in the course of his presentation. He narrows it when he argues that the worker produces 'not for himself, but for capital'. As a consequence, the 'labourer alone is productive, who produces surplus-value for the capitalist'

---

9   For more contemporary analyses, from a European perspective, of the changing roles of the state in socio-economic regulation, see Koch (2005) and (2008).

(MECW 35: 510). Marx extends it in so far as it is no longer necessary to do manual work in order to be productive when the 'co-operative character of the labour-process becomes more and more marked'. It is enough to be 'an organ of the collective labourer' and to perform 'one of its subordinate functions' (509).

The debate on productive and unproductive work has a long history, and there are a lot of different positions (Koch 1998: 33ff.). But one thing appears to be clear: Marx gives the example of a schoolmaster who is productive 'when, in addition to belabouring the heads of his scholars, he works like a horse to enrich the school proprietor', but unproductive if he carries out the same work as a civil servant. This makes it impossible without further ado to conclude from occupational statistics – the empirical raw material of most class analyses – whether occupations are productive or unproductive. If there is no difference for capitalists between investing in a 'teaching factory' and in a 'sausage factory' (MECW 35: 510), because surplus value is produced in both cases, an operationalization of Poulantzas's class boundaries between the working class and the new middle class becomes difficult. Not only can each type of work that produces use value be productive or unproductive in principle, but one and the same person might carry out both productive and unproductive tasks. Furthermore, empirical enquiries into the class 'consciousness' of wage labourers have undermined Poulantzas's claims rather than confirming them (Koch 1998: 78ff.; Wright 1997). It is above all differences in the hierarchy of the labour process – in particular different levels of education and control resources in the work process – that are correlated with negative or positive opinions about capitalism. Wright's additional observation that in the late 1960s less than 20 per cent of the US workforce constituted the working class according to Poulantzas's narrow definition should also make us think twice (Wright 1978: 55).

Another problem with Poulantzas's definition of class boundaries is his use of economic, political and ideological factors. If the old and new petty bourgeoisie are elements of one and the same class, he has to concede that both fractions have different market positions and different places in the relations of production. Moreover, the old petty bourgeoisie diminished quantitatively in the Fordist era, while the majority of the occupational groups belonging to the new petty bourgeoisie expanded (Koch 2006: 151ff.). In other words, the latter benefited from structural change and the former was threatened by it. This suggests that it is more appropriate to assume that the old and new petty bourgeoisie found themselves in opposed rather than just different market and class positions. In addition, Wright questions the postulated proximity between both groups at the level of politics: 'The new petty bourgeoisie in general has an interest in the expansion of the state; the old petty bourgeoisie is generally opposed to big government and large state budgets' (Wright 1978: 58).

I do not intend to discuss whether there is accordance between the old and new petty bourgeoisie at the level of ideology. It appears to be more important to stress that Poulantzas at this point implicitly renounces the primacy of the economy for class constitution: if alleged or real communalities in ideological orientations suffice for the construction of the biggest class in quantitative terms – the middle class as a whole – Poulantzas's original claim that classes should be defined 'principally but not exclusively by their place in the production process' cannot be upheld (CCC: 14). His attempt to distance himself from economism turned into an overestimation of ideas and ideologies that does not have much in common with Marx's original research programme regarding class analysis.[10] Marx proposed to *build* on the economic core determinations of class when examining their expressions in politics, ideology and culture.[11] There is, hence, no need to negate the role of the state in the *real* constitution of social classes. But if we choose to reconstruct classes at the level of theory on the foundation of an approach that proceeds by gradually removing levels of abstraction, the economic basis of class relations has to be the primary focus. This basis must be presented initially under the temporary abstraction from non-economic factors (Koch 1998: 12ff.).

However, it is not only that Poulantzas's theoretical construction of classes is unsatisfactory, but also his failure to check his model empirically.[12] This is obvious in the case of the working class: Poulantzas appears to see it as a largely homogenous social entity with uniform political positions and cultural preferences. In order to prove this claim, Poulantzas would have had to carry out an enquiry into the actual social practices and lifestyles of the working class. The critique of 'positivism' and 'historicism' should not turn into a general hostility to empirical and historical analysis.[13] If class analysis is to mean more than the abstract 'deduction' of classes from general socio-economic categories, hypotheses that are verifiable and falsifiable empirically must follow from the theoretical discussion. Ideally, the results of this empirical work are then reflected in modifications of the original

10 Bob Jessop (1985: 174) refers to the fact that Poulantzas at times gave 'strategic calculations' and political convenience priority over scholarly rigor. This might also explain the inconsistencies in Poulantzas's class theory.
11 See, for example, Bischoff et.al. (2002: 128).
12 An exception from this rule is Poulantzas's analysis of the 'Present Phase of Imperialism and the Domination of the USA' (CCC: 37ff.); see also my concluding remarks.
13 For further elaborations of this point, see Thompson (1978) and Bourdieu (1987).

theory. Poulantzas's class analysis may provide a range of hypotheses worth discussing, but their empirical validity is yet to be tested.

Finally, it is crucial to be aware of a concept's limits. The fact that this has often been ignored has led to fruitless controversies between scholars who try to explain almost any social phenomenon by referring to class relations, and those who totally disavow the existence of classes. Poulantzas falls under the former group. In his works, there are rather cautious indications of a concept of power not reduced to class domination: 'relations of power do not exhaust class relations and *may* go certain way beyond them' (SPS: 43; italics by M.K.). And yet, Poulantzas refrains from elaborating on what a systematic theory of social structure could be that considers different and coexisting relations of power and subordination, especially those of class, gender and ethnicity. Against this backdrop, it was only logical that scholars such as Frank Parkin, who attempted to understand the plurality of power relationships by making use of Weber's theory of social closure, were scathing in their critique of Poulantzas (Parkin 1979: 11ff.). In hindsight, it seems as if the dominance of themes such as the 'individualization beyond classes' and the 'new social inequalities' in the 1980s and early 1990s was the ideological riposte to certain 1970s discourses in the social sciences when the class character of society was exaggerated. Unfortunately, Poulantzas's class reductionism also affected his state theory: he tended to downplay the significance of social forces other than class in this area, too (Jessop 2001: 85).

5. Concluding remarks

Poulantzas left a range of concepts and ideas that are in part fragmentary. Nevertheless, it is worth discussing them today. This applies not only to his state theory, but also to his class analysis. His assertion that the social structure of contemporary social formations should be understood as a juxtaposition of different modes of productions and structural levels (economy, politics, ideology), for example, facilitates moving the debate beyond the 'deduction' of social classes from abstract economic categories. Building on this proposition would require considering principles of social stratification other than class and attempting to understand the complex structures of relations of power and subordination. In this context, class analysis has an important but not exclusive role. A possible step forward would be to combine Marxist class analysis with Weberian theories of exclusion and social closure (Koch 2006: 11f.). This could be beneficial for both sides, especially if the distinctiveness of class relations in comparison to other relations of power and subordination is not blurred: class conflicts are specific because they are not only based on exclusion, but also on exploitation. After all, the wealth of capitalists depends directly on the efforts of workers in the labour process. In contrast, patriarchy and ethnic conflicts are based on the advantages for men or ruling ethnic groups that arise out of women or ruled ethnic groups being denied access to certain resources and positions in society (Wright 1994: 40).

Similarly, Poulantzas's distance to empirical enquiry is not an insurmountable problem. It is encouraging that Poulantzas himself sometimes worked empirically. His preparedness to do so constituted a practical critique of the structuralist tendency to rely exclusively on theoretical models. Part one of CCC is inspiring in this respect: Poulantzas used statistical data to analyse the structural changes in the international division of labour and their impact on statehood. His approach to class boundaries could be improved in the same way: through operationalization and empirical validation. Today, empirical enquiry is no longer generally suspected of 'positivism' – as was the case during Poulantzas's lifetime. Accordingly, his hypotheses and concepts could indeed guide research projects. Whether this would validate his concepts and theories, however, must be answered elsewhere.

References

Beck, U. (1983) 'Jenseits von Stand und Klasse. Soziale Ungleichheit, gesellschaftliche Individualisierungsprozesse und die Entstehung neuer sozialer Formationen und Identitäten', in Kreckel, R. (ed.) *Soziale Ungleichheiten* (Göttingen: Schwartz), 35-74.
Bischoff, J. / Herkommer, S. / Hüning, H. (2002) *Unsere Klassengesellschaft. Verdeckte und offene Strukturen sozialer Ungleichheit* (Hamburg: VSA-Verlag).
Bourdieu, P. (1987) 'What Makes a Social Class? On the Theoretical and Practical Existence of Groups', *Berkeley Journal of Sociology*, vol. 32, 1-17.
Jessop, B. (1985) *Nicos Poulantzas. Marxist theory and political strategy* (Basingstoke: Macmillan).
Jessop, B. (2001) 'Globalisierung und Nationalstaat. Imperialismus und Staat bei Nicos Poulantzas', in Hirsch, J. / Jessop, B. / Poulantzas, N. *Die Zukunft des Staates* (Hamburg: VSA-Verlag), 71-100.
Koch, M. (1998) *Vom Strukturwandel einer Klassengesellschaft. Theoretische Diskussion und empirische Analyse* (Münster: Westfälisches Dampfboot).
Koch, M. (2005) 'Wage Determination, Socio-economic Regulation and the State', *European Journal of Industrial Relations* vol. 8, no. 3, 327-346.
Koch, M. (2006) *Roads to Post-Fordism. Labour Markets and Social Structures in Europe* (Aldershot: Ashgate).
Koch, M. (2008) 'The State in European Employment Regulation', *Journal of European Integration* 30 (2), 255-272.
Koch, M. (2009) 'Klassen- und Sozialstrukturanalyse in transnationaler Dimension',

in Burchhardt, H.-J. (ed.) *Nord-Süd Beziehungen im Umbruch. Neue Perspektiven auf Staat und Demokratie in der Weltpolitik* (Frankfurt am Main: Campus Verlag).
Lockwood, D. (1992) *Solidarity and Schism. 'The Problem of Disorder' in Durkheimian and Marxist Sociology* (Oxford: Clarendon Press).
Parkin, F. (1979) *Marxism and Class Theory. A Bourgeois Critique* (New York : Columbia Univ. Press).
Poulantzas, N. (1973) 'On Social Classes', in Martin, J. (ed.) *The Poulantzas Reader. Marxism, Law and the State* (London: Verso, 2008), 186-219.
Projekt Klassenanalyse (1973/1974) *Materialien zur Klassenstruktur der BRD* (Berlin: VSA Verlag).
Schelsky, H. (1965) *Auf der Suche nach Wirklichkeit. Gesammelte Aufsätze* (Düsseldorf: Diederich).
Thompson, E. P. (1978) *The Poverty of Theory and Other Essays* (London: Merlin Press).
Wright, E. O. (1978) *Class, Crisis and the State* (London: New Left Books).
Wright, E. O. (1997) *Class Counts* (Cambridge: Cambridge Univ. Press).
Wright, E. O. (1994) *Interrogating Inequality: Essays on Class Analysis, Socialism and Marxism* (London: Verso).

POULANTZAS, GENDER RELATIONS AND FEMINIST STATE THEORY

JÖRG NOWAK

One of the reasons why Marxism became marginalized within the Left in the 1990s was that it was enmeshed in relations of domination, which in turn were not analysed sufficiently. Marxist political theory tended to reproduce the objective position of dominance of the European labour movement in left-wing politics. Many Marxist scholars either completely ignored gender relations, racism and Eurocentric world views, or treated them as marginal phenomena. As a result, most Marxist approaches did not capture the multiple divisions in the working class that reflected relatively autonomous relations of domination contingent to the capital relation. In other words, Marxism failed to meet its own demand of producing a theory formulated from the proletarian standpoint.

It follows that Marxist theories which indeed did attempt to develop new theoretical concepts for over-determined forms of subaltern struggle are of particular interest. Louis Althusser emphasized the asynchronous nature of different dynamics of domination – a point taken up widely in feminist theories (Gimenez 1982; Burton 1985; Assiter 1990). Nicos Poulantzas linked gender relations to class struggles, but was mostly ignored by feminist authors (exceptions are Hartsock 1983; Sauer 2001). Nonetheless, certain core hypotheses from Poulantzas's *State, Power, Socialism* (SPS) figure in contemporary feminist approaches (Haney 1996; 2004; Daly/Rake 2003) – even if this influence is not usually acknowledged.

Since feminist state theory left unexplained the interaction of class and gender relations as discussed by Poulantzas, its failure to engage with his work constitutes a serious omission. In light of this, I will attempt to reconstruct Poulantzas's contribution to the debate about state power and gender and class relations. In the process, I will employ a conception of gender relations that combines social constructivism (Wetterer 2002) with theories of hegemony (Connell 1987; Hennessy 2000). Both approaches converge in emphasizing the importance of the social division of labour for the constitution of gender hierarchies. They point out that political power and economic interests influence the way in which certain types of labour are distributed along gender lines. There are two benchmarks for the existence of a dialogue between Poulantzas and feminist state theories: (a) the extent to which the autonomy of gender relations is accounted for, and (b) the extent to which the approaches in question take notice of changes in the capitalist mode of production.

1. Poulantzas's state theory

Poulantzas is important because he transfers Antonio Gramsci's rather empirical analysis of the interaction between the political and the economic into the realm of theory. He also radicalizes Louis Althusser's anti-economistic approach, according to which the capital-labour contradiction is 'never active *in the pure state*' (FM: 113). This does not mean, however, that Poulantzas gives up on the idea of economic determination in the last instance. Following Gramsci, he understands the economy and politics as specific arrangements whose object and extension vary in different phases of capitalism (SPS: 17ff., 196f.). This suggests that there is a specific configuration of societal 'spaces' (16f.) that mutually constitute one another in every mode of production.

Poulantzas places greater emphasis than Gramsci on the concentration of political power in the state, using the state and the political interchangeably (19). Poulantzas may distinguish political and state power, but he almost never engages in analysing non-state forms of political power. Similarly, he repeatedly emphasizes that the totality of struggles enjoys primacy over the state, but he does not conceptualize forms of political power existing in the family, trade unions and civil society. The rather vague concept of 'popular struggles' is no more than a placeholder. In contrast, Gramsci is able to capture ways of life, cultures, religion and folklore as non-state relations of power by using the concept of cultural hegemony. He recognizes the specific materiality of family structures and everyday traditions in the social relationships of forces, and thus is able to see how they function as foundation and object of state policies.

Poulantzas's orientation towards 'macro-structures' also shapes his engagement with Michel Foucault. Until 1976, Foucault had primarily analysed techniques of power, and described the historical emergence of the clinic, psychiatry and the prison, as well as their connection to the relations of production and the scientific disciplines. In *The Will to Knowledge* (WK), Foucault formulated, for the first time, a theory of power. He assumes that the 'manifold relationships of force that take shape and come into play in the machinery of production, in families, limited groups, and institutions, are the basis for wide-ranging effects of cleavage that run through the social body as a whole' (94). This highlights the plurality of power relations, but does not explain how they achieve global standardization, i.e., why there is such a remarkable geographical continuity. Poulantzas, in contrast, already used a relational concept of power in *Political Power and Social Classes* (PPSC). Here, he links this to 'class struggle' by emphasizing that 'power' refers to the effects of relatively stable structures – such as the capital relation – on the fields of practice of class struggle (PPSC: 108). Given these structural conditions, the power of a particular class arises in and through a dynamic, more or less polarized relationship to other classes. In this context, Poulantzas describes political power as a specific form of class organization, and the state as its key strategic site. In PPSC, he sees the state in capitalism as the 'centre of the exercise of political power' (115) and continues to use this definition in *State, Power, Socialism* (SPS: 44).

2. Gender relations in Poulantzas's work

What does Poulantzas's state theory have to offer to a critical analysis of gender relations?

(1) Poulantzas emphasizes that both class struggles and 'relations of power [...] in another sense' (SPS: 43) go beyond the state and enjoy primacy. This means that power relations are not only anchored inside the state but also in areas of life which remain outside the state in a formal sense and constitute its basis. He continues: '*relations of power do not exhaust class relations* and may go a certain way beyond them. Of course, they will still have class pertinency, continuing to be located, and to have a stake, in the terrain of political domination. But they do not rest on the same foundation as the social class division of labour, and are neither a mere consequence nor homologues or isomorphs of that division; this is so most notably in the case of relations between men and women' (ibid.).

Poulantzas thus establishes a connection between gender relations, political power, and class power. In other words, he recognizes that gender domination constitutes a component of political power. In his view, the instrumentalization of gender relations by capitalist interests is characterized by its limits: gender relations always partly evade instrumentalization.

There are, however, limits to the theoretical opening created by Poulantzas: he neither analyses the interpenetration of class and gender relations systematically, nor does he have a theoretical concept for what he provisionally refers to as the 'relations between men and women'. What he does emphasize, though, is that gender relations are always linked to 'specific apparatuses and institutions' (ibid.). Marriage and family are his cases in point. On the one hand, they belong to the foundations of the state. On the other hand, there is the state's function of condensation. This lies in bringing different power relations in line with the interests of the ruling class by articulating them (ibid.). Accordingly, gender relations are 'mediated and reproduced as a class relation' (ibid.) both within corporations and the state. In other words, gender relations structure the hierarchical effects of class relations. This is where Poulantzas's analysis breaks off.

It appears that theories of gender relations should take on board one of Poulantzas's insights: the primary significance of political power lies in the fact that substantial change in any social field of power depends on it (44). This implies that substantial changes in gender relations are legitimized and secured by the state. This in turn suggests that political power is not merely class power but also a position within gender relations. Following Poulantzas's assumption that there is a constitutive presence of the political in the relations of production, it is important to consider the over-determination of social conflicts. Regardless of the field within which struggles take place, they always affect a multiplicity of relationships: industrial action is also gender struggle, and struggles within and around the family also affect the relations between classes and within state apparatus.

Poulantzas emphasizes that power only exists 'insofar as it is materialized in certain apparatuses (and not just state apparatuses)' (44f.). However, he fails to specify the concept of the apparatus. If it is taken to include the family and relationships between couples, are there any social relations left that are not apparatuses?[1] This shows that the relation between 'structure' and 'social practice' remains ill-defined in Poulantzas's work. Transcending the argument in PPSC, where structures simply circumscribe forms of practice, he writes: 'Struggles always have primacy over, and constantly go beyond, the apparatuses or institutions' (45). This demonstrates that relations of forces are always the basis for any apparatus.[2] Furthermore, Poulantzas argues that the state 'plays a constitutive role [...] in the totality of power relations at every level of society' (ibid.).

State, Power, Socialism is thus defined by the tension between Poulantzas's

1   In PPSC (106f.) Poulantzas distinguished friendship from power and tried to define the former by using the concept of influence.
2   Poulantzas explains the primacy of struggles over the state by referring to the critical role of relations of production. For him, the force of the struggles within the relations of production constitutes the foundation of this primacy: 'To reject this as the foundation of struggle is to reject not only the determining role of the economic but the primacy of any kind of struggle over the state.' (SPS: 45).

attempts to (a) reconstruct the relatively stable interlocking of different structures of domination; and (b) to understand their dynamic and changing nature, which results from the constant restructuring of the social division of labour and the multiplicity of social struggles. It remains unclear how popular struggles that take place outside the institutional arena of the state are grounded in different types of relations of forces and apparatuses (SPS: 140ff., 259f.; cf. Demirović 1987: 143f.).

Regarding the interlocking of patriarchal relations of domination with class relations, Poulantzas identifies two dimensions: (a) the necessary and relatively durable connection of both sets of relations in the form of capitalist instrumentalization and state-led reproduction of gender relations; and (b) the independent foundation of gender relations and their basis in specific apparatuses. It remains unclear, however, what constitutes their independence. After all, Poulantzas does not describe, say, the family in its multiple determinations as state apparatus, economic unit and form of everyday life.

The strengths and weaknesses of Poulantzas's approach are also apparent in the following passage: 'We may [...] conclude that, in a society in which the State utilizes all power (e.g., phallocracy or the family) for the purposes of relaying class power, *every struggle*, be it heterogeneous to class struggles properly so called (e.g. the struggle between men and women), acquires its characteristic meaning only to the extent that class struggles exist and allow other struggles to unfold. (I am leaving untouched the question of whether these other struggles may be effectively articulated to class struggles, and of whether such articulation is desirable.)' (SPS: 148).

Poulantzas may understand the mutual determination and interpenetration of class and gender relations, but the fact that he brackets gender struggles shows that he does not possess theoretical concepts capturing them.

(2) Poulantzas's engagement with Foucault led him to move beyond his conception of state-based individualization that he had put forward in PPSC. In this book, it did not go beyond the ideological aspects of state legitimization such as the idea that the state embodies the general will and the political freedom of private individuals. In SPS, Poulantzas also points out that the state constitutes atomized individuals also through the 'materiality of the techniques for exercising power' (70). Each person's name is registered with the authorities, and people are forced to attend school. In this conception, the relations of production constitute the basis of individualization. Both the corporeality and the spatial and temporal organization emerging out of capitalist production are reproduced and

constituted within state apparatuses in a similar, yet not entirely congruent form. According to Poulantzas, the techniques of power and social technologies that Foucault called 'disciplines' point to the material rather than just the ideological constitution of atomized individuals. Foucault sees the dispositif of sexuality as the crucial link between economic-productive disciplining and the regulation of life through 'bio-politics'. In so doing, he describes production, state apparatuses and family structures as one integrated ensemble (WK: 145f.). In contrast, Poulantzas regards the state-driven process of individualization as the connection between the family and the capitalist economy. For him, the distinction between public and private is an element of the materiality of the state, which, in turn, is supported by the private institutions of the capitalist economy and the family.³ Hence, the private sphere is not external to the state. It constitutes a strategic terrain that belongs to it. The 'State [...], at the very time that it sets itself up as the public space, traces and assigns the site of the family through shifting, mobile partitions' (SPS: 72). Whenever the private sphere does indeed function as a space shielded from state interference, this should not be seen as resulting from a necessary effect of modern statehood, but rather as reflecting the force behind 'popular struggles'.⁴

It is striking that Poulantzas (like Foucault) does not even mention the hierarchical division of labour between men and women in general, and the distribution of non-waged labour in particular. Despite the fact that he refers to several modes of production, his concept of the economic remains restricted to capitalist wage labour. Poulantzas is so much focused on the family as a relational field of power dominated by the state that he completely ignores the autonomous logic of patriarchal power relations. For him, individuals are 'created' by the state without being embedded into the traditions of culture and the life-world. Here, Poulantzas more or less reproduces Foucault's 'neo-functionalism' (68).⁵ He fails to pay

---

3   Here Poulantzas follows the Marxian tradition of criticizing Hegel: 'Family and civil society are the premises of the state.' (MECW 3: 8).

4   For Poulantzas, representative democracy as well as civil and human rights are examples of the (historically contingent) institutional limits of state power (SPS: 73).

5   According to Poulantzas, Foucault portrays the diagram in *Discipline and Punish* (DP) as a fundamental mechanism of power that precedes all other functional social logics (economy, politics, ...) (SPS: 68) and that unfolds in a comprehensive, uninterrupted process: 'But the Panopticon must not be understood as a dream building: it is the diagram of a mechanism of power reduced to its ideal form; its functioning, abstracted from any obstacle, resistance or friction, must be represented as a pure architectural and optical system: it is in fact a figure of political technology that may and must be detached from any specific use.' (DP: 205) – 'The panoptic schema, without disappearing as such or losing any of its properties, was destined to spread throughout the social body; its vocation was to become a generalized function.' (207). Poulantzas's

attention to the fact that submission is always also a compromise and thus a constructive process of managing contradictions. It is surely correct to say that the capitalist relations of production and the family structures represent instances of the privatization of political power. And yet, Poulantzas fails to provide us with an up-to-date definition of the 'transformed' separation of the state, the capitalist economy and the family. He does not go beyond the commonplace argument that the boundaries of the family are transformed by the state and by political conflicts. Poulantzas neither discusses the reciprocal effects of the restructuring of capitalist production and the changes in family structures, nor the dependence of non-waged domestic labour on monetary incomes. Likewise, he does not see that the family structures constitute relations of forces. They may form an effective support for state domination, but they can also become a resource for popular struggles and struggles against patriarchy.

3. Feminist state theory

Feminist state theory emerged towards the end of the 1970s. Following the political division in the women's movement at that time, it was initially divided between socialist and radical feminists. The former (Wilson 1977; McIntosh 1978; Barrett 1983) stressed the functionality of state and patriarchy for the capital relation whilst paying little attention to the autonomous logic of gender relations. The latter (Werlhof 1985; MacKinnon 1989) dominantly understood the state in an essentialist way; state and patriarchy were held to be identical. The dissolution of this polarization in the 1980 and 90s created the space for more subtle and differentiated analyses.

Empirical research conducted from the 1980s onwards on the position of women in the welfare state put the relationship between the economy, the state and gender relations on the agenda. Initially, these studies were still influenced by socialist feminism, but due to the weakening of anti-capitalist politics, authors in the field increasingly adopted the theoretical premises of liberal feminism as well as its political strategy, i.e., the idea of achieving equality by reforming existing social structures. The institutionalization of the women's movement led to it losing political autonomy. This process was accompanied by a stronger orientation of feminist research towards the political mainstream. Many of the studies in question are therefore rather technocratic: they analyse the effects and occasionally also the mechanisms of patriarchal discrimination, but rarely discuss political strategies that

> analysis of individualization as a technique of power reproduces this mistake, because he deduces its expansion in a theoretical fashion without considering its historically concrete modifications.

address these problems.

In other words, feminist state theories increasingly turned towards examining theoretical premises through empirical case studies. In so doing, they departed from their theoretical origins, which were characterized by politically motivated generalizations, and also kept a critical distance to the frequently universalizing explanations offered by Marxism. As a result, they paid more attention than Poulantzas did to concrete policy patterns and specific constellations of actors and traditions. At the same time, however, they either refrained from discussing conceptions of the state altogether, or cobbled them together in a somewhat eclectic manner. Consequently, the concepts used were geared towards specific historical and geographic situations.

Marxist state theory has been discussing the crisis of Fordism and the Keynesian state since the 1970s. Similarly, feminist state theory has been emphasizing the particularly devastating effects of the neo-liberal capitalist offensive on women for at least 30 years. In the mid-1990s, it became clear that welfare state retrenchment was a new long-term orientation of state elites across all parties. In this situation, feminist analyses re-emerged that criticized the articulation of capitalism, gender relations and political power as a whole, and which drew more heavily on class-theoretical explanations. Below, I will discuss the particular difficulties arising out of paying equal attention to class and gender relations by portraying five approaches within feminist state theory. In this context, it must be emphasized that feminist state theories tend to examine *either* the consequences of successful neoliberal restructuring for gender relations, *or* the economic implications of specific gender regimes.

(1) In the Marxist state debate, Robert Connell (1979: 311) criticized Althusser and Poulantzas for their orthodox fixation on the economy, politics and ideology on the grounds that this would exclude gender relations. In so doing, he ignored Poulantzas's attempts to analyse gender relations. From the late 1980s onwards, Connell has been using a Gramscian concept of hegemony in order to portray masculinities as a dispositif of domination within the gender hierarchy (1987). However, he has severed any links of the concept to class theory. Connell argues that gender relations are anchored in the state as well as outside of it, and that the state is part of their structure (1990: 509). He sees the state as the 'central institutionalization of gendered power' and adds in turn that 'gender dynamics are a major force constructing the state' (519). According to him, the state is a node in a network of power relations. It constitutes the 'main organizer of the power relations of gender' (520) and its unity and the concentration of power in

it contrast markedly with the diffuse character of power relations within the family. For Connell, gender regimes result from social struggles, but get cemented by becoming institutionalized. They have a complex, non-linear relation to the dominant gender order anchored in everyday culture. The claim that the state is invested in the emergence and transformation of gender regimes shows clearly that Connell does apply some of Poulantzas's arguments to gender relations – e.g., the relational nature of state power and the inscription of struggles into state structures. However, he limits himself to highlighting individual links between the state and gender relations in an unsystematic fashion. Even when he insists that liberal feminism privileges the interests of a minority of highly qualified women whilst excluding working-class women (536), the only political goal he can envisage is participatory democracy. This prefigures the political confusion and modest strategic reach of the better part of left-wing feminism in the 1990s, whose lack of a class-theoretical perspective prevented it from opening spaces for political resistance against deregulation.

(2) In the 1990s, analyses of welfare regimes played a central role in the feminist state debate that referred critically to Gösta Esping-Andersen (1990). These centred on the assumption that Esping-Andersen's analysis of national class compromises and his distinction between liberal, conservative and social-democratic welfare regimes reproduced patriarchal perspectives. Feminist analyses argued that gendered structural patterns could only become the subject matter of social science research by expanding the meaning of welfare. Jane Lewis (1992) categorized welfare states according to how strongly they were dominated by the male breadwinner model. This resulted in a typology that cut across the one developed by Esping-Andersen. Lewis compared national gender regimes. She argued that different models of social provision constitute terrains in which structures of domestic and waged labour intersect, and that their variations are relatively independent from particular class compromises.

Drawing on this critique, Mary Daly (1994) integrated the family-state relation into a class-based analysis of the welfare state and demonstrated *how and to what extent* the family was located on the strategic terrain of the state – as Poulantzas had claimed. This point can be clarified by looking at the close interaction between the family and the state in the provision of welfare. The social policies of the state rest on prior assumptions about what families can provide; similarly, welfare responsibilities such as nursing are often shifted back and forth between families and the public sector. This implies that social policies have a decisive influence on family structures: 'the welfare state is a key actor in constructing the boundaries between what is considered as a public responsibility, a market option or a private obligation' (110). This is exactly what Poulantzas had argued: The 'State [...], at the very time that it sets itself up as the public space, traces and assigns the site of the family through shifting, mobile partitions' (SPS: 72). More detailed feminist analyses have proved this assumption correct, and have emphasized the importance of the gendered division of labour in the organization of the state and the polity.

For Mary Daly and Katherine Rake, the connection between gender and the welfare state rests on care work, wage labour, and state welfare. Their study thus focuses primarily on the division of labour, but they do not reduce it to class relations. Their assertions are highly relevant for a feminist critique of the debate over welfare state transformation that is also informed by class-theoretical considerations:

- Analyses of state policies that focus largely on the different social positions of men and women render a distorted picture because the interests of men and women vary strongly according to class, nationality, sexual orientation, etc. This ambiguity is becoming more important as social inequalities among women are currently on the rise in all OECD-countries (Daly/Rake 2003: 167).
- The state constitutes a terrain of political struggle. This implies that state policies are the result of conflicting strategies: 'Understanding the welfare state as a site of struggle means that one should not expect policy to be logical and coherent.' (165)
- National welfare regimes are characterized by different constellations of the state, markets, the family and the respective breadwinner model. These factors are in turn dependent on cultural traditions, ways of life and political struggles. Daly and Rake demonstrate how strongly concrete power relations determine the materiality and efficacy of the state, and that there is an interaction between collective ways of life and institutional regulation. They do not refer to Poulantzas, but this line of argument conforms to his assertion that both struggles and a specific separation of politics, the economy, and the family are inscribed into the state.

(3) Following regulation theory and discourse analysis, Janine Brodie has analysed the 'meso-narratives' constituting the philosophy that is inscribed into a particular state form. These meso-discourses contribute to the relative coherence of state action, social identities and political conflicts (1997: 227). They also constitute the state, the economy and the family as separate social spaces. The boundaries between these spaces vary according to whether

liberal, Keynesian and neoliberal states are examined. The neoliberal state form is characterized by the curtailment and the transformation of the public political sphere. The dominant discourse of 'efficiency' leads to novel convergences between the privatization of previously public services, the shifting back of responsibilities into families, and criminalization as a means of processing social problems in an individualized manner. Brodie describes how all these processes result in an 'increasingly unequal gender order' (239). She focuses on the new strategic link between state and capital, but views gender relations merely as an instrument of domination whilst neglecting counterstrategies. Moreover, there is the additional problem that her description of the relative coherence of the types of state glosses over contradictions and struggles. Her analysis discards a principle whose validity was obvious for Poulantzas: class-based analyses of formative phases should always be accompanied by considerations for the appropriate strategy on the part of the subaltern. In this respect, Brodie's approach resembles liberal feminism.

(4) Lynne Haney (1996; 2004) sees the state as an ensemble of multiple internally fragmented apparatuses that pursue a variety of policies and proclaim diverging gender norms. Political power and hegemonic discourses play a key role in subjecting these state apparatuses to common imperatives. Currently, there is a number of tools – also identified by Brodie – through which austerity is enforced, e.g., decentralization, individualization, cost efficiency, and additional repression. Moreover, new behavioural norms are established, which are no longer universal but selective, and direct violent oppression is increased. Haney's detailed institutional analyses show how feminist demands for more independence can be propagated as behavioural norms by state apparatuses, and can thus be turned into concepts of domination that target allegedly backward local communities. Although Haney lacks a political-strategic orientation, her analyses clearly show the effectiveness of 'penal welfarism', which links individual responsibility with coercion. The major part of her enquiries, however, remains purely descriptive. She claims that further research needs to determine 'why there appears to be a convergence among gender regimes, welfare regimes, and penal regimes'. (2004: 355).

(5) Birgit Sauer primarily analyses the connection between neoliberalism and gender regimes and explicitly refers to Poulantzas (2003: 86). She understands the state as relational and as constituted through struggles and conflicts, and connects this conception to gender relations. And yet, she does not draw on Poulantzas when she examines class relations. Sauer's analysis of neoliberal configurations demonstrates that gender inequality serves as a

resource during times of neoliberal restructuring (2001: 299). The growing numbers of working women makes it possible to reduce wages for working men (2003: 111). Her point that fractions of different classes in corporatist networks within the welfare state form alliances that discriminate against women (1997a: 47) is also illuminating. This particular aspect of corporatism continues to exist in the form of a transformed power bloc even after the end of the Fordist class compromise. Low-wage earners, the majority of which are women, are not represented in this configuration. Sauer coined the term 'gender-paradoxical state' [*geschlechterparadoxer Staat*] (1997b: 130) in order to describe the contradictory effects of neoliberal policies: they support equal opportunities, yet limit them through being invested in corporatist 'old boys' networks. Sauer emphasizes that feminist forces should enter into alliances with other opponents of neoliberalism to achieve more gender equality (140).

According to Sauer, the political constitution of market relations and economic exploitation as well as the structure of private households show that there is a tendency to shift the political steering of the relationships in households and wage labour onto sites that are inaccessible to public policy. She argues that this tendency can only be countered by re-politicizing the relationships in question (2001: 296). There may have been a 'partial feminization of the state' (2003: 108; translated), but currently there are tendencies towards its 'partial re-masculinization' (109; translated) by means of the 'masculinism' of competition. Sauer observes a 'decoupling and a new type of re-coupling of apparatuses within the state as well as between local, national, and international levels' (106; translated). Her research design, which focuses on the strategic axis between gender regime and neoliberalism, allows her to reconstruct the reciprocal dynamics of both structures in the current phase of capitalism. However, there are too few empirical elements in her analysis, which also means that they do not establish contradictions and possible sites for strategic intervention. Moreover, she has failed to incorporate Poulantzas's argument that popular struggles are inscribed into the state into her approach, which would have been important in the light of the fact that there is now a liberal feminist fraction anchored in the state.

4. Conclusion

Recent German family-related policies illustrate that there is a link between the strategic orientations of the neoliberal state and a more flexible, but also more hierarchical gender regime. The debates over new laws addressing childcare, child benefits and marital allowance show how struggles by the women's movement become inscribed into state strategies, and how the degree and form of this institutionalization depends on class relations. If we take into account the increasing number of precarious jobs, in particular the growth of female part-time labour and new labour market policies, we see 'a tendency in more deregulated employment situations towards the "gender-neutral" demand for, and the effective utilization of, the individual capacity to work' (Peinl 2004: 172; translated). Equal opportunity policies thus become a driving force of 'modernization' (Pühl 2001). They increase the labour force participation rate and reduce the value of labour power. Analyses that focus exclusively on gender relations may be able to understand the gender-specific effects of this development, but they fail to consider the situation of women as workers as well as the ongoing struggles against neoliberal policies.

A number of current feminist analyses take Marxist analyses of the transformation of the capital relation into account (Pühl 2001; Haug 2001; Brenner 2002; Acker 2003). Likewise, Marxist authors increasingly pay attention to feminist state theory (Demirović 1993; 1994; Jessop 1998; 2000; 2001). As a consequence, there is hope that the political success of neoliberalism may eventually be countered by a common 'culture of reception'. However, Marxist intellectuals still appear to have a harder time engaging with the other side than feminist intellectuals (see for example Hirsch 1995; 2002; 2005). Given that numerous analyses have proved the relevance of gender relations to the subject matter of Marxist social theory, this probably has to be attributed to male dominance within Marxism and to the understandable yet harmful fear that increased theoretical openness may lead to a diffusion of the Marxist project. And yet, there have also been some attempts from the Marxist side to break through these barriers (cf. Ryan 1982; Dickinson 1986; Fraad/Resnick/Wolff 1994). In the meantime, German-language feminist debates have also changed. Voices critical of the double-income model have become more pronounced, and it is increasingly recognized that the dominance of liberal feminism has resulted in material disadvantages for many women: 'Feminists and advocates of women's rights have for a long time demanded the inclusion of women into the labour market. Due to the pressures of commodification, this has proved to be a trap [...]. Instead of the individualization that women had hoped for, we are witnessing the opposite: the return of women's dependence on the male breadwinner' (Stecker 2003: 254; translated).

The long-term perspective of this analysis, however, remains the 'establishment of an "adult worker model" with gender parity' (ibid.; translated) and its supplementation by a dual carer model for non-waged labour (Björnberg 2003). Conversely, people criticize the fact that the growth in female participation in the labour force has been accompanied by a gender-specific reduction of the value of labour power. In order to reduce the political and social divisions among those directly or indirectly dependent on wage labour, the struggle for gender equality in exploitation will have to be combined with the struggle over the value of labour power. Yet the path there will remain blocked as long as the gendered nature of the social division of labour is not examined in connection with the class relations inscribed into it.

References

Acker, J. (2003) 'The Continuing Necessity of "Class" in Feminist Thinking', in Knapp, G.-A. / Wetterer, A. (eds.) *Achsen der Differenz* (Münster: Westfälisches Dampfboot) 49-72.
Assiter, A. (1990) *Althusser and Feminism* (London: Pluto Press).
Barrett, M. (1980) *Women's Oppression Today. Problems in Marxist Feminist Analysis* (London: NLB).
Björnberg, U. (2003) 'Sind Zwei-Verdiener-Familien "partnerschaftliche" Familien? Sozialpolitik und Geschlechtergleichheit in schwedischen Familien', in Leitner, S. / Ostner, I. / Schratzenstaller, M. (eds.) *Wohlfahrtsstaat und Geschlechterverhältnis im Umbruch* (Wiesbaden: VS-Verlag) 234-256.
Brenner, J. (2002) 'Feminism in the New Gender Order. Restructured Capital, Reconstructed Identities', *Against the Current*, vol. 17, no. 97, 8-14.
Brodie, J. (1997) 'Meso-Discourses, State Forms and the Gendering of Liberal-Democratic Citizenship', *Citizenship Studies*, vol. 1, no. 2, 223-242.
Burton, C. (1985) *Subordination. Feminism and Social Theory* (Sydney: Allen & Unwin).
Connell, R.W. (1979) 'A Critique of the Althusserian Approach to Class', *Theory and Society*, vol. 8, no. 3, 303-345.
Connell, R.W. (1987) *Gender and Power. Society, the Person and Sexual Politics* (Cambridge: Polity Press).
Connell, R.W. (1990) 'The state, gender, and sexual politics. Theory and appraisal', *Theory and Society*, vol. 19, no. 5, 507-544.
Daly, M. (1994) 'Comparing Welfare States. Towards a Gender Friendly Approach', in Sainsbury, D. (ed.) *Gendering Welfare States* (London: Sage) 101-117.
Daly, M. / Rake, K. (2003) *Gender and the Welfare State. Care, Work and Welfare in Europe and the USA* (Cambridge/UK: Polity Press).
Demirović, A. (1987) *Nicos Poulantzas. Eine kritische Auseinandersetzung* (Hamburg: Argument-Verlag).
Demirović, A. (1993) 'Politische Führung und Geschlechterverhältnis', *Mitteilungen des Instituts für Sozialforschung*, vol. 2, no. 2, 63-79.
Demirović, A. (1994) 'Hegemonie und Zivilgesellschaft. Metakritische Überlegungen zum Begriff der Öffentlichkeit', *Das Argument*, vol. 36, no. 206, 675-691.

Dickinson, J. (ed.) (1986) *Family, Economy & State. The Social Reproduction Process under Capitalism* (New York: St. Martin's Press).
Esping-Andersen, G. (1990) *The Three Worlds of Welfare Capitalism* (Cambridge/ UK: Polity Press).
Fraad, H. / Resnick, S. / Wolff, R. (1994) *Bringing it all back home. Class, gender and power in the modern household* (London: Pluto Press).
Gimenez, M. (1982) 'The Oppression of Women. A structuralist Marxist View', in Rossi, I. (ed.) *Structural Sociology* (New York: Columbia Univ. Press) 292-324.
Haney, L. (1996) 'Homeboys, Babies, Men in Suits. The State and the Reproduction of Male Dominance', *American Sociological Review*, vol. 61, no. 5, 759-778.
Haney, L. (2004) 'Introduction: Gender, Welfare, and States of Punishment', *Social Politics*, vol. 11, no. 3, 333-362.
Hartsock, N. C. (1983) *Money, sex, and power: toward a feminist historical materialism* (New York: Longman).
Haug, F. (2001) 'Zur Theorie der Geschlechterverhältnisse', *Das Argument*, vol. 43, no. 243, 761-787.
Hennessy, R. (2000) *Profit and Pleasure. Sexual Identities in Late Capitalism* (New York – London: Routledge).
Hirsch, J. (1995) *Der nationale Wettbewerbsstaat. Staat, Demokratie und Politik im globalen Kapitalismus* (Berlin: Ed. ID-Archiv).
Hirsch, J. (2002) *Herrschaft, Hegemonie und politische Alternativen* (Hamburg: VSA-Verlag).
Hirsch, J. (2005) *Materialistische Staatstheorie. Transformationsprozesse des kapitalistischen Staatensystems* (Hamburg: VSA-Verlag).
Jessop, B. (1998) 'Nationalstaat, Globalisierung, Gender', in Kreisky, E. / Sauer, B. (eds.) *Geschlechterverhältnisse im Kontext politischer Transformation* (Opladen: Westdeutscher Verlag) 262-292.
Jessop, B. (2000) 'Bringing the State Back in (Yet Again)', Web: http://www.lancs. ac.uk/fass/sociology/papers/jessop-bringing-the-state-back-in.pdf
Jessop, B. (2001) 'Die geschlechtsspezifischen Selektivitäten des Staates', in Kreisky, E. / Lang, S. / Sauer, B. (eds.) *EU. Geschlecht. Staat* (Wien: WUV) 55-85.
Lewis, J. (1992) 'Gender and the Development of Welfare Regimes', *Journal of European Social Policy*, vol. 2, no. 3, 73-91.
MacKinnon, C. A. (1989) *Toward a Feminist Theory of the State* (Cambridge: Harvard Univ. Press).
McIntosh, M. (1978) 'The state and the oppression of women', in Kuhn, A. / Wolpe, A. (eds.) *Feminism and Materialism* (London: Routledge) 254-289.
Peinl, I. (2004) 'Transformation von Erwerbsarbeit und Konturen des Geschlechterregimes', in Baatz, D. / Rudolph, C. / Satilmis, A. (eds.) *Hauptsache Arbeit?* (Münster: Westfälisches Dampfboot) 165-176.
Pühl, K. (2001) 'Geschlechterverhältnisse und die Veränderung von Staatlichkeit in Europa. Ansätze eines theoretischen Perspektivenwechsels', in Kreisky, E. / Lang, S. / Sauer, B. (eds.) *EU. Geschlecht. Staat* (Wien: WUV) 33-53.
Ryan, M. (1982) *Marxism and Deconstruction. A Critical Articulation* (Baltimore: John Hopkins Univ. Press).
Sauer, B. (1997a) 'Die Magd der Industriegesellschaft. Anmerkungen zur

Geschlechtsblindheit von Staatstheorien', in Kerchner, B. / Wilde, G. (eds.) *Staat und Privatheit* (Opladen: Leske + Budrich) 29-53.

Sauer, B. (1997b) 'Krise des Wohlfahrtsstaats. Eine Männerinstitution unter Globalisierungsdruck?', in Braun, H. / Jung, D. (eds.) *Globale Gerechtigkeit? Feministische Debatte zur Krise des Sozialstaats* (Hamburg: Konkret Literatur Verlag) 113-147.

Sauer, B. (2001) *Die Asche des Souveräns. Staat und Demokratie in der Geschlechterdebatte* (Frankfurt am Main: Campus Verlag).

Sauer, B. (2003) 'Gender makes the world go round. Globale Restrukturierung und Geschlecht', in Scharenberg, A. / Schmidtke, O. (eds.) *Das Ende der Politik? Globalisierung und der Strukturwandel des Politischen* (Münster: Westfälisches Dampfboot) 98-126.

Stecker, C. (2003) 'Der Fluch der Verheißung: Kommodifizierungszwang und De-Kommodifizierungsrisiko im adult worker model', in Leitner, S. / Ostner, I. / Schratzenstaller, M. (eds..) *Wohlfahrtsstaat und Geschlechterverhältnis im Umbruch* (Wiesbaden: VS-Verlag) 234-256.

Werlhof, C. v. (1985) 'Zum Verhältnis von Staat und Kapital und Patriarchat', *Beiträge zur feministischen Theorie und Praxis,* vol. 8, no. 13, 63-78.

Wetterer, A. (2002) *Arbeitsteilung und Geschlechterkonstruktion. 'Gender at Work' in theoretischer und historischer Perspektive* (Konstanz: UVK-Verl.-Ges.).

Wilson, E. (1977) *Women and the Welfare State* (London: Tavistock).

STATE, DOMINATION AND POLITICS: ON THE RELATIONSHIP BETWEEN POULANTZAS AND FOUCAULT

URS T. LINDNER

> Personally, I make a distinction between Foucault as a theorist of power [Foucault pouvoir] and Foucault as someone analysing particular practices and material techniques of modern power. It is the latter Foucault that I find interesting.
>
> Nicos Poulantzas (1978: 8)

Among the Marxist theorists of the 20th century, Nicos Poulantzas was the first and only one who was influenced strongly by Michel Foucault. Whereas Poulantzas's work in the late 1960s and early 1970s was largely a response to Louis Althusser, he became more and more attracted by Foucault's analytics of power during the 1970s. Therefore, we have to see Poulantzas's *State, Power, Socialism* (SPS) not only as an attempt to provide a systematic grounding for a Marxist theory of the state, but also as a first shot at a materialist appropriation of Foucault. In this respect, Poulantzas displayed an open-mindedness that to this day remains rare among Marxists: he was neither deterred by Foucault's ostentatious flirtations with Nietzsche, nor by his anti-Marxist polemics. Alas, Poulantzas's attempted dialogue remained unanswered by Foucault: although Poulantzasian figures of thought appear in the 1978-9 lectures on governmentality, Foucault never explicitly referred to the work of his former colleague at the reformist Vincennes University.

This refusal of a dialogue is probably one of the main reasons why scholars, with the exception of Bob Jessop (1990; 2005), have paid so little attention to the relationship between Poulantzas and Foucault.[1] I assume, like Jessop,

1   Another exception is Ajjaz Ahmad, who describes SPS as 'the most eclectic [book] in Poulantzas' overall *oeuvre*' because of the references to Foucault's work (Ahmad 1994: 336). However, Ahmad passes this scathing judgement on the grounds of focusing on the 'poststructuralist' Foucault who figures in debates about post-colonialism. This Foucault is characterized by discursive reductionism, 'judgmental relativism' and a

that Foucault was relevant for Poulantzas less as a philosopher than as an analyst of institutional techniques and practices. My conclusions, however, point in a different direction. Jessop seeks to reconstruct Poulantzas's work by means of Foucault's concepts of power and strategy; in contrast, I use Poulantzas as a source of inspiration for rethinking Foucault's analytics of power in the context of a critical social theory in the tradition of Karl Marx.

1. The equivocal concept of power

Poulantzas criticizes Foucault's concept of power, but he does so only after having adopted some of the results of the Foucault's material analyses. Poulantzas focuses his critique on the allegedly placeless character of power: for Foucault, 'the power relation never has any other basis than itself', rendering it a 'pure "situation"' (SPS: 149). Foucault supposedly detaches it from capitalist exploitation, a move that leads him 'into a logical impasse from which there is no possible escape: his famous resistances, which are a necessary element of every power situation, remain a strictly gratuitous assertion in the sense that they are given no foundation: *they are a pure affirmation of principle.*' (ibid.) Therefore 'no kind of resistance is possible [...]. For if power is always already there, if every power situation is immanent in itself, *why should there ever be resistance? From where* would resistance come, and *how would it even be possible?*' (ibid.)

Poulantzas observes in Foucault's work a 'constant sliding of the term power', which constitutes a symptom of its placeless character (150): 'It designates at one moment a *relation* (the power relation), at another, and often simultaneously, *one pole* of the power-resistances relation. In the absence of a foundation for resistances, power is in the end essentialized and rendered absolute, becoming the opposite "pole" of resistances, a substance which contaminates them by spreading, a pole that is primary and determining in relation to resistances.' (ibid.)

Poulantzas, in contrast, assumed the primacy of struggle and resistance: 'If struggle always has primacy over apparatuses, this is because power is a relation between struggles and practices (those of the exploiters and the

> fixation on 'difference'. Foucault clearly rejected at least the first of these attributions: 'The truth is, it wouldn't make much sense to say that only discourse exists. A very simple example: In a certain sense, capitalist exploitation became a reality without really having been formulated directly in a discourse. Later, it was revealed by an analytical discourse – an historical discourse or an economic discourse. But do historical processes proceed within a discourse or not? They proceed within the life of the people, within their bodies, within their work hours, within their lives and deaths' (Foucault 1974: 139, 637; translated). It is not quite as easy to dismiss the other two attributions: whether and to what extent they apply to Foucault depends on the importance one sees in his references to Nietzsche.

exploited, the rulers and the ruled) and because the State above all is the condensation of a relationship of forces defined precisely by struggle.' (151) In the case of class struggles, power designated 'the capacity of each class to realize its specific interests in a relation of opposition to that capacity in other classes' (36; cf. PPSC: 104).

To a certain extent, Poulantzas's critique is correct. Foucault may see himself as a 'nominalist' (cf. WK: 93), but time and again he talks about '*le* pouvoir', thereby lapsing into a substantializing manner of speaking. Beyond that, however, Poulantzas is off the mark. First, his critique is based on a misinterpretation: Foucault does not argue that power relations are grounded in themselves. For him, they are immanent in other kinds of relations – relations of knowledge, sexuality, production. Therefore, power is far from 'detached' from exploitation. Second, Poulantzas remains within a framework that is moderately class-reductionist. He speaks of power relations that 'may go beyond' class relations, and mentions in this context the '[gender] relations between men and women' (SPS: 43). However, according to him, '*every struggle*, be it heterogeneous to class struggles properly so called [...], acquires its characteristic meaning only to the extent that class struggles exist and allow other struggles to unfold' (148).² Third, Poulantzas's charge that Foucault fails to give an adequate justification for the existence of power applies to him just as well: his critique is grounded in a 'strugglist' ontology ('There are no social classes prior to their opposition in struggle'; SPS: 27) that deduces the primacy of 'struggles' from the fact that domination is never entirely stable.

Does this imply that Poulantzas's work is of no use for a critique of Foucault's *concept* of power? This is by no means a necessary conclusion. Foucault and Poulantzas can be read not only *against each other*, but also, in the spirit of an immanent critique, *against themselves*. Poulantzas's engagement with Antonio Gramsci as well as the structure of SPS, for example, offer a number of clues for a more plausible critique of Foucault. In PPSC, Poulantzas takes Gramsci to task for expanding the concept of hegemony into near-meaninglessness. Rather than focusing the concept on

---

2   The class reductionism of this statement certainly becomes apparent when we examine its political consequences. In certain political situations, it can be necessary to privilege a particular conflict. Poulantzas, however, implies that the category 'class' should be privileged out of principle. On these grounds, demands in, say, the field of gender politics can be rejected by arguing that the class struggles are not yet sufficiently developed to impart their 'own meaning' on other struggles. This does not imply, however, that Poulantzas's search for a form of subaltern political organization is pointless. On the contrary: building non-reductionist political projects becomes an even more pressing issue.

the relationship between the state and class struggle, Gramsci 'incorrectly extends it so that it covers the structures of the capitalist state' (PPSC: 137f.). In SPS, Poulantzas employs an analogous distinction between two ways of looking at the state. The first chapter deals with the 'institutional materiality of the state' and with the tasks that the state performs in the organization of domination on the basis of its position in the capitalist mode of production. The second chapter approaches the state as the 'condensation of relations of forces' that traverse it, but which also place it in a framework of domination.

If we draw on this distinction rather than on Poulantzas's more explicit critique, we find that Foucault's mistake in *Discipline and Punish* (DP) and *The Will to Knowledge* (WK) was not so much to substantialize a relational perspective, but to deploy an equivocal concept of power that referred to two different relationalities with the same term: domination and politics. When in operation, Foucault's *analytics* of power implies a distinction between permanently subjugating social forms constituting societies ('domination') and the collectively conducted conflict about this constitution ('politics'). However, at the level of categories and definitions, i.e., in his *concept* of power, Foucault simply short-circuits politics and domination. It is this equivocation that I believe to be the cause of the indeterminacy and elusiveness of Foucault's *concept* of power, which is criticized frequently. Against fruitless debates that take this as their starting point, it seems to me that a productive engagement with Foucault is only possible if we disregard for the time being the definitional inadequacies of his *concept* of power in favour of an investigation of his *analytics* of power: we should ask what Foucault can contribute to our understanding of both domination *and* politics.[3]

In his *analytics* of power, Foucault is looking for terminological tools that allow him to conceptualize both domination and politics in a manner

---

3   An argument frequently deployed in the literature on the subject is that the late Foucault drew an explicit distinction between 'power' and 'domination' (cf. Lemke 1997: 306ff.). In the 1980s, Foucault does indeed distinguish between power relations that can be overturned at any point, and within which free subjects are 'conducted' (1983: 138), and 'states of domination' within which power relations have become 'immobilized' and 'blocked' and where 'practices of freedom do not exist or exist only unilaterally' (1984: 27). This distinction, however, is not very useful at all. On the one hand, the relationship between leader and led already presupposes that it is not simply reversible. On the other hand, the capitalist mode of production by definition has to appear as 'free from domination' because of the legal subjectivity based on freedom and equality that co-constitutes it. And where Foucault's analytics of power is at its strongest during the seventies, i.e., in his analyses of disciplinary regimes, practices of normalization and governance of populations, it deals with relatively stable relations of subjugation that nonetheless leave a certain 'degree of freedom' [Freiheitsspielraum] and thus with something that can reasonably be identified as 'domination'.

that leaves behind fixations on the state. He tries to understand domination as 'productive', i.e., as a mechanism of subordination that exists in a wide variety of institutions. The effect of domination, combined with scientific knowledge, is to constitute subjects and regulate populations (cf. DP, WK).

According to Foucault, politics is by no means confined to a separate social instance. Although his thoughts on the subject remain vague, we learn that the political constitutes a strategic process that depends on specific 'schemas of politicisation' (1977: 190). In accordance with the two dimensions, Poulantzas reads Foucault in the first part of SPS as a theorist of domination, and in the second one as a theorist of politics. Poulantzas first deals with organizational services provided by the state that involve relations of subordination, and then with the role of the state in political conflicts. But his appropriation is hampered by a pronounced indeterminacy of his concept of the state: on the one hand he assumes a narrow definition, for example when he defines the bourgeois state as a 'specialized and centralized apparatus of a peculiarly political nature' (SPS: 54). On the other hand, he accuses Foucault and Gilles Deleuze of not using a broad concept of the state in the tradition of Gramsci and Althusser (cf. 36). Following Foucault, there can only be one solution to this problem: if state, domination and politics are not all to be dissolved into a situation where 'everything is the state', then the broad concept of the state has to be discarded.

2. The socio-technological state

Despite taking Foucault to task for having underestimated the effect and presence of state repression (cf. SPS: 77), Poulantzas turns the productive aspects of domination into a leitmotif of his own conception of the state: 'the State also acts in a positive fashion, *creating, transforming and making reality*' (30). His critical engagement with Foucault focuses on the conception of social disciplining developed in DP. In turn, he ignores the concept of 'bio-politics' introduced in the last chapter of WK (139). As a result, there are two important gaps in Poulantzas's reading of Foucault: He ignores one of the most important Foucauldian perspectives on the state; and he fails to use Foucault in order to establish connections between the state and modern gender domination.

Foucault employs terms like 'discipline', 'normalization', 'bio-politics' or 'security' to describe the productive aspects of domination. He tries to theorize the latter with the help of the concepts of 'power-knowledge' and 'technique of power'. In contrast to the 'poststructuralist' mainstream interpretation of Foucault, which does not distinguish between power and knowledge, Poulantzas is aware that the connection between the knowledge produced in the human sciences and the institutional practices of domination can only be theorized in a meaningful way if the two of them are not equated with one another from the outset. According to Foucault, the 'techniques of domination' (1981: 177) cross 'the "technological" threshold' at the beginning of the 19th century, and reach a level 'at which the formation of knowledge and the increase of power regularly reinforce one another in a circular process' (DP: 224; translation amended). His discussion of 'power/knowledge' and the 'technique of power' can be reformulated with the help of a concept of social technology that refers back to procedures of domination organized and authorized by scientific knowledge (cf. Lindner 2005). Poulantzas emphasizes the difference between the two aspects when he states that 'power is ideologically legitimized [...] as if it flowed automatically from a rational scientific practice' (SPS: 55). Similarly, he declares the scientific organization of the labour process a 'directly productive force' (ibid.) on a par with the natural sciences. He argues that both play a constitutive role for the relations within the process of production.[4] Initially, Poulantzas tries to ground the social technologies in the separation of mental and manual labour. He sees a continuum between the tendency towards the intellectual expropriation of the immediate producers in the process of production and the specialized administrative tasks performed by the state: '*In all its apparatuses [...] the State incarnates intellectual labour as separated from manual labour.*' (55f.) Government agents not only present themselves 'as bearers of a specific knowledge and an intrinsic rationality' (57); moreover, 'the capitalist State regiments the production of science' (ibid.) and thus plays an active role in the division of mental and manual labour.

In this context, the concept of 'discipline' becomes central for Poulantzas. Foucault uses it to denote a technique of domination that is standardized by way of scientific models. In institutions like the school, the workshop or the army, 'the body is reduced as a "political" force at the least cost and maximized as a useful force' (DP: 221). Surveillance devices and systems of tests and sanctions are employed to measure bodies in terms of their

---

4   It is a commonly held but mistaken view that Foucault dismissed *the* problematic of legitimacy. This issue first of all gives rise to the question of 'legitimacy'. If we start with the epistemological concept of legitimacy and accept as 'legitimate' any knowledge that is consistently justified, then Foucault – without denying the importance of such knowledge – does indeed shift the question towards the conditions under which something is seen as 'consistently justified'. If, however, we understand legitimacy sociologically as the acceptance of domination, then Foucault – and, following him in this regard, Poulantzas – is less concerned with the substantive justification of domination and more with the legitimacy effect with which practices of domination are endowed as soon as they are seen as 'scientific'.

performed differences and particularities. The aim is to improve efficiency through 'individualization'. Poulantzas applies this figure of thought to the state: 'It plays a role in forging this individuality through a set of *techniques of knowledge* (science) to which Foucault has given the name *disciplines*: "[...] They may be concisely designated as a modality of power for which individual differences are of relevance."' (SPS: 66). In contrast to PPSC, where Poulantzas admits to having fallen victim to the temptation of restricting the capitalist 'isolation effect' 'to mechanisms of juridico-political ideology and to the ideological role of the state, (...) Foucault's really original contribution' lay in having demonstrated 'that this role of the State finds expression in [...] the materiality of the techniques for exercising power' (69f.).

There are two objections to this that spring to mind immediately: one relating to the precise role played by the state in the process of 'individualization', and another relating to its possible theorization by means of an (Althusserian) concept of ideology. To begin with the state, Foucault and Marx would not disagree with Poulantzas, who argues that the state 'contributes' to, or 'consecrates and institutionalizes' (65), the production of individuality. A little further into the book, however, Poulantzas makes a different claim: 'Individualization and privatization of the social body are grounded on practices and techniques of power employed by a State which, in one and the same moment, totalizes the divided monads and incorporates their unity into its institutional structure. The private is a mere replica of the public' (72). Poulantzas reveals a statist tendency by perceiving the state as the institution that '*installs*' (63) the atomization of market subjects. He implies that both the systemic compulsion of market relations and micrological practices of domination, e.g., in the family or the factory, are subsumed by the state.

His thoughts on Althusser's concept of ideology are similarly skewed. By equating it with 'ideological inculcation' (30), and crediting Foucault with having identified, in the mechanism of discipline, a form of power that goes 'far beyond ideological inculcation' (67), Poulantzas falls victim to Foucault's strategy of denial, with which he sought to cover up his proximity to the Althusserian tradition. In DP, Foucault draws liberally on Althusser's theory of ideology. He takes from it, for example, the idea of *assujettissement*, a form of subjugation that is constitutive of subjects. At the same time, he maintains that *assujettissement* is not, as Althusser has suggested, 'only obtained by the instruments of violence or ideology' (DP: 26). However, Foucault uses the term discipline to describe violent practices that aim, sometimes very subtly, to 'externally discipline' (Treiber/

Steinert 2005: 108; translated) the subaltern. The concept of normalization deployed in WK is similarly influenced by Althusser's concepts of ideology and interpellation.

Althusser and Foucault show how institutional practices affix individuals to different socio-structural functional locations and positions. This process involves different degrees of violence and ideology, depending on an individual's class position. Poulantzas, too, is aware of this when he argues that the state must play the role 'of *apportioning-distributing* individualized agents among the classes. The State is thus called upon to shape and condition, train and subordinate these agents in such a way that they are able to occupy class positions to which they are not tied by nature or by birth' (SPS: 75). However, Poulantzas fails to recognize Foucault's originality in comparison with Althusser. By inquiring into the 'reproduction of the relations of production', Althusser roots his theory of ideology in the material reproduction of society (IISA: 148), that is, in the necessity of the stable production of foodstuffs and other articles of daily use. In WK, however, Foucault takes a different route. He looks at generative reproduction, i.e., the question of how a society organizes the procreation, education and care of its offspring.[5] Foucault assumes that over the course of the transition to modern society, the 'deployment (or dispositif) of alliance', based on a form of domination grounded in the extended patriarchal family, was replaced by a mode of regulation based on 'sexuality' and the nuclear family. Foucault refers to this new configuration as the 'deployment of sexuality': the behaviour of individuals is adapted to supposedly 'healthy' heterosexuality. This happens through governmental birth control policies ('biopolitics'), medical-pedagogic-psychiatric normalization, and bourgeois 'familiality'. Modern gender domination is thus based on the state's access to and control over women's ability to reproduce, as well as the hierarchically organized gender and sexual identities that bind individuals to specific places in the social division of labour.

In WK, Foucault also discusses the steering role of the state, albeit

5   Foucault is in good company here: the fundamental question 'according to the materialist conception' is 'the production and reproduction of immediate life. But this itself is again of a twofold character. On the one hand, the production of the means of subsistence, of food, clothing and shelter and the implements required for this; on the other, the production of human beings themselves, the propagation of the species.' (MECW 26: 131f.). As materialist feminists have repeatedly pointed out, however, Karl Marx and Friedrich Engels tended to naturalize the sphere of generative reproduction. One example of this is Engels's *The Origin of the Family, Private Property and the State*, where material reproduction is equated with 'work', but generative reproduction with 'family'. This is one of the key reasons why the problem of generative reproduction turned into a 'secondary contradiction' within Marxism.

somewhat bashfully. However, in his lectures on governmentality (STP; BP), which were held soon after the publication of SPS, Foucault starts to conceive of the state as a site of the deployment of social technologies in a programmatic sense. In these largely fragmentary lectures he, on the one hand, expands the concept of bio-politics to denote a deployment of security that pervades the entire state. On the other hand, by introducing the concept of guidance, he tries to shift the concept of normalization more towards to the practice of the self by the subjects and accuses state theory *in general* of essentialism and functionalism (BP: 75ff.; STP: 109f.). In so doing, he contradicts himself, given that he has developed his own state-theoretical perspective in his analyses of scientifically guided techniques and practices of domination.

3. The productivity of the law

Foucault constructs the 'juridico-discursive model of power' in order to highlight both the 'productive' dimension of domination and the strategic character of politics. In so doing, he creates an ideal-type of the 'negative' understanding of domination, which is centred on the obedience of the subjects. His critique of this model targets the common ground between Freudo-Marxist and Lacanian psychoanalysis and the philosophies of sovereignty of Thomas Hobbes, Jean-Jacques Rousseau and Carl Schmitt. All these approaches focus their analyses of domination and politics either on prohibition, or on the dichotomy between a law-making power and obedient subjects. Undoubtedly, Foucault outlines an important critique, in particular of the philosophical concept of sovereignty. And yet, he adopts the ideas about law held by these philosophers of sovereignty rather uncritically, and declares them a correct description of modern law: 'the famous old formal, bourgeois right' was 'in reality the right of sovereignty' (Foucault 2003: 39). The fact that contemporary capitalist societies can hardly be conceptualized as sovereign relations of obedience leads Foucault to conclude: 'We have entered a phase of juridical regression in comparison with the pre-eighteenth century societies' (WK: 144).

Poulantzas does not ask whether the assumption of an increasingly fast retreat of the legal system can be squared with the subsequent waves of legal codification since the 19th century. His target is Foucault's claims about the 'negativity' of the law, which the latter made in the course of his inquiries into the Freudo-Marxist hypothesis of repression. For Poulantzas, even in its repressive role, the law involves 'an eminently positive aspect: *for repression is never identical with pure negativity.*' It is '[m]ore than a conglomeration of prohibitions and censorship [...]; it lays down things to be done, dictates positive obligations, and prescribes certain forms of discourse that may be addressed to the existing power' (SPS: 82f.). This positive aspect applies especially to modern law, which is specific in so far as it constitutes 'an *axiomatic system*, comprising a set of *abstract, general, formal and strictly regulated norms*' (86). It is a precondition for the 'centralizing-bureaucratic-hierarchic framework' (88) of the capitalist state, which in turn creates the kind of predictability that is indispensable for the functioning of a capitalist economy.

Poulantzas undoubtedly grasps a central function of the modern legal system by emphasizing the authoritative regulation of horizons of expectations. And yet, his critique of Foucault is half-hearted. Just like Foucault, he does not manage to depart from the 'command theory of law' that is part of the philosophies of sovereignty (cf. Hart 1961). In other words, he sees legal norms as orders requiring obedience. Like his counterpart, he focuses one-sidedly on obliging norms and ignores enabling ones. The latter constitute much of both public and civil law, and endow individual and collective actors with legally enforceable claims (e.g., in contract law, collective bargaining clauses, definitions of judicial privileges, etc.). Poulantzas remains on the terrain of a law that is reduced to obliging norms when he criticizes Foucault for focusing on legal prohibitions and ignoring legal requirements. This critique completely obfuscates the enabling character of modern law, which, rather than committing actors to particular (positive) actions, enables them to take such actions out of their own accord and in a binding and orderly manner.

Maybe this is the price that Poulantzas paid for dismissing, for no good reason, the work of the most important Marxist legal theorist, Evgeny Pashukanis, as 'economistic' (1967: 146; translated). Pashukanis attempted to develop a social theory of the law that goes beyond the theory of natural law and legal positivism. He understood civil law as a legal relationship that played a co-constitutive role together with the capitalist economy and was not *created* but 'merely' codified and guaranteed by the state and its monopoly of violence (cf. 1924). In contrast, Poulantzas from the outset assumes the legal system and the law to be identical, thus negating any autonomy of the legal system vis-à-vis the state. For him, legal subjectivity based on freedom and equality is not a fundamental characteristic of modern legal systems. Rather, it is the function of laws to help 'establish and consecrate the new great Difference: *individualization*' (SPS: 87).

Although this criticique is partly grounded in legal positivism, Poulantzas raises an important objection to Foucault's one-sided assertion that there is a line of development leading from the legal system to social technologies that constitute subjects. Generalizing from certain developments in the rules governing criminal cases as well as the penal system, Foucault claimed that *the* law is being increasingly undermined by disciplining and normalising practices. Instead of emphasising 'free equality' as a defining characteristic of modernity, he presupposed a de-historicized understanding of legal subjectivity, according to which the legal subject in all social formations was characterized by a 'threat of death' exercised by the sovereign (WK: 143). In contrast, Poulantzas assumes that the modern legal system does play a role in the constitution of subjects. It contributes to their constitution by working 'either in a parallel, and more or less contradictory, relationship with other state techniques and practices (the normalization disciplines) or else by covering and moulding itself to them' (SPS: 87). Thus, Poulantzas's points are extremely relevant for 'mainstream' readers of Foucault, who tend to adopt the command model of the law from WK rather uncritically.

4. The state as strategic field

In the first section of SPS, Poulantzas locates the state in the capitalist mode of production and examines its role in the organization of domination. In the second section, he looks at it from the perspective of political conflict. He asks what role the state plays in conflicts about the organization of society, and *how* specific measures of the state come into being. Here, Poulantzas takes up a concept that Foucault used in his analytics of power in order to grasp politics: that of strategy. Poulantzas wants to explain 'the mode in which the class struggle, and especially political struggle [...] are inscribed in the institutional structure of the State' (125). The state has to be conceived as '*material condensation of* [...] a relationship [of forces]' (128). In Foucauldian terms: 'In locating the State as the material condensation of a relationship of forces, we must also grasp it as a *strategic field and process*' (136).

However, Foucault's concept of strategy is marked by a peculiar ambivalence. *On the one hand,* he deploys it in the context of a theory of action. Here, 'strategy' denotes unpredictable and unintended effects that arise from the intersection of several intentional actions: 'an implicit characteristic of the great anonymous, almost unspoken strategies which coordinate the loquacious tactics whose "inventors" or decision-makers are often without hypocrisy.' (WK: 95). At this point, 'anonymous strategies' are juxtaposed to 'intentional tactics'. *On the other hand,* Foucault also deploys 'strategy' in the sense of a 'directional' theory of politics: he sees politics as 'a more-or-less global strategy' aimed at 'co-ordinating and directing those relations' (1977: 189).

Poulantzas draws on both meanings of strategy. Despite remaining incomplete, Foucault's reflections on a theory of politics are still important for Poulantzas: what exactly does it mean to say that the state 'condenses' relations of forces? Poulantzas by no means views the state as a simple effect of the relations of forces: 'The State is not reducible to the relationship of forces; it exhibits an opacity and resistance of its own. To be sure, change in the class relationship of forces always affects the State; but it does not find expression in the State in a direct and immediate fashion. It adapts itself exactly to the materiality of the various state apparatuses, only becoming crystallized in the State in a refracted form that varies according to the apparatus' (SPS: 130f.). An example of what 'condensation' means in this context would be that decisions taken at the top level of a state due to a specific political conjuncture usually cannot be implemented in a simple top down fashion. In the different state apparatuses, there are 'fiefs, clans and factions', i.e., 'a multiplicity of diversified micro-politics' (135) rather than a 'completely unified mechanism' (133). Here, Foucault's concept of strategy comes into play insofar as it is grounded in a theory of action: within each particular apparatus, the behaviour of actors is guided by intentional tactics that are determined by the 'structural selectivity' specific to each apparatus, by the 'contradictory movement of decisions' (134), and by the respective 'determination of priorities' (ibid.). For Poulantzas, state activity does not consist in 'the (more or less successful) application of the global objective of the state apex'. According to him, it is 'essentially [...] the outcome' of the 'collision' of the multiple micropolitics specific to each apparatus (135f.).

And yet, this does not mean that the state is a 'mere assembly of detachable parts' (136). Poulantzas insists that there is a degree of centralized unity that 'finds expression in the fact that its global policy is massively oriented in favour of the hegemonic class or fraction' (ibid.). In order to explain this, he assumes that there is an 'organic' connection between the state and the ruling class. Here, the second meaning of Foucault's concept of strategy becomes relevant: the capitalist state constitutes 'the bourgeoisie as the politically dominant class' (125f.), while its apparatuses are 'permanently disorganizing-dividing the dominated classes' (140). Of course, this gives rise to the question: what does it means that the bourgeoisie is the 'politically dominant class'? Does the attribute 'politically dominant' refer to something more than the existence of a project shared by the capitalist state and different fractions of the bourgeoisie that (a) ensures the smooth accumulation of capital and (b) is more or less advantageous for each individual fraction, depending on the current balance of forces and refelecting an "unstable equilibrium of compromise" (127)? If so, how is this different from an instrumentalist perspective that views the state as a mere appendage of the 'ruling class'? Poulantzas struggles with finding a plausible explanation for the state's *relative autonomy* (ibid.). Sometimes, it appears to be a structural property held by the state *vis-à-vis* individual fractions of the bourgeoisie; at other times, it is not portrayed as 'a function of the State's capacity to remain external to them' (135), but as the exclusive result of fractional micropolitics.

In his lectures on *governmentality,* held shortly after the publication of SPS, Foucault used a particular phrase to characterize the state that was reminiscent of Poulantzas: 'The state is nothing else but the mobile effect of a regime of multiple governmentalities' (BP: 77). This is one of the few instances where Foucault put forward an argument that clearly hails from a theory of politics: the state does not simply employ social technologies; there are political arguments where, how and to what end this happens. However, this is all Foucault says on the issue. Following Poulantzas, it can be added that political conflicts within the state by no means take place on neutral territory, but that the interests of actors underpinning a conflict are in fact shaped by the state. In light of this, Poulantzas's concept of power (power as the 'ability to enforce collective interests') can be reformulated as a political concept that presupposes a theory of domination: collective, as opposed to individual, interests emerge as soon as groups of actors constitute themselves with a view to common goals. The state intervenes in this process through the disarticulation of subaltern forms of collectivity; and yet, the strength that actors develop is also dependent on the material and symbolic resources at their disposal.

5. Conclusion: beyond Foucault and Poulantzas

What conclusions can be drawn from the relationship between Poulantzas and Foucault, and how relevant are they today? Poulantzas's engagement with Foucault challenges us to distinguish different aspects in the latter's analytics of power, and to discuss what Foucault has to say on the subjects of social technology, law and politics. It also shows that Marxian theory, broadly conceived, can find inspiration in Foucault, as well as underlining the importance for a materialist theory of the state to distinguish between an approach informed by a theory of politics, and one informed by a theory of domination. Maybe this is where Poulantzas's lasting contribution to critical social theory lies: he was first to develop an integral approach to the capitalist state and always tried to capture the structural position of the state within the capitalist mode of production, and to its role with regard to the social relations of forces. In so doing, Poulantzas showed how to navigate between the Scylla of a simple 'functionalist' derivation of the state and the Charybdis of dissolving the state into 'struggles'.

Yet this also raises the question why Poulantzas's SPS was hardly ever read and understood in the comprehensive manner outlined above – that is, why those who drew on the text most of the time tended to view 'condensation' from the perspective of a theory of politics, often reducing it to the simple effect of relations of forces. I take this to be the result of the class reductionism that runs through Poulantzas's interpretation of the Critique of Political Economy. This leads him to disregard the 'the emergence of an independent existence for value' (MECW 36: 110; translation amended) vis-à-vis the class relation, i.e., the systemic compulsion to accumulate, which is mediated through competition. When Poulantzas inquires into the position of the state within the capitalist mode of production, he is ultimately only looking at the state's relationship to classes, rather than at the state's role in organizing the overall process of capitalist production.

Concerning the question of the organization of domination, we thus have to turn against Poulantzas and rehabilitate certain results of the West-German 'state derivation debate' (cf. Blanke et al. 1975). The relative stabilization of the capitalist economy, which remains crisis-prone on a fundamental level, is only possible if the state takes on certain organizational tasks that cannot be performed on the basis of the rationality of individual capitalists: the regulation of money, the codification and enforcement of the law, the provision of infrastructure, basic scientific research, and the maintenance of a healthy and somewhat qualified workforce. This is, by the way, the only way to explain the 'relative autonomy' of the state vis-à-vis the classes, which Poulantzas struggled with. State apparatuses have to be able to act against the interests of individual capitalists and fractions of capital and implement certain measures. From this, it does not follow that the state does not embody a higher reason or a 'general will'. As a fiscal state, it has a material interest in the smooth progress of capitalist accumulation.

Jacques Bidet (2004) has stressed that Marx's *Capital* includes not only a theory of the market, but also a theory of organization that refers to tasks performed by the state,[6] the process of production and the structuration of classes. From the perspective of a Marxian critical social theory, this is precisely where Foucault should be included. His analytics of social technologies constitute an improvement of Marx's ideas on the theory of organization in so far as he both expands them beyond the interrelation of economy and the state, and complements them with the problematic of the constitution of subjects that was first addressed by Althusser. As a result, the question of gender relations comes into focus, and the relevance

---

6   Bidet speaks of a 'state preceding the classes' (2004: 187; translated) when he refers to the preservation of legal relations and the regulation of the general equivalent.

of knowledge produced in the human sciences for issues of organization and legitimation is emphasized. Therefore, a materialist appropriation of Foucault can contribute to our understanding of the role administrative processes play in maintaining relations of domination, and of how this is related to scientific knowledge.

Yet what about Foucault's rather underdeveloped theory of politics? How are domination and politics 'mediated' within the capitalist state? Their 'mediation' is first of all grounded in the very character of the state as an institution of domination: the state needs to be a *public* coercive power in order to be 'relatively autonomous'. But this in turn implies that all measures taken by the state can in principle be contested, albeit within certain procedures and under conditions of highly unequal opportunities for participation that are historically rooted. Since conflicts about the organization of society also extend into the state there cannot be a millenarian dichotomy between 'evil' state domination and 'good' revolutionary class struggle. Some post-Marxist theories of politics were right to point out that there is a *continuum* of political conflict within which different political projects struggle against each other. Therefore, I agree with Bob Jessop's suggestion to go beyond Poulantzas by drawing upon Ernesto Laclau and Chantal Mouffe (1985), but propose to shift focus somewhat. Their post-Marxist theory of hegemony opens up the possibility of further developing *one particular* perspective on the state, namely that of a theory of politics. It is therefore not their rather reductionist concept of discursive articulation that I find 'highly relevant' (Jessop 2005: 36), but rather their description of the 'logic of equivalence': collective actors and interests emerge when individual concerns become 'equivalent' by way of a set of commonly shared signifiers. Such a theorization of politics, however, can neither ignore the question of domination, nor can it – as Laclau and Mouffe suggest – replace social theory in its entirety.

Theories such as that articulated by Laclau and Mouffe only have something to say about politics, but not about the state. A precondition of a critical theory of politics is that we understand that domination is enacted in the formation of politics through the state. This is especially important because even emancipatory projects are almost always implicated in relations of domination due to the complexity of society. Taking into account the tendency inherent in the state to de-politicize entire areas of society, we can use Jacques Rancière's distinction between 'police' and 'politics' (cf. Rancière 1999: 28ff.) to say that anti-authoritarian politics differ from a politics of domination not only with regard to their different goals, but more fundamentally by virtue of their politics of politicization.

References

Ahmad, A. (1994) *In Theorie. Classes, Nations, Literatures* (New Delhi: Oxford Univ. Press)
Bidet, J. (2004) *Explication et reconstruction du Capital* (Paris: Presses Univ. de France).
Blanke, B. / Jürgens, U. / Kastendiek, H. (1975) *Kritik der Politischen Wissenschaft. Analysen von Politik und Ökonomie in der bürgerlichen Gesellschaft* (Frankfurt am Main / New York: Campus Verlag).
Foucault, M. (1974) *Dits et écrits, vol. 2: 1970-1975* (Paris: Gallimard, 1994).
Foucault, M. (1977) 'The history of sexuality', in Gordon, C. (ed.) *Power/Knowledge: selected interviews and other writings 1972-1977* (New York: Pantheon Books, 1980) 183-193.
Foucault, M. (1981) 'Sexuality and solitude', in Rabinow, P. (ed.) *Ethics: subjectivity and truth* (New York: New Press, 1997) 175-184.
Foucault, M. (1983) 'The subject and power', in Rabinow, P. / Rose, N. (eds.) *The essential Foucault. Selections from Essential Works of Foucault 1954-1984* (New York: New Press, 2003) 126-144.
Foucault, M. (1984) 'The ethics of the concern of the self as a practice of freedom', in Rabinow, P. / Rose, N. (eds.) *The essential Foucault. Selections from Essential Works of Foucault 1954-1984* (New York: New Press, 2003) 25-42.
Foucault, M. (2003) *Society must be defended. Lectures at the Collège de France 1975-1976* (New York: Picador).
Hart, H.L.A. (1961) *The concept of law* (Oxford: Clarendon Press).
Jessop, B. (1990) *State Theory. Putting capitalist states in their place* (Cambridge: Polity Press).
Jessop, B. (2005) 'Macht und Strategie bei Poulantzas und Foucault', *Supplement der Zeitschrift Sozialismus*, no. 11.
Laclau, E. / Mouffe, C. (1985) *Hegemony and socialist strategy: towards a radical democratic politics* (London: Verso).
Lemke, T. (1997) *Eine Kritik der politischen Vernunft* (Hamburg: Argument-Verlag).
Lindner, U. (2005) *Die Ordnung der Gesellschaft. Sozialtechnologie und Recht in Foucaults Machtanalytik*, M.A. dissertation, Free University (Berlin).
Pashukanis, E. B. (1924) *Law and Marxism: A General Theory* (London: Pluto Press, 1989).
Poulantzas, N. (1967) 'A propos de la théorie marxiste du droit', *Archives de Philosophie du Droit*, vol. 12, 145-162.
Poulantzas, N. (1978) 'Les théoriciens doivent retourner sur terre', *Les nouvelles litteraires*, 26. janvier 1978, 55e année, no. 2619, 8.
Rancière, J. (2002) *Disagreement: Politics and Philosophy* (Minneapolis: Univ. of Minnesota Press).
Treiber, H. / Steinert, H. (2005) *Die Fabrikation des zuverlässigen Menschen. Über die 'Wahlverwandtschaft' von Kloster- und Fabrikdisziplin* (Münster: Westfälisches Dampfboot).

THE JURIDICAL CONDENSATION OF RELATIONS OF FORCES: NICOS POULANTZAS AND LAW

SONJA BUCKEL

Whenever contemporary authors refer to Nicos Poulantzas, they usually focus on his work on state theory. Bob Jessop has pointed out that in so doing, they tend to neglect the importance of Poulantzas's training as a lawyer. Nearly all of his early academic contributions dealt with the theory and philosophy of law. Even when he started engaging with the state, his analyses remained influenced by legal theory (Jessop 1985: 322f.). In fact, Jessop contends that legal theory was one of the three sources of his theoretical and strategic innovations; the other two were French philosophy and Italian Marxism (313).

I will reconstruct Poulantzas's contribution to the materialist theory of law by drawing largely on his later works[1] and presenting his legal theory in the context of his state theory. This will lead me to discuss how Poulantzas would need to be updated in order to overcome his class reductionism and to further develop his 'silent dialogue' (Adolphs 2011: 151) with both Michel Foucault and authors[2] drawing upon Marxian form analysis. First, however, I will outline the tradition in legal theory to which Poulantzas's arguments connect.

1. The law[3] as a technique of cohesion

1.1 Marxist legal theory between class interest and the legal form

Poulantzas's book *State, Power, Socialism* (SPS) was published during a brief

---

1   See Jessop (1985) for an account of the different phases of Poulantzas's work.
2   See Hirsch/Kannankulam in this volume.
3   Translator's note: In German, there is a distinction between 'Recht' and 'Gesetz', which is difficult to capture in English. Whereas 'Recht' denotes the abstract principle of law, 'Gesetz' is associated with the existence of a real-concrete, codified system of rules. In order to capture this difference, we have opted for using 'law' and 'the law' respectively in the translation.

historical phase when there was a wide Marxist debate on law. However, all in all, Marxists have usually treated legal theory like a 'neglected stepchild' (Negt 1975: 31; translated). Given that Marx himself did not leave behind an elaborated theory of law, the task of constructing it fell to his followers. Mostly, they portrayed the law as a 'mere reflex' of the 'economic base'. Once Marxist scholars became interested in the state, they assigned to the law a subordinate role by portraying it as an instrument for state interventions. As a result, they tended to overlook the autonomy of the law. Two Marxists working in the 1920s and 1930s were an exception: Franz Neuman, the jurist of the Frankfurt School, and the leading legal scholar in the Soviet Union, Evgeny Pashukanis.

Neumann reconstructed the state under the rule of law [Rechtsstaat] by looking at class relations. He stressed the bourgeoisie's interest to secure their economic freedoms by way of the law and to use the sovereignty of the state to destroy local and particular powers in order to create a unified and predictable economic space (1937: 23f.). Neumann argued that the law served to render processes of exchange predictable whilst 'obscuring' the 'actual distribution of power' under the outer form of the general law (46). This suggests that it also had the function of securing freedoms for the dominated classes. Herein lays its transhistorical character: the law's universal nature and the independence of judges contained elements that transcended their function under capitalism (ibid.). The law formed part of a totality, and yet its defining feature was 'relative independence' (1936: 16). Without this independence, law in the strict sense did not exist (ibid.). For Neumann, National Socialism was the classic example of a regime of direct domination that had dispensed with modern law.

In contrast, Pashukanis stressed the materiality of the law. He addressed the question of form. It was one thing, he argued, to explain the emergence of a legal regulation by referring to a society's material needs 'and thus [...] an explanation of the fact that legal norms conform to the material interests of particular classes'. But this would still leave unanalysed the reasons why these norms took on the *form* of law (1924: 55). Consequently, Pashukanis developed the 'legal form', following Marx's analysis of the value form. In his view, the legal form refers to the social relation expressed in the law, i.e., the exchange relation between commodity owners (93). Under capitalist conditions people do not encounter one another directly as social beings; due to the existence of a division of labour, private property and exchange, they satisfy their respective needs by exchanging commodities. In so doing, they recognize one another as individuals who are independent yet equal (151). According to Pashukanis, this meeting of the minds was the source of legal subjectivity. In his view, legal subjectivity was based on freedom, equality and the 'abstraction of man in general' (113). Under such circumstances, differences in interest would not lead to violent conflicts, but to legal action. Whereas Neumann's argument was grounded in class theory, Pashukanis was interested in the reification of social relations, or more precisely, the autonomization of commodity relations within the legal form.

In the 1970s, the 'state derivation school' was established. Pashukanis can be viewed as its 'patron saint' (Miéville 2005: 122). It was in this context that Poulantzas developed his state and legal theory. Nevertheless, he dismissed approaches based on 'derivation', as for him these were 'stuck in the sphere of circulation' because of their fixation on commodity exchange (Buckel 2007). Accordingly, he chose to draw upon Neumann instead, but transformed him by engaging with Antonio Gramsci and Foucault.

1.2. The organization of hegemony

Drawing on Gramsci's key concept 'relations of forces' (SPN: 175ff.), Poulantzas took the relations of production and the social division of labour to be the basis of power (SPS: 25f.). He viewed class power as resulting from different class places in the relations of production and as forming part of a web of relations and conflicts. Poulantzas's relational theory of power states that the law is neither a thing nor a subject, but a strategic location within power relations (Jessop 1985: 129).

This position is somewhat similar to Neumann's class-based theory of the law – even if Poulantzas did not take the law to be an instrument of the ruling class, but rather a technique for the organization of hegemony in and through the state. Moreover, Poulantzas did not accept the juridical self-description of the state and the law as 'sovereignty' – unlike Neumann, who followed the liberal tradition in this regard. Rather, Poulantzas saw them as a condensation of the relations of forces materialized in apparatuses.

Gramsci introduced the concept of hegemony in order to depart from repressive theories of power and to emphasize a peculiarity of bourgeois democracy: the ruling classes 'undergo catharsis, that is, they take other interests into account and compromise' (Demirović 2001: 61, translated). In other words, the concept captures *'the political practices of dominant classes in developed capitalist formations'* (PPSC: 137). The effectiveness of these practices depends on whether they involve concessions, and on how universal they are. This also means that different social forces are compelled to cooperate and form alliances. If such alliances prove to be stable over longer periods of time, they constitute a coherent 'hegemonic bloc' (Bieling/Steinhilber 2000: 105, translated).

Poulantzas integrated the concept of hegemony into his approach to state theory. He insisted that the capitalist mode of production made it impossible for competing bourgeois class fractions to pursue a common interest directly. In accordance with this, he proposed applying the concept to relationships between these *fractions*, arguing that one of them would have to play the hegemonic role. If it succeeded in unifying the other fractions behind its rule, there would be a 'power bloc' (SPS: 127ff.).

Poulantzas argued that the role of the state lay in the representation and organization of the long-term political interests of this power bloc (ibid.). Moreover, it had the task of producing the overall unity of the social formation by creating a balance of compromise between the classes. This entailed disorganizing the subaltern classes, i.e., preventing them from building political organizations capable of overcoming the individualization that results from the process of production (PPSC: 188f.). According to Poulantzas, disorganization resulted from the 'isolation effect' triggered by the existence of the capitalist state. The latter divides the body politic into 'individuals' whilst representing the unity of these individuals in the form of a 'people-nation' (SPS: 63ff.). In other words, it sets off a double movement that institutionalizes individualization by transforming socio-economic monads into juridico-political individuals (persons/subjects), and unifies them at the same time (65ff.). Similarly, Foucault would later write that state power was 'both an individualizing and a totalizing form of power' (Foucault 1983: 131). In sum, Poulantzas argued that the basic function of the state lay in it constituting a 'cohesive factor' in a society divided into classes and class fractions (PPSC: 187; cf. Jessop 1985: 61).

1.3. The law

Like Neumann, Poulantzas used the term 'state under the rule of law' ('Etat de droit'/'Rechtsstaat') to bring together law and the state. He did not, however, take the term to refer to a contradictory unity of law and violence and a permanent struggle between the two (Neumann 1937: 22f.). Poulantzas insisted that the law is an aspect of the repressive order from the very beginning (SPS: 76). Like Neumann and almost all other Marxist scholars, he conceived of the legal system as a 'subdivision' of the state. Its paradigmatic expression was the existence of laws. According to Poulantzas, the legal system is a central aspect of state practice, i.e., the organization of hegemony, as well as a technique for the creation of cohesion and consensus. It constitutes a 'set of *abstract, general, formal and strictly regulated norms*' (86) that allow the atomized monads produced by the social division of labour to be transformed into a unified entity. In other words, he saw it as a technique that had a generalizing effect on particular interests by virtue of its formal and abstract nature. This technique in turn rendered the fragmentation of society within the social division of labour manageable. In effect, relations of formal and abstract equality between individualized producers came into being, meaning that the latter were turned into classless subjects of the law.

For Poulantzas, the law not only produced the unity of subjects represented in the people-nation, it also led to the fragmentation of agents. It provided the code into which their differentiations could be inscribed: they became individual legal subjects with individual legal claims. 'The law is thus a hinge between the atomized individual and the unity of society' (Adolphs 2003: 87; translated). It is a mode of regulating differences as well as an ideological instance creating social cohesion (ibid.).

Consequently, Poulantzas saw the law as an 'important factor in organizing the consent of the dominated classes'; it endowed them with rights and prepared the ground for material compromises (SPS: 83). Moreover, it contributed to the organization of the power bloc by creating the possibility that modifications of the balance of forces could occur within it 'without provoking upheavals' (91). In other words, the law effected the 'organic circulation of hegemony among different fractions of the power bloc' (CD: 91).

1.4. Relative autonomy

The idea of 'relative autonomy' of the law already figures in Neumann's work (see above). And Poulantzas also had been fascinated by the autonomous reality of social relations that were in fact merely norms or ideas ever since he had concerned himself with Hans Kelsen's work. The unity of both the power bloc and the social formation is premised on a specific institutional structure (Jessop 1985: 56), that is, an ensemble of apparatuses with a specific materiality that ensures their independence. Consequently, Poulantzas was faced with the task of maintaining his relational theory and also conceptualizing the reification of relations of forces.

For him, relative autonomy was ultimately the result of the separation of the political from the economic in capitalism (SPS: 127). Producers are not subject to a *direct* political power – neither in the marketplace, where they have to sell their labour power, nor in the process of production. Poulantzas may have emphasized that the political, in a broader sense, is always present within the economy. But he also insisted that the political, more narrowly conceived as the institutionalized form of political domination, has come to be externalized [ausdifferenziert] into a separate political and administrative system. On the grounds of his theory of hegemony he added that the system's relative autonomy was the result of the structural presence of all classes within the state. For thanks to this presence, no single one class could monopolize all the state apparatuses for itself. According to Poulantzas, relative autonomy made the long-term hegemony of the power bloc vis-à-vis the dominated classes possible. It was achieved, for example, by imposing material compromises on the power bloc (140). If the state did not possess 'minimal autonomy', 'that is, if it were nothing but a political "space" within which contradictory interests clashed with one another', then the potential for social conflict would not be lessened but intensified (Esser et al. 1983: 15, translated).

This also applies to the law. According to Poulantzas, the bourgeois legal system was the 'necessary form of a State that has to maintain relative autonomy of the fractions of a power-bloc in order to organize their unity under the hegemony of a given class or fraction' (SPS: 91). Poulantzas assumed that the creation of consent always went hand in hand with the organization of violence (Adolphs 2003: 82ff.): consent is organized through the law because all social groups, in principle, can achieve power legally in parliament; but the state's ability to resort to the monopoly of violence in order to enforce consensus reveals its relative autonomy. In this context, Poulantzas drew on Neumann and criticized Foucault, emphasizing that political authority is founded on physical violence even in modern societies (SPS: 78). The law, he argued, is the code of organized, constitutionalized and public violence (Jessop 1985: 120f.). Such violence may be deployed less regularly in regulated relations of domination but it is still inscribed into the mechanisms of consent; after all, the deployment of techniques of consensus presupposes a state monopoly of violence. This is the case even if there are no direct violent acts carried out by representatives of the state.

2. Updating Poulantzas's theory of law

The potential of Poulantzas's contribution to the theory of law has not been sufficiently appreciated, and my intention is to fill this gap. It is obvious, however, that certain additions to his approach will be required. This is both a result of the 'crisis of Marxism'[4] and of the fact that the opposition

---

4   Louis Althusser deployed this term to demand that Marxism engage not only with the history made in its name, but also with the 'new social movements', whose politics could no longer be subsumed under the Marxist matrix. He also stressed the deficits of existing Marxism with respect to the sphere that Marx had sometimes referred to as the 'superstructure', i.e., the state, the law and ideology. These had often been simply derived from the 'economic base'.

between post-structuralism and critical theory, which shaped Poulantzas's thoughts on the subject, is a matter of the past.[5]

2.1. Expanding the concept of 'relations of forces'

The relations of production were Poulantzas's point of departure, but he did not accord priority to the economy. For him, there could not be a purely economic space, and the political and the ideological were always already present in the economy. In other words, he took the relations of production to contain all the social relations within which production occurs. Later, Ernesto Laclau and Chantal Mouffe would repeat in almost identical words what Poulantzas stated at the beginning of SPS – that 'the space of the economy is itself structured as political space' (Laclau/Mouffe 1985: 76f.).

Yet there was one flaw that pervaded his approach: the classic Marxist emphasis on one particular relation of domination. In earlier phases of his work, Poulantzas had entirely ignored non-class relations of domination (Jessop 1985: 76). Later, in SPS, he recognized that power relations exceeded class relations, and that their base could lie in aspects other than the social division of labour. Above all, he took notice of gender relations (SPS: 43), and yet, he was unable to leave his class reductionism behind.

According to Poulantzas, all power in class societies has an element of class power within it – despite the fact that the division between classes is not the only terrain on which power is constituted (ibid.). In principle, this is correct – just as all power in patriarchal societies produces a matrix of two hierarchically organized genders. However, it does not follow that both the state and law can be explained solely with reference to class relations. Yet this is what Poulantzas infers, and consequently his theory does not do justice to the multiplicity of relations of domination in capitalism. Upon closer inspection the material condensation of relations of *forces* turns out to be simply a condensation of *class* relations and not one of gender or 'race' relations, which suggests that it is impossible to grasp sexual and racist violence with the help of this framework.

Laclau and Mouffe have argued that Gramsci's conception of hegemony is deficient due to its exclusive focus on class practices (1985: 69, 137f.). Buci-Glucksmann and Therborn add that the elites of the working class

---

5   This opposition emerged under historically specific conditions. Instead of reifying it in a dogmatic fashion, Marxists ought to enter a dialogue with post-structuralists. This dialogue should not 'seek to simply level important differences (…), but to understand that both [approaches] contain potentials for social criticism that are developed to different degrees. These potentials can cross-pollinate productively and complement one another if people manage to engage in concrete social criticism' (jour-fixe-initiative-berlin 1999: 11, translated).

have taken position in the Fordist state with the help of social democratic parties. Consequently, it appears that the state exceeds the field of the power bloc. If institutional frameworks are no longer created exclusively by the bourgeoisie, and if they cease to be external to the workers, 'the problem of hegemony becomes – *for all political forces* – the problem of creating a ruling bloc, which is necessarily a construct' (1981: 126; translated).

As a consequence, an up-to-date materialist legal theory requires a broader conception of relations of forces. Gender relations, for example, are also constituted and reproduced by the state and law (Pühl/Sauer 2004: 169), and feminist state theory in particular has reflected on the inscription of the women's movement into legal (Dackweiler 2002) and state apparatuses (Sauer 2001). Furthermore, it is hard to imagine the existence of constructs such as 'race', 'nation' and 'sexuality' without state and legal regulation.

A relational theory of law should be grounded in a more plural conception of 'relations'. This would involve conceptualizing subjects as 'ensemble[s] of the social relations' (MECW 5: 4) and 'different subject positions' (Laclau/Mouffe 1985: 20). In these ensembles, relations of domination such as class, gender, sexuality and ethnicity constitute and interpenetrate one another. Feminist legal theorists have captured this with the concept of 'intersectionality'.[6] The point is not to merely to add one relation of domination to the next but to investigate the differences *within* each, for example by linking the hierarchical system of gender relations to the capitalist reproduction of labour power (Brunner 2005: 84). Expanding the concept of 'relations of forces' has consequences for how we see the two effects of the law that were of central importance for Poulantzas: consent and cohesion. If we assume a plurality of social spaces then hegemony can no longer emanate from a single social force (Laclau/Mouffe 1985: 141); instead, there is a 'multitude' (Hardt/Negri 2000) of social subjects involved in struggles for hegemony.

The law, in the sense of a technology of cohesion, is involved both in fragmenting agents through constructing them as abstract legal subjects, and in re-composing them into a 'people-nation'. The 'isolation effect' plays a major role for the first aspect of cohesion. Initially, Poulantzas mostly focused on the issue of juridical individualization because it generates the modern, rational, non-gendered individual subject imbued with subjective rights. In SPS, he expanded this conception and included in it the *disciplines* analysed by Foucault in *Discipline and Punish* (DP), i.e., the production of bodies that are individualized, drilled, and ordered hierarchically. At this point, a 'secret dialogue' between Poulantzas and Foucault ensued (Adolphs

6   For an overview see Elsuni (2006: 180ff.), Engel et al. (2005), and Knapp (2005).

2011: 151, translated). As a result, their approaches moved closer together – despite the fact that Poulantzas criticized Foucault in public, and that Foucault ignored Poulantzas. From today's vantage point, we can describe the isolation effect as a form of subjectivation. In other words, the law is an aspect of the modern regime of subjectivation, which in turn generates the modern 'human being'. According to Foucault, the 'juridical practices' are crucial here (1974: 4).

At the same time, and this is the second dimension, the law connects the monads thus produced: through laws, contracts, administrative acts, punishments and court rulings. The law regulates differences and at the same time manages their fragile unity (cf. Buckel 2007). It is a technology of consent, because its universalizing mode of operation provides an ideal type for the multiple hegemonic projects emanating from different social forces. Thanks to the existence of the law, juridical intellectuals are able to transform these projects into concepts of legal theory (Buckel/Fischer-Lescano 2009).

2.2. The legal form

My second revision of Poulantzas concerns his concept of 'relative autonomy'. In this context, Esser et al. speak of an 'almost magical hyper-functionalism' (1983: 17, translated): the state needs to possess relative autonomy because it guarantees the long-term hegemony of the bourgeoisie. Of course, Poulantzas can show that at any time, different social classes are present within the state, so that the latter cannot be seen as an instrument in the hands of a single class. But on closer inspection we find that the state's relative autonomy is not explained but simply presupposed – by asserting that there is a separation of the political (in a narrow sense) from the economic.

Jessop agrees that Poulantzas did not manage to clarify this concept. According to Jessop (1985: 131), Poulantzas's emphasis on class struggles was meant to inject an element of contingency into his account of the capitalist state, but also to show that the latter maintains class domination in the long run – even if this was 'only' the result of a multiplicity of micro-politics. But Poulantzas, Jessop suggests, did not explain the 'how' of this process: 'He erred in assuming that somewhere in the state there is something which can somehow guarantee bourgeois class domination' (136).

Unlike Jessop, however, I do not believe that Poulantzas should have given up on the concept of 'relative autonomy'. It is a key characteristic of the legal system that it possesses its own materiality. This is reflected in the fact that it follows its own 'laws', i.e., its own internal logic. Legal systems theory can claim credit for highlighting the fact that the 'legal system' determines its own limits (Luhmann 2004: 58f.): legal operations are recursively linked only to other legal operations but not to economic or political ones (98f.). Extra-legal communication has to be translated into legal communication before it becomes relevant for the legal system.

There is one materialist approach that could have remedied this deficit in Poulantzas's theory – had it not been for the alleged opposition of (post-) structuralism and critical theory: form analysis in the tradition of Pashukanis. Although Poulantzas explicitly distanced himself from this tradition (1972; SPS: 50ff.), there is evidence of yet another secret dialogue,[7] and some of the arguments are similar in spite of differences in terminology.

Form analysis enables us to examine instances of reification in capitalist societies. It is based on a reading of Marx's *Capital* according to which the legal form is a social form, i.e., a reified and fetishized figure. Social forms are expressions of 'the reciprocal relations between social individuals', but they appear to be 'autonomous vis-à-vis their conscious will and actions' (Hirsch 1994: 161). They can only be decoded by way of theoretical critique. In other words, *social relations* congeal into a materiality imbued with its own dynamic, which at the same time obfuscates the fact that they are social relations. Thus form analysis is a theory that traces the autonomization [Verselbstständigung] of the results of human actions. Social entities are, of course, the result of practices and struggles within certain relations of forces, though these practices are usually carried out as part of a routine. Social forms allow for the perpetually regulated repetition of a particular practice by virtue of their autonomization, and in this way they cause structural effects.

Marx showed this to be the case for the value form: value is a social relation, but it appears as a property of labour products. Thanks to the processes of societalization that occur behind the backs of the individual actors (CI: 82f.), value exists only in the form of its appearance; it is 'natural-supernatural' [sinnlich-übersinnlich] – a thing and a relation, reified yet still purely social (82; translation amended).

The 'reification' of the legal form takes on the particular shape of legal procedures, and these operate on the grounds of specific knowledge. It is not everyday practices that define what is 'legal' or not, for processes of decision-making concerning such matters are codified in a juridical manner. Following Habermas (1996: 340f.), legal procedures organize information, issues, contributions, and justifications in such a way that only juridical arguments pass the 'procedural filters'. They exclude subaltern

---

7   See Hirsch/Kannankulam in this volume.

people and are the terrain of juridical intellectuals who have not only been disciplined through their training, but who are also versed in the techniques of legal argument. Legal methodology plays a crucial role here. Its specific language produces the self-referential nature of the legal form. As a result of these procedures, social relations (of forces) are transformed into legal relations: court rulings, files, codes of law, street signs, incarceration, deportation, etc. The legal form creates a new reality imbued with its own dignity: a 'counterfactual factual arrangement' [kontrafaktische Faktizität] (Brunkhorst) that is insulated against direct interventions from the outside. For example, parties to a civil action cannot simply make an appeal to 'justice'. Instead, they need to base their claims on legal norms and be aware of the legal methods for interpreting them. Furthermore, they need to prove their claims on the basis of particular rules of evidence: facts are only seen as 'true' if they can be substantiated with the help of admissible documents or witness statements. Moreover, the arguments put forward by the parties have to be presented in a specified form: usually only juridical intellectuals are allowed to present arguments and return verdicts; such a verdict becomes legally binding (i.e., enforceable by state institutions) only if it can be sustained at the next level of jurisdiction. Once a verdict has been confirmed it becomes part of the literature, i.e., of legal commentaries and treatises on legal theory. It informs other verdicts and becomes part of a sprawling web of legal operations. Thus the legal form is far more than just 'laws'.

Its autonomy, however, is *relative*. To be sure, autonomy and relativity appear irreconcilable principles at first glance. Yet if we accept that the autonomy of the law is the historically specific product of the autonomization of social relations under capitalism, it becomes obvious that it is always already part of a social totality. The law is only autonomous in abstraction from this totality, yet relative *in relation* to the other practices and relations or technologies of power. To avoid misunderstandings, one should really speak of '*relational* autonomy'. The concrete conditions that generate relational autonomy, however, need to be analysed in their respective historical specificity. They cannot be reduced to the state's monopoly of violence.

Accordingly, decisions about whether or not a social norm is part of the technology of law are made within the legal system itself. Every specific case has to be woven into the fabric of previous rulings, so that any arbitrary act responding to direct violence will be seen as an obvious breach of the law. The autonomy of the legal form breaks down when the latter ceases to adhere to its own laws of motion and instead follows extra-legal rationalities.

In this case, we are left with nothing but a 'dummy of legality' (Luhmann 2004: 109). *Only if* the legal form displays relational autonomy and powerful social actors find it impossible or very difficult to gain direct influence on the legal system, does it become possible to speak of 'law' in bourgeois-capitalist societies.

This point was crucial for Neumann in the context of the erosion of the rule of law under National Socialism: 'If law and the Leader's will are identical and if the Leader can have political foes killed without legal trial and this action is then celebrated as the highest realization of law, then one can no longer speak of law in a specific sense. Law in this case is nothing but a technical instrument for the execution of certain political objectives; it is nothing but the command of the ruler.' (1937: 61).

Seeing the law as the legal *form* allows us to connect these thoughts to Poulantzas's concept of relative autonomy. The political and the legal form are imbued with their own materiality and as such prepare the ground for the organization of hegemony. They take on the form of reified and fetishized entities, whose internal logic compels our obedience. The law does not exist *in order to* stabilize a society pervaded by relations of domination; however its reified *modus operandi*, which constitutes an unintended consequence of the autonomization of social relations, might indeed have this *effect* (cf. RC; Foucault 1977: 196).

2.3. Governmentality

Poulantzas's discussion of the law was little more than a by-product of his state theory. This reflects his 'methodological statism' or, as Jessop has it, his 'enduring politicism' (1985: 141). Following Poulantzas, the state, as a central factor of cohesion, constitutes the one instance in capitalist societies that guarantees the reproduction of the social whole (Demirović 1987: 60). With the help of form analysis, however, it becomes possible to show that other technologies of cohesion or social forms also play important roles. Society does not exist as an objectively given totality, but as the complex and unstable result of multiple political articulations.

Similar insights can be had from looking at Foucault's approach to state theory. First of all, it should be noted that he took a significant step in Poulantzas's direction at the beginning of the 1980s – a fact that he never disclosed. He expanded his conception of social technologies of power so that it included the state and 'governmentality', and this strategy bore similarities to Poulantzas's. Instead of viewing the state as an antecedent substratum and deducing the totality of practices from the "essence of the state" as though the latter were an autonomous source of power (BP: 77),

Foucault proposed seeing it as an ensemble of practices, 'a way of governing' (STP: 248, 277)". It was 'not that kind of cold monster' (248), no 'state-thing' (277). Foucault wanted to apply his analysis of micro-powers to state institutions (381). Thus it appears that Foucault was also talking about the 'material condensation of relations of forces': for him, 'materiality' was always the materiality of practices and dispositifs of power that inscribe themselves into bodies or institutions (Balibar 1991: 55).

Foucault conceptualized law and the state as technologies of power that maintain their relative autonomy. The relationship of the various technologies of power – i.e., the disciplines, biopolitics, law and government – to one another is determined by a system of correlations constituted by these technologies. According to Foucault, in the age of the modern nation state all technologies are over-determined by the practice of governing. His concept of governing shows many parallels to the idea of hegemony. Governing is not the same as reigning, commanding or ordering (STP: 115); rather, it describes the manner in which everyday behaviour is conducted. 'Hegemony' refers to the practices of social forces, while 'government' starts from power relations that get transformed into anonymous strategies. Both concepts are based on rejecting a repressive take on power: while hegemony is based on active consent, government is the art of persuasion. It is based on subjects that are either active or at least capable of being activated (Krasmann 2003: 136f.) and links the subjects' relationship to themselves ('governance' or 'technologies of the self') with technologies of domination.

When Foucault started investigating the problem of the population, he turned to looking at state practice – an unavoidable move if the goal is to analyse 'management of a whole social body' (BP: 186). He contemplated whether governmentality should be conceived as a kind of 'general technology of power' (STP: 120) that constitutes the exterior of the state apparatus. The state was not simply one of the forms or loci of power relations; rather, all power relations had become increasingly 'statified' so that they became linked to it. As a result, the technology of power inscribed into the apparatuses of the state, i.e., government, had achieved a position of dominance (STP: 108f.)

This approach takes into account the close historical relationship between the state and law whilst remaining aware of their respective relational autonomy. The legal form functions according to its own logic and cannot be reduced to an instrument for state intervention and steering. Together with the other technologies of cohesion, it processes a fragile mode of societalization, which emerges behind the back of actors. The fact that it is 'governmentalized' implies that it is also involved in the governance of the population: it prepares the organization of hegemony and the consent to a specific mode of governance with the help of juridical subjectivation and cohesion.

Due to the transnationalization of social relations, the legal form and governmentality are no longer limited to the national state.[8] Today, questions of cohesion, hegemony and governance have to be discussed against the background of an expanded ensemble of apparatuses that cut across national, sub- and transnational spaces. Once again, a problematic comes to the fore that reflects a paradox: although the law is a reified social phenomenon and a technology of power, its relational autonomy means that power can be 'suspended'. Of course, this aspect of relational autonomy had to be fought for. Both the bourgeoisie and various social movements (e.g., the labour movement, the women's movement, the black power movement) managed to achieve, in principle, the recognition of their members as free and equal legal subjects. The practice of governing, however, over and over again produces subjects without rights. The latter's exclusion from the legal form in fact constitutes their biopolitical 'productivity', as is demonstrated by the example of 'illegal' migration. Transnationalization does not make borders redundant, quite the contrary: border regimes regulate cross-border labour mobility by way of the 'flexible decoupling of labour from its loci of reproduction, resources and rights' (Karakayali/Tsianos 2005: 49, translated). In so doing, they strip people of their rights and force them into clandestine life-styles.

Poulantzas maintained that every juridical system includes illegal zones, which in turn constitute gaps in its discourse (SPS: 84f.). A theory of law in the tradition of Poulantzas has to start from this paradox: from the simultaneous presence *and* absence of the legal form; and from demands to implement and, at the same time, go beyond the juridical conception of democracy. After all, the latter recognizes processes of social self-organization only on the grounds of the law, whose mechanisms of reification in turn work to derail such processes.

References

Adolphs, S. (2003) *Der Staat nach der Krise des Fordismus. Nicos Poulantzas und Michel Foucault im Vergleich*, diploma thesis, Faculty of the Social Sciences, Goethe University (Frankfurt am Main).

Adolphs, S. (2010) 'Biopolitik und die anti-passive Revolution der Multitude', in Pieper, M. / Atzert, T. / Karakayali, S. / Tsianos, V. (eds.) *Biopolitik – in der Debatte* (Wiesbaden: VS Verlag), 141-162.

8   See Wissel (2007) and his chapter in this volume.

Balibar, É. (1991) 'Foucault und Marx. Der Einsatz des Nominalismus', in Ewald, F. / Waldenfels. B. (eds.) *Spiele der Wahrheit. Michel Foucaults Denken* (Frankfurt am Main: Suhrkamp), 39-65.

Bieling, H.-J. / Steinhilber, J. (2000) 'Hegemoniale Projekte im Prozess der europäischen Integration', in Bieling, H.-J. / Steinhilber, J. (eds.) *Die Konfiguration Europas. Dimensionen einer kritischen Integrationstheorie* (Münster: Westfälisches Dampfboot) 102-130.

Brunner, G. (2005) 'Sexualität und Spätkapitalismus - revisited? Queer-politische Praktiken im Kontext neoliberaler Verhältnisse', *femina politica*, vol. 9, no. 1, 82-92.

Buci-Glucksmann, C, / Therborn, G. (1981) *Le défi social-démocrate* (Paris: Maspero).

Buckel, S. (2007) *Subjektivierung & Kohäsion. Zur Rekonstruktion einer materialistischen Theorie des Rechts* (Weilerswist: Velbrück Wiss.).

Buckel, S. / Fischer-Lescano, A. (2009) 'Gramsci Reconsidered: Hegemony in Global Law', *Leiden Journal of International Law*, vol. 3, 437-454.

Dackweiler, R.-M. (2002) 'Staatliche Rechtspolitik als geschlechterpolitische Handlungs- und Diskursarena. Zum Verrechtlichungsprozess von Vergewaltigung in der Ehe', in Dackweiler, R.-M. / Schäfer, R. (eds.) *Gewalt-Verhältnisse. Feministische Perspektiven auf Geschlecht und Gewalt* (Frankfurt am Main / New York: Campus Verlag) 107-131.

Demirović, A. (1987) *Nicos Poulantzas. Eine kritische Auseinandersetzung* (Hamburg: Argument-Verlag).

Demirović, A. (2001) 'Hegemoniale Projekte und die Rolle der Intellektuellen', *Das Argument*, vol. 43. no. 239, 59-65.

Elsuni, S. (2006) 'Feministische Rechtstheorie', in Buckel, S. / Christensen, R. / Fischer-Lescano, A. (eds.) *Neue Theorien des Rechts* (Stuttgart: Lucius & Lucius) 163-186.

Engel, A. / Schulz, N. / Wedl, J. (2005) 'Queere Politik: Analysen, Kritik, Perspektiven. Kreuzweise queer: Eine Einleitung', *femina politica*, vol. 9, no. 1, 9-23.

Esser, J. / Fach, W. / Väth, W. (1983) *Krisenregulierung. Zur politischen Durchsetzung ökonomischer Zwänge* (Frankfurt am Main: Suhrkamp).

Foucault, M. (1974) 'Truth and juridical forms', in Faubion, J. (ed.) *Power: Essential Works of Foucault 1954-1984*, vol. 3 (London: Penguin Press, 2000) 1-89.

Foucault, M. (1977) 'The Confession of the Flesh', in Gordon, C. (ed.) *Power/ Knowledge: selected interviews and other writings 1972-1977* (New York: Pantheon Books, 1980) 183-193.

Foucault, M. (1983) 'The subject and power', in Rabinow, P. / Rose, N. (eds.) *The essential Foucault. Selections from Essential Works of Foucault 1954-1984* (New York: New Press, 2003) 126-144.

Habermas, J. (1996) *Between Facts and Norms: Contributions to a Discourse Theory of Law and Democracy* (Cambridge: MIT Press).

Hardt, M. / Negri, A. (2000) *Empire* (Cambridge: Harvard Univ. Press).

Hirsch, J. (1994) 'Politische Form, politische Institutionen und Staat', in Esser, J. / Görg, C. / Hirsch, J. (eds.) *Politik, Institutionen und Staat* (Hamburg: VSA-Verlag) 157-212.

Jessop, B. (1985) *Nicos Poulantzas. Marxist theory and political strategy* (Basingtoke: Macmillan).
jour-fixe-initiative-berlin (1999) 'Einleitung', in jour-fixe-initiative-berlin (ed.) *Kritische Theorie und Poststrukturalismus. Theoretische Lockerungsübungen* (Berlin/ Hamburg: Argument-Verlag) 5-12.
Karakayali, S. / Tsianos, V. (2005) 'Mapping the Order of New Migration. Undokumentierte Arbeit und die Autonomie der Migration', *Peripherie. Zeitschrift für Politik und Ökonomie in der Dritten Welt*, vol. 97/98, 35-64.
Knapp, G.-A. (2005) 'Intersectionality - ein neues Paradigma feministischer Theorie? Zur transatlantischen Reise von Race, Class, Gender', *Feministische Studien*, vol. 24, no. 1, 68-81.
Krasmann, S. (2003) *Die Kriminalität der Gesellschaft. Zur Gouvernementalität der Gegenwart* (Konstanz: UVK).
Laclau, E. / Mouffe, C. (1985) *Hegemony and socialist strategy: towards a radical democratic politics* (London: Verso).
Luhmann, N. (2004) *Law as a Social System* (New York: Oxford Univ. Press).
Miéville, C. (2005) *Between equal rights. A Marxist theory of international law* (Leiden: Brill).
Negt, O. (1975) '10 Thesen zur marxistischen Rechtstheorie', in Rottleuthner, H. (ed.) *Probleme der marxistischen Rechtstheorie* (Frankfurt am Main: Suhrkamp).
Neumann, F. (1937) 'The Change in the Function of Law in Modern Society', in Neumann, F. *The Democratic and The Authoritarian State: Essays in Political and Legal Theory* (Glencoe, Illinois: The Free Press, 1957) 22-68.
Neumann, Franz (1936) *The Rule of Law. Political Theory and the Legal System in Modern Society* (Leamington Spa: Berg, 1986).
Pashukanis, E. B. (1924) *Law and Marxism: A General Theory* (London: Pluto Press, 1989).
Poulantzas, N. (1972) 'Aus Anlass der marxistischen Rechtstheorie', in Reich, N. (ed.) *Marxistische und sozialistische Rechtstheorie* (Frankfurt am Main: Athenäum Fischer Taschenbuch Verlag) 181-199.
Pühl, K. / Sauer, B. (2004) 'Geschlechterverhältnisse im Neoliberalismus. Konstruktion, Transformation und feministisch-politische Perspektiven', in Helduser, U. / Marx, D. / Paulitz, T. / Pühl, K. (eds.) *Under construction? Konstruktivistische Perspektiven in feministischer Theorie und Forschungspraxis* (Frankfurt am Main: Campus Verlag) 165-179.
Sauer, B. (2001) *Die Asche des Souveräns. Staat und Demokratie in der Geschlechterdebatte* (Frankfurt am Main: Campus Verlag).
Wissel, J. (2007) *Die Transnationalisierung von Herrschaftsverhältnissen. Zur Aktualität von Nicos Poulantzas' Staatstheorie* (Baden-Baden: Nomos).

THE ORDER OF KNOWLEDGE: THE STATE AS A KNOWLEDGE APPARATUS

INGO STÜTZLE

Statistics is the premier political science! I know a man's head when I know how many hairs grow on it. (MECW 1: 133)

The constitution of a knowledge (*savoir*) of government is absolutely inseparable from the constitution of a knowledge of all the processes revolving around population in the wider sense of what we now call "the economy". (STP: 106)

I don't care who writes a nation's laws [...] if I can write its economics textbooks.
Paul A. Samuelson cited in *The Economist*, 08/23/1997

1. Introduction

The capitalist state does not constitute an omniscient meta-subject. Nevertheless, it articulates the 'general interest' of capital as opposed to the particular interests of competing individual capitals. According to Friedrich Engels, it represents the 'ideal collective capitalist' (MECW 26: 266; translation amended). He postulated that the 'total capitalist interest' is both a *necessary condition* of existence of the capitalist mode of production and a *result of state policies*. The state neither possesses direct knowledge of the 'total capital interest', nor does it represent the arithmetic mean of all particular societal interests and relations of forces. Rather, its constitution requires it to produce knowledge that brings government in line with the 'total capitalist interest'.

But how can this insight be integrated into state theory? The state has rarely been discussed as a 'knowledge apparatus' (cf. Foucault 1976: 33) – not even by Johannes Agnoli (1975), who defined the form and function of the state in a similar fashion. He saw it as a comprehensive organizer, but neglected analysing the specific process by which the total capitalist interest is constituted. Poulantzas's *State, Power, Socialism* (SPS) is one of the few exceptions in so far as the category of 'knowledge' is prominent in this work. But he is ambivalent with regard to the 'total capitalist interest' – which in his work appears as 'general capitalist interest'. On the one hand he describes it as an ideological element forming part of idealizing or idealist conceptions of the state, according to which all social contradictions are sublated in the latter (cf. SPS: 156, 183f., 241, 243; PPSC: 133, 190). On the other hand he frequently uses arguments similar to those of Agnoli and Engels. This applies not only to his general definition of the state as a 'factor of cohesion' in capitalist social formations (cf. PPSC: 45ff.). More specifically, he also argues that it is 'a political necessity' for the state to perform functions 'of *general interest* for the bourgeoisie *as a whole*' (SPS: 182). Similarly, he remarks that the state possesses 'relative autonomy [...] so that it may ensure the organization of the general interest of the bourgeoisie' (129). In light of this, I contend that it is possible to integrate Poulantzas's ideas into a form-analytical theory of the capitalist state. In fact, integrating Poulantzas may allow us to answer the question of how total capitalist interest is constituted. In this context, Michel Foucault's analyses also constitute a source of inspiration. However, they are more difficult to integrate because they are not grounded in a theory of the capitalist mode of production. Nevertheless, I will demonstrate that Foucault's ideas contribute to the reconstruction of Poulantzas's theory and help us dealing with its occasional lack of differentiation.

2. The state form and its functions

Inquiries into the form of the state have produced a lot of misunderstandings. They have, for example, been accused of functionalism. As Bob Jessop argues (1982: 120), functionalist theories of the state assume that the capitalist state is functional for the stabilization of the capitalist mode of production. In so doing, they essentialize the state form. But this critique needs to be qualified: the charge of functionalism only holds if and when functions are simply posited rather than reconstructed in their constitution and realization (Barben 1999: 1141). Versions of state theory that conceive of the state as knowledge apparatus are particularly suited for reconstructing the realization of state functions.

In order to do this, it is important to distinguish between form analysis and functional analysis. Whereas the former only explains the 'state form" (Agnoli 1975: 23)[1] itself, the latter identifies necessary conditions of existence

1   The point of departure here should be a proposal made by Marx in the third volume of *Capital* (CIII: 777f.). He suggests inquiring into the political form as such rather than

of the capitalist mode of production. An analysis of functions is necessary because it is the only way to distinguish existential requirements from contingent functions that do not affect the capitalist mode of production directly. Such an analysis can establish in which social fields the state, as a knowledge apparatus, plays a particularly important role, and according to which criteria social hegemony needs to be organized. In other words, it demonstrates which contradictions are to be minimized and where consent needs to be manufactured.

The point of departure for this kind of functional analysis is Karl Marx's presentation in *Capital*. Marx shows that the capitalist mode of production can only exist as a political and economic system, i.e., by virtue of the existence of political forms. The mode of production itself cannot, however, generate these elements by itself – despite the fact that they are necessary for its existence.[2] Michael Krätke (1998: 148, 152, translated) thus refers to 'entry points and toeholds' of politics in the economy. These 'entry points' constitute different political areas that are processed in an open 'system' of political forms. Note, however, that these forms do not necessarily need to be guaranteed by the state. Nevertheless, the question how and where the economic and the extra-economic connect is negotiated on the terrain of the state.

Poulantzas describes contradictions and conflicts located *within* the state apparatus (SPS: 123ff.). These can be explained and analysed only on the grounds of the conception of the state outlined here: the state is a composite institution and a unified apparatus in the formal sense. It constitutes a terrain on which different types and fields of knowledge are generated. The total capitalist interest in turn is produced on the grounds of this knowledge.

3. Knowledge and the separation of mental and manual labour

Before I start examining the various fields of knowledge, I will establish the differences and communalities between the explanations for the separation of mental and manual labour in Foucault's and Poulantzas's theories of knowledge. This allows me to use them both in concert. Whereas Foucault

---

postulating the existence of a specific starting point for state 'derivation'. This political form is based on the existence of an 'extra-economic coercive force'. In the context of the existence of a monopoly of violence, the latter guarantees and enforces the legal form by creating a *general norm* and a *general law* that are both *public* and *impersonal* in character (Blanke et al. 1975).

2   This points to an inadequate understanding of the logic of presentation in *Capital* that characterizes many contributions to the so-called state derivation debate. The point of functional analysis – as opposed to the theoretical explanation of the state form – is not to derive both the state form and its functions from one foundational economic principle.

views the nexus between power and knowledge as a general feature of modern societies (Foucault 1971), Poulantzas takes knowledge and its 'function' to be the specific result of the separation of mental and manual labour, and identifies mental labour with the ruling class (CCC: 237f.). Poulantzas explicitly refers to 'the classics', giving most weight to the work of Marx and Engels (cf. MECW 35: 326ff.; MECW 5: 28ff.; Demirović 2001).[3] According to him, the separation of mental and manual labour points to the political and ideological importance of the state within the relations of production, and takes 'specific forms' in the capitalist mode of production (CCC: 234). He states: '*In all its apparatuses [...] the State incarnates intellectual labour as separated from manual labour.* [...] And it is within the capitalist State that the organic relationship between intellectual labour and political domination, knowledge and power, is realized in the most consummate manner. Separated from the relations of production, the State takes up position alongside an intellectual labour that has itself been divorced from manual labour: it is the corollary and the product of this division, and at the same time plays a specific role in its constitution and reproduction.' (SPS: 83; italics by I.S.) Although Poulantzas emphasizes that the state is not the result of this specific division of labour alone (60), he fails to explain the peculiar status of this explanation vis-à-vis others.

For Foucault, there is neither an 'origin' nor a central subject of knowledge. Yet he does argue that the separation of mental and manual labour produces privileged 'sites of speech' as well as privileged actors, particularly the intellectuals and experts located within the different fields of knowledge (e.g., DP: 231ff.; WK: 53ff.). Under capitalism, knowledge is said to take on a new quality with the separation of mental and manual labour, due to the emergence of a genuine link between truth and power. The argument that 'sovereigns surrounded themselves with pedagogues, that kings were advised by philosophers, scholars or wise men' (Foucault 1979b: 63; cf. Hobbes 1651: 302ff.) may have been made before, but Foucault argued that knowledge under capitalism did indeed take on a different significance. From 'the 19th century on, knowledge as such became statutory, equipped with a definite quantity of power. [...] Precisely because it is knowledge it disposes of power, and it is not the good will of power or its curiosity that opens it to knowledge' (Foucault 1979b: 63). Knowledge is infused with power because the 'rationality' of social relations is no longer

---

3 In the *German Ideology*, the social division of labour is used as a 'universal category' (Heinrich 1999: 140, translated) explaining the capitalist social formation. Poulantzas accords it a similar status in his explanation of capitalist societality, treating it almost on a par with the relations of production (e.g., SPS: 14, 27, 49, 110).

simply 'proven' by the existence of god; it has to be produced the the help of 'true' knowledge. This implies that state power is subject to the requirement of justifying and legitimizing itself through 'true' knowledge.

In sum, both Poulantzas and Foucault assume that in modern capitalist societies the significance of knowledge within social power relations has undergone a transformation. This transformation coincides with the specific way in which mental and manual labour are separated.[4] Foucault is primarily interested in mental labour and the importance of knowledge for power. Poulantzas, in contrast, focuses on the class theoretical dimension of this division of labour, which provides his analysis of the state with a materialist foundation.[5] Against this background, what follows below is a systematic reconstruction of those fields of knowledge production discussed by Poulantzas in SPS.

4. The significance of knowledge production and fields of knowledge in Poulantzas's state theory

4.1. Strategic knowledge

Poulantzas criticizes that Louis Althusser's distinction between repressive and ideological state apparatuses remains merely descriptive (SPS: 29f., 33) and leaves no conceptual space to consider the 'material substratum' (31) of social consensuses. Moreover, Poulantzas departs from Althusser by focusing on the role of the state in the production of knowledge and discourses. He highlights the *productive* character of 'law' and 'power'. The state develops discourses and mechanisms for 'organisation and consent' (82) by virtue of its correspondence with the 'forms of struggle under capitalism' (ibid.). It does not, however, produce a 'uniformly mystifying discourse' (31), but a 'discourse that is broken into segments and fragments according to lines intersecting the strategy of power' (32), on account of the fact that capital is not only divided into fractions, but also into competing individual capitals. According to Poulantzas, the organization of this consensus – the total capitalist interest – is a result of this process rather than its precondition. He argues that 'at a certain level tactical elaboration is an integral part of

---

[4] The differences between the two with respect to the relationship between knowledge and the social division of labour are therefore smaller than Poulantzas thought. In SPS, he had argued that 'Foucault objects to any interpretation of this materiality of power (and thus of the State) as rooted in the relations of production and social division of labour.' (67).

[5] It would be interesting to investigate the relationship between knowledge and ideology in the works of Poulantzas and Foucault in a separate paper. Poulantzas occasionally uses the latter term in an entirely un-theorized manner. Nevertheless, he implicitly concedes that Foucault's rejection of a dichotomous conception separating knowledge/science and ideology is in fact justified. After all, Poulantzas states that '*the break between science and ideology is far from possessing the radical character that we ascribed to it some years ago*' (SPS: 111).

the State's provisions to organize the dominant classes: it appears on the state arena by virtue of its role in *representing* these classes' (ibid.). There is a variety of tactics expressed across different state apparatuses: The central bank, for example, promotes stable prices and a strong currency, thus acting in line with the interests of the financial fraction of capital and classes depending on imports. Its policies, however, have a negative effect on classes depending on exports.

These tactics develop in and through government statements, policy initiatives and their justifications, consciously launched or accidentally leaked 'reform proposals', commissions, corporative structures, and hearings and debates in parliament. According to Poulantzas, state apparatuses organize capital by directing different discourses at the different fractions of capital (ibid.). Individual capitals, in turn, attempt to generalize their view of a given problem through public statements and positions articulated by employers' federations, public attempts at blackmail (e.g., by threatening to move production abroad), negotiations in corporative structures, and by major public relations campaigns.

The divergence of state tactics becomes visible only in the form of the contradictions and conflicts between the different apparatuses and channels of information. These arise because individual capitals and fractions of capital not only compete with one another, but also have to deal with very different economic conditions. According to Poulantzas, the state is not aware of its own strategy in advance and cannot formulate it at the level of discourse either (ibid.). Although the 'state discourse' 'is the supreme realization of the injunction between knowledge and power, it has *no inherent unity of its own*' (58; italics by I.S.).[6] It should rather be seen as an attempt to combine the different tactics of accumulation into a relatively coherent *general strategy of accumulation* representing the total capitalist interest. If this strategy reaches a degree of unity, it still does not remove the conflicts that are inscribed into the capitalist mode of production. Rather, it renders them manageable. Accordingly, the state constitutes a form in which social contradictions move, become apparent and get articulated. The interests and tactics of different social forces thus find their expression on the terrain of the state. The knowledge articulated in the discourse of the state forms *strategic knowledge*. After all, it constitutes the state as a strategic

6   This shows that it is not only the formal unity of the various state apparatuses that constitutes the framework in which the total capitalist interest is determined, but also the 'societal form of movement' (Gerstenberger 1990: 489) that emerged together with the bourgeois state – the bourgeois public sphere. Poulantzas focuses on the latter far more in the context of his discussion of 'public opinion' in PPSC (217f.) than he does in SPS.

field by giving expression to class interests in a selective manner consistent with the social relations of forces.

4.2. Abstract and administrative knowledge

For Poulantzas, the 'state discourse' always needs to be '*heard* and *understood*, even if not in a uniform manner: it is not enough that it be uttered as an incantation' (SPS: 58). 'Incantations' are the domain of the pre-bourgeois state, in which the sovereign was seen as having insight into true, god-given 'laws', with the only challenge being how to use them wisely (88f.). Foucault explains how and, to some extent, why this changed. Until the 17th century the rationality of 'government' was immanent to the *raison d'état*. From this point onwards, the relationship between government and stores of knowledge necessary for the maintenance and development of the state changed fundamentally (STP: 273f.). Foucault notes: 'That is to say, the sovereign's necessary knowledge (savoir) will be *a knowledge (connaisance) of things* rather than knowledge of the law, and this knowledge of the things that comprise the very reality of the state is precisely what at the time was called "statistics".' (274;italics by I.S.)

In turn, Poulantzas shows that the state does not only 'proclaim the truth of its power [...]; it also adopts the necessary means to elaborate and formulate' (SPS: 32). He refers to bourgeois statistics and state-run statistical institutes in this context. But the knowledge produced by these institutes has little in common with the strategic knowledge discussed above. Rather, it constitutes *abstract knowledge,* which refers to an already existing social reality (modern property, quantities of value expressed in prices), but also constitutes a new one: 'Cadastre, conscription and cartography therefore produce the state, they make societies governable. They may be regarded as "machines" that have the function to render *orderly, calculable* and *productive,* through the application of special techniques what is chaos, mess, confusion from the point of view of the government; people are supposed to be transformed into the population, nature into landscape, and goods into values.' (Tantner 2002: 149, translated; italics by I.S.; cf. Bourdieu 1998: 45).[7] These data are not simply the product of pre-existing 'facts', but a specific social construction (Poovey 1998). They are based on abstract statistical categories like 'gender', 'nation', 'family', 'birth rate', 'occupation', 'income' that cover up any social dimension. Knowledge about 'people and country' transpired in parallel to modern statehood. It developed with the enforcement of private property and the appearance of the legal person who needed to be identifiable (Groebner 2002, Tantner 2002). Moreover,

---

7 Cf. Gottschalk (2004), Porter (1986), John (1884) und Desrosières (1998).

it surfaced with the emergence of the tax state, which required predictable data about tax payers and their wealth. Similarly, 'bio-politics'[8] were based on marital status, birth rates, etc., whilst the existence of a standing army required knowledge about the numbers and whereabouts of healthy male nationals of military age. Finally, active economic policy was only possible if there was awareness of the structure and capacities of production for reasons beyond preparing for war.

Poulantzas sees abstract knowledge as a historical fact, and discusses it – probably as a result of his reading of Weber – as the mode of operation of state bureaucracies (Weber 1922: 956ff.).[9] The same applies to the 'secrecy of power and bureaucracy' (SPS: 32). However, the *arcana imperii* are the result of a historical process. They functioned as the means of production of abstract knowledge, which in turn served to develop the potential of state power. This knowledge had to be a 'state secret', because potential enemies could not be allowed to have information about a country's ability to wage war (STP: 275, 316).

Abstract knowledge is characterized by standardization (cf. Weber 1922: 223f.). Given that administrations rely on standardizations, it became a problem for the state that there was a multiplicity of dialects[10] and of names for tools and measures of surface area.[11] Accordingly, the field of knowledge thus produced constitutes an abstract measure of social relations and economic potency. However, it is not just the basis for decisions about economic policy. Capitalist society and the social relations constituting it appear controllable and governable in and through this abstract knowledge (cf. Miller/Rose 1990).

4.3. Scientific knowledge and the techniques of power

Poulantzas points out that in the early bourgeois age, politics and law were also legitimized through 'the model of scientific technique and apodictic *episteme*' as 'a form of knowledge opposed to what they termed utopia' (SPS:

8   Cf. Lindner in this volume.
9   Poulantzas mentions the mode of operation of bureaucratic administration and the circulation of knowledge without going into any detail. Max Weber views it as 'administrative knowledge' [Dienst-Wissen] (cf. 1922: 225).
10 Poulantzas discusses the standardizing effects of abstract knowledge only with regard to the national language. This, he argues, is not a side effect of state domination, but an essential 'material feature' (SPS: 59) of the existence of the specific separation of manual and mental labour. Poulantzas probably focuses on the problematic of language because the standardization of language was central to the emergence of the French nation (cf. Bourdieu 1998: 37), and because the 'nation' becomes the central subject of the further discussion in SPS.
11 For example, as late as the 18th century, more than 20 different definitions of the measure 'foot' were still used in Prussia (Spittler 1980: 585).

57; cf. CCC: 238). But it was only with the capitalist state that a specific link between power and knowledge emerged, that is power was 'ideologically legitimized in the modality of scientific technique' (SPS: 55). The scientific techniques that Poulantzas discusses are not just the human sciences repeatedly criticized by Foucault, but also criminology and law. In this context, knowledge takes on the material form of practices of power within state apparatuses. It guarantees the '*primary forms of ideology* secreted by the state' that resulted in the state's self-legitimization (57). The law is purported to represent the 'incarnation of Reason' (89); but amongst the techniques of power we also find the apparatuses of individualization, the repressive-ideological apparatuses (military, police, prison) and ideological-pedagogic institutions like universities and schools.

The state's incorporation of knowledge occurs on two separate levels. First, the state constitutes a materialization of the sciences in the form of disciplinary techniques. When Foucault argues that the state rests on the 'institutional integration of power relationships' (WK: 96), he has the process in mind whereby techniques of power turn into tools of the state. He nevertheless assumes that there is a decentralization of techniques of power and knowledge. Poulantzas, in contrast, views the sciences in general as 'state science': 'The capitalist State regiments the production of science in such a way that it becomes, in its innermost texture, a *state science* locked into the mechanisms of power; [...] More generally, this State structures intellectual labour through a whole series of circuits and networks [...]: it subordinates and marks down for itself the *intellectual-scientific corps* [...]. In the universities, institutes, academies and societies of learning, these bearers of knowledge-science have become state functionaries through the same mechanisms that made intellectuals of this State's functionaries.' (SPS: 57)

This 'scientific corps' constitutes the second aspect of the scientific character of modern statehood: the state organizes scientific discourses through committees of enquiry, scientific advisory boards and testimonies. Their goal is not to provide space for the political articulation of a variety of interest groups, but to make politics more 'rational'.

4.4. The state and the discourse of political economy

Within the state's field of knowledge, there is one central social dimension that follows its own laws – the capitalist economy. The idea of the economic as a 'specific domain of reality' (STP: 108) emerges together with bourgeois society. The discourse of political economy is established in the second half of the 18th century together with and within bourgeois society. Its autonomy was on the one hand the effect of the increasing importance of the capitalist mode of production, on the other a result of a particular form of 'criticizing the reality' (Foucault 1979a: 204) that challenged then-dominant assumptions about social reality. This critique was successful insofar as political economy became a central terrain of societal self-reflection (Heinrich 1999: 28).

Foucault argues that the transition from mercantilist to physiocratic ideas as dominant paradigms in 'political economy' coincided with a change in the latter's relationship to sovereign power. For mercantilists, rationality was immanent to the *raison d'état* – the state's end was the state itself. In other words, it was supposed to be capable of producing social reality according to its will. The physiocrats questioned this. According to them 'things [are] not flexible' (STP: 344). State-determined prices (for example for grain) had the opposite effect of what had been intended: increased scarcity (Reichelt/Zech 1985: 580ff.). According to Foucault the physiocrats concluded from this that 'a regulation *based upon and in accordance with the course of things themselves must* replace a regulation by police authority' (STP 344; italics by I.S.) Political economy saw their inflexibility as a result of the materiality of an independent economic sphere. The real basis of this interpretation lies in the establishment of the dominance of the capitalist mode of production, its naturalizing effects (which were analysed by Marx in *Capital*), and the resulting, largely self-referential compulsion to valorize capital. Whereas Marx demonstrated that economic processes emanate from specifically capitalist relations of production, classical bourgeois economic theory simply assumed them to be natural processes (MECW 35: 81ff.). The classical political economists suggested that the economy works according to the 'natural' laws of the market; they ignored the dictates of the disciplinary techniques centralized in the state and flanked by scientific knowledge. Accordingly, they assumed that it is the state's task to subject its 'art of government' to a 'higher logic'.[12]

From a historical point of view, the emergence of the discipline of 'political economy' represents the discursive effect of the societal separation of the economy and politics.[13] This discourse also emerged as a reaction to and a criticism of the 'Polizeystaat' [police state], i.e., of a government bound by the *raison d'etat* (STP: 262ff.). The real relationship between the state and economic science is thus the precise opposite of Poulantzas's conception of science as a state science: the state is bound to follow 'economic reason'

---

12   Foucault argues that as a result, the market became the locus of truth-formation (BP: 29ff.).
13   The fact that political economy nowadays seems to have taken a back seat to other social sciences is simply the result of the fact that the latter have largely adopted the essential principles of the former as their own presuppositions.

as proclaimed by political economy; its task as a knowledge apparatus is to discover the latter's structures and laws. Otherwise, 'good' governance is not possible. Thus an entire 'truth field' emerges of which the state must have knowledge. Decisions about whether state actors acted correctly or incorrectly are no longer made within the ensemble of disciplinary techniques centralized in the state, but by the 'market'. Political economy as an epistemic form [Erkenntnisform] is 'not a knowledge of government itself [...] a knowledge internal to the art of government. [...] *You have a science which is, as it were, tête-à-tête with the art of government, a science that is external to the art of government*'. (STP: 351; italics by I.S.).

As a result, '[...] economics cannot be the internal principle, law, rule of conduct, or rationality of government. *Economics is a science lateral to the art of governing*. One must govern with economics, one must govern alongside economists, one must govern by listening to the economists, but economics must not be and there is no question that it can be the governmental rationality itself.' (BP: 286; italics by I.S.).

This statement is valid in so far as there is a separation of the economy and politics in capitalism. But since each sphere constitutes a condition of existence for the other, the discourse linked to economic theory is not capable of taking into account what Poulantzas described as their 'separation as form' (SPS: 18f.). This does not mean that the state is external to the discipline of political economy as a specific process of knowledge production, let alone to the economy as such. Quite the contrary: there are constant discussions about which techniques of power and domination need to be deployed where, and to what extent, especially with regard to the successful reproduction of capital. As a consequence, political economy constitutes the key discourse where discussions based on 'reasonable' and 'balanced' criteria are taking place about the constitutive presence of the state in the capitalist economy.[14]

Therefore, the discourse of political economy structures the field of conflict in which the total capitalist interest is formulated. To a great degree, this field is shaped by the naturalizing effects of the categories of bourgeois political economy. Accordingly, there are particular forms of social conflict that strongly suggest themselves to social actors.[15] These forms gain

14 This discourse is taking different forms, depending on its respective theoretical basis. Following Kuhn we can speak of three paradigms (neoclassical economics, Keynesianism, Marxism), each of which tries to define the object of the 'economy' in their different ways (cf. Heine/Herr 2000; Heinrich 1999: 28ff.).

15 The classic example of this is the struggle for a just wage: it is, on the one hand, a collective struggle about the payment for labour time, but it does not, on the other hand, break through the obfuscation of exploitation effected by the wage form and

additional force by virtue of the 'dull compulsion of economic relations' (CI: 726) and the external disciplining that occurs thanks to techniques of power. In the process, the state constitutes the central terrain on which arguments take place about how these effects interact.

5. Conclusion

The point of departure for this chapter was the question how the state establishes the total capitalist interest. My key assertion was that it is possible to identify this process by drawing on Poulantzas and seeing the state as a knowledge apparatus. However, it also emerged that some of Poulantzas's claims lack differentiation. He fails to analyse the different relations of power in the respective fields of knowledge sufficiently. In reality, these are always interlinked and form conditions of existence of one another to some extent. But their analytical separation is crucial for their reconstruction because it allows for examining their different functions as well as their relationship to the state. A more detailed analysis could provide concrete data on the fields of knowledge and establish their specific articulations.

Another result is that Poulantzas's conception of knowledge is strongly state-centric: by arguing that the state monopolizes mental labour, he denies that the power relations analysed by Foucault produce valid knowledge. In effect, he subordinates claims to knowledge directly to the state. For future theoretical discussions, it would be useful to pick up the idea of condensation, which emphasizes that relations of power and force do indeed condense in the state, but they certainly do not emanate from it alone.

In conclusion, the type of *abstract knowledge* discussed is based on specifically capitalist modes of societalization. It emerged with the marginalization of personalized relations of domination and reflects the mutual interrelatedness of the capitalist economy and the state, i.e., – in Poulantzas's words – their co-constitution. Abstract knowledge is not only the 'data' on the basis of which the state decisions are taken. It also serves as the foundation for the formulation of a general strategy of accumulation.[16] Accordingly, it does not reflect trans-historical social relations but is a form of social reality produced by the state.

In contrast, the term *strategic knowledge* emphasizes the organizing role

therefore fails to transcend capitalist forms of intercourse (cf. CI: 535ff.).

16 This suggests that there is a problem for the organization of post-capitalist economies: Poulantzas stresses that the existence of stores of 'abstract' knowledge always coincides with the general monopolization of knowledge by the state and the exclusion of the popular masses. The capitalist separation of direct producers from 'organizational functions' (SPS: 56) raises the question how their knowledge about production could be organized in a post-capitalist society. Charles Bettelheim (1976: 140) has at least recognized this problem, even if his system of planned prices fails to resolve it.

played by the state. The different state apparatuses formulate political tactics regarding the conditions of accumulation for the class fractions represented within them. The conflicts *within* the state that arise from this are thus conflicts about the capitalist common interest, which are transposed onto the state's terrain. Attempts made by class fractions to generalize their respective interests and strategies condense into a general strategy on this terrain: If strategic knowledge exists in the form of an accumulation strategy formulated by the state, this reflects that particular interests have been generalized through compromises. Thus strategic knowledge expresses existing relations of forces, and reproduces and reinforces them. After all, certain conditions of accumulation favourable to specific fractions of capital are privileged over others in the making of state policies.[17]

Finally, the term *scientific knowledge* refers to a condition of existence of any kind of power. It serves as a foundation for the state's monopolization of authorized techniques of domination, which aim to engage in the 'fabrication of reliable human beings'. Political economy plays a special role in this, because the state depends on government knowledge based on economic theory. Without the latter it is neither possible to interpret abstract knowledge, nor to formulate strategic knowledge. Accordingly, political economy constitutes *overarching knowledge*. It is the discourse within which the field of the bio-political debate is formed.

Although drawing on Foucault is indeed helpful for the reconstruction of these fields of knowledge, the central insights of Marxist state theory remain inaccessible on these grounds. Foucault is capable of giving a *historical* account of the separation of the economy and politics, but he does not provide a *theoretical* explanation for it. His description of power and knowledge is limited in so far as he does not possess concepts for ordering and weighting the phenomena observed and portraying their relationship to the state.

This is also apparent in Foucault's work on governmentality. He demonstrates how the discourse of political economy emerged, but he neither explains the existence of the economic forms that are the backdrop to this process, nor does he shed light on the articulation between the state and the process of capital accumulation. Moreover, he also refrains from elucidating why the relationship between political economy and the state appears in the form of an external relationship. Marxist approaches, in contrast, do all that: In *Capital*, Marx lines out a theory of the economic forms that constitute the capitalist mode of production. Poulantzas shows that the state is constitutively present in the accumulation of capital as a

17   Following Bourdieu (1998: 60), this could be thought of as 'profit of universalization'.

producer of knowledge, among other things. With the help of Althusser's concept of structural causality, it is possible to explain the external relationship between the state and political economy: the economic sphere and that of the state mutually determine each other; their separation is politically determined. In other words, the state is present in the economy in its 'absence'. The inverse is true as well: the fact that certain use values are provided by the state in the form of non-commodified public goods does not mean that this is not an economic process. Public education, for example, is often highly functional for the realization of capital (Nuss/ Stützle 2006).

The fact that Marxist approaches to social and state theory do not share the deficits of Foucault's analyses does not mean that they are flawless. For example, Poulantzas fails to differentiate relations of power and knowledge sufficiently, which result in him taking a state-centric position: he subordinates all the fields and forms of knowledge discussed to the state. The counter-argument that the state is present in the production of all forms of knowledge is not really convincing, because Poulantzas does not explain how this happens. As a consequence, some authors (e.g., Demirović1990: 27) dismiss Poulantzas's conception of knowledge in its entirety. I have shown, however, that Poulantzas's ideas can be used for developing a theory of the capitalist state based on conceiving it as an apparatus of knowledge that acts as the 'ideal collective capitalist'. Accordingly, I do not propose to look for the 'authentic' Poulantzas, but to further develop motives found in his state theory.

References

Agnoli, J. (1975) 'Der Staat des Kapitals', in Agnoli, J., *Der Staat des Kapitals und weitere Schriften zur Kritik der Politik, Gesammelte Schriften*, vol. 2 (Freiburg: Ca-Ira-Verlag, 1995) 21-89.
Barben, D. (1999) 'Funktionalismus', in Haug, W. F. (ed.) *Historisch-kritisches Wörterbuch des Marxismus*, vol. 4 (Hamburg: Argument-Verlag) 1141-1157.
Bettelheim, C. (1976) *Economic calculations and forms of property* (London: Routledge and Kegan Paul).
Blanke, B. /Jürgens, U. /Kastendiek, H. (1975) 'Das Verhältnis von Politik und Ökonomie als Ansatzpunkt einer materialistischen Analyse des bürgerlichen Staates', in Blanke, B. / Jürgens, U. / Kastendiek, H. *Kritik der Politischen Wissenschaft. Analysen von Politik und Ökonomie in der bürgerlichen Gesellschaft* (Frankfurt am Main / New York: Campus Verlag) 414-444.
Bourdieu, P. (1998) *Practical reason: on the theory of action* (Cambridge: Polity Press).
Demirović, A. (1990) 'Der Staat als Wissenschaftspraxis. Hegemonietheoretische

Überlegungen zur intelektuellen Produktion von Politik und Staat', *KultuRRevolution*, vol. 9, no. 22, 23-27.
Demirović, A. (2001) 'Geistige und körperliche Arbeit', in Haug, W. F. (ed.): *Historisch-kritisches Wörterbuch des Marxismus* vol. 5 (Hamburg: Argument-Verlag) 124-137.
Desrosières, A. (1998) *The Politics of Large Numbers. A History of Statistical Reasoning* (Cambridge: Harvard Univ. Press).
Foucault, M. (1971) *L'ordre du discours* (Paris: Gallimard).
Foucault, M. (1976) *Society must be defended. Lectures at the Collège de France 1975-1976* (New York: Picador, 2003).
Foucault, M. (1979a) 'The Birth of Biopolitics', in Rabinow. P. / Rose, N. (eds.) *The essential Foucault: selections from essential works of Foucault 1954-1984* (New York: New Press, 2003) 202-207.
Foucault, M. (1979b) 'Power and Norm: Notes', in Morris, M. / Patton, P. (eds.) *Michel Foucault: Power, Truth, Strategy* (Sydney: Feral Publications).
Gerstenberger, H. (1990) *Die subjektlose Gewalt. Theorie der Entstehung bürgerlicher Staatsgewalt* (Münster: Westfälisches Dampfboot).
Gottschalk, K. (2004) 'Wissen über Land und Leute. Administrative Praktiken und Staatsbildungsprozesse im 18. Jahrhundert', in Collin, P. / Horstmann, T. (eds.) *Das Wissen des Staates. Geschichte, Theorie und Praxis* (Baden-Baden: Nomos) 149-174.
Groebner, V. (2002) 'Das Wissen von der Bezeichnung der Körper. ›Complexio‹ und die Kategorien der Personenbeschreibung zwischen dem 13. und dem 16. Jahrhundert', in Landwehr, A. (ed.) *Geschichte(n) der Wirklichkeit. Beiträge zur Sozial- und Kulturgeschichte des Wissens* (Augsburg: Wißner) 173-188.
Heine, M. / Herr, H. (2000) *Volkswirtschaftslehre. Paradigmenorientierte Einführung in die Mikro- und Makroökonomie* (München/Wien: Oldenbourg).
Heinrich, M. (1999) *Die Wissenschaft vom Wert. Die Marxsche Kritik der politischen Ökonomie zwischen wissenschaftlicher Revolution und klassischer Tradition*, 2nd ed. (Münster: Westfälisches Dampfboot).
Hobbes, T. (1651) Leviathan (Baltimore: Penguin Books, 1968).
Jessop, B. (1982) *The Capitalist State. Marxist Theories and Methods* (Oxford: Robertson).
John, V. (1884) *Geschichte der Statistik. Ein Quellenmässiges Handbuch für den akademischen Gebrauch wie für den Selbstunterricht* (Stuttgart: Enke).
Krätke, M. R. (1998) 'Wie politisch ist Marx' Politische Ökonomie?', *Z. Zeitschrift marxistische Erneuerung*, vol. 8, no. 33/34, 114-127.
Miller, P. / Rose, N. (1990) 'Governing economic life', in Gane, M. / Johnson, T. (eds.) *Foucault's New Domains* (London: Routledge, 1993) 75-105.
Nuss, S. / Stützle, I. (2006) 'Was ist und welchen Zweck hat Privatisierung? Anmerkungen zu einer linken Politik öffentlicher Güter', *ak – Zeitung für linke Debatte und Praxis*, no. 507, 16.6.2006, 13.
Poovey, M. (1998) *A History of the Modern Fact. Problems of Knowledge in the Sciences of Wealth and Society* (Chicago: Univ. of Chicago Press).
Porter, T. M. (1986) *The Rise of statistical thinking 1820-1900* (Princeton: Princeton Univ. Press).

Reichelt, H. / Zech, R. (1985) 'Nationalökonomische Theorien: Merkantilismus, Physiokraten und Klassiker', in Fetscher, I. / Münkler, H. (eds.) *Pipers Handbuch der politischen Ideen*, vol. 3 (München: Piper) 561-615.

Spittler, G. (1980) 'Abstraktes Wissen als Herrschaftsbasis. Zur Entstehungsgeschichte bürokratischer Herrschaft im Bauernstaat Preußen', *Kölner Zeitschrift für Soziologie und Sozialpsychologie*, vol. 32, no. 3, 574-604.

Tantner, A. (2002) 'Vermischung vermeiden. Seelenkonskription, Hausnummerierung und Vermischung um 1770', in Landwehr, A. (ed.) *Geschichte(n) der Wirklichkeit. Beiträge zur Sozial- und Kulturgeschichte des Wissens* (Augsburg: Wißner) 147-172.

Weber, M. (1922) *Economy and society: an outline of interpretive sociology* (Berkeley: Univ. of California Press, 1978).

TERRITORY AND HISTORICITY: SPACE AND TIME IN NICOS POULANTZAS'S *STATE, POWER, SOCIALISM*[1]

MARKUS WISSEN

1. The theoretical context

The engagement of the social sciences with space and time has developed in a way comparable to the movements of a pendulum. For a long time, scholars in the field paid little attention to space and focused on time. This also applies to Marxist approaches in the social sciences – not least the works of Karl Marx and Friedrich Engels (cf. Jessop 2002: 101). Marx and Engels concentrated on analysing the relationship between time and society and rather than that between space and society. The *Communist Manifesto* may capture the tendency towards globalization inherent in capitalism, but it embeds this tendency in a teleological narrative that culminates in the sublation of all class contradictions (MECW 4: 447). In *Grundrisse*, Marx uses the phrase 'space must be annihilated by time' (MECW 28: 448) to mark the fact that 'by its very nature, capital strives to go beyond every spatial limitation' (ibid.). This suggests that spatial limits are less important than the time it takes to overcome them.

From the 1970s, in contrast, social scientists started to pay closer attention to the social meaning of space. Henri Lefebvre's book *La production de l'espace* (The Production of Space, 1974) took a pioneering role. Drawing an analogy with Marx's analysis of the fetishistic character of the commodity, Lefebvre investigated the social relations that produce space and are in turn structured by it. He was followed by, among others, David Harvey and Neil Smith, whose points of departure were a critique of the 'spatial blindness' of historical materialism. Harvey and Smith would go on to develop

---

[1] I would like to thank the editors as well as Bernd Belina, Herbert Böttcher, Uli Brand, Wiebke Dreier and Matthias Naumann for important and inspiring suggestions and comments.

'historical-geographic materialism'.²

In spite of these developments, it was not until the 1990s that the (critical) social sciences took their *spatial turn*. At this point, globalization had thoroughly shaken up the spatial configuration of Fordism that had been seen as 'natural' for so long. At the level of theory, the *spatial turn* built on Marxist research, in particular Lefebvre's *The Production of Space*, first published in English in 1991. However, the work of Michel Foucault and feminist social theory also played a central role. These more-or-less explicit critiques of the abstractions of Marxist social theory established the problem of space as 'the realm of the concrete and the particular' (Harvey 1985: 144). Other important contributors to the debate were Doreen Massey (1994) and Edward Soja (1989), who also consolidated the influence of Lefebvre's work.³

Most contemporary approaches in the (critical) social sciences treat space and time as categories holding more or less equal importance. Bob Jessop goes so far as to argue that space has surpassed time in importance, so that the latter now needs to be 're-valued': 'The spatial turn associated with the interest in the globalization of capital has been overdone and [...] a temporal (re)turn is overdue: time and temporality are at least as important as, if not more important than, space and spatiality in the logic of economic globalization' (2002: 97).

2. Poulantzas's concept of the *matrix*

It makes sense to re-engage with Poulantzas in the light of this oscillating emphasis upon time and space in the social sciences. His relevant work, which is mostly from the 1970s, already pays equal attention to both, especially in his discussion of 'the nation' in *State, Power, Socialism* (SPS). Here Poulantzas aims to establish the specificity of the capitalist forms of both space and time through a method based on historical comparison. His starting point is a critique of conceptions of the nation dominant within Marxism. According to Poulantzas, Marxist approaches in the field

2   See especially *The Limits to Capital* (Harvey 1982) and *Uneven Development* (Smith 1984). A reconstruction of the 'spatialization' of Marxist thought can be found in Soja (1989: ch. 2).

3   In *The Production of Space*, Lefebvre developed the category of 'differential space' to provide a counterpoint to capitalist space, which is abstract and destroys difference. Accordingly, he can be seen as providing a link between the Foucauldian-feminist theoretical tradition and that of Marxism. There remain, however, fundamental differences between these traditions, for example as regards the viability and importance of (macro-)theory. This disagreement is particularly visible in Harvey's statement (1996: 111) that '[t]he inference that there can be no theory of the production of space or that the search for any sort of general or meta-theory must be abandoned, is plainly wrong'.

usually fall short of their self-professed goals because they remain tied to the level of commodity circulation. They see the modern nation as relying on the homogenization of the space in which 'competing individuals or commodity traders constantly move' (SPS: 96). Speaking from a class analytical perspective, they portray the nation as having been 'created by commodity capital' and account for it with reference 'to the mercantile bourgeoisie of early capitalism' (ibid.). This leaves unexplained why the processes of homogenization and the removal of barriers to the circulation of commodities and capital within a domestic market happen to take place on the national scale, as opposed to any other. Moreover, it remains unclear how far the constitutive elements of the nation – territory, language and tradition – are connected to capitalism. They become naturalized, that is, they are portrayed 'as transhistorical essences possessing an immutable nature' (ibid.).

In contrast, Poulantzas emphasizes that territory and tradition are socially produced and thus subject to historical change. Both territory and tradition are inscribed into temporal and spatial *matrices* whose meanings vary between epochs. Taking this into account is a prerequisite for understanding that the emergence of the modern nation forms part of the constitution of the capitalist mode of production: 'The fact that capitalist space and time are not at all the same as their counterparts in previous modes of production implies that considerable changes have taken place in the reality and meaning of territory and historicity. These changes both allow and entail the constitution of the modern nation' (97).

The central role that Poulantzas accords to space and time is underscored by his use of the term *matrix*. Poulantzas uses it as a 'metaphorical reference to its original meaning, namely "ancestral mother" or "causal force"'.[4] The term informs Poulantzas's main critique of dominant understandings of space as something essentially neutral appropriated in diverging ways in different historical epochs, a container that remains independent of the social processes that occur 'within it'. The term 'matrix' refers to the structuring effect of space on social processes, which varies between different modes of production. This is because the spatial and temporal matrices and the mode of production mutually constitute each other: 'Themselves implied by the relations of production and social division of labour, these matrices appear at the same time as their presupposition' (99). Just like Lefebvre, Poulantzas develops a materialist conception of space and time. Both understand 'the spatial and temporal "matrices" of capitalism, its material groundedness,

---

4   See Läpple (1991: 196), whose terminology in his *Essay über den Raum* (Essay on space) follows Poulantzas's in this respect.

as simultaneously presuppositions and embodiments of the relations of production' (Soja 1989: 118f.).

3. The spatial matrix of capitalism

Poulantzas develops the characteristics of the capitalist spatial and temporal matrices by comparing them to those of antiquity and feudalism. He uses the distinction between homogeneity and fragmentation, as well as, for the spatial matrix, the distinction between inside and outside as references of his comparison.

According to Poulantzas, the space of antiquity was characterized by openness and homogeneity. It was dominated by a system of cities whose architectural and spatial structures were all based on a similar pattern. Cities were open towards their surroundings, with the latter sometimes taking on the fundamental spatial patterns of the former. The space that emerged was homogeneous, continuous and undifferentiated. In it, people could not really change their location because 'each point in space is an exact repetition of the previous point' (SPS: 101). Leonardo Benevolo's analysis of the Roman Empire illustrates this point: 'It established on the shores of the Mediterranean Sea a continuous network of several thousand cities, both large and small, walled and unwalled, and frequently conforming to a unified geometric design that ordered the various public and private architectural elements. Within the enduring and peaceful setting of the Roman Empire, this rational design flowed from the cities to the hinterland and ordered the countryside according to the regular forms of agricultural plots, roads, bridges, aqueducts, borders, canals and ports: the functional supports and omnipresent image of a homogeneous civilization spread over a vast geographic area' (1993: 5f.).

It is important to understand that this space did not have boundaries in the modern sense. To be precise, there was no 'outside' in ancient conceptions of space. Accordingly, the areas bordering the Roman Empire, which were inhabited by 'barbarians', were seen as non-places. Poulantzas argues that they did not constitute different aspects of the same space, but 'the definitive end of all possible space' (SPS: 102).

Compared to their counterparts of antiquity, cities in medieval feudalism were more clearly closed off from their surroundings. Under the protection of the *pax romana*, cities had flourished. After its demise, however, the area that today is Western Europe came to be characterized by a far less consolidated territorial order, where cities protected themselves with the help of strong walls. These walls delimited a space in which certain freedoms had been obtained, contrary to the countryside, with its persistent feudal relations of dependency. Yet unlike cities in other medieval empires (e.g., China, Byzantium) or in the Arab Caliphate, occidental cities did not play a significant role again before the 11th century (Benevolo 1993). Until then, occidental relations of production and political authority had been shaped by the feudal lien system and its tensions, which led to a permanent cycle of borders dissolving and being redrawn (Elias 1939). Unlike in the modern state system, however, external borders did not mark the transition between two equivalent spaces. In fact, the situation was rather more similar to that which prevailed in ancient times: beyond the imperial borders lay non-places; the only difference was that the barbarians were replaced with heathens and unbelievers (SPS: 103).

According to Poulantzas, the homogeneity of medieval space was mostly the result of the dominant role of religion and its transnational, universal character. Due to the close link between spiritual and secular power, religion was 'directly present in the forms of the exercise of power and it patterned space by setting the seal of Christianity upon it' (102f.). Accordingly, the homogeneity of medieval space was embodied in the sovereign. The paths he travelled in order to exercise his authority delimited space, and the unity of his empire depended on his physical existence.

The homogeneity of medieval space was also the result of the weakly developed social division of labour and its limited effects in terms of differentiating space. This is a crucial difference between the feudal and the capitalist mode of production. Capitalism is characterized by a highly developed division of labour, resting on the private ownership of the means of production and on the subdivision and enclosure of communal land. Its development is extremely dynamic: it is continuously valorizing spaces which have not yet been penetrated, while simultaneously devalorizing others (Harvey 1982). Uneven spatial development is a feature inherent in capitalism. It constitutes 'the geographical expression of the contradictions of capital' (Smith 1984: 152). According to Poulantzas, it is these discontinuities and segmentations that shape the spatial matrix of capitalism and distinguish it from those of previous epochs. Segmentation governs capitalist space all the way down to the arrangement of bodies in the labour process: the worker, separated from the means of production, is a mere appendage of the machine. She is forced – for example in assembly line work – into a precisely delimited space that is subdivided into sections and cells (SPS: 64).

If segmentation or discontinuity constitutes one defining aspect of capitalist space, homogeneity forms another.[5] Yet in capitalism, spatial

---

5 Thus, Lefebvre (1978: 86) describes capitalist space as 'both homogenous and broken'.

homogeneity signifies something very different from what it referred to in feudalism or antiquity. Whereas the homogeneity of feudal and ancient space was anchored in the constitution of the mode of production and the forms of political authority, this relationship has now been reversed: capitalist relations of production and the capitalist division of labour go hand in hand with spatial discontinuity and segmentation. The problem of homogeneity becomes one of *homogenization*, or, more precisely, of 'second-degree [...] homogenization' (103).

The state plays a central role in this process. It shapes the individuals that have become detached from their traditional surroundings by establishing affinities and normalizing social hierarchies. It unifies the individuals within a given territory 'into a group of formally equal legal subjects separated from their socio-economic relations' (Hirsch 1990: 45; translated; cf. SPS: 86ff.). Finally it draws borders and creates binding internal rules, which create the legal certainty necessary for the functioning of a domestic market. The state does not suspend the discontinuities and segmentations of the spatial matrix of capitalism, but renders them controllable, manageable and 'negotiable' (Lefebvre 1974: 282), thus fortifying them in the very same act. It even contributes to their establishment by constituting 'individuals not as members of antagonistic classes, or cultural and social milieus, but as abstract market subjects and citizens' (Hirsch 1990: 45) and by 'trapping them in a grid' (SPS: 105) that includes schools, armies, prisons, hospitals. Accordingly, individualization is also the 'material effect of state practices and techniques' (67).

In this way the state fragments and homogenizes the population at the same time. It 'realizes the unity of the individuals of the people-nation in the very movement by which it forges their individualization. It secures the political-public (nation-State) homogenization of the "private" dissociations in the very movement by which it contributes to their establishment' (106). In the process, the modern nation emerges, bound inseparably to the capitalist mode of production. The decisive role played by the state here should not be taken to imply historical succession. The state and the nation, the latter understood as a simultaneously homogenized and fragmented territory, mutually presuppose each other. The state not only makes a crucial contribution to national unity, 'but sets itself up in constructing this unity – that is, in forging the modern nation' (105).

The contradictory relationship between homogenization and fragmentation corresponds to the relationship between the in- and outside of the modern nation. On the one hand, the homogenization of space into a national territory with stable external borders (the 'political expression of an enclosure'; ibid.) is a necessary precondition for the functioning of a domestic market. On the other hand, the circulation of capital tends to constantly transgress borders. Capital can only reproduce itself *trans*nationally – that is, by transgressing borders –, but it moves within a spatial matrix that is itself *inter*national, i.e., it relies on the existence of separate, bordered territories. The drawing of borders implies that they can also be moved. There is a demarcated interior 'that is always capable of being extended *ad infinitum*' (106).

However, this shifting of borders does not constitute an expansion into a continuous and homogeneous space – as was the case in ancient or medieval conquests. Rather, it entails the homogenization of territory and the assimilation or, in extreme cases, the annihilation of its inhabitants. In this context, Poulantzas refers to (a) the valorization of non-capitalist spaces through imperialist expansion, (b) the massacres inflicted on minorities in the course of the creation of national states,[6] and (c) some forms of the exercise of power in the 'exceptional forms of capitalist State' (80) such as the creation of concentration camps. The latter internalize the borders into the national space and serve as a form of incarceration for those who stand 'outside the nation' yet inside the national territory. Accordingly, the contradictory relationship between inside and outside, characteristic of the spatial matrix of capitalism, engenders a tendency towards expansion that entails the targeted destruction of difference, distinguishing it from the 'undifferentiated massacres' (107) that accompanied the expansion of ancient and feudal empires. Thus 'the roots of totalitarianism are inscribed in the spatial matrix concretized by the modern nation-State – a matrix that is already present in its relations of production and in the capitalist social division of labour' (ibid.).[7]

4. The temporal matrix of capitalism

As is the case with spatial matrices, Poulantzas discovers a number of similarities between antiquity and feudalism with regard to their temporal matrices. These in turn distinguish them from capitalism. His initial assumption is that both epochs were dominated by modes of production that, unlike capitalism, were characterized by simple rather than expanded

---

6   Poulantzas mentions the example of the genocide of Armenians during the foundation of the Turkish nation state under Mustafa Kemal Atatürk (SPS: 107).
7   This is not the place to discuss Poulantzas's tendency to apply terms such as 'genocide' and 'concentration camp' universally, nor to discuss his references to 'totalitarianism'. It is worth, however, pointing out that the Nazi policies of annihilation, which Poulantzas does not mention explicitly, cannot be explained sufficiently with this theoretical framework. Similarly, his concept of the 'capitalist exceptional state' is unable to capture the character of the National Socialist state.

reproduction. Thus, their historicity is not directional. It is, just like pre-capitalist space, *'continuous, homogeneous, reversible and repetitive'* (SPS: 108).

Antiquity was dominated by a circular conception of time. In analogy to the constant repetition of one and the same fundamental pattern in the spatial matrix, the temporal matrix was characterised by 'eternal recurrence' (ibid.). This is illustrated by the theory of the transmigration of the soul held by the Pythagoreans, a pre-Socratic philosophical school that Poulantzas mentions in passing. It held that the soul is the real, immortal essence of the human being. Upon birth, the soul enters into the mortal body, from which it is released in death, only to enter into another body again. There is a goal to this cycle, namely cleansing the soul from the impurities of the physical. But this goal is always both an end and a beginning. Although it 'halts the spiral of freshly-begun cycles, it does so by looping the loop, by knitting both ends together' (ibid.). The notion of a cycle also informs Plato's epistemology. He argues that the soul has already 'beheld' the 'ideas' (the Good, the Beautiful, God) before entering into the mortal body. Once within the body, the sensual prevents the soul from being aware of this fact. By ridding itself of the sensual through training the mental capacities, the soul then becomes capable of 'recollection' (*anamnesis*). Hence, knowledge is nothing but the recollection of what has already been seen (cf. Anzenbacher 1981: 48)[8].

The Middle Ages, in contrast, were dominated by a Christian, linear perception of time that viewed creation as the beginning, and judgement day as the end of history. Yet it would be wrong to take this as a chronology, because this would mean overlooking 'the eschatological independence of the future from the passage of time' (Link-Wieczorek 1996: 1369). In fact, the linearity of the Christian conception of time only *appears* as such: Jesus' activities render the future kingdom of God a present reality to some extent. The 'succession of past, present and future is determined asymmetrically by a future filled by God. The latter not only affects the present but can also turn the past into it again'. Therefore, the 'messianic understanding of time' entails that the past and future are not arranged '"on a line", but that the temporal modes are intertwined with one another' (1368). In Poulantzas's words, 'beginning and end, *before* and *after* are fully *co-present* in the constant essence of the divine' (SPS: 109). The annually recurring Christian holidays, which commemorate the birth, death and resurrection of Christ, are everyday expressions of this. At the political level, the constant 're-concretization of the past' (ibid.) in the middle ages is evident in the

8   This is the foundation for Plato's allegory of the cave in *Politeia*.

translatio imperii, that is, the transfer of the mantle of Roman Emperor first to the Francs and then to the German-Roman kings. It shows that history was not understood as a progression from the past into the present, but as a continuum within which the past is continuously present. Thus, the middle ages neither knew territory in the modern sense, nor historicity. And just like the medieval spatial matrix, the sovereign embodied the medieval temporal matrix ('political time is the time of the prince-body', SPS: 110) and formed part of a continuum of authority.

The temporal matrix of capitalism is entirely different. The expanded reproduction typical of capitalism gives rise to directional, linear historicity. In contrast, in antiquity and the Middle Ages simple reproduction corresponded to a cyclical understanding of time, that is, to the co-presence of the past and the future in the present. In other words, the present in capitalism 'marks a transition from the before to the after. Modern historicity is thus of an evolutionary and progressive character' (ibid.). Moreover, time becomes segmented, i.e., divided into equal parts. Poulantzas sees a direct connection to the 'new relations of production' (ibid.) and the capitalist division of labour, which is characterized by large industry and assembly line work. These presuppose time that is measurable with a punch clock (i.e., that is segmented and divisible into equal parts). Finally, the temporal matrix of capitalism is characterized by asynchronous development, the temporal correlate to the spatially uneven development of capitalism.

The parallels between the spatial and temporal matrices of capitalism are obvious. Poulantzas further emphasizes them by using the same attributes to describe each ('segmented', 'discontinuous'). Yet if capitalist time, like capitalist space, is characterized by segmentation and discontinuity, this means for Poulantzas that it also gives rise to a similar problem, namely that of homogenization.

Homogenization implies that individuals are forced into temporal rhythms and practices which are compatible with the capitalist relations of production and the capitalist division of labour.[9] This way, the dominance of the linear time of production over other times (e.g., the cyclical times of the reproduction of the body, of nature, etc.) are produced. In the process, the state plays a central role. It regulates the length of the working day and of educational and training periods, and the relationship between work and leisure.

Tradition is a key aspect of the homogenization of the temporal matrix

---

9   See also Gramsci's remarks on the 'the new type of man demanded by the rationalization of production and work' in 'Americanism and Fordism' (SPN: 297) and Harvey (1996: 225ff.).

of capitalism. It imbues societies with a common historical orientation characterized by individualization and discontinuity. In other words, it creates a frame of reference within which the asynchrony of the capitalist social formation can unfold without endangering social cohesion. Accordingly, the role played by tradition in the temporal matrix of capitalism is the same the national territory plays for the spatial matrix: it is the precondition, medium and result of homogenization and a constitutive element of the modern nation. Like territory, tradition is inescapably tied up with the state: the latter legitimizes itself by way of the foundational acts contained in the former. Moreover, the state 'monopolizes' tradition 'by storing up the memory of the people-nation' (SPS: 113). At the same time – and herein lie the roots of 'totalitarianism' – it eliminates other traditions, turning them into mere 'variations of its own history' (ibid.). Thus the state creates a close relationship between the spatial and temporal matrices, as well as between tradition and territory: the genocides committed during the constitution of the modern nation constitute expulsions 'beyond space and time' (114). They destroy not only the physical and, hence, spatial existence of social groups, but also the collective memory of their existence and their history. Accordingly, modern camps spatially enclose those individuals and social groups 'for whom time and national historicity are *in suspense*' (115). In turn, people's demands for their own state and territory are at once demands for their own history.

5. Critical appraisal

Although Poulantzas deals at length with 'totalitarianism' and exceptional states in capitalism, his analyses of the spatial and temporal matrices of capitalism refer more to the interventionist state and the Fordist mode of development prevalent in Western societies. The key terms he uses to describe the spatial and temporal matrices reflect the idea of the assembly line and the Taylorist organization of the labour process: 'segmented', 'linear', 'irreversible' (in the sense of unidirectional) on the one hand, and 'homogeneous' and 'levelling' (in the sense of obliterating particularities) on the other. At one point, he states explicitly that the capitalist space-time matrix is 'materialized *par excellence* in the production line' (SPS: 65).

Taylorism may not have disappeared completely, but Poulantzas tends to generalize from spatial and temporal forms predominant in a particular phase of capitalist development, thus losing sight of the spatio-temporal specificities of other phases. Consider, for example, some of the characteristics of 'post-Fordist' capitalism: in some key sectors and for certain employees, the spatial and temporal matrices that Poulantzas took to be characteristic of capitalism in general have become dysfunctional from the perspective of the valorization of capital. Castells emphasizes this when he discusses the temporal regime in the so-called 'network enterprise'. He states: 'Because the value-making potential of labor and organizations is highly dependent on the autonomy of informed labor to make decisions in real time, traditional disciplinary management of labor does not fit the new production system. Instead, skilled labor is required to manage its own time in a flexible manner, sometimes adding more work time, at other times adjusting to flexible schedules, in some instances reducing working hours, and thus pay.' (1996: 437).

Similarly, novel forms of dealing with nature also deviate from Poulantzas's spatial and temporal matrices of capitalism. The valorization of biological diversity, for example, presupposes that spatial and temporal particularities are taken into account to some extent, instead of simply inserting these particularities into rigid matrices. The conservation of nature and the preservation of cultural specificities in the form of indigenous knowledge and practices have become central elements in the process (Görg 2003: 286).[10]

This reveals yet another gap in Poulantzas's considerations. He lacks a concept of space as the *physical and material precondition* of social processes. Such a concept is necessary in order to grasp that societal relations with nature also form part of the spatial and temporal matrix. Moreover, it is also necessary to capture what Harvey (1982) called the 'built environment' (buildings as well as the infrastructures of traffic, supply and communications). The dynamics and contradictions of social relations with nature and the built environment are key aspects of the transformation of the capitalist relations of production and division of labour, and they are also reflected in the transformation of its spatial and temporal matrices. In the built environment, this effect is visible in the 'compression' of space and the 'acceleration' of time made possible by modern information and communications technology. Harvey refers to this process as 'time-space-compression'. It not only transforms economic interactions,[11] but also representations of space, approximating them to the kind of *co-presence* that Poulantzas assumed had been abolished by the temporal and spatial matrix of capitalism: 'As space appears to shrink to a "global village" of telecommunications and a "spaceship earth" of economic and ecological

---

10   There is no space to discuss here that this again entails entirely different forms of destruction (see Brand/Görg 2003). And of course, post-Fordist and Fordist-fossilistic forms of the appropriation and valorization of nature also coexist with one another (Altvater 2005).

11   Consider, for example, the stock exchanges, which have come to form a global network.

interdependencies – to use just two familiar and everyday images – and as time horizons shorten to the point where the present is all there is (the world of the schizophrenic), so we have to learn how to cope with an overwhelming sense of compression of our spatial and temporal worlds' (Harvey 1990: 240).[12]

Poulantzas's conception of space primarily refers to the *spatial scale* of social processes (which was in fact revolutionized through the constitution of the modern nation) rather than to their physical and material preconditions. The fact that he mostly examines just one dimension of space is at once a weakness and strength. After all, his focus allows us to capture the contemporary shifts in space and scale that are visible in the emergence of supranational and international forms of statehood – and does so without minimizing the importance of the national state. Poulantzas demonstrates that capitalism and the national state are joined at the hip: Although they co-exist under conditions of tension, it is only within the framework of the national state, i.e., on the grounds of territory and tradition, that the contradictions of capitalism become manageable. This insight guards against a premature delivery of the national state's swan song in the face of globalization: The 'hard core of the modern nation is to be found in the unchanging kernel of the *capitalist* relations of production' (SPS: 117). This statement exhibits functionalist leanings, implying the roots of the national state lie in the problem of ensuring social cohesion, and this problem in turn stems from the spatio-temporal segmentations and discontinuities inherent in the capitalist mode of production. Yet Poulantzas's implicit functionalism is moderated by his reference to the social struggles and relations of forces[13] that are materialized in the national state: he views the state as a 'strategic field ploughed from one end to the other by working-class and popular struggle and resistance' (119).[14] Accordingly, the 'spatiality and historicity' of the working class constitutes an 'integral part' of the nation (118).

Poulantzas emphasizes how the national scale is *produced* in the wake of

---

12 Consider Castells's (1996: 466) remark that a significant and increasing number of financial transactions rely on 'the capture of future time in present transactions', or Altvater and Mahnkopf's verdict that there is a 'preponderance of the present': 'The present rules over the past and the future. The future appears as nothing but present discounted value, as "*presented future*" (Anders) or as a simple extrapolation, as a "de-futurised future" (ibid.). This way, it is transformed into a present disembedded from its history that will emerge at a later time' (Altvater/Mahnkopf 1996: 121; translated).
13 There is a tension between functionalist explanations and arguments starting from social struggles throughout *SPS* (cf. Jessop 1985: 336ff.; Demirović 1987).
14 Poulantzas primarily focuses on class struggles and largely ignores conflicts that result from other contradictory social relations – e.g., gender relations – and their materializations in state apparatuses.

social conflicts. This suggests he is aware of the possibility that the relation between the national and other scales of the organization of politics can shift. However, he was not able to conduct an in-depth analysis of the changes that accompanied globalization. In his analyses of the internationalization of capital, he does little more than giving some hints on this matter. He asks, for example: 'what exactly are the new relationships between the imperialist social formations (United States, Europe, Japan), and what are the effects of these on the state apparatuses? Is it still possible today to speak of a *national state* in the imperialist metropolises? What connections are there between these states and the internationalization of capital or the multinational firms? Are new super-state institutional forms tending to replace the national states, or alternatively, what modifications are these states undergoing to enable them to fulfil the new functions required by the extended reproduction of capital on the international level?' (CCC: 38) He analyses these spatial and scalar transformations not so much from the perspective of the 'internationalization of the state' (Hirsch 2001), instead emphasizing the question how relations between the imperialist states are changing in light of the 1970s crisis of US hegemony (cf. CD).[15] He still identifies, however, 'certain [...] visible strains between state and nation' (CCC: 80). These do not take on the form of a 'supranationalization' of political authority, but of a revival of regionalism (e.g., in the Basque Country). He concludes that the internationalization of capital leads 'more towards a fragmentation of the nation, such as it is historically constituted, than to a supranationalization of the state' (ibid.).

Even under conditions of globalization, the fragmentation of states is a widespread phenomenon. The recent history of Eastern Europe and the Balkans, as well as the independence movements in regions like Flanders speak to this tendency. In these cases, we see the construction of a national tradition and a national territory along the lines described by Poulantzas. Yet the contemporary spatial and scalar transformations at the subnational level are not limited to separatism; they also give rise to the emergence of a worldwide network of *global cities*. In addition, there are important changes at the inter- and supranational scale: (a) European integration, which has accelerated since the second half the 1980s; and (b) the creation or upgrading of international institutions such as the World Trade Organization (WTO) and the International Monetary Fund (IMF).

15 We have to bear in mind that the *internationalization of the state* was not as evident in the 1970s as it is today. Quite the reverse: the collapse of Bretton Woods and the stagnation of European integration revealed that supra- and international state institutions were in a deep crisis.

It was impossible for Poulantzas to predict these changes. The important point is that his theory can accommodate them. Attempts to use Poulantzas's conceptual tools in order to analyse changes in the contemporary spatial and scalar organization of the state are evidence of this. Some scholars try to describe international governmental institutions as 'second-order condensations', drawing on Poulantzas's conception of the national state as the condensation of social relations of forces (Brand 2005; Brand et al. 2011). The idea is that different national interests condense within international institutions, and that these interests are in turn already condensations of social relations of forces (first-order condensations). Moreover, the debate among Anglophone geographers about the *politics of scale* (Brenner 1998; 2004; Smith 1995; Swyngedouw 1997) can also be linked to Poulantzas. It analyses the emergence of new scales of the economy and politics. These are results of social conflicts and remain constantly contested, whilst also making a key contribution to the management of the contradictions of capitalist socialization.

Just like Lefebvre's oeuvre, that of Poulantzas has played a pioneering role for materialist conceptions of space and time. This is their lasting contribution. Today, their added value lies in guarding us against the many simplifications in the debates on globalization. Poulantzas points out that the existence of nations is a constantly contested result of social conflict. This is highly relevant for our present struggles. There is potential for political progress if we constantly address the question of how to overcome capitalism and the national state itself.

References

Altvater, E. (2005) *Das Ende des Kapitalismus, wie wir ihn kennen: Eine radikale Kapitalismuskritik* (Münster: Westfälisches Dampfboot).
Altvater, E. / Mahnkopf, B. (1996) *Grenzen der Globalisierung: Ökonomie, Ökologie und Politik in der Weltgesellschaft* (Münster: Westfälisches Dampfboot).
Anzenbacher, A. (1981) *Einführung in die Philosophie* (Wien: Herder).
Benevolo, L. (1993) *The European City* (Oxford: Blackwell).
Brand, U. (2005) *Die politische Form der Globalisierung: Politische Institutionen und soziale Kräfte im internationalisierten Staat*, professorial dissertation (Kassel).
Brand, U. / Görg, C. (2003) *Postfordistische Naturverhältnisse: Konflikte um genetische Ressourcen und die Internationalisierung des Staates* (Münster: Westfälisches Dampfboot).
Brand, U. / Görg, C. / Wissen, M. (2010) 'Second-order Condensations of Societal Power Relations. Environmental Politics and the Internationalization of the State from a Neo-Poulantzian Perspective', *Antipode. A Radical Journal of Geography*, vol. 43, no. 1, 149-175.

Brenner, N. (1998) 'Between fixity and motion: Accumulation, territorial organization and the historical geography of spatial scales', *Environment and Planning D: Society and Space*, vol. 16, no. 4, 459-481.
Castells, M. (1996) *The Rise of the Network Society: The Information Age: Economy, Society and Culture* (Cambridge / Oxford: Blackwell).
Demirović, A. (1987) *Nicos Poulantzas. Eine kritische Auseinandersetzung* (Hamburg: Argument-Verlag).
Elias, N. (1939) *The Civilizing Process* (Oxford: Blackwell, 1982).
Görg, C. (2003) *Regulation der Naturverhältnisse: Zu einer kritischen Theorie der ökologischen Krise* (Münster: Westfälisches Dampfboot).
Harvey, D. (1982) *The Limits to Capital* (London: Verso, 1999).
Harvey, D. (1985) 'The Geopolitics of Capitalism', in Gregory, D. / Urry, J. (eds.) *Social Relations and Spatial Structures* (New York: St. Martin's Press) 128-163.
Harvey, D. (1990) *The Condition of Postmodernity* (Malden: Blackwell).
Harvey, D. (1996) *Justice, Nature and the Geography of Difference* (Cambridge: Blackwell).
Hirsch, J. (1990) *Kapitalismus ohne Alternative? Materialistische Gesellschaftstheorie und Möglichkeiten einer sozialistischen Politik heute* (Hamburg: VSA-Verlag).
Hirsch, J. (2001) 'Die Internationalisierung des Staates: Anmerkungen zu einigen aktuellen Fragen der Staatstheorie', in Hirsch, J. / Jessop, B. / Poulantzas, N. *Die Zukunft des Staates* (Hamburg: VSA-Verlag) 101-138.
Jessop, B. (1985) *Nicos Poulantzas. Marxist Theory and Political Strategy* (Basingtoke: Macmillan).
Jessop, B. (2002) 'Time and Space in the Globalization of Capital and their Implications for State Power', *Rethinking Marxism*, vol. 14, no. 1, 97-117.
Läpple, D. (1991) 'Essay über den Raum. Für ein gesellschaftswissenschaftliches Raumkonzept', in Häußermann, H. et al. (eds.) *Stadt und Raum. Soziologische Analysen* (Pfaffenweiler: Centaurus-Verlag) 157-207.
Lefebvre, H. (1974) *The Production of Space* (Oxford: Blackwell, 1991).
Lefebvre, H. (1978) 'Space and the State', in Brenner, N. / Jessop, B. / Jones, M. / MacLeod, G. (eds.) *State/Space: A Reader* (Malden: Blackwell, 2003) 83-100.
Link-Wieczorek, U. (1996) 'Zeit und Ewigkeit: 2. Systematisch-theologisch', in *Evangelisches Kirchenlexikon*, vol. 4 (Göttingen) 1367-1370.
Massey, D. (1994) *Space, Place and Gender* (Minneapolis: Univ. of Minnesota Press).
Smith, N. (1984) *Uneven Development: Nature, Capital and the Production of Space*, 2. ed. (Oxford: Blackwell, 1990).
Smith, N. (1995) 'Remaking scale: Competition and cooperation in prenational and postnational Europe', in Eskelinen, H. / Snickars, F. (eds.) *Competitive European Peripheries* (Berlin: Springer) 59-74.
Soja, E. W. (1989) *Postmodern Geographies: The Reassertion of Space in Critical Social Theory* (London: Verso).
Swyngedouw, E. (1997) 'Neither Global nor Local: "Glocalization" and the Politics of Scale', in Cox, K. R. (ed.) *Spaces of Globalization. Reasserting the Power of the Local* (New York: Guilford Press) 137-166.

EUROPEAN STATEHOOD

HANS-JÜRGEN BIELING

There can be no doubt that forms of 'coordination' of the economic policies of different states have proved to be a contemporary necessity (various international institutions, including the EEC). But these institutional forms do not in fact amount to apparatuses supplanting the national states or superimposed on them. And the reasons for this include one that we have not so far touched on, i.e. that these economic interventions by the state are not, as a well-established tradition would have it, neutral technical functions imposed by the necessities of a "production" that is itself considered as neutral in character. The economic functions of the state are in fact expressions of its overall political role in exploitation and class domination; they are by their nature articulated with its repressive and ideological roles in the field of class struggle of a social formation, which brings us back once more to the points made above. It is impossible to separate the various interventions of the state and their aspects, in such a way as to envisage the possibility of an effective transfer of its "economic functions" to supranational or super-state apparatuses, while the national state would retain only a repressive or ideological role; at the very most, there is sometimes a delegation in the exercise of these functions. (Poulantzas, CCC: 81)

Introduction

Nicos Poulantzas did not deal with European integration in depth. The chapter on 'The Internationalization of Capitalist Relations and the Nation State' in *Classes in Contemporary Capitalism* (CCC) is an exception. Here, Poulantzas discusses Ernest Mandel's theoretical reflections (1970) on the integration process. Responding to Jean Jacques Servan-Schreiber's book *The American Challenge* (1968), Mandel argued that the accelerated integration of capital in Western Europe had given rise to the possibility that a supra-national state would form. Mandel declined to forecast whether this potential would ever become relevant politically. In his view, only an economic crisis could reveal this. There would be either a dominantly national or a dominantly European strategy for overcoming it (1970: 84ff.).

Poulantzas objected to this on empirical grounds. He argued that there was no basis for talking about an independent European integration of productive and financial capital given the quantity and structure of US foreign direct investment (CCC: 50ff.). Poulantzas also objected to Mandel on the grounds of his state and integration theory, claiming that even a strong degree of capital integration does not automatically trigger the supranationalization of state functions. In contrast to Mandel's instrumentalist view of the state, Poulantzas has a much more comprehensive understanding. He sees the state as a specific material condensation of social relations of forces (SPS: 128). Not only does the state play the role of articulating and executing capital's collective interest in valorization it also has to meet general requirements of societal reproduction. In so doing, it ensures a minimum of social cohesion and political legitimacy. Particularly in times of acute social conflicts, the national state remains indispensable for Poulantzas. Despite the internationalization of capital, it continues to serve as an arena for the production of social consent and compromise (CCC: 78ff.).

In hindsight, this has proven to be a fairly useful perspective. Yet it was obviously shaped by specific historical conditions such as crisis tendencies in the world economy and the upsurge of socialist movements and parties, which largely remained focused on the national state. Since then, economic, social, and geopolitical conditions have changed considerably, and so has the quality and social character of European integration (cf. Bieling/Steinhilber 2000). Evidence of this is, first, the push for integration in the 1980s and 90s, which centred on the single market project and the Economic and Monetary Union (EMU); second, the repeated rounds of enlargement that have expanded the EU from originally six to 27 member states; and third, a number of revisions, from the mid-1980s, to contracts at the European level, which have 'communitized' political regulation.

The question remains whether Poulantzas's perspective is still useful for understanding European integration. I will argue that this is indeed the case. There are basically two approaches to integration theory that borrow from Poulantzas. The first is based on his empirical analyses and his theory of imperialism, and focuses on the developmental dynamics of US-dominated transatlantic capitalism (cf. Panitch/Gindin 2003). The second connects to his state theoretical concepts at a more abstract level and argues that there are supra-national forms of statehood today (cf. Demirović 2000; Bieling 2001).

It is difficult, however, to relate the two approaches to each other, let alone to combine them. The former reduces the EU to a merely regional power centre within the transnational US empire, whilst the latter emphasizes the EU's autonomous role vis-à-vis its member states as well as the US. Yet it may be possible to make productive use of this divergence. It could help us clarify the state and integration theory – both at the conceptual level and with regard to research strategy.

1. US imperialism and European integration

The first theoretical approach (which follows Poulantzas rather closely) largely avoids the question of the statehood of supra-national institutions. Instead, it emphasizes the analysis of dominant patterns of economic reproduction and inter-state power relations in the international political economy. This approach is distinctive because it portrays economic processes and intergovernmental relations as expressions of social (power) relations. This way, it departs from the state-centred approach of the realist school.[1] Leo Panitch and Sam Gindin (2003), among others, emphasize the advantages of grounding an analysis of the state in social theory. They question the assumption that there is a necessary trade-off between the power of the state and the power of transnational capital. This line of argument explicitly targets the 'varieties of capitalism' approach of Peter Hall and David Soskice (2001), but also goes against (neo-)functionalist, institutionalist, and liberal-intergovernmentalist approaches (see Bieling/Lerch 2005) that conceptualize the relationship between the market and the state as a form of competition between two separate spheres. Such approaches neither allow for giving precise accounts of the developmental dynamics of political-economic structures, nor of social and, more specifically, of transnational power relations (cf. Apeldoorn et al. 2003). When Panitch (2000: 8f.) draws upon Poulantzas, he looks at the interweaved nature of economic and political power in capitalism: 'Poulantzas' outstanding contribution was to explain: (i) that when multinational capital penetrates a host social formation, it arrives not merely as abstract "direct foreign investment", but as a transformative social force within the country; (ii) that the interaction of foreign capital with domestic capital leads to the dissolution of the national bourgeoisie as a coherent concentration of class interests; (iii) but far from

---

1 ' Some of the core assumptions of the 'realist' school are (a) that thanks to the absence of a central coercive power, the international system is characterized by anarchy; (b) that states are the most important actors in this system; (c) that the foreign policies of any state are primarily influenced by the international system; and (d) that there is a zero-sum-game over power, influence, and resources among states' (Scherrer 2000: 14, translated).

losing importance, the host state actually becomes responsible for taking charge of the complex relations of international capital to the domestic bourgeoisie, in the context of class struggles and political and ideological forms which remain distinctively national even as they express themselves within a world conjuncture.'

Panitch (2000: 9f.) and Panitch/Gindin (2003: 118ff.) also take up Poulantzas's reformulation of arguments found in Marxist theories of imperialism. This does not so much hold for concepts that refer back to Lenin (1964), namely those of the 'imperialist chain' and 'uneven development'. These do not sufficiently take interdependence in global relations of dominance and dependence into account, and over-emphasize inter-state rivalry. Both Poulantzas, in *Classes in Contemporary Capitalism* (CCC), and Panitch/Gindin (2003) avoid such one-sided conceptions. Among others, they refer to Karl Kautsky's hypothesis of 'ultra-imperialism' (1914: 922, translated), i.e., to the assumption that there is a common politics of exploitation and a 'holy alliance of imperialists'. In other words, they balance Lenin's assumption of inter-imperialist rivalry with reference to Kautsky's assumption of ultra-imperialist cooperation. However, theoretical reflections based on Kautsky, in what is almost an inverted mirror-image of Lenin, tend to focus in a one-sided manner on inter-state agreement. Accordingly, they overlook the contradictions, conflicts, and asymmetric power relations that are equally characteristic of the relations between imperialist states (cf. CCC: 38ff.).

As a consequence, it is not helpful to just base one's analysis on *either* Lenin *or* Kautsky. We need to grasp the transformations in the imperialist chain, especially the processes of economic (inter-)penetration and the modification of political forms of control, in order to better understand the patterns of competition and interdependence as well as conflict and cooperation. Following Poulantzas, Panitch and Gindin (2003; 2004; 2005) have demonstrated that the dynamic of internationalization is primarily organized by US capital. This applies to economic relations narrowly conceived, i.e., trade and foreign direct investment, but also to class relations and political relations of power. US capital does not need to be immediately present in the 'power bloc' of its subaltern European partners in order to assert its interests. It suffices if there are domestic fractions of capital introducing the interests of US capital into domestic political bargaining because they want to get access to US markets (CCC: 75).

Thirty years later, Panitch and Gindin take up this argument and some of the other points made by Poulantzas (e.g., the one about distinctive features of the national arenas of class struggle) (2003; cf. Panitch 2000:

8ff.). They agree that US-dominated 'Atlantic capitalism'[2] constitutes the central analytical frame of reference for understanding the progress of European integration, but also its crises and phases of stagnation. However, Panitch and Gindin (2003: 14) are also critical of Poulantzas. They believe his analyses need to be amended and expanded both at the empirical and the theoretical level: 'Yet Poulantzas's admirable concern to demonstrate that globalization was not about "the virtual disappearance of national state power" in Europe led him to consider American capital primarily in terms of its effects on European social formations and states. He did not examine in any detail the forces within the American economy that were impelling foreign direct investment in Europe and the contradictions this represented for American capitalism. Even more crucially, he also failed to examine the modalities and mechanisms of American neoimperialism as it was expressed in and through the apparatuses of the American state and the international institutions it dominated'.

Gindin's analyses (2003; 2004; 2005) transcend Poulantzas insofar as they try to gain a more precise understanding of the imperial or hegemonic practices of the US state. Above all, Poulantzas (CCC: 71ff.) asserted that there are unequal power relations between US capital and the Western European 'interior bourgeoisie'[3] subordinated to it. In contrast, Panitch and Gindin argue that US direct investment is certainly important for understanding the imperial state, but that there are also other mechanisms for ensuring domination. According to them, these need to be analysed carefully, especially the unique position of the US in the international financial structure (Panitch/Gindin 2004) and the integration of European capital into the transnational American empire (Panitch 2000).

Panitch and Gindin (2004; 2005: 107ff.) demonstrate how the US succeeded in integrating other capitalist societies into its own financial and monetary circuit of reproduction and into their system of control after World War II. During the era of Bretton Woods this happened mainly through international aid. The US not only launched the Marshall Plan. It also tolerated the under-valuation of other capitalist currencies,

---

2   Kees van der Pijl (1984) even talks about an 'Atlantic ruling class'.
3   Poulantzas (CCC: 71f.) defines the *'interior bourgeoisie'* by distinguishing it from the 'national bourgeoisie' and the 'comprador bourgeoisie'. The national bourgeoisie possesses relative autonomy in economic and political-ideological terms by virtue of being a 'fraction of the indigenous bourgeoisie'. It represents itself as a single unit. In contrast, the comprador bourgeoisie lacks its 'own base for capital accumulation' and is little more than an 'intermediary of foreign imperialist capital'. The 'internal bourgeoisie' occupies the middle ground. It is characterized by possessing a basis for accumulation *sui generis*, but is also dependent on the dominant international capital in a number of economic and political ways (cf. Kannankulam/Wissel 2004).

gave military and technological aid to its allies and stimulated European integration. After the end of Bretton Woods and with the emergence of the 'Dollar-Wall Street regime' (Gowan 1999), the parameters of control changed. The primary goal was no longer to give financial and military support to the allies, but to ensure that there was a share of internationally disposable capital available for the modernization of the US economy, This was achieved by relying on the US Dollar and Wall Street, i.e., on the global reserve currency and the dominant global financial centre.

Accordingly, the *modus operandi* of the dollar-centred international financial system and of global structures of production are tightly coupled. This is also highlighted by the second mechanism through which US domination is reproduced: the affirmative references to the US made by leading representatives of European and Asian capital. In order to emphasize the economic, political, and cultural integration of managers and other executives, Panitch (2000: 16ff.) refers to Susan Strange (1989).[4] She argues that even in Europe many leading cadre and professionals regard themselves as 'semicitizens' of a transnational American empire that is not defined in territorial terms: 'As in Rome, citizenship is not limited to a master race and the empire contains a mix of citizens with full legal and political rights, semicitizens and noncitizens like Rome's slave population. Many of the semicitizens walk the streets of Rio or of Bonn, of London or Madrid, shoulder to shoulder with the noncitizens; no one can necessarily tell them apart by color or race or even dress. [...] They include many people employed by the large transnational corporations operating in the transnational production structure [...]. They include the people employed in transnational banks [...]. They often include many academics in medicine, natural sciences, and social studies like management and economics who look to U.S. professional associations and to U.S. universities as the peer group in whose eyes they wish to shine and to excel. They include people in the press and media for whom U.S. technology and U.S. examples have shown the way, changing established organizations and institutions' (Strange 1989: 170f.).

However, Strange did not explain systematically what the significance of different transnationally oriented forces was for the reproduction of the American empire. Drawing on authors such as Shaw (2000), Hudson (2003) and Gowan (1999), Panitch and Gindin transcend Strange insofar as they seek to find a more precise explanation for the political-economic

---

4   Panitch (2000: 17) is well aware of the theoretical differences between Poulantzas's neo-Marxist state theory and Strange's more neo-Weberian approach. He emphasizes that in contrast to Poulantzas, Strange does not conceptualize state power as class-based, changing, and decentralized, but as autonomous, static, and centralized.

foundations and developmental dynamics of transatlantic capitalism. They present the mechanisms of the socio-economic and political-strategic reproduction of the transatlantic network of power as multi-faceted and complex. With regard to European integration and the EU, however, their analysis remains one-dimensional. They refrain from looking closely at the internal dynamics of the integration process, that is, the politico-economic interests and strategies of dominant states and fractions of capital, as well as the institutional and regulatory setting of the European economy. As a consequence, Panitch and Gindin (2003: 131) arrive at a simplistic conclusion: 'transatlantic integration' has turned the EU 'into an agency of neoliberal discipline, regardless of whatever social policies and human rights issues were on its agenda'.

Panitch and Gindin are not alone in understanding the EU as a sphere of reproduction of the transnational US empire (see for example Hirsch 2005: 185ff.). However, a number of authors in Critical International Political Economy are questioning the notion of US hegemonic control (e.g., Gowan 2003). They assert that the nature of US hegemony has changed due to a dual structural rupture: (a) the collapse of Bretton Woods and (b) the erosion of the bipolar world order. US administrations initially succeeded in stabilizing transatlantic relations of forces in the course of the transition of the US from international creditor to international debtor, and the corresponding transformation from integral to minimal hegemony (cf. Cafruny 1990). It is doubtful, though, whether this mode of stabilization will prove sustainable under the conditions of the 'new world order', the tendency of the US towards imperial overstretch, and the increased instability of exchange rates and financial markets.

The process of European integration has taken place parallel to the weakening of US hegemony. It accelerated strongly from the 1980s – through market and monetary integration, as well as a number of contractual revisions. The latter enlarged step-by-step the number of policy fields under supranational jurisdiction. This process started with the Single European Act (SEA), the EU treaties of Maastricht, Amsterdam and Nice, and went all the way to the emergence of the option of a constitutional treaty (cf. Bieling/Deppe 2003).[5] The political constitutionalization of common,

5   The repeated enlargements of the EU are another important instance of the revitalization of European integration. It is debatable, of course, whether the EU has been strengthened or weakened economically by the respective rounds of enlargement. What is not debatable, however, is the fact that enlarging it to currently 27 member states has increased the EU's internal heterogeneity – in socio-economic, political, and cultural terms. This in turn has made (socio-)political processes of bargaining and decision-making significantly more complicated.

competitive market relations, which are regulated in a uniform fashion, is not just a product of intergovernmental bargaining. It also a result of transnational capitalist strategies. Regarding the integration process, the US economy is still the model aspired to. This is because US capital disposes of multiple ways of exercising influence in the European decision-making process. At the same time, however, the regional cohesion of European capital has increased significantly (cf. Holman/Pijl 2003). This is revealed by the existence of corporate networks and of strategic planning bodies such as the European Rounds Table of Industrialists (ERT). In other words, European transnational capital has created its own, politically independent fora of representation.

2. Europe en route to statehood?

The increasing autonomy of European integration is also the basis for the second way of conceptualizing European statehood that is inspired by Poulantzas. It is based on the assumption that the acceleration of integration also reveals limits to external control. After World War II, the capacities of the US for coordination and control were seen as multi-layered and far-reaching. The US fulfilled the role of a continental hegemonic power by giving numerous vital boosts to European integration (cf. Ziltener 1999: 84ff.) that propelled the latter into a direction compatible with US interests. Examples are the Marshall Plan, the European Payments Union (EPU), and NATO.

However, the main motivation for the states participating in the integration process from the start was increasing their strength through 'communitization'. Following Albert Statz (1989: 16), the central function of European integration can be described as follows: 'Regional integration within the framework of the EC can be [...] seen as a relative solution to the contradiction between the internationalization of the valorization of capital (trade, investment, financial relations) and the narrow limits of national markets and the boundaries of national states. The "territorial incongruence" of the economy and politics in the international system requires the expansion of markets as well as the internationalization of state functions. It can be overcome partially in a regional context.'

Initially, both the European Coal and Steel Community (ECSC) and the European Economic Community's (EEC) subsequent plan for a customs union represented rather modest attempts at bridging the territorial incongruence between the economic and the political space. The projects of the 1980s and 1990s (Single Market, EMU), however, were of a different nature. First, they aimed at the creation of an integrated, not merely liberalized, European economic space in which non-tariff barriers to trade (technical and product standards, tax rules, etc.) would be largely abolished. This was supposed to be achieved through minimal harmonization and the principle of mutual recognition. Second, the steps taken towards economic integration corresponded to a process of contractual constitutionalization. Political competencies and national sovereignty rights were transferred to the supranational level, which also meant that they were partly removed from democratic control by national parliaments. An example of this is the expansion of qualified majority voting in the Council of Ministers. This was accompanied, third, by a partial shift in focus in terms of political discourses and activities: from the 1980s, the EU has become a more important arena of political activity and struggle for social (or civil society) forces, mostly for (business) associations, but also for trade unions and NGOs.

These developments can also be read as reflecting the superimposition of a European economic space, a European mode of regulation and nascent forms of a transnational civil society on national models of capitalism (cf. Bieling 2001; Demirović 2000). In other words, 'communitization' gives rise to elements of a European state. However, this rudimentary form of statehood disposes only of limited financial resources (e.g., the Agricultural Fund, the Regional Fund) that can be used for compensatory payments aimed at strengthening cross-border social cohesion. Supranational state apparatuses such as the European Commission, the European Court of Justice (ECJ) or the European Central Bank (ECB) are instead first and foremost core elements of a new type of technocratic regime, i.e., of a 'complex institutionalized structure of autonomized governmental activity' (Hueglin 1997: 95). This regime aims to promote competition between firms and national modes of regulation within the common economic space (cf. Ziltener 1999: 138ff.). Stephen Gill (1998: 5) refers to this as a 'new constitutionalism' aiming to divorce the liberalizing dynamic of economic policy from overall political accountability. The purpose is to subject governments to the discipline of markets and competition: 'New constitutionalism is the politico-legal dimension of the wider discourse of disciplinary neoliberalism. Central objectives in this discourse are security of property rights and investor freedoms, and market discipline on the state and on labour to secure 'credibility' in the eyes of private investors, e.g. those in both the global currency and capital markets'.

The political process of constitutionalization – above all the Single European Act (SEA) and the treaties of Mastricht, Amsterdam and Nice – has strengthened the European institutional system to such an extent that it is appropriate to speak of emerging European statehood. The *acquis communautaire* now encompasses a very large array of common and binding regulations. Consequently, it can be assumed that there is a European level of the capitalist state. The latter can be looked at from a Poulantzasian angle: According to Poulantzas, the capitalist state should 'not be regarded as an intrinsic entity [...], *it is rather a relationship of forces, or more precisely the material condensation of such a relationship among classes and class fractions, such as this is expressed within the State in a necessarily specific form*' (SPS: 128f.).

Poulantzas rejected analyses that saw the state either as a more or less neutral instrument or object that could be conquered and used by influential social (class-)actors, or as a subject hovering above society that steered the latter in an autonomous fashion: 'In locating the State as the material condensation of a relationship of forces, we must also grasp it as a *strategic field and process* of intersecting power networks, which both articulate and exhibit mutual contradictions and displacements. [...] At this level, to be sure, the policy is still decipherable not only as a strategic calculation, but even more as the result of a conflictual co-ordination of explicit and divergent micro-policies and tactics, and as the national formulation of a coherent global project.' (136)

Poulantzas's emphasis on the flexibility of state arenas as well as forms and practices of institutionalization allows us to avoid confining his state theory to the national level. However, simply transferring 'national' concepts would be problematic because of the fragmentation of civil society structures and public sphere. The condensation of social relations of forces in transnational space is a highly complex, selective and contradictory process.

Following Ulrich Brand and Christoph Görg (2003: 222ff.), European statehood can be seen as a 'second-order condensation'.[6] However, they assume the structural primacy of the national level of regulation, implying that international condensation is nothing but the ensemble of national processes of condensation. This analytical perspective, which largely focuses on intergovernmental bargaining processes, is probably adequate for most international institutions. Within the EU, however, condensation is also based on other processes of mediation that are supported by nascent forms of a transnational civil society (cf. Bieling 2001).

'New constitutionalism' is not just organized through neoliberal economic modernization strategies on the part of national governments, but also through transnational forces – be they corporations, capital groups

---

6   Michael Felder (2001: 93) makes a similar point. For him, international regulatory complexes represent forms of 'secondary interweaving'.

or business associations. The latter may not be able to avoid involving the governments of major EU member states in the formulation and implementation of their strategies, but they also frequently address the Commission and the European parliament directly in order to influence the European political agenda.

3. European statehood? Open research questions for state theory

The two theoretical approaches to European integration described here show that Poulantzas's analytical tools are certainly still useful. However, the more they are removed from their original historical context, the more they cease to form a theoretical framework and become a mere heuristic source of inspiration. This is also revealed by the fact that the two approaches diverge significantly regarding their theoretical assumptions and empirical conclusions:

• The first approach to the theoretical conceptualization of European statehood chooses a transatlantic analytical perspective. It tends to deny that European institutions exhibit features of statehood. Panitch and Gindin (2003; 2005) base their arguments on a territorialized conception of the state that at least implicitly assumes a hegemonically produced spatial congruence between the people, state power and national territory. With one exception, of course: the US state is capable of establishing a transnational empire, of penetrating the economic, social and political spaces of other societies, and of incorporating national power blocs into the empire (cf. Panitch 2000; Panitch/Gindin 2005).

• The second approach assumes a perspective internal to European integration. It argues that European statehood is emerging (Felder 2001: 193ff.). The state is viewed as the ensemble of political, legal, and administrative forms of regulation that have become at least partially decoupled from national-territorial bonds. Some authors talk about 'second-order condensation' in order to capture this partial decoupling (Brand/Görg 2003: 222). In this view, elements of supranational statehood emerge as a result of a transfer of sovereignty that is partly intergovernmental and partly transnational, yet always mediated by hegemony and highly selective.

To conclude, I will take the differences between the two approaches as an instructive provocation. I will try to make use of the disagreements between both camps by refining, on their grounds, contemporary conceptions of state theory. In my view, there are three issues that ought to be looked at more closely:

First, analyses grounded in Poulantzas's work generally assume that the national, European and global patterns of reproduction are not mutually exclusive, but form components of a contradictory yet unified whole (cf. Bieling/Beckmann/Deppe 2003: 10f.). Furthermore, it is almost certainly the case that a transnational constellation of control has been emerging from the 1980s, and that the European arena has become more and more important (cf. Röttger 1997: 119ff.). However, there is disagreement as to how far-reaching this process is, and what forces actually determine integration. There could be a productive turn to this disagreement. This would lie in defining criteria for the analysis of transnational relations of forces in a precise and systematic fashion and in applying these to case studies.

Second, it seems plausible to treat international institutions such as the EU as 'second-order condensations'. However, as soon as authors try to explain what that means, their views diverge. In this respect, such efforts resemble attempts to determine transnational relations of forces. Accordingly, some argue that processes of condensation are primarily being organized by national states, i.e., they constitute inter- or transgovernmental processes (cf. Hirsch 2005). Others emphasize the crucial role of transnational forces. From a neo-Gramscian, transnational perspective, politically organized transnational capital is the leading force in the process of supranational condensation (cf. Holman 2004). Others again view complex, strategically selective networks as important mediating links in the emergence of European statehood (cf. Felder 2001; Jessop 2004).

Third, Poulantzasian approaches to state theory generally assume that transformations at the national level are being organized and given a neoliberal direction at the European level of regulation (cf. Ziltener 1999). However, beyond this generic function of European statehood, they leave (de-)regulation ill-defined. This may be due to the fact that they are based on a traditional conception of the national state: one in political, legal, and administrative state forms are tightly bound up with one another, and where there is, thanks to civil society and the welfare state, a relatively high degree of social cohesion. However, it is evident that these state forms in the EU are diverging. In other words, the emergent supranational statehood is fragmented and developed unevenly. It is supported by a transnational yet incomplete set of laws and regulations (cf. Buckel 2003), and there are only limited administrative apparatuses, weak forms of democratic participation and control, and restricted financial resources targeting social cohesion.

The issues discussed imply that Poulantzas's work on social theory and state theory remains instructive with regard to analysing and defining (1) national, European, and global relations of forces, (2) the processes of their political-institutional condensation in the EU, and (3) their specific properties. Poulantzas views the state as a complex strategic terrain whose social and institutional structures are not static or pre-given but constantly changing. This seems to apply to developments in Europe. Ultimately, however, it is obvious that current processes of state transformation are taking a course that transcends Poulantzas.

References

Apeldoorn, B. v. / Overbeek, H. / Ryner, M. (2003) 'Theorizing European Integration. The Case for a Transnational Critical Approach', in Cafruny, A. W. / Ryner, M. (eds.) *A Ruined Fortress? Neoliberal Hegemony and Transformation in Europe* (Lanham: Rowman & Littlefield) 17-46.
Bieling, H.-J. (2001) 'Staat, Zivilgesellschaft und New Governance in der Europäischen Union', *Kurswechsel*, vol. 16, no. 3, 26-35.
Bieling, H.-J. / Steinhilber, J. (eds.) (2000) *Die Konfiguration Europas. Dimensionen einer kritischen Integrationstheorie* (Münster: Westfälisches Dampfboot).
Bieling, H.-J. / Beckmann, M. / Deppe, F. (2003) '"Euro-Kapitalismus". Begriffliche Provokation oder heuristische Analysekonzeption', in Bieling, H.-J. / Beckmann, M. / Deppe, F. (eds.) *Euro- Kapitalismus und globale politische Ökonomie* (Hamburg: VSA-Verlag) 7-17.
Bieling, H.-J. / Deppe, F. (2003) 'Die neue europäische Ökonomie und die Transformation von Staatlichkeit', in Jachtenfuchs, M. / Kohler-Koch, B. (eds.) *Europäische Integration* (Opladen: Leske + Budrich) 513-539.
Bieling, H.-J. / Lerch, M. (eds.) (2005) *Theorien der europäischen Integration* (Wiesbaden: VS-Verlag).
Brand, U. / Görg, C. (2003): *Postfordistische Naturverhältnisse. Konflikte um genetische Ressourcen und die Internationalisierung des Staates* (Münster: Westfälisches Dampfboot).
Buckel, S. (2003) 'Global "Non-State". Überlegungen für eine materialistische Theorie des transnationalen Rechts', in Buckel, S. / Dackweiler, R.-M. / Noppe, R. (eds.) *Formen und Felder politischer Intervention* (Münster: Westfälisches Dampfboot) 50-68.
Buckel, S. (2005) *Subjektivierung & Kohäsion. Zur Rekonstruktion einer materialistischen Theorie des Rechts*, Ph.D. thesis, Faculty of Social Sciences, Goethe University (Frankfurt am Main).
Cafruny, A. (1990) 'A Gramscian Concept of Declining Hegemony. States of US Power and the Evolution of International Economic Relations', in Rapkin, D. P. (ed.) *World Leadership and Hegemony* (Boulder: Rienner) 97-118.
Demirović, A. (2000) 'Erweiterter Staat und europäische Integration', in Bieling, H.-J. / Steinhilber, J. (eds.) *Die Konfiguration Europas. Dimensionen einer kritischen Integrationstheorie* (Münster: Westfälisches Dampfboot) 51-72.
Felder, M. (2001) *Die Transformation von Staatlichkeit. Europäisierung und Bürokratisierung in der Organisationsgesellschaft* (Wiesbaden: Westdeutscher Verlag).

Gill, S. (1998) 'European Governance and New Constitutionalism. Economic and Monetary Union and Alternatives to Disciplinary Neoliberalism in Europe', *New Political Economy*, vol. 3, no. 1, 5-26.

Gowan, P. (1999) *The Global Gamble. Washington's Faustian Bid for World Dominance* (London: Verso).

Gowan, P. (2003) 'U.S. Hegemony Today', *Monthly Review*, vol. 55, no. 3, 30-50.

Hall, P. / Soskice, D. (2001) 'An Introduction to Varieties of Capitalism', in Hall, P. / Soskice, D. (eds.) *Varieties of Capitalism. The Institutional Foundations of Comparative Advantage* (Oxford: Oxford Univ. Press) 1-68.

Hirsch, J. (2005) *Materialistische Staatstheorie. Transformationsprozesse des kapitalistischen Staatensystems* (Hamburg: VSA-Verlag).

Holman, O. (2004) 'Asymmetrical regulation and multidimensional governance in the European Union', *Review of International Political Economy*, vol. 11, no. 4, 714-735.

Holman, O. / Pijl, K. v. d. (2003) 'Structure and Process in Transnational European Business', in Cafruny, A. / Ryner, M. (eds.) *A Ruined Fortress? Neoliberal Hegemony and Transformation in Europe* (Lanham: Rowman & Littlefield) 71-94.

Hudson, M. (2003) *Super Imperialism: The Origins and Fundamentals of US World Dominance* 2nd ed. (London: Pluto Press).

Hueglin, T. (1997) 'Regieren in Europa als universalistisches Projekt', in Wolf, K. D. (ed.) *Projekt Europa im Übergang? Probleme, Modelle und Strategien des Regierens in der Europäischen Union* (Baden-Baden: Nomos) 91-107.

Jessop, B. (2004) 'The European Union and Recent Transformations in Statehood', in Puntscher Riekmann, S. / Mokre, M. / Latzer, M. (eds.) *Transformations of Statehood from a European Perspective* (Frankfurt am Main: Campus Verlag) 75-94.

Kannankulam, J. / Wissel, J. (2004) 'Innere Bourgeoisie', in Haug, W. F. (ed.) *Historisch-kritisches Wörterbuch des Marxismus*, vol. 6/II (Hamburg: Argument-Verlag) 1135-1142.

Kautsky, K. (1914) 'Der Imperialismus', *Die Neue Zeit*, vol. 32, no. 21, 908-922.

Lenin, V. I. (1964) 'Imperialism, the Highest State of Capitalism', *V.I. Lenin Collected Works*, vol. 22, 185-304.

Mandel, E. (1970) *Europe versus America? Contradictions of Imperialism* (London: New Left Books).

Panitch, L. (2000) 'The New Imperial State', *New Left Review*, vol. 1, no. II.2, 5-21.

Panitch, L. / Gindin, S. (2003) 'American Imperialism and Eurocapitalism: The Making of Neoliberal Globalization', *Studies in Political Economy*, vol. 25, no. 71/72, 7-38.

Panitch, L. / Gindin, S. (2004) 'Finance and American Empire', in Panitch, L. / Leys, C. (eds.) *The Empire Reloaded. Socialist Register 2005* (London: Merlin Press) 46-81.

Panitch, L. / Gindin, S. (2005) 'Superintending Global Capital', *New Left Review*, vol. 6, no. II.35, 101-123.

Pijl, K. v. d. (1984) *The Making of an Atlantic Ruling Class* (London: Verso).

Röttger, B. (1997) *Neoliberale Globalisierung und eurokapitalistische Regulation. Die politische Konstitution des Marktes* (Münster: Westfälisches Dampfboot).

Scherrer, C. (2000) 'Global Governance: Vom fordistischen Trilateralismus zum neoliberalen Konstitutionalismus', *Prokla*, vol. 30, no. 118, 13-38.

Servan-Schreiber, J.-J. (1968) *The American Challenge* (London: Hamilton).

Shaw, M. (2000) *Theory of the Global State. Globality as an unfinished Revolution* (Cambridge: Cambridge Univ. Press).

Statz, A. (1989) 'Die Entwicklung der westeuropäischen Integration. Ein Problemaufriss'; in Deppe, F. / Huffschmid, J. / Weiner, K.-P. (eds.) *1992 – Projekt Europa. Politik und Ökonomie in der Europäischen Gemeinschaft* (Köln: Pahl-Rugenstein) 13-38.

Strange, S. (1989) 'Toward a Theory of Transnational Empire', in Czempiel, E.-O. / Rosenau, J. N. (eds.) *Global Changes and Theoretical Challenges. Approaches to World Politics for the 1990s* (Lexington: Lexington Books) 161-176.

Ziltener, P. (1999) *Strukturwandel der europäischen Integration. Die Europäische Union und die Veränderung von Staatlichkeit* (Münster: Westfälisches Dampfboot).

THE TRANSNATIONALIZATION OF THE BOURGEOISIE AND THE NEW NETWORKS OF POWER

JENS WISSEL

In recent decades, the crisis of Fordism has called into question many of the allegedly fixed assumptions concerning the constitution of societies and the role of the national state. For some, the national state is in a condition of progressive dissolution, whilst others still view it as the most important actor on the international stage. In turn there are those who point to a process of fundamental transformation. The conceptualization of its relationship to the processes commonly referred to as 'globalization' is particularly contentious.

There seems to be broad agreement that globalization has fundamentally altered the national state's conditions of existence (cf. Hirsch 2002; Jessop 2002; Candeias 2004). In the 1970s, Nicos Poulantzas wrote an article entitled *Internationalisation of Capitalist Relations and the Nation-State*.[1] He argued that the changing global constellation of power has internationalized and transformed the national state. By internationalization, he understood the emergence of a new inside/outside dialectic. He held that internationalization was not a process influencing the state from the outside, but a development internal to it.

Conflicts over the reconstitution of the economic and political world order reveal a transformation of the national state and the inside/outside dialectic within the world system. Thus, social scientists have begun to conceptualize this dialectic in different ways. Dualistic approaches do not recognize it at all, because they see societal spaces as being external to one another. At most, they assume that the inside and outside interact in a

---

1 Translators' note: This article was published as Part One of Classes in Contemporary Capitalism (CCC), but also separately in the journal *Economy and Society*, 1974, Vol.3, No. 2, 145-179. In our translation we refer to the version in CCC because it is closer to the German version used by the author than the other one.

reciprocal fashion. In approaches centred on the national state, the outside tends to disappear; in 'hyperglobalist' approaches, it is the inside, that is, the national state. None of these views are convincing: dualistic approaches do not do justice to the complexity of the situation, and the other two fail to grasp the interconnectedness of the processes in question because they restrict themselves to generalizing certain aspects.

In contrast, I will demonstrate that the national state *is being transformed* in the processes of globalization, and that its position in the world capitalist system is shifting. In doing so, I will draw on both Poulantzas's state theoretical as well as his class theoretical considerations concerning internationalization. After all, Poulantzas rejects dualistic models of explanation, and he refrains from reifying social spaces and relations. He sees neither the economy and politics nor national territoriality and internationalization as discrete units. Following him, it becomes possible to understand both the concurrence and interdependence of these different developments.

The questions Poulantzas dealt with in the 1970s (CCC: 38) are not substantially different from those discussed here. Nevertheless they reflect a situation in which the neoliberal turn and the new global constellation connected to it were not yet foreseeable. Therefore, connecting to Poulantzas in the 'here and now' requires us to develop his theory of internationalization further.

1. The state as a material condensation of relations of forces

Poulantzas views the state neither as an instrument in the hands of a particular class, nor as a neutral actor, let alone as the embodiment of the general interest. For Poulantzas, the state constitutes a strategic terrain. On this terrain, the bourgeoisie organizes itself. Constant competition divides the bourgeoisie in multiple ways, which means that it cannot directly become the class which is politically dominant. Thus, maintaining the structure of bourgeois society requires an entity that is able to act independently of the particular fractions of the ruling class.

The state is the terrain where the power bloc can be organized, and where the ruling class can forge a preliminary general interest from the heteronomous constellations of interests within the power bloc. However, not only are the 'relations of forces'[2] inside the power bloc condensed in the state, but also those of subaltern interests. The state achieves its autonomy vis-à-vis individual fractions of the power bloc in and through these processes, and it is therefore not merely a condensation, but a material condensation of relations of forces. This implies that social change is not reflected in the

---

2   See Wissel (2010) for a detailed discussion of the concept.

state in an unmediated fashion. The condensation is *material* in so far as the state represents a form of practice *sui generis*.³ However, changes in the social relations of forces do affect the state because the different social spheres are not external to one another. Thus the separation of politics from the economy should not to be understood in an essentialist way, but rather as '*the capitalist form of the presence of the political in the constitution and reproduction of the relations of production*' (SPS: 19).

Similarly, the relationship between national states and the process of internationalization should not be seen as external. Rather, national states are internationalized from within, so that it is no longer merely national relations of forces that are condensed, but increasingly also international ones. In short, the fact that struggles address themselves to the nation state does not imply that they are national struggles (cf. CCC: 70ff.). The crucial mediating step that allows us to conceptualize this process of interiorization is the analysis of class relations.⁴ The internationalization of class relations thus implies a corresponding shift of the power base within national states.

2. The emergence of the interior bourgeoisie

Poulantzas's arguments regarding the transformation of relations of forces in *State, Power, Socialism* are more abstract than his earlier class analytical investigations. The key difference is that the latter build on a more differentiated account of the relations of forces in the power bloc. According to Poulantzas, the differentiation between the national and the comprador bourgeoisie, which had been common in materialist discussions, no longer adequately described processes of internationalization (CCC: 72ff.).

Poulantzas argues that the national bourgeoisie is 'that fraction of the indigenous bourgeoisie which, on the basis of a certain type and degree of contradictions with foreign imperialist capital, occupies a relatively place position in the ideological and political structure, and exhibits in this way a characteristic unity' (71). Depending on circumstances, the national bourgeoisie either develops its own imperialist interests, or takes part in struggles for national liberation. It has its own material basis and develops

---

3   Cf. Foucault's lectures at the Collège de France (STP). On the necessary combination of Poulantzas's approach with a form-analytical approach see Hirsch/Kannankulam in this volume. Regarding problems and contradictions in Poulantzas's conceptualisation of the state cf. Wissel (2007: 84ff.).

4   It is plausible to assume that class relations play a unique role in processes of transnationalization (Altvater/Mahnkopf 1999: 267). However, Poulantzas's theory needs to be expanded to take into account that relations of production are overdetermined by sexualized and racialized social relations as well as struggles over society's relationship with the natural environment (cf. Buckel, Nowak and Lindner in this volume).

mostly autonomously. In contrast, the comprador bourgeoisie is merely a deputy bourgeoisie and as such entirely dependent on foreign capital. Yet this distinction, whose main purpose was to analyse the relations between the capitalist centres and peripheries, did not capture the newly emerged 'demarcation line' between the USA and Europe. In order to deal with this problem, Poulantzas developed the concept of the 'interior bourgeoisie', which denotes a new form of imperialism and inside/outside-relationship. By referring to the 'interior', Poulantzas tries to show that the interior bourgeoisie's reproductive base lies inside the national state – despite its entanglement with foreign capital. At the same time, the interior bourgeoisie is no longer a national bourgeoisie developing endogenously. Thus Poulantzas writes in *The Crisis of the Dictatorships* (CD: 43): 'The development of this domestic bourgeoisie coincides with the internationalization of labour processes and production, and with the internationalization of capital, in other words with the induced reproduction of the dominant relations or production actually within these various social formations'. The interior bourgeoisie is thus neither a merely externally determined bourgeoisie nor a self-centred national one. While it is dependent on US capital because the latter is embedded into it, 'significant contradictions thus exist between the interior bourgeoisie and American capital' (CCC: 72).

The crucial point is that with the concept of the 'interior bourgeoisie' Poulantzas captures the interiorization of internationalized relations of power within the national state. *Internationalization should be understood – and herein lies Poulantzas's innovation – as a process that takes place chiefly within national states.* 'It deeply affects the politics and institutional forms of these states by including them in a system of interconnections which is in no way confined to the play of external and mutual pressures between juxtaposed states and capitals. These states themselves take charge of the interest of the dominant imperialist capital in its development within the "national" social formation, i.e. in its complex relation of internationalization to the domestic bourgeoisie that it dominates. This system of interconnections does not encourage the constitution of effective supra-national or super-state institutional forms of agencies' (73).

3. From the internationalization to the transnationalization of capitalist relations of production

Poulantzas assumed that Europe was penetrated by US capital when he described the internationalization of the national state in the 1970s. He saw this as a new form of US imperialism. According to him, national power blocs in Europe 'can scarcely be located any more on a purely national level;

the imperialist states take charge not only of the interests of their domestic bourgeoisies, but just as much of the interests of the dominant imperialist capital and those of the other imperialist capitals, as these are articulated within the process of internationalization. On the other hand, however, these "foreign" capitals do not directly participate as such, i.e. as relatively autonomous social forces, in each of the power blocs involved' (CCC: 75).

These shifts are connected to a new international division of labour and the transformation of international class relations. Poulantzas saw these processes as taking place under the unambiguous leadership of US capital. US capital exports dominated in the 1970s, which is why he failed to apply the concept of the 'interior bourgeoisie' to the US itself. Alnasseri et al. comment (2001: 38; translated; cf. Kreile 2000: 276; Hübner 2003: 105): 'Inasmuch as the superiority of US capital is disappearing and the interpenetration of the centres of the triad is becoming mutual, this also applies to the American bourgeoisie'. In the US, there is now an interior bourgeoisie oriented towards transnationalized accumulation, which tends to lose its ideological and political autonomy due to the interiorization of foreign capital and transnational interpenetration. As a result, there has been an increase in the number of authors who deploy the concept of *transnationalization* (cf. Gill 1990; Bieling/Deppe 1996; Röttger 1997: 106ff.; Candeias 2004; Wissel 2007: 108ff.).

Poulantzas drew attention to the fact that the interior bourgeoisie undergoes a process of decentring; the relations among its members 'proceed by way of the interiorization of American capital within the bourgeoisies themselves' (CCC: 77; translation amended). This applies even more to the transnationalized interior bourgeoisie: here relations function through the interiorization of transnational capital.

Accordingly, transnationalized corporations differ from each other only in their varying relations to national states and regions. As large corporations need to be *native* to all the important markets, there is no 'foreign capital' in the strict sense.[5] Large corporations are a part of the relations of forces not just in their 'home states'; they are present in all the essential national states through their goods and their participation in production and research (cf. Pries 2002: 103ff.; Köhler 2002: 126ff.; Lütje/Schumm/Sproll 2002: 69ff.). However, the mere emergence of transnational corporations is not a sufficient justification for speaking of the transnationalization of

5 This is not to deny that transnational corporations usually have special 'national connections' because they are usually related to one national state in particular. These connections can result from national corporate cultures (cf. Hartmann 1999) as well as privileged relations to the national states in which the corporate headquarters are located (cf. Hack 2002; see also Hübner 2003).

class relations. Transnationalization has to be shown to be a *political project*, too. Accordingly, a number of neo-Gramscian studies look at the national, regional, and transnational intellectual networks that are part of this project (among others Pijl 1989; Gill 1990; Apeldoorn 2002; Walpen 2004).[6] The Trilateral Commission, the European Round Table and the Mont Pélerin Society are all elements of a far-reaching web whose links and channels are often barely visible. The invisibility of these connections makes the institutions in question appear as individual publishing houses, institutes, or research centres (Walpen 2004: 362). Yet, it is here that the neoliberal project is being advanced. By looking at the networks in question, neoliberalism can be identified as a strategic project of the transnational capitalist class. This class is progressively detaching itself from class compromises organized within national states, or indeed trying to tear these compromises apart.

It is not merely thanks to the resources of neoliberal think tanks or the skilful tactics of particularly savvy neoliberal intellectuals that the neoliberal project has had such tremendous global success. There are also a number of structural reasons. In the 1970s and 1980s, it became increasingly clear that Fordist strategies of crisis management had stopped working. Reasons for this are the crisis of US hegemony in the 1980s; the failure of industrialization via import-substitution and the debt crisis in the countries of the global 'South'; the overaccumulation crisis and growing resistance to Taylorist forms of production in metropolitan countries; and the collapse of the Eastern bloc (Hirsch 1993). All these events have contributed in different ways to accelerating the process of internationalization which had already started under Fordism. Moreover, they pushed it in a particular direction which was eventually condensed into the neoliberal project.

It is impossible to understand this project on the grounds of Poulantzas's focus on national social formations. His concept of the 'imperialist chain' is inadequate for this purpose. Not only have relations of forces within states shifted. A new type of power bloc has emerged at the transnational level that organizes itself in and through flexible and polycentric networks. Groups of intellectuals (NGOs, think tanks, publishers etc.) are as much a part of these networks as transnationalized regimes of private law (*lex mercatoria*) and regional, national, or transnational institutions and organizations (WTO, IMF, NATO, UNO etc.). National states constitute actors and nodal points in these arrangements, too (Robinson 2004: 85ff.; Hirsch/Wissel 2010).

In other words, global relations of power and control are condensed in transnational networks. These cannot be compared to the apparatuses of

6 Their empirical foundation, however, is still weak because they usually only focus on sectors and are often based on elite rather than class theory.

the national state, which are characterized by a higher degree of autonomy. Transnational networks do not possess the same materiality and are therefore more immediately affected by short-term fluctuations in the relations of forces (cf. Wissen 2003: 154). Michael Hardt and Antonio Negri are right to insist that the new formation is *not* a state (2000: xiiff.). Politics and the economy are no longer separate in the way they were at the national level. And yet, Hardt and Negri overlook the fact that the political autonomy of the national state is also being restructured. The tendency of transnational groups to become detached from national spaces of regulation destabilizes such autonomy. This is due to the presence of transnational capital within national power blocs and the resulting shifts in the relations of forces as well as increasing external pressure on national states.

4. The new power bloc

The new transnational power bloc[7] is constituted through national states and power blocs that are in turn themselves transnationalized. The transnational power bloc is neither a reflection of the sum of national power blocs, nor are the latter concrete national manifestations of transnational relations of control. The new power bloc is present in each national state in a specific form, depending on national relations of forces, traditions etc. While the presence of the transnational power bloc modifies the structure of individual national power blocs, this does not necessarily imply the former's leadership over the latter. The position of the transnational power bloc is constantly contested and depends not just on the relations of forces in the individual national and supranational power blocs (e.g., the EU), but also on the position of the bloc at the transnational level.

The fields and networks in and through which the transnational power bloc is constituted do not possess materiality in the same way as national states. This has resulted in the emergence of a highly flexible structure. At the transnational level, there is a far-reaching structural autonomization of political forms, which remains unaffected by the 'logic of condensation and displacement' (Demirović 1987: 90; translated) dominant at the national level. This means that sectoral shifts and overlays, the 'dissolution or continued but irrelevant existence' (ibid.) of apparatuses and the shifts of formal and real power have much stronger effects than at the level of the national state.[8] This flexibility makes possible the maintenance of the

7   According to Poulantzas, the power bloc constitutes 'a contradictory unity of *politically dominant* classes and fractions *under the protection of the hegemonic fraction*' (PPSC: 239). This suggests that the emergence of a transnational power bloc is a process that affects only certain parts of the bourgeoisie.

8   Ulrich Brand and Christoph Görg (2003: 223) describe these processes in their account

selectivity of interests inherent in the imperial network.

Struggles over the selectivity of the varying transnational regulatory nodal points are also always about the insulation of institutions and organizations from subaltern interests. Thanks to the flexibility of the transnational network, achievements of subaltern groups can be circumvented. If the conflicts taking place at one node of the network fail to bring about the desired results, the terrain of struggle is shifted to other institutions (*forum-shifting*) (Wissen 2003: 129). This type of flexible shifting and displacing of power can make influential organizations irrelevant and irrelevant ones influential. Examples include the UNCTAD (*UN Conference on Trade and Development*; cf. Ricupero 2004: Xff.) and the MAI (*Multilateral Agreement on Investment*). The MAI is no longer going to be implemented via the OECD but through other channels (Mark-Ungericht/Fuchs 2004: 140). Similarly, the Cancún negotiations revealed that the WTO is not the only option for the leading industrialized nations and the new power bloc. The one-sided opening-up of markets can sometimes be achieved more effectively with the help of bilateral free trade agreements because these are marked by even more clear-cut power relations (Wissel 2007: 161ff.). *In conclusion, the position, constitution and institutional manifestation of the regulatory network through which the transnational power bloc is constituted remain unstable and are subject to constant transformations.* Thus, the formation of the power bloc takes on a complex shape that includes different scales and areas of regulation.

5. The new inside/outside-dialectic

Poulantzas argued that national states are not disappearing, but becoming actors in the processes of transformation. According to him, the inside/outside dialectic within the world system is not dissolved but restructured. The transnationalization of the national power blocs and the emergence of a transnational power bloc mean there can no longer be a clear-cut separation between the inside and outside – either with regard to the state and global relations of control, or to to politics and the economy. Such polar opposites do not only refer to and define one another by way of negation, they are also present within one another. This is not new per se; what is new is the quality of the processes of interpenetration.

Therefore, conceptions of external determination (dependency theory, world systems theory) and conceptions of the primacy of the interior (regulation theory) must be formulated in a more nuanced way. Poulantzas made some important points in this regard: 'Maintaining the primacy

of the international conflicts over genetic resources. See also Wissen (2003: 154f.).

of internal factors in this way already takes us a step further; we have to break once and for all with a mechanistic and almost topological (if not "geographical") conception of the relation between internal and external factors. In the present phase of imperialism there is really no such thing as external factors on the one hand, acting purely from "outside", and opposed to internal factors "isolated" in their own "space" and outclassing the others. If we maintain the primacy of internal factors, we simply mean that those coordinates of the imperialist chain that are "external" to a country – the global balance of forces, the role of a particular great power, etc. – only act on the country in question by way of their internalization, i.e. by their articulation to its own specific contradictions. But these contradictions themselves, in certain aspects, represent the induced reproduction of the contradictions of the imperialist chain within the various individual countries. To talk of internal factors in this sense, then, is to discover the real role that imperialism (uneven development) plays in the evolution of the various social formations.' (CD: 22).

In fact, the significance of the interiorization of external relations of control described by Poulantzas has increased since he wrote this. The national state is no longer the centre of regulation, as it had been during Fordism (Hirsch 1995: 98); it is but one – albeit important – nodal point within a complex and far-reaching regulatory network. Hence, Poulantzas's conceptualization of the relation between inside and outside needs to include the new power dispositifs that have emerged on the transnational level.

Poulantzas never viewed politics and the economy as separate social spaces external to each other. Thus, what is at stake is not the dissolution of the separation between politics and the economy inherent in capitalism, nor the alleged subversion of the regulatory powers of the state by economic globalization. Rather, it is the reconfiguration of this separation, which results from shifts in the relations of forces.

The socially dominant understanding of politics and the economy has changed in and through these processes. According to the neoliberal point of view, politics is now a mere 'event' with the purpose of creating framework conditions for an economy that has become autonomous and cannot be influenced. The economy is thrust into the centre of society and dominates all other social issues (cf. Hirsch 2001: 189): 'Management literature propagates the unrelenting expansion of the market model to all social relations as "best practice" and disregards all objections by assuming that what ought to be is what is already given' (Bröckling 2000: 133; translated). Besides these discursive shifts, there is also an apparent reconfiguration of politics and the economy through transnationalization. The economization of transnational politics is manifested precisely in the fact that there is no such thing as a global state or a similar institutional condensation. Thus economic interests can be translated more directly into political decisions. The boundaries between politics and the economy become blurred, not only causing political autonomy gained within in civil society to be short-lived, but also leading to increased pressure from transnational terrains of conflict on the political autonomy of national states (cf. Hirsch 2002: 139). Within the national state apparatuses, those apparatuses that serve as bases of the transnationalized bloc are becoming more dominant. It is mainly economic state apparatuses such as central banks and finance ministries that gain political importance and increasingly escape democratic control. The economization of political discourse is accompanied by an increasing importance of so-called expert groups that make ever more open attempts at evading parliamentary control, thus precipitating a new form of authoritarian statism (cf. Kannankulam 2008). The economization of politics is therefore a fundamentally political process.

6. Empire and the new imperialism

The developments in question caused Poulantzas to talk of a new phase of imperialism. According to him, what is crucial is that imperialism – by which he mainly meant US imperialism – is not external to other social formations, but becomes part of them. Yet in the course of transnationalization, interiorization becomes generalized. This is because the US is also penetrated by transnational relations of forces and even in the US the national bourgeoisie has lost influence. In addition to the various imperialisms that have been materializing under the changed conditions, a transnational power bloc has emerged that organizes itself in and through the fields and networks of a highly flexible empire.

If these arguments are correct, then the disappearance of the US bourgeoisie represents the disappearance of the last endocentric bourgeoisie in Poulantzas's theory. Thus the national basis of his concept of imperialism can no longer be maintained.[9] National imperialisms have become part of a global imperial constellation; that is, imperialist expansion is no longer necessarily linked to a *specific* national state. At the same time it is obvious that transnationalization is accompanied by a new imperialist politics supported by national states (cf. Deppe et al. 2004; Panitch/Leys 2003). But how can we understand the relationship between the new imperial network-

---

9 On the problems concealed in Poulantzas's concept of imperialism see Wissel (2007: 151ff.).

power and national imperialisms?

Imperialism is a specific form of global power relations by which political and economic categories are mediated. The concept describes the relationship of states and power blocs to other states and power blocs in the context of the expansive tendency inherent to capital. The historical transformations of economic and political spaces described above have transformed this configuration and its specific political and economic mediation. National imperialism is now materialized in a transnationalized environment and mediated through the imperial politics of the new power bloc. Thus national imperialisms now take second position, which, however, does not make them any less dangerous or aggressive. Thus, new imperialism cannot be understood in isolation from the processes of transnationalization outlined here.

Compared to the phase of classical imperialism, the current constellation of power has become much more complex due to the creeping dissolution of national economies and the ensuing transnational forms of accumulations and regulation. Today, when national states pursue their 'economic interests' they are always also pursuing those of the transnational capitals embedded within them. This does not lead to the disappearance of national competition. This is evidenced in the political scheming in the UN before the Iraq war and in conflicts over economic policy that flare up time and again. Imperialist politics has always allowed the externalization of conflicts within a social formation. Currently, this becomes more obvious because of the internal fragmentation of national states: 'The structural political crisis and the crisis of representation that accompany the transformation of the state into a competition state can trigger a dynamic that in turn propels inter-state rivalries. This applies in particular where there are attempts to compensate for the crisis of representation through populist, nationalist, and racist strategies of legitimation' (Hirsch 2004: 685; translated). This also implies that it is no longer entirely plausible to identify a spatial imperial centre as Poulantzas did with respect to the US.

The US may represent the most important condensation of power relations in the world. However, it is neither a condensation of relations of forces that are, as in earlier times, primarily national in character, nor is it a power centre that can be understood in isolation from the global constellation of power. It is therefore somewhat unsatisfactory to use the term 'American Empire' to describe the current situation: the new network-like empire is not American, but transnational. It is a configuration within which national states have not quite ceased to exist, but which cannot be understood by simply analysing individual states (not even the most powerful one). Accordingly, empire is the constantly changing terrain on which the transnational power bloc is constituted. In this network of power, the US is merely one – albeit important – nodal point at which hegemonic struggles are concentrated and materialized. Hardt and Negri (2000) recognized the novel quality of this imperial network, yet they were unable to explain this novelty at the level of theory. Poulantzas allows us to analyse more clearly particular condensations of power relations and the multiple spatial layers, shifts, and nestings of empire, and to relate them to one another.

New imperialism results from the failure to establish a developmental model guaranteeing hegemonic integration, at least temporarily. Due to the ever more radical exclusion of large parts of the world, inclusion increasingly has to be organized on a military basis. This can be done in an imperial manner with the help of a coalition, formed by the UN or NATO, of transnationalized national states and the new power bloc; or, if conflicts within the empire make joint action impossible, in a national manner through the US's quasi-monopoly of 'legitimate' violence. But even unilateral action by the US takes place within the imperial configuration. US imperialism – like that of other states – is an aspect of the transnationalized relations of power, meaning that under certain conditions parts of the transnationalized power bloc may wager on the imperialism of individual states. National imperialisms can nevertheless endanger the imperial structure if hostilities between the metropolitan states spiral out of control.

Accordingly, the conflicts under the cover of empire are becoming ever more visible. *Since national capitals have become less important,* imperialist contradictions between metropolitan states depend more strongly on societal conjunctures and on concrete constellations of power (cf. Albo 2003; Panitch/Gindin 2003: 15). The relationship between the metropolitan states is one of *competitive cooperation.* This means that under changed circumstances conflicts such as those surrounding the military intervention in Iraq can rapidly lose intensity. Future armed confrontations between the metropolises remain unlikely, not least because of the undisputed military superiority of the US. Rather, contradictions and competition will surface in conflicts over economic policy, or in the refusal to provide troops for military interventions.

7. Conclusion

Concerning the direction of emancipatory struggles against the globalizing relations of control, it is necessary to expand on Poulantzas's statement that the struggle of the people 'against their own interior bourgeoisies and their own state (...) is fundamental' (CCC: 88). It should be added that transnational relations of control do not merely manifest themselves in the changed composition of national power blocs. Emancipatory resistance also needs to take seriously the new power dispositif that has emerged at the transnational level. It follows that resistance must also become transnational, and that it must be as flexible in utilizing potential connections and possibilities for organization as the power bloc is in making use of the networks and terrains of empire. Even a partial rupture in the selectivity of crucial condensations of power can transform the terrain of struggle in such a way as to create opportunities for more expansive confrontations.

The new global movements display some promising signs of this. The heterogeneity of these movements, which are traversed and divided by different relations of domination (sexism, racism, anti-Semitism, class relations), should not lead their radical factions to give up the terrain of struggle so as to enjoy the 'purity of doctrine' within their own circles. We should not forget that struggles always contribute to the awareness of oppression and the desire for its theorization.

References

Albo, G. (2003) 'The Old and New Economics of Imperialism', in Panitch, L- / Leys, C. (eds.) *The New Imperial Challenge. Socialist Register 2004* (London: Merlin Press) 88-113.
Alnasseri, S. et al. (2001) 'Raum, Regulation und Periodisierung des Kapitalismus', *Das Argument*, vol. 43, no. 239, 23-43.
Apeldoorn, B. v. (2002) *Transnational Capitalism and European Integration* (London: Routledge).
Altvater, E. / Mahnkopf, B. (1999) *Grenzen der Globalisierung. Ökonomie, Ökologie und Politik in der Weltgesellschaft* (Münster: Westfälisches Dampfboot).
Bieling, H.-J. / Deppe, F. (1996) 'Gramscianismus in der internationalen politischen Ökonomie', *Das Argument*, vol. 38, no. 217, 729-740.
Brand, U. / Görg, C. (eds.) (2003) *Postfordistische Naturverhältnisse. Konflikte um genetische Ressourcen und die Internationalisierung des Staates* (Münster: Westfälisches Dampfboot).
Bröckling, U. (2000) 'Totale Mobilmachung. Menschenführung im Qualitäts- und Selbstmanagement', in Bröckling, U. / Krasmann, S. / Lemke, T. (eds.) *Gouvernementalität der Gegenwart. Studien zur Ökonomisierung des Sozialen* (Frankfurt am Main: Suhrkamp) 131-167.
Candeias, M. (2004) *Neoliberalismus, Hochtechnologie, Hegemonie. Grundrisse einer transnationalen kapitalistischen Produktions- und Lebensweise. Eine Kritik* (Hamburg: Argument-Verlag).
Demirović, A. (1987) *Nicos Poulantzas. Eine kritische Auseinandersetzung* (Hamburg: Argument-Verlag).
Deppe, F. et al. (2004) *Der neue Imperialismus* (Heilbronn: Distel-Verlag).
Gill, S. (1990) *American Hegemony and the Trilateral Commission* (Cambridge:

Cambridge Univ. Press).
Hack, L. (2002) 'Organisationsvermögen. Gesellschaftliche Formbestimmungen von Wissen in globalisierten Kontexten', *Das Argument*, vol. 44, no. 248, 668-683.
Hartmann, M. (1999) 'Auf dem Weg zur transnationalen Bourgeoisie? Die Internationalisierung der Wirtschaft und die Internationalisierung der Spitzenmanager Deutschlands, Frankreichs, Großbritanniens und der USA', *Leviathan*, vol. 27, no. 1, 113-141.
Hardt, M. / Negri, A. (2000) *Empire* (Cambridge/MA: Harvard Univ. Press).
Hirsch, J. (1993) 'Internationale Regulation. Bedingungen von Dominanz, Abhängigkeit, und Entwicklung im globalen Kapitalismus', *Das Argument*, vol. 35, no. 198, 192-222.
Hirsch J. (1995) *Der nationale Wettbewerbsstaat* (Berlin: Ed. ID-Archiv).
Hirsch J. (2001) 'Postfordismus: Dimensionen einer neuen kapitalistischen Formation', in Hirsch, J. / Jessop, B. / Poulantzas, N. *Die Zukunft des Staates* (Hamburg: VSA-Verlag) 171-210.
Hirsch, J. (2002) *Herrschaft, Hegemonie und politische Alternativen* (Hamburg: VSA-Verlag).
Hirsch, J. (2004) 'Was bedeutet Imperialismus heute', *Das Argument*, vol. 46, no. 257, 669-689.
Hirsch, J. / Wissel, J. (2010) 'Transnationalisierung der Klassenverhältnisse', in Thien, H. G. (ed.) *Klassen im Postfordismus* (Münster: Westfälisches Dampfboot) 287-309.
Hübner, K. (2003) 'Ausländische Direktinvestitionen, internationale Produktionsverflechtung und nationale Arbeitsmärkte', in Mahnkopf, B. (ed.) *Management der Globalisierung. Akteure, Strukturen und Perspektiven* (Berlin: Ed. Sigma) 101-119.
Jessop, B. (2002) *The Future of the Capitalist State* (Cambridge: Polity Press).
Kannankulam, J. (2008) *Autoritärer Etatismus im Neoliberalismus. Zur Staatstheorie von Nicos Poulantzas* (Hamburg: VSA-Verlag).
Köhler, H.-D. (2002) 'Lokale Vernetzung in der globalen Produktion am Beispiel der Automobilkonzerne', in Mückenberger, U. / Menzl, M. (eds.) *Der Global Player und das Territorium* (Opladen: Leske + Budrich) 125-152.
Kreile, M. (2000) 'Die Internationalisierung von Produktion und Dienstleistung', in Kaiser, K. / Schwarz, H.-P. (eds.) *Weltpolitik im neuen Jahrhundert* (Bonn: Schriftenreihe Bundeszentrale für politische Bildung) 271-278.
Lüthje, B. / Schumm, W. / Sproll, M. (2002) *Contract Manufacturing. Transnationale Produktion und Industriearbeit in der IT-Branche* (Frankfurt am Main: Campus Verlag).
Mark-Ungericht, B. / Fuchs, M. (2004) 'Vom GATT zur OECD (MAI) zur WTO. Versuche der Durchsetzung eines multilateralen Investitionsabkommens', in ATTAC (ed.) *Die geheimen Spielregeln des Welthandels. WTO-GATS-TRIPS-MAI*, 2nd ed. (Wien: Promedia) 136-149.
Panitch, L. / Leys, C. (2003) *The New Imperial Challenge: Socialist Register* 2004 (London: Merlin Press).
Panitch, L. / Gindin, S. (2003) 'Global capitalism and the American empire', in Panitch, L. / Leys, C. *The New Imperial Challenge: Socialist Register 2004* (London:

Merlin Press) 1-42.

Pijl, K. v. d. (1989) 'The International Level', in Bottomore, T. / Brym, R. J. (eds.) *The Capitalist Class. An International Study* (New York: Harvester Wheatsheaf) 237-266.

Pries, L. (2002) 'Transnationale Konzerne zwischen globaler Strategie und lokaler Einbettung. Das Beispiel der großen deutschen PKW-Hersteller', in Mückenberger, U. / Menzl, M. (eds.) *Der Global Player und das Territorium* (Opladen: Leske + Budrich) 99-113.

Röttger, B. (1997) *Neoliberale Globalisierung und eurokapitalistische Regulation. Die politische Konstitution des Marktes* (Münster: Westfälisches Dampfboot).

Ricupero, R. (2004) 'Nine Years at UNCTAD: A personal Testimony', in Kasahara, S. / Gore, C. (eds.) *Beyond Conventional Wisdom in Development Policy. An intellectual History of UNCTAD 1964-2004* (New York: United Nations) IX-XX.

Robinson, W. I. (2004) *A Theory of Global Capitalism: Production, Class, and State in a Transnational World* (Baltimore: Johns Hopkins Univ. Press).

Walpen, B. (2004) *Die offenen Feinde und ihre Gesellschaft* (Hamburg: VSA-Verlag).

Wissel, J. (2007) *Die Transnationalisierung von Herrschaftsverhältnissen. Zur Aktualität von Nicos Poulantzas' Staatstheorie* (Baden-Baden: Nomos).

Wissel, J. (2010) 'Kräfteverhältnisse', in Haug, W. F. / Haug, F. / Jehle, P. (eds.) *Historisch-Kritisches Wörterbuch des Marxismus*, vol. 7.II, forthcoming (Hamburg: Argument-Verlag) 1941-1955.

Wissen, M. (2003) 'TRIPs, TRIPs-plus und WIPO. Konflikte um Eigentumsrechte an genetischen Ressourcen', in Brand, U. / Görg, C. (eds.) *Postfordistische Naturverhältnisse. Konflikte um genetische Ressourcen und die Internationalisierung des Staates* (Münster: Westfälisches Dampfboot) 128-152.

CRISIS AND STATEHOOD IN THE WORK OF NICOS POULANTZAS

THOMAS SABLOWSKI

Nicos Poulantzas deserves credit not only for having developed an extraordinarily subtle concept of the capitalist state, but also for having created tools for the analysis of different state forms and forms of regime change. At the same time, his writings – even where they seem abstract or largely focused on historical processes – always referred directly to problems of socialist strategy. His analyses of political crises are particularly pertinent in this regard. Political crises are relatively open situations. The existing state form can either be reproduced or be succeeded by a different one; given specific circumstances, transformations in the social formation or even a transition to a different mode of production become genuine possibilities. In this chapter, I will try to show how Poulantzas conceptualizes the connections between economic crises, political crises, and statehood. I will first summarize his general discussion of economic and political crises, and then discuss one of his analyses of a concrete situation: the rise of fascism in Italy and Germany.

1. The link between economic crisis, political crisis, and statehood

Like other members of the Althusser School, Poulantzas conceives of historical materialism as an *ensemble* of theories that analyse different subject areas, or the same subject area from different viewpoints and levels of abstraction. He distinguishes between the *general theory* of historical materialism – which defines terms like mode of production, social formation, class, politics and so forth – and *particular theories* of specific modes of production (such as the theory of the capitalist mode of production) and of different social formations (e.g., France in the 1970s). This distinction is important because it allows us to understand concrete social formations as *combinations* of different modes of production, forms of production, and social relations instead of reducing them to manifestations of just *one* mode of production. Poulantzas also assumed that in all modes of production and social formations, it was possible to distinguish at least between an economic, political and ideological level, and that it was necessary to develop *regional theories* for these levels in order to arrive at a conception of a complex, structured whole. According to Poulantzas, Marx's specific achievement lay in elaborating the general theory of historical materialism, the particular theory of the capitalist mode of production and the regional theory of the economic level within that mode of production – even if these theories remained incomplete (cf. PPSC: 11ff.). Poulantzas intended to complement these achievements by further developing (a) the concept of the political in general, (b) the particular theory of the capitalist mode of production, and (c) the regional theory of the political within the capitalist mode of production. I contend that Poulantzas essentially stuck to this basic framework until his death, even if he took the criticism levelled against his 'structural formalism' very seriously and modified certain aspects of his approach significantly.[1] This continuity is visible, for instance, in the fact that, even in his later work, he maintained a rigid distinction between economic, political and state crises.

In addition to state theory, Poulantzas also aimed to advance Marxist class theory.[2] In each social formation he distinguishes between a 'power bloc', composed of the ruling classes and class fractions, and the subordinated popular classes (i.e., the working class, poor and somewhat wealthier peasants, the old and the new petty bourgeoisie). The dominance of a particular mode of production in all social formations suggests that the struggle between the main classes plays a determining role for the development of the social formation in question. In social formations dominated by the capitalist mode of production, this is the struggle between the bourgeoisie and the working class. However, Poulantzas particularly emphasizes that there are contradictions within the power bloc, and he uses the distinction between determination and dominance to relate the determining role of the conflict between the main classes in a particular social formation to the dominance of different contradictions among the ruling classes.

Since the ruling classes are pervaded by deep contradictions and do not necessarily share a common concrete interest beyond the general interest in maintaining their rule, their unity must be produced by the capitalist state. Following Poulantzas, alternative political strategies that are discussed and elaborated in the 'ideological state apparatuses' (the churches, the mass media, educational institutions, etc.) often reveal contradictions within the

1   Cf. Barrow in this volume.
2   Cf. Koch in this volume.

ruling classes rather than fundamental conflicts between the ruling and subordinate classes. This is because the struggles of the subordinate classes affect the state only indirectly, while the ruling classes and class fractions partake directly of state power and are directly represented in the state apparatuses. In this situation, individual ruling classes or class fractions, but also the power bloc as a whole may be able to mobilize the support of particular subordinate classes or class fractions (e.g., the petty bourgeoisie or certain elements of the peasantry). Thus any concrete configuration of state power and state apparatuses represents *directly* an unstable compromise between the different ruling classes and class fractions, and represents *indirectly* one between the ruling and the subordinate classes: the state is a material condensation of social relations of forces.

1.1. Economic crises

Poulantzas distinguishes between crises and phases of the successful reproduction of capitalism. The former are divided into economic crises, political crises, and state crises. Interestingly, he never properly defines these concepts.[3] In my reading, *economic crises* for Poulantzas are situations in which capital accumulation stalls.[4] He draws on Marx's 'law of the tendency of the rate of profit to fall', but rejects a deterministic understanding of it. For him, it is not meant to predict a fall in the rate of profit that can be measured empirically. Rather, it depends on class struggle whether this tendency asserts itself or is compensated by countervailing tendencies such as a depreciation of constant capital or an increase in the rate of surplus value (SPS: 173f.). During crises, these counter-tendencies become effective in a condensed and 'wild' manner. Far from being dysfunctional, economic crises are actually necessary for the reproduction of capitalism, provided that they do not turn into political crises in which the possibility of abolishing capitalism may arise.

Poulantzas rejects the mechanistic and economistic conception of crisis that was prevalent in the Communist International (Comintern), and which he felt had not been overcome properly in later years. The Third International alleged that capitalism, in its monopoly phase, found itself in a constant state of crisis. Hence it was common to speak about a 'general

---

3   This absence of definitions is in line with Marxist conceptions of theory according to which the meaning of a concept can only be defined and developed within the context of a *particular* theory, and through a gradual transition from abstract to concrete and from simple to complex determinations. However, it may also be indicative of a lack of clarity evident in the works of many other Marxist theorists. The ubiquitous use of the term 'crisis' in Marxist discourse is also linked to the difficulty of defining criteria for when it does and does not make sense to speak of a crisis.

4   Poulantzas does not state this explicitly; it is my own interpretation.

crisis of capitalism' that would last until capitalism would be abolished. Yet if capitalism is conceived as *always* being in crisis, the specificity of the concept of crisis is erased. In order to avoid this kind of conclusion, Poulantzas drew a distinction between the *elements that generate crises*, which are always at work in the reproduction of capitalism, and the crises themselves, which represent specific situations characterized by a condensation of capitalist contradictions (1979: 360). According to Poulantzas, teleological conceptions of crisis need to be avoided: It is not crisis but class struggle that potentially ends capitalism (ibid.).

1.2 Political crises and state crises

What is the relationship between economic, political and state crises? Poulantzas employs the concept of *political crisis* exclusively to refer to a particular situation of condensation of contradictions in the political sphere (1979: 362). I take him to mean that political crises are situations in which the existing mode of political domination is called into question. According to Poulantzas's theory of political domination, this implies that the relationship between leaders and led, between representatives and represented, enters into crisis on two levels: the hegemonic class or class fraction in the power bloc is no longer able to exercise hegemony within the power bloc; and the power bloc's hegemony over the subordinate classes starts to crumble. All political crises are relatively open situations that allow for various solutions. But not every political crisis is a revolutionary situation or a crisis that triggers the rise of fascism (365). For Poulantzas, political crises are above all the result of substantial modifications of the relationship of forces within class struggle. This touches upon the contradictions between the classes in struggle; the configuration of class alliances on the part of the power bloc as well as on the part of the exploited and dominated classes; the emergence of new social forces; the relationship between the forms of organization and representation of certain classes and those classes themselves; and, finally, the emergence of new contradictions between the power bloc and certain classes supporting it (365f.).

Poulantzas also distinguishes the concept of *state crisis* from the concept of political crisis. Within the context of his state theory, it can be argued that state crises are situations in which the state can no longer fulfil its function of organizing the power bloc and disorganising the subordinate classes. Political crises entail state crises as one of their elements but cannot be reduced to them. Poulantzas stresses the difference as well as the connection between state crises and political crises, because bourgeois sociology and political science saw political crises primarily as institutional crises or as crises of the 'political system' and thus tended to reduce political crises to state crises. In contrast to this, Poulantzas attributes crises at the level of state apparatuses to crises of state power, and the latter in turn to changes in the relation of forces within class struggle. However, due to the capitalist state's relative autonomy vis-á-vis the power bloc and the specific separation of the state's organizational framework from the economic space, this definition is neither direct nor uniform (366). Countering economistic conceptions, Poulantzas insists that economic crises do not necessarily become political crises and state crises; the transition neither happens automatically nor in a uniform manner. Politics is not a simple expression or reflection of the economic, because political class struggle, whose objective is state power and the state apparatus, cannot be reduced to economic struggle (or a simple reflection thereof) (363). Therefore, it is impossible to determine in general *if* and *when* an economic crisis becomes a political crisis.

When economic crises do indeed become political crises, Poulantzas speaks of *structural crises* or, drawing on Antonio Gramsci, *hegemonic* or *organic crises*. The attribute 'structural' here should not to be taken to constitute the antonym of 'conjunctural'. Rather, it suggests that the entire ensemble of social relations is in crisis: the crisis is economic *and* political; it is manifested in a *conjuncture*, i.e., a concrete situation in the condensation of contradictions inherent to the social structure (363f.).

The fact that economic crises turn into a political crises does not imply that they (or their respective processes) necessarily coincide. The specificity of the political terrain frequently produces lags and displacements between the two crises. A political crisis may set in belatedly, i.e., at a point in time when the economic crisis is already past its climax, which is what happened, for instance, in the case of the 1929 economic crisis and the political crisis in Germany that led to the National Socialists taking power in 1933. But the political crisis may also precede the economic crisis and may indeed lead to it: according to Poulantzas, this was the case in France in May 1968, and in Chile during the Allende era (365).

This argument is informed by a non-economistic conception of the economy: if political struggles can interrupt economic reproduction, it becomes possible to argue that the hegemony of a class or class fraction in the power bloc as well as the hegemony of the power bloc over the whole of society are constitutive of the expanded reproduction of capital. However, this also problematizes Poulantzas's earlier conception of discrete regional theories of the economic and the political.

There is also a terminological and conceptual problem regarding the distinction between political crises and hegemonic crises that becomes apparent at this point: on the one hand, Poulantzas only speaks of hegemonic crises when economic crises become political crises, that is, when the entire ensemble of social relations is in crisis, which in his view is not always necessarily the case. Within the framework of his theory of political domination, on the other hand, the concept of political crisis can only be defined with reference to a crisis of hegemony. But what causes a hegemonic crisis? Is it shifts in the balance of forces between classes and class fractions in the context of the dynamic of capital accumulation? Is it perhaps the state's insufficient autonomy vis-á-vis classes and class fractions, rendering problematic its role in the organization of hegemony? Or even an ideological crisis – something that has not even been mentioned yet?

1.3 Ideological crises

For Poulantzas, a political crisis is always accompanied by an *ideological crisis*. The latter is a constitutive element of the former, primarily because ideological relations are themselves directly present in the constitution and reproduction of social classes. These relations – the dominant ideology in particular – are organically present in the constitution of state apparatuses. The role of the state apparatuses in turn is to reproduce the dominant ideology in its relation to the ideologies or ideological sub-ensembles of the subordinate classes. Poulantzas, like Antonio Gramsci and Louis Althusser, sees ideology as incorporated into the material practices, customs and ways of life of a social formation. The ruling classes cannot control the exploited classes simply by means of physical violence. Rather, the use of violence must be legitimized by the ruling ideology, which presupposes that the state produces the consensus of the subordinate classes and class fractions (1979: 367; SPS: 31).

The dominant ideology also has a role to play inside the state apparatuses, acting as cement that binds the people working in different apparatuses together and turning them into servants of the ruling classes. All political crises are necessarily connected to ideological crises, which in turn become so-called legitimation crises. This articulation arises out of changes in the balance of forces within class struggle, as well as through the fissures within the state apparatuses caused by political crises. Moreover, political crises are manifested within the apparatuses of economic state intervention as well as the repressive state apparatuses (the army, the police, the judiciary) (1979: 367).

Although ideological crises are among the constitutive elements of political crises, the latter cannot be reduced to 'value crises' or 'legitimation crises'. This happens in bourgeois sociology and political science insofar as some bourgeois scholars see political conflict merely as an expression of contradictory ideas or opinions and the 'political system' as a self-regulating whole whose harmonious working is interrupted by external 'shocks'. In opposition to that, Poulantzas stresses that the elements inducing political crises, which can be attributed to class struggle, are inherent in the reproduction of institutionalized political power, and that political and state crises play an organic role in the reproduction of class domination. Provided that class struggle does not lead to socialism, crises can be a way of restoring the hegemony of the ruling class and of adapting the capitalist state to the new realities of class struggle (361). Hence, political crises may be just as functional as economic ones, although this can only be stated *ex post*.

2. Crisis and the rise of fascism

Fascism and Dictatorship (FD), Poulantzas's analysis of Italian fascism and German National Socialism, was published in 1970. Even though the topic of the book seems merely historical, it was actually motivated by strategic problems that the communist movement was facing towards the end of the 1960s. It was above all the military coup in Greece in 1967 that pushed Poulantzas to look at the issue of fascism. The left tended to dangerously expand the concept and to refer to the Greek military dictatorship, among others, as fascist – as if this was beyond doubt. Poulantzas also saw the danger of democratic regimes being replaced with exceptional states or even fascism as a result of ongoing political crises. He did not believe that fascism was restricted to one historical period of capitalist development only, yet argued that all forms of exceptional states needed to be analysed carefully in order to develop an adequate strategic response (FD 11: 357ff.). According to Poulantzas, it is important to distinguish between the different forms of the exceptional state, such as Bonapartism, fascism and military dictatorship, which are characterized by varying degrees of political support from the population. Unlike military dictatorships, fascism, for instance, has a genuine mass basis that lends it a certain flexibility and stability. It also produces its own ideology and its own channels of mass mobilization, such as the fascist mass party and other mass organizations, which set it apart from military dictatorships. Bonapartism, in turn, stands between fascism and military dictatorship as regards mass support and flexibility (Jessop 1985: 97). For our purposes, it is of particular interest to examine the relationship between economic crisis, political crisis, and the rise of fascism. According to Poulantzas, the concrete historical form of exceptional state is closely linked to the form of the political crisis and the period of capitalist development from which it emerges (FD: 16). He locates historical fascism in the context of the transition from competitive to monopoly capitalism, which was characterized by (a) the expansion of forms of production that were typical for monopoly capitalism, (b) an unstable balance between these forms and those belonging to competitive capitalism, and (c) the dissolution of other, subordinate modes of production (FD: 20ff.; CCC: 134f.).

Poulantzas strongly rejected economistic interpretations of fascism as held by the Comintern. He stressed that neither the economic crisis following World War I nor the world economic crisis from 1929 onwards could, by themselves, explain the victory of Italian fascism or National Socialism. After all, other countries were also affected by these crises, but they did not show the same type of condensation of contradictions that was visible in Italy and Germany (FD: 34-5, 53f.). Poulantzas argues that fascism took hold in both countries when the low point of the preceding economic crises had already been passed: 'The conjuncture of the class struggle which led to them was not directly determined by any one "economic crisis".' (54)[5].

According to Poulantzas, fascism was victorious in the weakest links in the 'imperialist chain' (after Russia). The weakness of a particular link is not necessarily or exclusively the result of the respective country's economic backwardness. After all, Germany was one of the most highly developed capitalist countries. Instead, this weakness is the result of an aggregation of economic, political, and ideological contradictions (22ff.).

Fascism emerged out of a specific political crisis characterized by a peculiar constellation of class struggle. Poulantzas's hypothesis is that the political crisis that led to fascism was preceded by a defeat of the working class and a phase of relative stabilization, and that the rise of fascism was characterized by an offensive of the bourgeoisie and a defensive of the working class (78ff., 107, 130f.). Therefore, the political crisis that led to fascism is not the direct result of the working class challenging the bourgeoisie; it rather arises out of the struggle between monopoly and non-monopoly capital, because neither fraction was able to establish itself as the leading force within the framework of the existing political order (71ff.).

This crisis of hegemony was accompanied by an ideological crisis threatening internal cohesion in the power bloc and its control over the masses (76ff.). According to Poulantzas, the ruling ideology in Germany,

---

5   Regarding Germany, Poulantzas states (FD: 95): 'The economic crisis of 1929, which had a specific effect on the aggravation of contradictions within the power bloc, began to ease off around 1932'. However, while it is correct that the economic crisis reached its low point in summer 1932 (Peukert 1993: 251f.), Poulantzas seems to over-emphasize the lagged and contingent relationship between the economic crisis, the political crisis, and the rise of fascism, given that he himself identifies a 'point of no return' in the final phase of the Brüning government (FD: 101f.). According to this, the 'point of no return' even precedes the low point of the economic crisis!

which consisted of a specific combination of feudal and imperialist elements, found itself in a state of dissolution. Reactionary feudal romanticism, medieval corporatism, the technocratic-imperialist ideology of organized capitalism, and the 'liberal' pretensions of medium capital became increasingly independent from one another (103ff.). The organic intellectuals of the power bloc increasingly turned their backs on traditional ideology and embraced fascist instead.[6] Demands for an exchange of governing elites and attacks on parliamentarism were spreading. This was not merely a crisis of the dominant ideology, but a generalized ideological crisis: it also involved crises of various 'ideological subsystems' that were strongly influenced by the dominant ideology (i.e., working-class and petty bourgeoisie ideologies), as well as a crisis of Marxism-Leninism (76ff., 105ff., 129ff.). This crisis of hegemony was accompanied by a crisis of representation in parliament, the growing incoherence of government policies, chronically unstable governments, the emergence of paramilitary forces, and a shift of power away from constitutional channels towards informal power networks (73ff., 100ff.).

2.1 The class character of fascism

The solution to the political crisis consisted in developing the hegemony of monopoly capital. But this was only possible through new forms of political organization, new economic strategies, and new forms of ideological cohesion that would favour the interests of monopoly capital at the same time as facilitating an attack on the labour movement. The function of fascism was to carry out exactly this reorganization of the hegemony of the power bloc and to increase the exploitation of the working class (FD: 72f., 74, 154, 171f.).

In defining the class character of fascism, Poulantzas sets himself apart from three traditional conceptions:

1. The official position dominant within the Comintern saw the fascist party as a 'military weapon in big capital's fight' that could be manipulated at will. It recognized neither the autonomy of the fascist state, nor the mass basis of fascism and the support it received from other fractions in the power bloc (83f.).

2. The idea of an equilibrium of forces between the bourgeoisie and the working class exaggerates the autonomy of the fascist state. This leads to a number of erroneous judgements, such as the assumption that the fascist war economy contradicted the interests of monopoly capital (84f.).

---

6   Poulantzas's analysis of the ideological dynamic of the rise of fascism remains underdeveloped. He barely mentions anti-Semitism – a topic of central importance to the first generation of the Frankfurt School, which is also at the centre of current debates in Germany and beyond.

3. The view of fascism as a political dictatorship of the petty bourgeoisie, which was widespread among social democrats, correctly pointed to the political link between fascism and the petty bourgeoisie that was neglected by the Comintern. However, it exaggerates the autonomy of fascism vis-á-vis monopoly capital by hypostatizing the petty bourgeoisie as a 'third force' (85).

Poulantzas argues that fascism had a specific relative autonomy vis-á-vis the power bloc in general, and the fraction of monopoly capital whose hegemony it established. This relative autonomy rested, on the one hand, on the power bloc's internal contradictions: it was necessary in order to reorganize the latter and create the hegemony of monopoly capital. On the other hand, it was based on the contradictions between the power bloc and the subordinate classes. Given the general crises of the Italian and German social formations, as well as their multifaceted relationship with the subordinate classes, fascism was able to organize the restabilization of political domination by virtue of its relative autonomy.

2.2 Phases in the rise of fascism

Poulantzas distinguishes four phases within the rise of fascism: the first period covers the time from the start of the process until the 'point of no return', that is, the moment 'after which it appears difficult to turn it back' (FD: 66). In this period the fascist party, which previously had mostly represented the short-term political interests of the petty bourgeoisie, increasingly garnered support from monopoly capital and created organizational links with the various elements within the power bloc (86f.). The 'point of no return' is not to be confused with the 'accession to power' of fascism, which 'seems such a simple, final act, occurring only when the essentials are already decided and done with' (66). The more the fascist party turned into a mass party and toned down anti-capitalist and petty bourgeois elements in its ideology, the more it was embraced by the power bloc. The second period, which spans the time from the 'point of no return' until the 'accession to power', is less important for the political rise of fascism, but more 'for its nature and specific political character' (66, 87, 109ff., 131f.). This period was characterized by a successful alliance of monopoly capital and petty bourgeoisie, which was mediated by the fascist party (87).

The third period of the rise of fascism immediately follows the 'accession to power'. It was characterized by a high degree of instability and the initially highly complex class character of fascism. Due to 'the very ambiguous character of the popular support it has when it reaches power', fascism found 'itself generally obliged to make compromise measures of a kind to bolster many illusions' (66f.). Fascist policies favoured monopoly capital, but at the same time they tried to secure support from the other parts of the power bloc and the masses. Through the fascist party the petty bourgeoisie became the *ruling class*, but it did so without also becoming the *politically dominant class* (87, 111, 134). In contrast to this, the fourth period of the rise of fascism – the phase of the stabilization of fascism – was characterized by a kind of fascism ridding itself 'of the ambiguity of its origins; this becomes evident with widespread, bloody purges of its own ranks'. In other words, it brutally removed 'a part of the class weight under which it labours' (67). The fascist party itself was subordinated to the state apparatuses. Monopoly capital thus realized its hegemony and became the ruling as well as the dominant class, while the petty bourgeois individuals staffing the state apparatuses no longer represented their class of origin. At the same time, the contradictions within the power bloc resurfaced: 'Fascism is obliged to be evasive in this respect [vis-à-vis big capital], sometimes putting a distance between itself and the hegemonic fraction. Although it does conduct a policy which is, in the last analysis, overwhelmingly in the *long term* interests of this fraction, it is not an agent under its orders. [...] fascist policy in the end comes to antagonize big capital' (88, cf. 112f., 134f.).

2.3 The mass basis of fascism

Although Poulantzas conceived of the petty bourgeoisie as the primary mass basis of fascism, the latter nevertheless managed to attract considerable support from the various rural classes because of the crisis of agriculture and the transformation of the relations of production in that sector. The workers' parties in Italy and Germany had neglected forming an alliance between the industrial proletariat and poor peasants and agricultural labourers. Thus populist appeals to 'blood and soil', the redistribution of land, and colonization were quite effective. Nevertheless, Poulantzas argued that fascism in the countryside was not a sufficient basis for the reorganization of hegemony and that, in the end, it was the support from the urban classes and state apparatuses that proved decisive (FD: 278ff.).

Poulantzas believed that working-class support for fascism was limited. Yet for him the category 'working class' only comprises workers who produce surplus value, while he sees 'non-productive' wage labourers located in the sphere of circulation and the state apparatuses as the 'new petty bourgeoisie' (FD: 238ff.; CCC: 94f., 209ff.[7]). Poulantzas attributes the

---

7   For Poulantzas, productive labour should not simply formally defined formally as labour that produces surplus value. In his view, a physical criterion should also be considered: Services cannot be productive labour even when they assume the character of commodities. Regarding the critique of Poulantzas's narrow concept of the working class and his wide concept of the new petty

influence of fascism among the working class to the strategic failure of its organizations and the influence of 'petty bourgeois' ideological elements (FD. 144ff.). This demonstrates that he tended to idealize the working class and Marxism-Leninism as its 'proper' ideology (cf. Jessop 1985: 238f.; Demirović 1987: 47). According to Poulantzas, fascism neutralized the working class and rendered it passive through a combination of repression, ideological interpellations (i.e., nationalism and corporatism, which included 'socialist' and 'anti-imperialist' ideological elements), and relative material compromises (FD: 165ff., 190f., 221f.).[8]

Poulantzas explains the strategic failure of workers' organizations in the face of the rise of fascism by referring to the role and 'objective class character' of social democracy whose policy of class cooperation led to its gradual surrender to the fascist movement. He sees the social democrats' constant search for compromises, as well as their support for bourgeois governments as the allegedly 'lesser evil' as resulting in a continuous shift to the right. The legalistic wait-and-see attitude, the renunciation of political strikes and mass action, and the failure to mobilize their own paramilitary units also proved fatal (107f., 147ff., 177ff., 204ff.). But Poulantzas also criticizes the communist vanguard organizations' theoretical and strategic mistakes, as well as their economism, the absence of a mass line and their failure to form alliances with peasants and the petty bourgeoisie. During the process of fascization, the Italian and German Communist Parties (PCI and KPD, respectively) pursued a disastrous 'ultra-left' line (156ff.). The KPD, for example, followed the Comintern and the position established at its 6th World Congress in viewing social democracy as its primary enemy (the notorious allegation of 'social fascism'). It also demobilized its paramilitary forces after 1931. Finally, it neglected building up an underground apparatus in case of a fascist takeover, which meant that its resistance against the National Socialist regime was bound to fail (180ff.).

---

bourgeoisie cf. Demirović (1987: 38f., 46ff.).

8   Ernesto Laclau (1977: 81ff.) criticizes the class reductionism in Poulantzas's analysis of fascism and in Marxism more generally. According to Laclau, ideological elements do not possess a fixed meaning; they only receive it through their articulation within a discourse (i.e., the manner of their combination). This suggests that Poulantzas is wrong to speak of 'petty bourgeois ideological elements'; terms like 'socialism', 'democracy', or 'nationalism' can assume varying class-specific meanings, depending on their articulation. Although Laclau's critique of the class reductionism in the Marxist theory of ideology is plausible, his conception leads to a number of problems. First, it reduces class struggle to ideological struggle and neglects the economic level. This problem is even more obvious in Laclau's later, 'post-Marxist' work (cf. Sablowski 1992). Second, Laclau may concede that popular-democratic traditions which can be detached from the dominant bourgeois discourse and can be integrated into socialist discourse display different degrees of development in different countries (they were stronger in Italy at that time than, for instance, in Germany; cf. Laclau 1977: 133f.). But in my opinion he still underestimates the peculiarity and stability of historical traditions.

I do not agree with Bob Jessop's critique that Poulantzas implicitly assumes that a correct communist strategy would have been sufficient to prevent fascism (1985: 262). In my view, Poulantzas develops a fairly subtle account of the rise of fascism, in which the communists were but one force among many. It is possible, however, to criticize Poulantzas's analysis for its insufficient complexity, especially with regard to contradictions within the power bloc. In *Fascism and Dictatorship* he focuses on the contradictions between three classes or fractions of the power bloc: monopoly capital, non-monopoly or medium capital, and large landowners. In *Classes in Contemporary Capitalism* (CCC: 130ff.), he points to the contradictions between industrial, banking, and merchant capital, which also pervade monopoly capital itself. If we accept Kurt Gossweiler's view (1971), these contradictions were also relevant during the era of the Weimar Republic. Moreover, while Poulantzas in *Fascism and Dictatorship* does point to the 'imperialist chain' and to Italy and Germany as its weakest links after Russia, the international context and the contradictory strategies of internationalization and self-sufficiency on the part of different capital fractions only seem to play a marginal role for him. In contrast, Gossweiler (1971), Alfred Sohn-Rethel (1987) and David Abraham (1981) have emphasized the importance of those contradictions within German industrial capital (the 'modern', internationally oriented fraction vs. the 'traditional' heavy industry focused on self-sufficiency).

Moreover, Jessop (1985: 279f.) is surely right in criticizing a functionalist trait of Poulantzas's analysis: in spite of its complexity, Poulantzas essentially argues that fascism was functional for monopoly capital, and uses this to explain the latter's consolidation. In doing so, Poulantzas downplays the internal contradictions of fascism and stresses that in the end it could only be destroyed with the help of a military intervention from the outside. As a result, he evaded the question to which extent the internal contradictions of fascism contributed to its military defeat.

3. Concluding remarks

Apart from the rise of fascism in Italy and Germany, Poulantzas also looked at two other political crises in detail: the crisis of the military dictatorships in Greece, Portugal and Spain in the mid-1970s (cf. CD), and, to some extent, the simultaneous crisis in the capitalist metropolises that is today referred to as the crisis of Fordism (cf. SPS 163ff.). Due to a lack of space, these analyses cannot be discussed here, but in conclusion I would like to draw attention to a general problem in Poulantzas's analyses of crises. They are fairly strong whenever he looks at political crises as well as transformations and critical moments of state power and state apparatuses, but fairly weak with regard to the economic dimension of concrete analyses. Today there are much more concrete analyses of capitalist development after World War II, especially with regard to the economy. Examples include Ernest Mandel's account of late capitalism (1978), the analyses of the regulation approach (Aglietta 1979 et al.), and the more recent work of Robert Brenner (1998; 2003).

It seems to me that the strengths and weaknesses in Poulantzas's analyses of crisis are two sides of the same coin, and that they result, to a large degree, from his assumption that there should be two separate regional theories of the economic and the political, which was influenced by Althusser. Perhaps Poulantzas was only able to make his undeniably great advances in the analysis of political crisis and the concrete forms of statehood by neglecting the economic. The works of Marxist economists, on the other hand, frequently neglect the political. This is surely an effect that disciplinary boundaries have on academic Marxism. It is the task of future generations to integrate the advances made in different fields of Marxist theory and to apply them in concrete analyses of historical situations.

Today, it is obvious that the crisis specific to the 1970s has been overcome – at least in so far as it was conditioned politically by an offensive of the working class and socialist forces and characterized economically by stagflation. Like historical fascism, the neoliberal offensive of the bourgeoisie was preceded by a defeat of the working class and socialist forces.[9] But the characteristics of the present solution to the crisis are still hotly debated: are we witnessing, on the international level, the continued dominance of US capital? Or, rather, its decline? Are we really looking at a renewal of bourgeois hegemony, or maybe at a new form of political domination that can almost completely dispense with the material concessions or class compromises so central to Gramsci's concept of hegemony? How economically and politically stable or crisis-prone is the present phase of capitalist development? Can the changes in statehood that result from the current 'war on terror' be understood as a new step in the development of what Poulantzas called 'authoritarian statism' (cf. SPS: 203ff.)? Are they political safeguards for neoliberal developments or rather a symptom of their crisis? Does the current world economic crisis point to the end of neoliberalism or the end of a finance-led regime of accumulation? We may not be able to find direct answers to those questions in Poulantzas's works, but reading the latter is still necessary because he provided us with a number of indispensable theoretical concepts for answering them.

9   See my own analysis of the links between the crisis of Fordism and the rise of the new right in Italy (Sablowski 1998).

References

Abraham, D. (1981) *The Collapse of the Weimar Republic* (Princeton: Princeton Univ. Press).
Aglietta, M. (1979) *A Theory of Capitalist Regulation* (London: New Left Books).
Brenner, R. (1998) 'The Economics of Global Turbulence', *New Left Review*, vol. 39, no. I 229, 1-265.
Brenner, R. (2003) *The Boom and the Bubble: The US in the world economy* (London: Verso).
Demirović, A. (1987) *Nicos Poulantzas. Eine kritische Auseinandersetzung* (Hamburg: Argument-Verlag).
Gossweiler, K. (1971) *Großbanken, Industriemonopole, Staat: Ökonomie und Politik des staatsmonopolistischen Kapitalismus in Deutschland 1914-1932* (Berlin: VED).
Jessop, B. (1985) *Nicos Poulantzas. Marxist Theory and Political Strategy* (Basingstoke: Macmillan).
Laclau, E. (1977) *Politics and Ideology in Marxist Theory: Capitalism – Fascism – Populism* (London: New Left Books).
Mandel, E. (1978) *Late Capitalism* (London: Humanities Press).
Peukert, D. J.K. (1993) *The Weimar Republic: the crisis of classical modernity* (Harmondsworth: Penguin Books).
Poulantzas, N. (1979) 'The Political Crisis and the Crisis of the State', in Freiberg, J.W. (ed.) *Critical Sociology: European Perspectives* (New York: Irvington) 357-393.
Sablowski, T. (1992) 'Vom Sozialismus zur radikalen Demokratie: Zum Postmarxismus von Laclau/Mouffe', *links*, vol. 24, no. 262, 12-14.
Sablowski, T. (1998) *Italien nach dem Fordismus. Regulation und organische Krise einer kapitalistischen Gesellschaftsformation* (Münster: Westfälisches Dampfboot).
Sohn-Rethel, A. (1987) *The economy and class structure of German fascism* (London: Free Association).

'INSIDE' AND 'OUTSIDE': THE STATE, MOVEMENTS AND 'RADICAL TRANSFORMATION' IN THE WORK OF NICOS POULANTZAS

ULRICH BRAND AND MIRIAM HEIGL

By the late 1970s, Poulantzas had experienced the advance of authoritarian statism, the crisis of left-wing parties, and the emergence of new social movements. Moreover, his own theory had reached a new stage of development. As a result, he chose to look for a new political strategy. His conception of the state as a social relation suggested that neither the 'inside' nor the 'outside' of the state should be the privileged terrain of the fundamental transformation of society: 'In the democratic road to socialism, these two forms of struggle must be combined', he wrote in *State, Power, Socialism* (SPS: 260). Accordingly, it was impossible for Poulantzas to imagine socialist transformation without changes to the state. After all, he argued that the latter neither constituted an instrument of the ruling class nor a neutral instance, but an asymmetric field of compromises.

Against this background, this chapter discusses Poulantzas's thoughts on the relationship between the state and emancipatory movements. First, we give a critical account of his line of argument and expand on it. Then, we discuss the distinct contribution of political analyses in the Poulantzasian vein, using the example of anti-privatization struggles. Last but not least, we highlight some theoretical problems of radical transformation under the current social conditions.[1]

1. 'Inside', 'outside' and transformation

Poulantzas distinguishes his approach to the relationship between social movements and the state from other political and theoretical positions. For him, the state is neither a neutral instance committed to the 'common good' and the effective management of social problems, nor is it an

---

1   We thank the editors for their valuable comments.

instrument of the ruling classes. Accordingly, emancipatory movements would be mistaken to assume that state actors necesssarily implement policies in line with the 'common good', or that the state can be 'taken over' and transformed into an instrument they can control. Poulantzas rejects both the statism of social democratic and communist parties and 'autonomist' and 'subjectivist' perspectives. He criticizes social democratic and communist parties, arguing that their statism is based on a profound 'distrust of mass initiatives' (SPS: 251). After all, their approach implies that the party and its vanguard cadre are needed to guide the popular masses. In contrast, the autonomist perspective primarily focuses on autonomous struggles and on building counter-power at the grassroots level, while the state is viewed as an uncontrollable Leviathan. In his critique of this position, Poulantzas follows Rosa Luxemburg, who pointed to the danger of underestimating the achievements of representative democracy and of reconstituting authoritarian political relations by way of introducing a political system supposedly based on grassroots democracy. The 'institutions of representative democracy are at the same time expressions of the bourgeoisie and conquests of the popular masses' (Poulantzas 1979a: 32; translated). Poulantzas points to how this is demonstrated by the Russian and Portuguese experiences, where relatively strong radical left-wing forces focused only on autonomy and paid too little attention to the state, thus allowing the 'statists' to take it over (1979b: 7). He also regards 'subjectivist' anti-statism as deficient, arguing that its analysis and transformative practice are overly focused on the innumerable forms of micro-power, whilst ignoring the institutional specificity of the capitalist state.

Poulantzas's understanding of the relationship between the state and social movements is based on his distinction between (a) state power as the condensation of social relations of forces that traverse the state apparatus and are shaped by it at the same time and (b) state apparatuses as the institutional materialization of these relations of forces. There is, however, no necessary correlation here. The power of the state comprises all social forces that act within and through it, but not all of them are present to the same extent. There are social forces, in particular social movements, that constitute themselves outside of the state apparatuses affecting the latter only from a distance. It is essential to bear this relationship in mind in the transition to socialism.

Deploying a Poulantzasian 'double perspective', we show how social movements can act within the state, what room for manoeuvre they have at their disposal, and what sort of influence they can develop. We also elaborate the role the state plays (or ought to play) in the strategic considerations and struggles of social movements.

1.1 The organization of bourgeois hegemony

According to Poulantzas, the state is tasked with reproducing the hegemony of the ruling class, which can only be stabilized in the context of the institutional foundation of bourgeois hegemony and of the social relations of forces linked to it: 'The state apparatuses consecrate and reproduce hegemony by bringing the power bloc and certain dominated classes into a (variable) game of provisional compromises' (SPS: 140). In any given historical phase, the state provides a certain stability and form to the relations of forces through temporary compromises. This also applies to the achievements of emancipatory struggles. However, Poulantzas (1979b) also points out that repression is frequently used against left-wing forces. In order to stabilize bourgeois hegemony, the state deploys a variety of techniques: the state apparatuses disorganize and divide the dominated classes and movements, they insulate institutional power centres against subaltern actors, but they also initiate compromises by forcing certain fractions of the power bloc to grant material concessions to some of the dominated forces.

In capitalist societies, the state embodies the 'general interest', which is always constructed in and through conflicts and compromises. However, this general interest is not given *a priori*, but has to be created and made hegemonic. The state is the terrain on which political strategies become binding and generally accepted policies. Poulantzas describes this task of generalization as the state exercising the 'global role as the cohesive factor in a social formation' (PPSC: 53; cf. 44ff.). Thus the state is always a focus of struggles that target society as a whole. However, the matrix of the state is not a neutral terrain. Rather, the state constitutes a strategic terrain that is equipped with structural selectivity, which is why different social forces have different degrees of access to it.

Accordingly, the state is not an instance that is unified and external to the struggles of the subaltern. Rather, the dominated forces are present in the state (SPS: 141) and exist in its institutional structure 'in a specific manner', that is, in the form of 'centres of opposition' (142). Poulantzas does not expand on this term, and it is difficult to imagine such centres as the term suggests a degree of conscious organisation of forces in selected state apparatuses.

Poulantzas also argues that the struggles of social movements are present not only through the establishment of centres of opposition, but also by virtue of the fact that the terrain of the state is pervaded by contradictions within the power bloc and contradictions between the latter and the dominated classes. Therefore, divisions within the state are not just the result of the representation of different interests of the bourgeoisie by different apparatuses: *'for those processes depend equally, or even above all, on the State's role vis-à-vis the dominated classes'* (140). The state and social movements are always interlinked. Even if movements constitute themselves at a distance from the state they always affect its institutional configuration and become part of it. Poulantzas was very concise on this subject: 'the class enemy is always present within the State.' (141). This means that it is always possible for movements to affect concrete policies and the structure of the state apparatus. They do so by shifting the social relations of forces.

Poulantzas has been criticized for focusing too much on forces and struggles, and paying insufficient attention to the structural solidifications of capitalist social formations. Partly as a result of this, Bob Jessop speaks of the state as a 'form-determined condensation of the balance of forces in political and politically-relevant struggle' (1985: 338).[2] An expansion of this discussion in a form-analytical fashion enables us to focus systematically on the fact that the means by which the state acts are far from neutral. These means (e.g., law, money, and taxes) are structured in a bourgeois-capitalist manner. After all, the state is dependent on a functioning capitalist economy. This has far-reaching effects on how we can conceptualize the transformative potential of movements.

Furthermore, Poulantzas deserves to be criticized for overstating the extent to which social relations are formed by the state. Alex Demirović's charge of 'overrating of the state' politically and conceptually (1987: 133; translated) is justified. A more useful approach lies in a Gramscian understanding of the processes through which hegemony is established, which accords a larger role to conflicts within civil society. Such an approach looks more closely at how particular interests, identities and values become generalized into a social project through processes of coercion and consent-compromise. Gramscian approaches are superior to those inspired by Poulantzas in so far as they enable us to theorize the constitution of social forces 'outside' and 'beyond' the state.

1.2 'Radical transformation' and state in the strategic calculus of movements

Undoubtedly, Poulantzas was aware that many left-wing forces do not aim to fundamentally transform social relations. Nonetheless, he consistently argued for such a transformation. In his later works he no longer speaks of revolution, but of 'radical transformation' (SPS: 43). He still identifies the need for rupture and for escalation, but no longer for a moment of

---

2   See Hirsch/Kannankulam in this volume and – for the internationalized state – Brand (2005).

revolutionary transformation. He envisages a long road to socialism, 'during which the masses will act to conquer power and transform the state apparatuses' (254). This refers to all state apparatuses, including the repressive ones (1979b: 7), whose importance Poulantzas had long underestimated (Jessop 1985: 348). Given that the ruling classes held a systematic advantage in the unstable balance of compromises, the task was to transform the terrain upon which compromises were formed. This constituted a 'double strategy' that aimed at transforming the state in the sense of specific relationships of forces, and modifying the materiality of state apparatuses: 'It is true that the State retains a specific materiality: not only is a shift in the relationship of forces within the State insufficient to alter that materiality, but the relationship itself can crystallize in the State only to the extent that the apparatuses of the latter undergo transformation. [...] In this context, I talked above of a *sweeping transformation* of the state apparatus during the transition to democratic socialism' (SPS: 260f.). The transformation of the state on the basis of broad mass movements also matters because Poulantzas is alert to the danger that the state, and in particular the bourgeoisie, might resort to repression when faced with a strengthening of left-wing movements (188f.). Thus for Poulantzas 'the choice is not [...] between a struggle "within" the state apparatuses (that is, physically invested and inserted in their material space) and a struggle located at a certain physical distance from these apparatuses' (259). Struggles at a distance are always also 'refracted' within the apparatuses and present 'through intermediaries' (ibid.). Poulantzas's metaphor of the 'physical investment/insertion' of struggles in the state suggests that what is being transformed are specific orientations of the state personnel, concrete constellations of forces, and conflicts within and between apparatuses in the institutional ensemble that is the state.

Socio-economic and political crises, which sometimes turn into crises of the state, are an important precondition for radical transformation (257).[3] More windows of opportunity open up during such phases than under conditions of hegemony. But what is radical transformation? For Poulantzas, it requires massive and diverse struggles by mass movements. There is no longer a master plan: 'History has not yet given us a successful experience of the democratic road to socialism: what it has provided [...] is some negative examples to avoid and some mistakes upon which to reflect' (265; cf. 1979b: 7f.). However, a general feature of radical transformations would be the 'increased intervention of the popular masses in the State' and the expansion of mechanisms for democratic conflict resolution and

3   Cf. Sablowski in this volume.

discussion (SPS: 261).

Mass struggles aim to strengthen their own base, which includes gaining the support of other social groups for these struggles. In a Poulantzasian vein, what is required is a policy of broad alliances and the integration of a multiple demands (e.g., those of the women's or the green movement). An implicit assumption here is that a mass movement shares an interest that is relatively homogeneous, or that at least remains unproblematized. At the same time, Poulantzas suggests that such a movement should increase tensions within state apparatuses, and expand networks of resistance within the institutional framework of the capitalist state. Shifting the relationship of forces within the State 'denotes nothing other than a *stage of real breaks*, the climax of which – and there has to be one – is reached when the relationship of forces on the strategic terrain of the State swings over to the side of the popular masses' (258f.). Poulantzas not only has in mind elections, parliamentary activity and the occupation of ever-higher posts in government (259f.). He always also indicates that one should aim for the transformation of the relations of forces in all the apparatuses and dispositifs of the state – a transformation that has to occur both within and at a distance to the state apparatuses.

By using the metaphor of rupture, Poulantzas is cautioning us not to focus on successive reforms, important though they may be. Specific ruptures are expressions of shifting relations of forces. True, it remains hard to imagine the 'tipping of the relations of forces on the strategic terrain of the state in favour of the popular masses'. Yet, what Poulantzas does is delineate a kind of bottom line: 'It is necessary to transform the state radically, not just to transform the relations of forces in order to transform the state' (1979a: 32; translated).

Following Poulantzas, struggles over the relations of forces within the state have to be accompanied by struggles over forms of grassroots democracy and self-management. If the latter are absent, the former risk turning into a form of social democracy: 'This [the global perspective of the withering away of the state; U.B./M.H.] comprises *two* articulated processes: transformation of the State and unfurling of direct, rank-and-file democracy' (SPS: 262f.). The attempt to establish and subsequently expand elements of grassroots democracy takes place on the strategic terrain of the state and at the same time transforms representative democracy. Poulantzas advocates social forms of opinion formation and of the coordination of interests whose establishment would render the political form of the state superfluous (cf. Demirović 1987: 145). But he ignores some important problems of representative democracy, namely the separation of 'public' and 'private' or 'politics' and 'economics', as well as the relationship of this separation to forms of direct democracy. If these relations are taken seriously, then social movements need to take into account not only the state, but also other forms of social reproduction (see below).

Poulantzas views the emancipatory democratic transformation of the state as riddled with risks, because movements operate in a terrain with a highly uneven structure. The state might be able to integrate movements into its 'circuits' because they are already reactions to and products of statism themselves (SPS: 234). Unless they are able to transform the state apparatuses, they run the risk of becoming part of the self-modernization of the power bloc (cf. 1979a).

Poulantzas develops his ideas about the relationship between the state and movements against the backdrop of authoritarian statism, the crisis of the state, the centralization and personalization of state power, the growing importance of state bureaucracies for the organization of social classes, and the crisis of the bourgeois and workers' parties. One of the defining characteristics of authoritarian statism is that public administration 'tends to play a monopoly role in politically organizing social classes and ensuring hegemony', and that parties become 'veritable transmission belts for executive decisions, rather than being centres engaged in political elaboration and in working out compromises and alliances around a more or less precise programme' (SPS: 229). And since social democratic and communist parties 'ground their organization too much in the inner contradictions of the factory' (1979c; translated), they do not have a response to this. Therefore, they have to change fundamentally and be present within the movements that Poulantzas views as the answer to authoritarian statism. The 'cultural rebellions' (1979a: 31; translated) or 'revolts', which often do not take place at the centre of production, 'condense diffuse popular protest by transferring it into the cultural domain'. Contrary to the interpretations dominant back then, Poulantzas did not see any contradiction between these movements and class struggle: they 'have repercussions on class conflicts yet cannot be reduced to the latter' (1979c; translated). Nevertheless, Poulantzas still claims that other axes of conflict become relevant primarily in the form of class conflict (SPS: 43f., 148).

Regardless of this, Poulantzas remains sceptical about the capacities of social movements to affect social transformation. In his view, their activities result mostly in neo-corporatism and social segmentation: 'If there is no moment of political generalization, [...] these movements march side by side – each without knowing what the one next to it wants' (1979a: 31; translated).

At the same time, Poulantzas rejects Pietro Ingrao's[4] proposal for the integration of movements into the democratized state, because state apparatuses and parties have a tendency to absorb movements and their procedures of grassroots democracy. Total autonomy, on the other hand, is also deeply problematic. Poulantzas suggests looking for a 'middle way' that preserves the 'unrelenting tension' between movement and party (1979b: 9; translated; 1979c: 10). However, he does not specify what exactly this means.

Poulantzas's scepticism vis-à-vis the new social movements appears exaggerated. He seems to fall victim to his own class reductionist idea that potentials for social generalization can only be found in the working class, and is in turn expressed by the workers' parties. In addition, due to his theoretical and political focus on the state, the existence of strong movements and weakened representative institutions lead him to sound warnings of the disintegration and atomization of the social whole. He underestimates the transformative dynamics of mobilization and politicization unleashed by the movements, as well as the learning processes they entail. Why should autonomous movements only represent particular interests? Why should a generalization of interests, norms and identities that is based on experience and geared towards compromise only occur via parties and the state? Poulantzas's reference to possible 'particularist' orientations does, however, highlight one important point: the state can weaken or even dissolve movements if such moments of generalization do not occur.

In sum, Poulantzas helps us to ask important questions, but he does not supply the answers: how does the claim by particular movements to embody universal moments of an emancipatory society affect these movements, and how does it affect the 'movement of movements'? What are the consequences of a particular movement claiming to embody universalized, emancipatory aspects of society – both for this particular movement and for the 'movement of movements' ? Which role do parties play? Today, it is common to answer that no one specific actor – not even a party – represents a project of universal emancipation, but that such a project needs to be approached and thought through collectively. Universality under bourgeois-capitalist conditions always implies inclusion and exclusion, as well as the identification of people and collectives as dominated subjects. The recognition of the particular is more important than Poulantzas thought. He is far too quick to dissolve it in the universality of the working

---

4   When Ingrao made this statement, he was a member of the national directorate of the PCI [Italian Communist Party – translator's note]. In 1976, he became president of the Italian chamber of deputies.

class and its parties, and thus underestimates an important characteristic of radical transformation and the role of the state: under bourgeois-capitalist, antagonistic conditions, there is a tendency for structures of domination to enforce the universal against the particular.

Of course, this line of argument does not specify any positive criteria for an emancipatory process, nor can such criteria really be specified in advance. They have to emerge in and through processes of struggle, through learning and experience. When engaged in abstraction, we can only say that the non-hierarchical articulation of interests, norms and identities and their reflexive institutionalization are fundamental for developing forms of post-capitalist universality. But this also suggests that radical transformations in the vein of Poulantzas have to be seen as open, searching processes that do not put the state centre-stage. The whole of society, i.e., all mechanisms of reproduction that reinforce divisions of labour and logics of domination, have to be transformed (see below). This also has consequences for counter-hegemonic strategies.

2. Privatization struggles as an example

The political situation today cannot be compared with the siuation when Poulantzas wrote his central works. Nowhere is the transition to socialism an immediate possibility. Yet we believe that Poulantzas's concept of radical transformation can still serve as a source of inspiration for emancipatory struggles. Below we discuss Poulantzas's ideas using the example of privatization struggles. We assume that there is a multiplicity of struggles in society, and that in every conjuncture, some of them become charged with particular importance. Privatization struggles have often been among the 'important' struggles because they usually affect people directly and visibly in their everyday lives. In the 1990s, they developed into a focal point of social conflict.

2.1. Privatization and the transformation of the state

The idea that the state is the instrument of the bourgeoisie or of individual fractions of capital is still prominent in many critical analyses of privatization processes (cf. Boris et al. 2005; Gill 2002). In contrast to this, we outline a Poulantzasian understanding of privatization policies.

The implementation of privatization policies, which constitute a core element of the neoliberal transformation of the state, have been implemented rigorously for about twenty years. The push for privatization in the 1980s and 1990s was preceded by a massive push for state ownership. State ownership was consistent with the generalized model of the Keynesian state that also played an important role in the construction of specific peripheral

Fordist modes of development in the context of decolonization. Thus, policies of transferring assets into state ownership reflected a historically specific configuration of social relations of forces.

Privatizations were (a) an attempt to solve what was perceived, by the end of the 1970s, as the crisis of Fordism (for example in France and Mexico), and (b) a specific strategy for restructuring social relations. It was an expression of specific political and accumulation strategies supported by national and international actors. The interiorization of external interests is particularly important in peripheral formations. The dynamic of accumulation emerging in the transition to post-Fordism relied crucially on the privatization of formerly state-owned industries and services. This strategy was favoured in particular by transnational fractions of capital that owned major stakes in transnational corporations. Sometimes fractions of the national bourgeoisie were also interested in privatizations, because it allowed them to penetrate more deeply into particular niches and recover areas for private capital accumulation. However, privatization proved a contradictory process. Not every privatization was profitable. The water company *Suez*, for example, pursued an expansive global strategy up until the millennium. In 2000, however, it began retreating from the countries of the South. Its strategy had turned out to be insufficiently profitable. Nevertheless, privatization also formed a political strategy that furthered the neoliberal vision of society. It constituted an activity that was aimed at shifting social relations of forces.

In this regard, the forces pushing for privatization managed to institutionalize their vision in the apparatuses of the internationalized state. In so doing, they transformed the latter's institutional materiality. The post-Fordist state became a 'national competition state' (Hirsch 1997) – a process through which those economic state functions connected to competitiveness became more important. In this context, privatization became a measure of competitiveness.

In sum, privatization was crucial to the neoliberal project of restructuring the state and society. This does not mean that all privatization attempts were smooth. In fact, privatization remained a heavily contested issue inside and outside state apparatuses. Within the matrix of the state, there were frequent attempts to 'depoliticize' privatizations by changing the setting in which decisions are taken – usually by switching to the international level. These processes of institutional restructuring contributed to establishing a strategic selectivity on the terrain of the state that rendered this terrain 'conducive to privatization'. Thus, they had significant feedback effects on the effectiveness of different actors' strategies within conflicts around privatization.

2.2. Struggles against privatization

What is Poulantzas's contribution to the analysis of struggles against privatization? He shows that struggles are extremely diverse and emerge in a variety of locations, but can nonetheless develop certain universalizing dynamics. Based on these ideas we develop below a typology of anti-privatization struggles.

Struggles against privatization arose for a multiplicity of reasons (e.g., to save jobs or maintain access to clean and affordable drinking water) and involved multiple actors. Some of these actors constituted themselves directly on the terrain of the state, others at a distance from it. For example, state personnel and public sector employees conducted struggles aimed at defending public service jobs. They felt that certain tasks should remain in the hands of the state. In other words, they subscribed to the idea of the state as the representative of the common good. Often, their resistance took subtle forms, e.g., isolated acts of sabotage, and sometimes it was publicized by trade unions. Although their self-understanding was usually not anti-capitalist, their resistance did constitute a centre of opposition in Poulantzas's sense.

Anti-privatization struggles also developed at a certain distance from the state, and were carried by social movements that often represented highly diverse interests: sometimes these actors were engaged in purely defensive battles, e.g., when they resisted the sale of a company or service provider. Consumer rights movements, which remained largely within the confines of capitalist discourses, are another example. These movements demanded the protection of their living conditions, e.g., they requested that privatized companies refrain from increasing user fees.

There were also attempts to develop longer-term strategies for anti-privatization struggles that went beyond capitalist societalization. One example was the anti-GATS-campaign under the motto 'Our World is not for Sale', which connected defensive struggles with the expansion of political visions at the discursive level.

Ultimately, these struggles aimed to reconstruct the matrix of the state, although this was not necessarily a conscious goal. They were about trying to avert the neoliberal transformation of the state in a particular economic sector, industry or company. Thus struggles against privatization were often struggles against the internationalization of the state, which frequently went hand in hand with privatizations, and *for* strengthening national parliaments.

At the same time, the terrain of the state also shaped these struggles because at one point or another people ended up utilizing the state's strategic capacities. Employees usually sought to avert the threat of privatization-induced job losses through recourse to labour law. Even when people were facing more confrontational strategies and felt the coercive force of the state, they regularly took recourse to the law and to questions of legitimacy to protect themselves.

In conclusion, amongst the various strategies used by opponents of privatization, the ones that were successful tended to be those that were anchored in broad alliances and took institutional actors into account. For example, alliances between demonstrators and parliamentarians increased the chance to significantly disrupt processes of privatization. But we should not be tempted to re-embrace a naïve conception of the state and assume that it represents the common good. Rather, future campaigns against privatizations still require a radical critique of the state and should take the form of *strategic interventions* (cf. Heigl 2010, 2011).

Such strategic interventions encompass a whole range of strategies, including demonstrations, targeted lobbying strategies by NGOs, and hearings organized by parliamentarians. Yet, what remains crucial, is that the protagonists of the various strategies are in contact with one another, so that the movement is both diverse and harbours contradictions. Similarly, it is essential to develop equitable ways of dealing with one another within a movement – through grassroots democracy – as well as forms of resistance to the transformation of the state that make use of representative democracy.

3. Perspectives: radical transformation in global capitalism

Poulantzas poses a political and theoretical question: to what extent can particular struggles defend and promote not only particular interests, norms and identities, but also transform the terrain of struggles in itself, and organize the general features of society in a non-hierarchical way? He sees no alternative to acting both inside and outside of the strategic terrain of the state. But this only provides a general framework that needs to be filled with specific strategies by specific forces and coalitions.

The radical transformation of society is riddled with uncertainties and dilemmas: To what extent can emancipatory forces exploit contradictions and crises within hegemonic constellations? How is a far-reaching transformation of the institutional materiality of the state possible that takes competing actors into account? To what extent can emancipatory forces enter into coalitions with other forces whose fundamental interest lies in the maintenance of bourgeois-capitalist society? What is the role of international relations? To what extent does the practical critique articulated by anti-capitalist forces generate a modernizing dynamic for capitalism?

Poulantzas's term 'radical transformation' refers to the state, i.e., to its power and its institutional materiality. A post-capitalist or socialist strategy, however, has to fundamentally transform all social relations, not just the state: ways of producing, reproducing and living; ethnic and gender relations; relations with nature; and the forms of international exchange. Poulantzas can help us to make sense of this theoretically, but his strategic considerations fall far short of it.

Since the 1980s, however, the concept of radical reformism has provided a necessary change of perspective (Hirsch 1990; Esser et al. 1994; Brand 2001). Radical reformism focuses more on the step-by-step transformation of all social relations in and through conflicts, experiences, and learning processes. The perspective shifts to include the existing divergences within emancipatory movements, as well as the need to address them. Generally speaking, radical reformism envisages action that occurs within and transforms institutions. In so doing, it also affects wider social structures (Esser et al. 1994: ch. 5).

Poulantzas intervened in political debates that were shaped by the failed socialist experiments in Chile or Portugal, but also by offensives of emancipatory forces. In contrast, radical reformism developed in the context of the emergence of post-Fordism, the neoliberal counter-revolution and the resulting transformation of the state. To simplify somewhat, it emphasizes the autonomous aspects of political transformations without losing sight of the state's materiality. But it is far more critical of states and parties than Poulantzas's 'radical transformation' and relies more on the creativity of social movements and their ability to universalize their claims. Poulantzas in turn emphasizes more strongly than radical reformism the need to transform the state apparatuses themselves, including the repressive ones.

'No one can escape their times', Poulantzas stated in his critique of Gramsci (1979b: 13; translated). This of course also applies to himself. Today we need to reflect upon the fact that there is an enormous diversity of struggles and actors, and that some of these actors are not able or willing to cooperate in a more or less coherent project.

Both Poulantzas's strategic ideas and those of radical reformism largely refer to the national state and have to be thoroughly rethought in the face of globalization. The challenge is to develop a 'neo-Poulantzasian' research programme for International Political Economy (IPE) (Brand et al. 2008; Brand/Görg 2008). The 'inside' and 'outside' of the state are changing, and so are the strategies of those involved in transformative struggles. One of the important theoretical tasks of the coming years will be to conceptualize, from the perspective of social forces and their strategies, the transformations of economic, ideological and political relations and the transformation of the state that is occurring within them. In so doing, we must not lose sight of the materiality of the state and its specific functions in the process of reproducing bourgeois-capitalist domination. The state as a condensed relationship of forces and as an institutional materiality is becoming increasingly multi-scalar. Useful approaches to these processes already exist in concepts like the internationalization of the state (Hirsch 2005), within neo-Gramscian IPE (Bieling 2005; Bieler/Morton 2004; Cox 1993) and feminist IPE (Sauer 2003; Bakker/Gill 2003). Normatively, there is the question of how – on a global level – we can envisage a post-capitalist society with forms of conflict resolution and compromise that exceed the logics of domination and rule-orientated behaviour. The 'inside' and 'outside' of the internationalized state and the 'general perspective' of its withering away also need to be investigated. The general principles of these investigations are the following: to produce and consume in a sustainable and non-hierarchical manner; to deal with conflicts in a way that does not reproduce domination; and to enable people to formulate desires and represent and live their interests, values and identities. Social problems (potentially concerning the whole world) should be dealt with where they emerge; but this might have to be coordinated globally.

A precise analysis of the state, of its small adjustments and fundamental transformations, and of its contradictory role in the process of bourgeois-capitalist reproduction remains an important condition for practices of transformation and emancipation. However, even the most precise analyses will not guard us against the risks and problems attached to transformative strategies and actions – and nothing shields us from the fact that they can fail.

References

Bakker, I. / Gill, S. (eds.) (2003) *Power, Production and Social Reproduction* (Basingstoke: Palgrave Macmillan).Bieler, A. / Morton, D. A. (2004) 'A Critical Theory Route to Hegemony, World Order and Historical Change: Neo-Gramscian Perspectives in International Relations', *Capital & Class*, vol. 82, 85-114.
Bieling, H.-J. (2005) 'Die Konflikttheorie der Internationalen Politischen Ökonomie', in Bonacker, T. (ed.) *Sozialwissenschaftliche Konflikttheorien* (Wiesbaden: VS-Verlag) 121-142.
Boris, D. / Schmalz, S. / Tittor, A. (eds.) (2005) *Lateinamerika: Verfall neoliberaler Hegemonie* (Hamburg: VSA-Verlag).
Brand, U. (2001) 'Radikaler Reformismus im globalisierten Kapitalismus: Neubestimmungen nach "Seattle" und "Genua"', *ila*, vol. 26, no. 248, 5-7.
Brand, U. (2005) *Gegen-Hegemonie. Perspektiven globalisierungskritischer Strategien*

(Hamburg: VSA-Verlag).
Brand, U. / Görg, C. (2008) 'Post-Fordist governance of nature. The internationalization of the state and the case of genetic resources: a Neo-Poulantzian Perspective', *Review of International Political Economy*, vol. 15, no. 4, 567-589.
Brand, U. / Görg, C. / Hirsch, J. / Wissen, M. (2008) *Conflicts in Environmental Regulation and the Internationalization of the State. Contested Terrains* (London: Routledge).
Cox, R. W. (1993) 'Gramsci, Hegemony, and International Relations: An essay in method', in Gill, S. (ed.) *Gramsci, Historical Materialism and International Relations* (Cambridge/UK: Cambridge Univ. Press) 49-66.
Demirović, A. (1987) *Nicos Poulantzas. Eine kritische Auseinandersetzung* (Hamburg: Argument-Verlag).
Gill, S. (2002) 'Privatization of the State and Social Reproduction? GATS and New Constititutionalism', conference paper (Warwick).
Esser, J. / Görg, C. / Hirsch, J. (eds.) (1994) *Politik, Institutionen und Staat: Zur Kritik der Regulationstheorie* (Hamburg: VSA-Verlag).
Heigl, M. (2011a) 'Social Conflict and Competing State Projects in the Semi-Periphery. A Strategic-Relational Analysis of the Transformation of the Mexican State into an Internationalized Competition State', *Antipode. A Radical Journal of Geography*, vol. 43, no. 1, 129-148.
Heigl, M. (2011b) 'An Operationalization of the Strategic-Relational Approach: The Contested Privatization of the Mexican Oil Sector (1982-2006)', *Globalizations* vol. 8, no. 1, 81-96.
Hirsch, J. (1990) *Kapitalismus ohne Alternative?* (Hamburg: VSA-Verlag).
Hirsch, J. (1997) 'Globalization of capital, nation-states and democracy', *Studies in Political Economy*, vol. 54, 39-58.
Hirsch, J. (2005) *Materialistische Staatstheorie. Transformationsprozesse des kapitalistischen Staatensystems* (Hamburg: VSA-Verlag).
Jessop, B. (1985) *Nicos Poulantzas. Marxist Theory and Political Strategy* (Basingstoke: Macmillan).
Poulantzas, N. (1979a) 'El Etatismo Autoritario recorre Europa. Entrevista con Nicos Poulantzas', *El Viejo Topo*, vol. 4, no. 35, 28-32.
Poulantzas, N. (1979b) 'Problemas de Implementación de una Vía Democrática al Socialismo: Entrevista con Nicos Poulantzas', *Argumentos*, vol. 3, no. 28, 6-14.
Poulantzas, N. (1979c) 'La crise des partis', *Le Monde Diplomatique*, 26-09-1979.
Sauer, B. (2003) 'Die Internationalisierung von Staatlichkeit: Geschlechterpolitische Perspektiven', *Deutsche Zeitschrift für Philosophie*, vol. 51, no. 4, 621-637.

RULE OF THE PEOPLE?
DEMOCRACY AND THE CAPITALIST STATE
IN THE WORK OF NICOS POULANTZAS

ALEX DEMIROVIĆ

There is a division of labour in political science and in Marxist debates: political theory and philosophy deal with values, e.g., equality, liberty and justice, while policy analysis looks at the actual processes of state power being exercised, that is, at parties, legislative procedures, and administration. Material necessities are divorced from the notions of freedom and emancipation as well from potentials for autonomous action. Nicos Poulantzas rejects this separation; he analyses the state in the context of an integral theory of politics. This covers power and the state (SPS: 11) as well as democratic progress and the emancipation of subaltern groups. Poulantzas discusses democracy not as an empty normative abstraction, but in the context of how it is exercised; through parliamentary democracy, state domination and concrete social struggles. His aim is to establish that democracy is a contradictory form of state rule. For him, the capitalist state is not simply an institution with dictatorial qualities that executes the will of the ruling class. Accordingly, he also suggests moving beyond a critique of ideology that contents itself with pointing out that the state is just the form bourgeois domination takes under capitalist conditions, and that the common interest it represents is an illusion.

This may be correct at a high level of abstraction, but from a historical perspective, things become particularly interesting if we start investigating the concrete ways in which bourgeois class rule is exercised. Poulantzas emphasizes how, under normal circumstances, state rule in capitalism takes the form of the democratic republic: 'why, in general, does the bourgeoisie seek to maintain its domination by having recourse precisely to the national-popular State – to the modern representative State with all its characteristic institutions?' (12). It is clear, however, that in many modern states the principle of the republic and democracy prove to be either short-lived or severely restricted. This indicates that the bourgeoisie does not necessarily perceive this state form as being adequate to the pursuit of its interests, and that its support is not unconditional in the normative sense. In fact, the bourgeoisie's relationship to the democratic form is a tactical one, and more often than not it appears as though it has to be forced into accepting the rules of democracy.

1. Democracy: self-determination of the people or a mechanism of integration?

Wolfgang Abendroth's works are of key importance for the Marxist analysis of state domination and democracy. They reflect the specific constellation of class compromise that expressed the weakness and demoralization of bourgeois forces after the defeat of National Socialism. This constellation was enshrined in the West German Basic Law[1] and constituted a framework for the democratic conduct of conflicts of interest. Abendroth assumes that in monopoly capitalism, the liberal separation of society and state comes to an end. Given the concentration of capital, the legislature no longer enacts general laws to be applied in a competitive market, but intervenes on behalf of leading corporations that enjoy privileged access to political decision-making. The Basic Law should be seen as a class compromise because the dominance of capital is counterbalanced by juxtaposing it to the idea that justice and the common good are not simply the result of unregulated markets, but that the state must instead intervene and balance the unequal distribution of power on the grounds of collective decisions by political and social forces. Accordingly, the state is understood as a social and democratic state under the rule of law [Rechtsstaat]. In turn, the society represented in and through this democratic state has the opportunity to rule itself through the state and to modify its own foundations (cf. Abendroth 1954a: 122).

According to Abendroth, the essence of democracy lies in the equal participation of all in the regulation of common tasks. Parliamentary forms of legislation and the formation and control of governments should not be equated with democracy. It was only through universal suffrage, allowances for MPs, and democratic mass parties – which emerged due to the pressure from the labour movement – that pluralistic opportunities for the political participation of all citizens and for shaping public life were created. Parliament was thus able to gain true political power, and the state was democratized.

---

1   Editors' note: The Basic Law or 'Grundgesetz' was enacted in 1949 in West Germany as a substitute for a constitution. This reflected the provisional status of the Federal Republic of Germany. Under the terms of the 1990 Contract of Reunification between both German states, the Basic Law was transformed into a constitution with a permanent status.

Yet Abendroth does not fall prey to parliamentary delusions. Parliament can only be a 'democratic means of integration' to the extent 'to which it is aware that it is merely the coordinator and decision-making unit of the manifold forces of modern society whose interior is organized democratically' (1954b: 29, translated). He also rejects any form of abstract faith in the law: a constitution does not by itself guarantee democracy; it is, rather, a kind of 'class truce' supported by the prevalent social forces. A regression into authoritarianism remains possible unless there is a deepening of democracy that embeds the achievements of the Basic Law more deeply, above all by restricting the decision-making power and the influence of monopoly capital. It is crucial for Abendroth that the Basic Law does not rule out the possibility of a peaceful transition to socialism. Without neglecting the fact that the use of physical violence may become an issue again, he states unambiguously that it is in the best interest of the labour movement to avoid such violence and to go about the dismantling of political domination in a democratic manner (cf. 1977: 188f.).

Johannes Agnoli (1968) was the most vocal opponent of Abendroth's ideas. According to him, the ruling classes' fear of social emancipation through universal suffrage and the constitution leads them to transform democracy. They ensure that the capitalist structures serve as the framework of the parliamentary 'game'. This happens by reducing the degree of control exercised by parliament, as well as its sovereignty and representative character, subordinating it to the executive. Accordingly, the parliamentary oligarchy gets linked symbiotically with the upper echelons of the executive apparatus. For Agnoli, parliament is no longer a decision-making body, but an instrument of peaceful manipulative integration. It integrates subaltern groups by exposing a section of holders of power – the parliamentary oligarchy – to public scrutiny and creating the impression that this is the place where decisions are really made. Agnoli argues that western parliamentary democracy is a product of capitalism and a type of public-legal rule adequate to the 'market economy'. It renders class antagonism invisible by transforming it into a pluralistic contest between parties and leaders. Parties get detached from their respective social bases and become catch-all parties, so that class consciousness is supplanted by 'citizens' consciousness'. The state appears as a power above and beyond the arguments of particular groups, committed exclusively to the common good.

Both Abendroth's and Agnoli's approaches share the assumption that society is determined by the state. For Abendroth, there is an equilibrium of forces which ensures that the state also remains open to the interests of the working class. It depends on the democratic structure of the parties whether this openness is utilized effectively. This is also Agnoli's initial assumption. In his view, however, the parliament and the parties have changed fundamentally. They now act as filters that selectively process the interests of subaltern groups, and serve to create the illusion that these interests are still being considered in discussions and decision-making. This way, they adapt subaltern interests to the ideological universality of the state.

Both accounts have serious flaws. Abendroth takes parliament to be the centre of political power. In fact, he focuses on this part of the state so much that he loses sight of other parts. Agnoli, on the other hand, is so caught up in his critique of the ideology of parliament and the parties that his analysis neither convincingly renders the state as a whole nor the complexity of the balance of forces and of class compromises.

2. The capitalist state as the material condensation of relations of forces

Poulantzas's work is original because he develops a concept of the capitalist state that combines both class struggle and class compromise, as well the solidification of the state into a function for domination. All these aspects are linked in the hypothesis that the capitalist state is the material condensation of the relationship of forces between ruling and dominated classes. The state is itself a form of class struggle; it operates in a field of unstable balances of compromise in order to maintain bourgeois rule and the hegemony of some of the individual fractions of this class (cf. SPS: 30f.). Accordingly, it can be seen as a condensation in which an unstable balance of social forces materializes. It constitutes a compromise not only when there is an exact equilibrium of forces – as Otto Bauer (1924) or Wolfgang Abendroth have it – but also when there is an asymmetrical configuration.

This definition is based on two assumptions: (1) there is a primacy of social struggles; and (2) the state embodies political-ideological relations and materially condenses such struggles and the relationships of forces between classes and class fractions, thereby becoming the central *locus* for the exercise of political power (SPS: 128, 26f., 44f.). The field of power and the field of social struggles are wider than the field of class struggles, which in turn encompasses effects that go beyond the state. Social struggles cannot be reduced to class struggles, which themselves cannot be reduced to struggles over the state – as has often been argued by representatives of communist, anarchist, and socialist movements. In spite of also being a consequence of struggles, the state does not enter their field *ex post facto*, intervening into them from the outside only. Instead, it is constitutively present within them and in the field of power. In other words, it 'is organically present in the generation of class power' (45, cf. 39). The field of power, social struggles and compromises is always already over-determined by the state, which acts as the conduit for these struggles and compromises as well as a potential force for intervention.

All this follows from Poulantzas's explanation for why the capitalist state is marked by a peculiar material structure. According to him, the capitalist mode of production is characterized by the fundamental separation of the economy and politics. Thus, he rejects Abendroth's idea – influenced by Hegel – that society determines itself through the state. According to the classic contractual model, the state represents the common interest of society because, due to the presence of self-interested individuals, it is incapable of doing so for itself. Poulantzas argues, however, that the state is itself a social relation that is drawn into social struggles, albeit in a privileged position. This is a convincing point: the state cannot be a part of society and at the same time direct it as a whole or overcome its conflicts. Poulantzas therefore strongly rejects functionalist explanations according to which the state produces the cohesion of society by externally securing the conditions for the reproduction of capital (29f.). The state is a strategic terrain of power in so far as social struggles are partly displaced in and through it. As a result, they take place on its terrain. The particular role of the state results from its separation from the relations of production, which, in turn, is the result of the separation of the immediate producers from the means of production, and of owners of capitals controlling the latter. This separation and appropriation has to be supported by a separate political apparatus, because the class that owns the means of production organizes the apparatus of production and the private appropriation of surplus labour, but does not exert direct, personal control over wage labourers.

Moreover, owners of capital are not only engaged in local struggles with the working class; they are also in conflict with other owners of capital who all want their share of the total profit. What is therefore required is the emergence and reproduction of a sphere of political domination and of a relatively autonomous state, whose separation from the relations of production allows for the formation of an autonomous economic sphere appearing to be governed by something akin to the laws of nature. Yet with the help of its many apparatuses, the capitalist state can still unify the bourgeoisie in its entirety, give stability to its rule, and fulfil some of its organic tasks in its place. The state is able to do so thanks to its separation from the relations of production. Accordingly, Poulantzas argues that the capitalist state emerges as an autonomous apparatus that integrates the bourgeoisie and other ruling classes in a power bloc. This does not mean that the state simply represents the collective interest of the bourgeoisie. It does not transcend the bourgeoisie or other classes. Instead, there are conflicts within the power bloc over the strategy for controlling the popular classes and the distribution of profits. In the power bloc, one fraction is hegemonic. This fraction is the one that defines the common interest of the power bloc, the long-term strategy, as well as the criteria for reaching compromises between the fractions in the power bloc and with the popular classes. The relationships of forces in the power bloc are materialized in the state apparatuses and their relations to one another. Just as the state, as a strategic terrain, organizes the rulers as rulers, it also disorganizes and divides the subaltern social classes. It does so by (a) individualizing their members through turning them into legal subjects and citizens, (b) uniting and representing them as the people/nation, and (c) making compromises with particular groups (cf. PPSC: 133ff.).

In contrast to Abendroth and Agnoli, Poulantzas concludes that the popular classes cannot be directly organized and represented within the capitalist state; but they are also never entirely external to it. In other words, the material structure of the state has excluding effects in a strategic sense (cf. SPS: 151f.). However, thanks to possessing relative autonomy, the state can impose certain compromises on the power bloc. In so doing, it is able to win over sections of the subordinate classes for supporting or entering alliances with the power bloc. The popular masses are therefore inscribed into the state through the conflicts between themselves and the ruling-class fractions. They are also inscribed into the state through the strategies that the ruling fractions choose for exercising domination, which either weaken or strengthen the position of the popular masses in the power bloc: 'The dominant classes and fractions exist in the State by means of apparatuses or branches which, although subject to the unity of the state power of the hegemonic fraction, nevertheless crystallize a power that is peculiar to these classes and fractions. By contrast the dominated classes exist in the State not by means of apparatuses concentrating a *power of their own*, but essentially in the form of centres of opposition to the power of the dominant classes' (142).

The popular classes are effective in the state from a distance. Yet whereas some state apparatuses (e.g., the police, the judiciary) are capable of producing compromises only to a very limited extent, others are much better at this, so that individuals from the popular classes may attain relevant positions within them (e.g., the schools, higher education, the armed forces) (152). The more 'successful' state apparatuses often attain dominance precisely because they organize these very compromises. Finally, the popular classes are present in parliaments and – more rarely – governments through their elected representatives. These positions hand them considerable control and knowledge (cf. 221ff.). Hence, the subordinate classes are present in the state – but always as subordinates. In Germany, this is reflected in the common perception that CDU and CSU are the structural parties of government, which are deemed fit to govern despite their corruption, mistakes and failures, while SPD-led governments seem to be in constant need of legitimation.[2]

Thus, the state constitutes a strategic terrain on which the ruling classes are represented and organized, and establishes their hegemony over the subordinate classes. In other words, it is the place where the balance of forces between the ruling groups and claims for leadership are negotiated and restructured. This applies particularly to the relationships of forces in and between state apparatuses. Each state apparatus is thus the *locus* of condensation for a particular constellation of forces. This is true for state apparatuses as diverse as (1) the repressive state apparatuses military and police, (2) state apparatuses engaged in economic regulation such as the ministries of economics and finance, the central bank or scientific and statistical institutes, and (3) ideological state apparatuses such as the parliament, the parties, higher education institutions, the schools, the media, and the churches. The political unity of these apparatuses is established through the hegemony of a particular fraction of capital in the power bloc. The latter in turn contains all the contradictions and conflicts between the different fractions.

Following Althusser (IISA), Poulantzas views both the parliament and the parties as ideological state apparatuses. If we take Germany as a test case, we have to distinguish, however, between different houses of parliament such as *Bundestag* [lower house] and *Bundesrat* [upper house], the chancellor and her/his office, the president, the speakers of the houses, the leaders of the parliamentary parties, the parliaments of the federal states[3], and the constitutional court. This list shows that the functions of state apparatuses cannot be defined in an essentialist manner, because their functions change (cf. SPS: 33). Political power runs through them and can become condensed in particular constellations of people, representative roles and functions. As a result, the appointment of particular individuals

2   Translators' note: the CSU (Christian Social Union) and the CDU (Christian Democratic Union) are two closely allied centre-right parties operating in Bavaria and the rest of Germany respectively. They form a single parliamentary party in the Lower House of the Federal Parliament (Bundestag). For the better part of the history of the Federal Republic of Germany, they held government. The SPD is the Social Democratic Party of Germany.

3   Editors' note: Germany consists of 16 federal states, which all have their own parliaments [Landtage], governments and prime ministers [Ministerpräsidenten].

with distinct opinions and strategies may become either more or less important than the formal and legal authority of an office, an agency, or a government body. It is impossible to determine once and for all whether the parliament is the privileged *locus* of opinion formation. This not only comes down to the state of the parties – as Abendroth and Agnoli suggest. It also depends, to an even higher degree, on whether the forces in the power bloc see themselves as being represented in parliament and organize themselves through it, or whether they are unwilling to make compromises (as indicated by the conservative criticism that legislation is always watered down in parliament). The national parliament is just one of these places. If representative democracy and the pluralism of political parties work, and members of parliament represent the interests of the population not just in parliament but also directly vis-à-vis the administration, then this is usually accompanied by expanding political liberties (169f., 182f.). However, the political process does not guarantee a particularly powerful position for parliament. It may well be the case that the latter's role is restricted to producing and reproducing ideology. At worst, parliament hosts 'theatrical' events characterized by non-binding discussions, while the legislative process is dominated by the heads of the executive, administrative agencies, lobby groups and their lawyers. Yet parliament should not be underestimated even in such a configuration. After all, there may still be conflicts of interest between different lobby groups, so that parliamentary decision-making becomes important again. In addition, MPs backing the government can become dissatisfied with it and withdraw their support if they fear for their re-election or feel that they are not taken seriously.

Under normal circumstances, parliament remains an important node of political power because it is the place where political decision-making is directly accessible for the public, and where decisions become collectively binding legal rules. Accordingly, Poulantzas distinguishes four levels of state organization and power:

(1) The capitalist type of state, which is characterized by its separation from the economy, its organizational role for the power bloc, and its individualizing and unifying effect in terms of producing a people/nation.

(2) Different state forms, which can be distinguished by looking at how they articulate the state and the economy, i.e., whether the relations between both fields are liberal or interventionist in character. The state forms correspond to particular combinations of ownership and property of the means of production and the social division of labour at a certain phase of the capitalist mode of production.

(3) The different types of political regimes located at an even more concrete

level. Here, the question is how the policies of the power bloc are formulated and what kind of strategies are pursued, that is, how the power bloc is organized. This concerns different forms of the distribution of tasks among the apparatuses, the role of parties, and the mode of separation of powers between the executive, legislative and judicial branches of government as well as between central and federal governments. The power bloc can, for instance, organize itself through a single party (such as the LDP in Japan) and conduct its fractional conflicts within this party, but it can also be organized as a two- or multi-party system. It is also possible that political crises and conflicts inside the power bloc lead to (a) power being displaced and shifted into a specific part of the executive, and (b) an increase of the state's autonomy vis-à-vis the fractions in the power bloc. Such a crisis can throw the entire political scene and regime into crisis (cf. PPSC: 319).

(4) Different forms of the exceptional capitalist state: Bonapartism, military dictatorship, and fascism (cf. FD: 313ff.).

I would now like to highlight three implications of Poulantzas's approach for the assessment of parliamentary democracy:

(1) Agnoli's analyses suggest that any left-wing participation in parliamentary elections will only serve to integrate protest into the pacification agenda pursued by the state, which in turn contributes to the reproduction of the capital relation. In contrast, Abendroth argues that socialist parties which integrate the different factions of the left and have trade union support should advocate a transition to socialism in parliament that is supported by legislative activity. Poulantzas, too, is clearly in favour of left-wing parties entering parliament. There is, after all, a particular relationship of forces in parliament. This concerns parties, the parliamentary representation of the popular masses and public discussion as well as the connections and exchanges between MPs and the administration. As a result, there is a certain degree of public control over the administration.[4] However, parliament is also a specific and local relationship of forces, and it is not at all clear whether the formulation of the policies of the power bloc are even made in the political scene. The effects of left-wing parties in this regard are ambivalent. If their parliamentary politics are successful, they will try to drag more political issues and decisions into the ambit of parliament, which will, in turn, force the power bloc to organize itself more strongly in and through parliament. At the same time, however, such successes may also cause the power bloc to retreat from parliament, at least temporarily.

(2) According to Poulantzas, society is not grounded in the state and the

---

4 Accordingly, Poulantzas stood for the Greek Euro-communist party in general elections.

parliament-as-legislator; rather, the state is located in the strategic field of social struggles and compromise. Therefore, the democratization of society cannot be achieved simply by the democratization of parliament or even of multiple state apparatuses. Even in cases where the occupation of relevant positions of power by representatives of the popular classes results in a successful reversal of the balance of power in individual state apparatuses, the power bloc will simply move into others. Bearing in mind that the private/public separation is itself defined politically, there is also the possibility for the power bloc to obtain the support of semi-private forces that come to be its *de facto*-representatives: fascist or mafia-type groups, certain media or coteries. In so doing, the power bloc may be able to reverse the constellation of forces inside a certain state apparatus. This implies that civil society must be democratized, too. Poulantzas underlines the multiple contradictions and conflicts between different fractions of the power bloc on the grounds of the experience of the military dictatorships in Southern Europe and their decline in the 1970s. Popular struggles can cause such contradictions to become more intense and lead to the implosion of regimes (cf. CD: 85). The Portuguese case constitutes Poulantzas's prime example: the dictatorship was brought down by a group in the military that supported socialist goals. If popular struggles are effective from a distance and intensify the power bloc's internal contradictions it will become more difficult for the latter to pursue a consistent strategy. This can even trigger a political crisis in which no individual fraction is able to become hegemonic. Given the situation of the 1970s, Poulantzas therefore calls for the multiplication of popular struggles and social movements and argues that these must not be reduced to a single contradiction (wage labour/capital) or to a single form of domination.

(3) Poulantzas warns against falling prey to illusions of autonomy, i.e., policies that are deemed to remain outside power and the state, but do not. At the same time, he supports such policies to an extent. According to him, it is impossible to remain outside the state because political actors cannot leave the strategic field of struggles and compromises. Grassroots movements and networks of self-management are important, but Poulantzas rejects the idea that autonomy can only be achieved outside of the field of relations of forces. After all, movements emerge in the field of power and cannot but act in it and in the field of the state (cf. SPS: 152f.). Accordingly, autonomy is not the starting point, but the result of political struggle. It can only be achieved when centres of resistance emerge and democratization and transformation are pursued as explicit strategic goals.

3. Radical transformation and the goals of democratic socialism

Poulantzas's explicit aim is democratic socialism. For him, Lenin's main mistake lay in seeing representative democracy as the dictatorship of the bourgeoisie, and in pursuing a strategy of dual power. According to Lenin, state power was concentrated in one place, and the popular masses were located outside of it. Consequently, the popular masses were supposed to conquer the bourgeois state apparatus and substitute it with the 'real' democracy of Soviets. This also meant there was no conception of transforming the state apparatus itself. The existing state was seen as an instrument of the bourgeoisie, and this was accompanied by the belief that one could use it for certain tasks by exchanging the leadership and controlling it from the top. In this conception, a parallel state-like structure emerges that is characterized by top-down control through the party; the latter in turn is structured like the state. The implementation of this strategy results in a technical-bureaucratic statism imposed by experts, with a concomitant distrust of grass roots-democratic movements.

In light of this, Poulantzas highlights a false choice that the left needs to reject. There is the Social Democratic option of accepting representative democracy, which means that pushes for democratization can always be reversed. Alternatively, there is a strategy based on direct rank-and-file democracy, which, however, becomes inevitably transformed into the despotism of state experts. Therefore, Poulantzas suggests a strategy of transformation that incorporates both approaches. This strategy is two-pronged:

(1) One aim must be the 'sweeping transformation' of the state (SPS: 261, cf. 43) through a strategy for democratization, combined with a shift in the balance of compromise in the state apparatuses. This is meant to strengthen the institutions of representative democracy and to reinforce political liberties (258). Poulantzas stresses that this strategy is not narrowly focused on merely electoral successes. It only makes sense if it leads to an extension of real breaks, 'the climax of which [...] is reached when the relationship of forces on the strategic terrain of the State swings over to the side of the popular masses', i.e., the entirety of its apparatuses and dispositifs (258f.). The state, however, should not be destroyed. Following Rosa Luxemburg, Poulantzas emphasizes that the institutions of representative democracy need to be maintained as positive conditions of political liberty and democratic socialism. The separation of the state and the economy can be overcome and the state can gradually wither away to the extent to which new forms of rank-and-file democracy emerge with the expansion of new

networks and centres of self-management (261f.).

(2) The transformation of the state has to be combined with a continuous struggle at a distance from the state and the development of grass-roots democracy in the form of social movements and practices of self-management. However, these struggles for grass-roots democracy should not become an alternative power base claiming to be outside the state. A unilateral 'shift of the centre of gravity towards the self-management movement would likewise make it impossible, in the medium term, to avoid techno-bureaucratic statism and authoritarian confiscation of power by the experts' (262). In contrast to the sceptical, occasionally sterile discussion on the left about whether or not it makes sense to participate in elections, Poulantzas's answer is clearly affirmative. Depending on circumstances, however, it may be more effective to pursue interests outside parliament or without government participation. Social movements are not simply an instrument at the disposal of other forces that can be used in random ways. Poulantzas's writing was strongly influenced by Euro-communist debates that took place at the same time as the development of broad social movements in many European countries. In Germany, these processes led to the Green party entering parliaments, councils, and governments of federal states, and eventually even the federal government. Yet partial successes in the areas of legislation and financial and political sponsorship notwithstanding, this has hardly led to a reversal of the relationship of forces. Instead, the Green party became subject to the logic of statism. In this process, it changed its membership as well as its electoral basis. This has not strengthened its cooperation with social movements; in fact, the movements have lost popular support and influence in important political areas in the process.

From the point of view of a theory of democracy, Poulantzas's thoughts on radical transformation provide some interesting insights. He argues that social movements should not try to compete with the state over who can claim to represent the general will of society. There are good reasons why the state should continue to embody the latter: when particular forces start positing themselves as universal, others might do the same. There is a risk that conflicts of interest are no longer dealt with under conditions of democracy and political freedoms. This suggests that social movements should participate in processes of democratic competition while continuing to struggle over the definition of the general interest. This in turn suggests that on the terrain of the state, the relationship of forces and the structure of the state have to be modified. The state apparatuses may have to allow for new and different aggregated interests to become predominant. Nevertheless, the state remains the central *locus* of political power and continues to hold the monopoly on universality.

At this point, however, Poulantzas's arguments regarding the theory of democracy remain fairly general and insufficient:

1. It would have been useful to discuss the relation between interventions in the relationships of forces on the terrain of the state and the practice of social movements in more detail. This is one of the main problems social movements face when they deal with parties that are represented in parliaments or governments at the local, regional, or federal level. How this should be coordinated so as to avoid the logic of statism and the division of labour between professional politicians and radical spokespeople from the movements remains an open question.

2. Another unanswered question concerns the relationship between different movements of the popular classes. Poulantzas rejects reducing the activities of these movements to class struggle, but that is not enough to provide us with a positive definition of their relationship. Such a definition can only be produced by analysing the relationship between (a) the relations of production and class contradictions and (b) other social conflicts, emancipatory goals and broad processes of democratization.[5] Of course, abolishing class antagonism is especially important for creating the necessary conditions for development of all other forms of freedom, and all emancipatory struggles should share an interest in doing so. Even so, it remains unclear how different forms of emancipation can be coordinated.

3. Poulantzas's arguments remain at a fairly general level as regards the democratization of the social division of labour. It is even more surprising that he also neglects the question of democracy in the relations of production. He only mentions in passing the principle of self-management. In the 1970s, there were many experiments with alternative forms of labour and cooperatives in the western world, mostly in small enterprises. Yet there were problems with such experiments similar to those identified by Poulantzas with regard to the relation between movements and state. If the principle of self-management is applied with a view to remaining outside the state, this can result in a reversal of its dynamic, that is the emergence of a new type of entrepreneur and work ethic. These aspects of the reversed dynamic can then be appropriated by business associations and integrated in new strategies of domination in the workplace. Even though Poulantzas implies that the firm is a political form and a terrain of struggles and relations of forces, he rarely pays attention to struggles for the democratic organization of production and the division of labour. Analyses like his, which portray

5   See also Brand/Heigl in this volume.

the social division of labour and in particular the division between manual and intellectual labour as the foundation of the capitalist state, ought to be more concerned with the everyday conflicts over democracy that take place at the workplace and in the firm.

4. The most difficult problem may lie, however, in the dialectics of politics. How can a process of democratization that aims for the expansion of politics and collectively binding decision-making, mediated by the state, ever achieve transformations that lead to its withering away? How can the contradiction between the particular and the universal in the political sense be rendered obsolete? Poulantzas fails to discuss the relationship between the two goals of extended democracy *and* the abolition of the state – despite the importance of this issue for his arguments. Following Althusser, he would surely have had to reject the idea that socialism could ever be transparent and free from conflict. After all, socialist societalization can only aim for the elimination of conflicts that are related to class contradiction and state domination.

4. Democratization of the imperial network state

In conclusion, I want to address an issue that Poulantzas could not address, perhaps in part due to his untimely death: the transformation of statehood and transnational democracy. Poulantzas apparently believed that only the national state materially condenses relationships of power, which is why a strategy that aims at democratization and transformation sets its sight on the national state apparatuses as the target and object of its political practice. Today, however, such a strategy would be off-target by some distance. Thanks to the transnationalization of capital – the beginning stages of which Poulantzas observed – capital now frequently escapes the need to make compromises. Accordingly, the balance of class forces has shifted – to the disadvantage of the working class. The national state, too, loses importance as an instance of the condensation of compromises. Transnational capital reorganizes the accumulation of capital: it does not commit to particular locations of production, and thus compels states to support accumulation through deregulation, the systematic depreciation of a part of the capital stock and the commodification of public goods. The apparatuses of the national state frequently become dismantled and fragmented. The state's political actions no longer aim at the national territory as a whole; instead they create social and spatial hierarchies within society. In many places, politics abandons its responsibilities in order to resolve the 'crisis of governance' that Poulantzas witnessed in the 1970s. The dominant fraction in the power bloc becomes represented and reproduced in and through the Wall Street/US-Treasury/IMF/credit rating agencies-complex (cf. Harvey 2003). This forms part of a flexible geometry of power that links the dominant fraction with regional coordination and decision-making centres, such as the European Commission, European Central Bank or Council of Ministers; but also with national state apparatuses, or sections of the latter, that act as nodes and bases of a transnational-imperial network state (cf. Demirović 2001: 161ff.; 2005: 78ff.; Wissel 2007).

This development is a reaction to the difficulties linked to the valorization of capital, the crisis of governance in the 1970s and 1980s, successful anti-colonial struggles, demands for the democratization of production and distribution, and the emergence of diverse social movements. Many of these factors have fed into comprehensive global demands for the democratization and sustainable development of the global economy and the international state system. Since the 1990s, social movements and a great number of non-governmental organizations, whose character remained ambivalent, have increasingly been intervening in transnational political processes (cf. Demirović 1997: 239ff.).

This relocation of political issues and decisions has inevitably led to de-democratization at the national level, confirming to some degree Poulantzas's notion of authoritarian statism, but at the same time going beyond it.[6] The new state form is supposed to combine the formal continuity of parliamentary procedures with (a) increasing economic state interventionism, (b) the transfer of decision-making to the administration, and (c) the subordination of the latter to the top ranks of the executive branch. Parties and MPs lose their capacities for exchange with and control over the administration, and their role is reduced to transmitting decisions made at the top to parties and voters. The past years have shown, however, that administrations become fragmented into networks that traverse individual state departments, that state hierarchies are being destroyed, and that 'deficits in implementation' are being created. This is accompanied by the outsourcing of state responsibilities to the private sector and a huge increase in international cooperation and integration between armed forces, police forces, secret services, banks, telecommunication firms, and private-public dispositifs of surveillance. Moreover, there is the practice of selectively calling states of emergency, which allows doing away with the separation between the executive and the judicial branch and suspending human and civil rights (cf. Butler 2004: 50ff.). Accordingly, the parties, the parliament and the government enjoy little trust among the population.

These developments have led to the emergence of new forms of resistance

---

6   Cf. Jessop in this volume.

to neoliberalism by some governments (especially in Latin America), new liberation struggles (Zapatismo), new social movements of various kinds, and a new form of social movement unionism. In this situation, it is well worth seriously re-engaging with Poulantzas's ideas, and formulating a democratic strategy towards the radical transformation of the state that is aimed at the transnational level.

References

Abendroth, W. (1954a) 'Zum Begriff des demokratischen und sozialen Rechtsstaats im Grundgesetz der Bundesrepublik Deutschland', in Abendroth, W. *Antagonistische Gesellschaft und politische Demokratie. Aufsätze zur politischen Soziologie* (Neuwied: Luchterhand) 109-138.
Abendroth, W. (1954b) 'Demokratie als Institution und Aufgabe', in Abendroth, W. *Arbeiterklasse, Staat und Verfassung* (Frankfurt am Main: Europäische Verlagsanstalt, 1975). 21-32.
Abendroth, W. (1977) 'Contribution to the discussion', in Abendroth, W. et al. *Der Kampf um das Grundgesetz: Über die politische Bedeutung der Verfassungsinterpretation* (Frankfurt am Main: Syndikat) 188-194.
Agnoli, J. (1968) 'Die Transformation der Demokratie', in Agnoli, J. *Die Transformation der Demokratie und andere Schriften zur Kritik der Politik* (Freiburg: ça ira-Verlag, 1990) 21-106.
Bauer, O. (1924) 'Das Gleichgewicht der Klassenkräfte', in Bauer, O. *Werkausgabe*, vol. 9, (Wien: Europaverlag, 1980) 55-79.
Butler, J. (2004) *Precarious Life: The Powers of Mourning and Violence* (London: Verso).
Demirović, A. (1997) *Demokratie und Herrschaft. Aspekte kritischer Gesellschaftstheorie* (Münster: Westfälisches Dampfboot).
Demirović, A. (2001) 'NGO, Staat und Zivilgesellschaft. Zur Transformation von Hegemonie', in Brand, U. et al. (eds.) *Nichtregierungsorganisationen in der Transformation des Staates* (Münster: Westfälisches Dampfboot) 141-168.
Demirović, A. (2005) 'Der kapitalistische Staat', in Kaindl, C. (ed.) *Kritische Wissenschaften im Neoliberalismus* (Marburg: BdWi-Verlag) 51-84.
Harvey, D. (2003) 'Accumulation by Disposession', in Harvey, D. *The New Imperialism* (Oxford: Oxford Univ. Press) 137-183.
Wissel, J. (2007) *Die Transnationalisierung von Herrschaftsverhältnissen. Zur Aktualität von Nicos Poulantzas' Staatstheorie* (Baden-Baden: Nomos).

CONJUNCTURE OF THE INTEGRAL STATE?
POULANTZAS'S READING OF GRAMSCI

PETER THOMAS

Nicos Poulantzas's reading of Antonio Gramsci is marked by recurring ambivalences that are not easily ranked under the label of either affiliation or repudiation. Poulantzas's explorations of the nature of the capitalist state are unthinkable without Gramsci's earlier development of the concepts of the state 'in its integral meaning' and of 'proletarian hegemony'. Gramsci famously described his 'general notion of the state' as 'political society + civil society, in other words hegemony armoured with coercion' (SPN: 262f.; PN 3: 75f.). Poulantzas, for his part, defined the state as a material condensation of relations of forces and thus overcame both instrumental conceptions of the state as well as the limits of the social fields that the Marxist tradition had characterized as 'state' and 'civil society'. Bob Jessop has argued that 'it is as an Althusserian structuralist that Poulantzas is most often presented' (1985: 317), particularly in the Anglophone world, influenced by the structuralist excesses displayed in the famous Poulantzas-Miliband debate in *New Left Review*.[1] There is, however, an alternative line of affiliation that perhaps better characterizes Poulantzas's problematic: that of a 'philosophy of praxis', understood in the broadest sense, running from his earlier engagement with the praxis-oriented dimensions of Sartrean existentialism (Jessop 1985: 26ff.) to his increasingly pronounced articulation of his own project with that of Gramsci. From this perspective, Poulantzas appears as a theorist of political and institutional praxis who 'traversed' the Althusserian problematic in order to concretize research questions founded upon a different terrain. In other words, if, viewed from a particular and by no means exhaustive perspective, Marxist theory in France in the 1960s and 1970s can be characterized as a spectrum whose poles are defined by the proper names of Gramsci (praxis) and Althusser (structure). Poulantzas,

---

1 Cf. Barrow's contribution to this volume.

despite received wisdom, is perhaps more properly located closer to the former rather than the latter.²

1. Dual power: a first approach

The early phase of Poulantzas's engagement with Gramsci effectively reproduces charges levelled by Althusser in *Reading Capital*: Gramsci's putative (idealist) historicism, expressivist model of the social totality, tendency towards voluntarism, pan-politicism and so forth. It is notable that the 'young' Poulantzas often deploys rhetorical strategies similar to those of Althusser when discussing Gramsci: first, rapprochement and praise for the intelligence and fertility of Gramsci's researches, followed by qualification and distancing from his substantive theses. Thus, he asserted in *Political Power and Social Classes* that 'Gramsci, whose political analyses, though always valuable, are often tainted by the historicism of Croce and Labriola' (PPSC: 39; cf. 138f., 194, 197, 201). At another moment, he argued that 'on the one hand Gramsci, with amazing acuteness, perceived the problems posed by the political functioning of bourgeois ideology in a capitalist formation; on the other hand, though his analyses are distinct from the typical historicist conception of ideologies as presented for example by Lukács, because of the historicist problematic which essentially governs his work, they demonstrate very clearly the impasses and errors to which this problematic of ideology leads' (*PPSC* 195). Poulantzas's objection to Gramsci's historicism, however, more often than not functions as a concession to prevailing Parisian fashions, essentially discontinuous with or rhetorically external to his concrete analyses of Gramsci's theses.³ Given the serious misunderstandings upon which Althusser's repudiation of Gramsci's historicism was based, there is little need to consider its almost mimetic and inessential repetition by the early Poulantzas at length here.⁴

2   Christine Buci-Glucksmann (1969) was the first to suggest such a close affinity, noting the presence of Gramscian themes even from the time of PPSC. The connection was later emphasised by Bob Jessop (1985).
3   In *PPSC*, for example, Poulantzas argued that in Gramsci there is 'a confusion of the areas in which hegemony is exercised [...] according to which force is exercised by the state in "political society", hegemony in "civil society"' (226). The proposition manifestly calls for philological justification and a deeper engagement with the *Prison Notebooks*, in order to determine if such a confusion is indeed present in Gramsci's text itself. At this stage, however, Poulantzas left such an engagement to one side, reverting to the Althusserian shibboleth. The foundation of Gramsci's confusion and 'distinction between force and hegemony', it seemed, lay in 'the historicist conception of [the] relation' of the 'economic and political spheres', according to which the political would be a motor of 'the "economic laws" conceived in a mechanistic fashion' (ibid.).
4   I have previously analysed the errors of Althusser's interpretation of Gramsci's notion of 'absolute historicism' in Thomas (2004). Cf. also Haug (1996) and for a more

Much more interesting are the ambivalences of the 'final' Poulantzas's engagement with Gramsci in *State, Power, Socialism* (SPS). Here Poulantzas elaborates a critique that is in many respects diametrically opposed to the Althusserian-inflected perspective of the earlier work. The Althusserian moment had asserted the distinctiveness of its own temporality, at least in part, by consigning Gramsci to a superannuated historical phase of Marxism's development. In effect, it forced Gramsci to step forward as a voluntarist who had failed to break with the theoretical presuppositions of the Second International. In Poulantzas's final texts, however, Gramsci comes on stage as a theorist who had thoroughly internalized the Leninist and, in a different version, Third Internationalist strategy of 'dual power'. For Poulantzas, that constituted a problem, in so far as he claimed that Gramsci, despite all the sophistication of his notion of the state, had ultimately remained a prisoner to the topographical metaphors of the Leninist tradition.

Poulantzas argued that 'all Lenin's analyses and actions are traversed by the following *leitmotif*: the state must be entirely destroyed through frontal attack in a situation of *dual power*, to be replaced by a second power – soviets – which will no longer be a state in the proper sense of the term, since it will already have begun to wither away' (SPS: 252).[5] Lenin developed the concept of 'dual power' implicitly in the *April Theses* (1964a), explicitly in the article *On Dual Power* (1964b) published in *Pravda* in April 1917, and then most famously in *The Task of the Proletariat in our Revolution* (written on April 10th/23rd, but not published until September; cf. 1964c). The latter text described the situation during the interregnum of 1917 in which there was the '*interlocking of two* dictatorships' (60): the soviets ranged against the provisional government. Poulantzas was quick to acknowledge the difference between this analytical thesis and strategic perspective and its later degeneration under Stalinism into a 'refusal of the political' (that is, a refusal of engagement with the forms of bourgeois democracy, which were conceived as merely instruments of class rule). Nevertheless, he was equally as quick to argue that there was a line of continuity between the perspectives that had informed the Bolsheviks' practice in 1917 and the

extended account, Tosel (1995).

5   Two corrections to Poulantzas's presentation should be immediately entered. First, the thesis of dual power only emerges explicitly in Lenin's thought at a very specific moment, namely, between the two revolutionary upheavals of 1917, as an attempt to comprehend the specificity of the revolutionary conjuncture. In an article in *Pravda*, Lenin notes that '*Nobody* previously thought, or could have thought, of a dual power' (1964b: 38). Second, Lenin's argument that the soviets were not 'a state in the proper sense of the term' (1964c: 68) was not due to the state having begun to wither away, but because it conformed to what he called 'the special type of state' of the Paris Commune (1964b: 38), in which power was based on direct initiative 'from below'.

state theory canonized by the Third International. In particular, they shared perspectives on, first, the *location* of 'the struggle of the popular masses for state power' (SPS: 254), outside the state, in that area nebulously defined, in the sense of a remainder, as civil society; second, the *means of struggle*, in the 'creation of a situation of dual power' (252); third, the *concept of social and political power* as 'a quantifiable substance' presently sequestered by the bourgeoisie (254); and fourth, the *goal* of the capture and destruction of the 'fortress' state, to be replaced 'by the second power (soviets) constituted as a state of a new type' (255).

These perspectives were also, according to Poulantzas, to be found in Gramsci's *Prison Notebooks* (PN). Cognisant with the earlier mode of simultaneous invocation and critique, Poulantzas argued in SPS that 'Of course, there is no disputing Gramsci's considerable theoretical political contributions, and we know the distance he took from the Stalinist experience. Still [...] the fact remains that Gramsci was also unable to pose the problem in all its amplitude. His famous analyses of the differences between war of movement (as waged by the Bolsheviks in Russia) and war of position are essentially conceived as the application of Lenin's model/strategy to the "different concrete conditions" of the West' (256). Such Leninist residues had a decisive impact on Gramsci's ability to theorize the state. Gramsci had not understood that 'to take or capture state power is not simply to lay hands on part of the state machinery in order to replace it with a second power' (257f.). Rather, he had remained enthralled by a notion of the state as 'a fortress that may be penetrated by means of a wooden horse', or 'a safe that may be cracked by burglary' (258). Gramsci had not conceived the state as a condensation of 'a series of relations among the various social classes' (ibid.) – a conception according to which the state is to be comprehended as a form of movement of class contradictions, thus rejecting the distinction formulated by the Marxist tradition between 'state' and 'civil society' (*bürgerliche Gesellschaft* or *Zivilgesellschaft*).[6] Rather, following the spirit of the Leninist formulation, Gramsci posited civil society as a lowlands external to the state, the *locus* for the construction of a possible counter-power. From here, the working-class movement could wage a 'war of position' that would eventually permit it to launch an attack

6   'Zivilgesellschaft' is used in the German translation of the critical edition [*Die Gefängnisheften*] in order to translate Gramsci's concept of *società civile*, and in order to emphasise its difference from Marx's term 'bürgerliche Gesellschaft' (literally in Italian: *società borghese*) (a distinction that is not possible, for example, with the English *civil society*, used for the translation of both terms). The historical and political specificity of the term is decisive (no *Zivilgesellschaft* before the rise of political power of the bourgeoisie; no *Zivilgesellschaft* without the integral state, etc.).

upon the citadel of the bourgeois state, in order to smash it and replace it by a more adequate form of social organisation. Alex Demirović summarizes Poulantzas's reading of Gramsci in the following way: 'To take the fortress in a war of position means to persevere patiently for a long time and to conquer gradually all of the advance posts and points of fortification (the democratic institutions). Once the enemy, the bourgeoisie, has been driven out of the fortress, you can use if for your own defence' (1987: 49).[7]

In the end, therefore, though more sophisticated and less prone to vulgar instrumentalism than either Stalinist or social democratic variants, Gramsci's proposal for the working-class movement in the West had remained within the problematic of the strategy of 'dual power' (SPS: 258). Gramsci had failed to comprehend, according to Poulantzas's reading, the extent to which the capitalist state was already traversed by the class antagonisms and struggles from within. That is, politics did not occur 'outside' the fortress of the state, but constituted its very materiality of the state as a condensation of power relations. In particular, Poulantzas rejected the topographical metaphor according to which there lay some place 'beyond the state' in which the forces for a future state of a different type could be mustered (cf. Jessop 1990: 230). As all social relations were always already relations of power within the given state, they were interpellated by and simultaneously constitutive of it (cf. SPS: 39). In effect, for Poulantzas, the state became an enduring state of affairs [*Dauerzustand*].[8]

2. War of position and war of movement

The novelty of this reading of Gramsci's state theory is striking, and not merely because it represents a significant departure from the critique of Gramsci elaborated within the Althusserian problematic. Much more significantly, Poulantzas here proposes a very different reading of Gramsci from two widely diffused and reductive (and highly politically overdetermined) interpretations. According to the first of these interpretations, Gramsci's 'war of position' is a proposal for a 'long march through the institutions' of the bourgeois state. The state itself is conceived as the mere sum of its parts and thus divisible. Individual outposts or institutions are supposed to be conquered, subtracting them from bourgeois political domination

---

7 Demirović goes on to note that Poulantzas's ascription of a war of position of this type to Gramsci was not entirely legitimate; cf. Demirović (1987: 49).

8 Demirović succinctly summarizes this position, while simultaneously revealing some of its more troubling conceptual consequences for an historical materialist analysis of the historicity of the state: 'It is the state that is comprehended as a social relation; it is not the concrete social relations that take on the state form. [...] and because it is everywhere, it [the state] cannot be abandoned, nor can it be attacked, but rather, only transformed' (96, translated).

in a simple arithmetical progression, until sheer force of numbers forces open the inner sanctum and the working class takes possession of the state (conceived as instrument of government or state apparatus). Unlike a 'war of manoeuvre', the war of position does not attempt to storm the citadel in a great set-piece battle, but involves undermining the bourgeois state from within. Left social democrats proposed this interpretation in good faith in the 1970s; its logic has since been cynically perverted and redeployed in certain aspects of the neo-liberal 'third way'.

According to the second interpretations, the privileged terrain of Gramsci's 'war of position' is civil society. The distance of the war of position from the state implies that such a war of position does not deploy any great forces straight away, and that the state has no immediate effect on struggles and manoeuvres beyond itself. In opposition, according to this interpretation, the war of manoeuvre is an immediate confrontation with the state. The Bolsheviks were only able to deploy this strategy in the East because there civil society was underdeveloped and unable to act as a bulwark or trench complex defending the state from direct assault, as is argued to be the case in the West.[9] The legacy of such readings can still be seen today in those versions of the concept of hegemony that posit it as a 'logic of the social' with little to say about the specificity of *state* power, because it has been dissolved into a pervasive and indeterminate 'discursivity'.[10]

For Poulantzas, on the other hand, Gramsci's metaphor is not to be read according to a simplistic binary opposition of strategies 'internal' to the state or to civil society (the two variants of 'war of position') versus those oriented to an 'external' state ('war of manoeuvre'). Rather, he argues that the distinction between Gramsci's metaphors consists not in their topographical presuppositions (both strategies posit the state and civil society as distinct *loci* of the capitalist social formation) but their differential temporalities. Gramsci's war of manoeuvre is 'essentially conceived' (SPS: 256) as an 'encirclement of a fortress state' (258) or 'the application of Lenin's model/strategy to the "different concrete conditions" of the West' (256). According to Poulantzas, the war of movement is thus in effect a 'war of manoeuvre in slow time'. It occurs outside, not within, the state, in civil society, but it has an *immediate* relation to bourgeois state power insofar as it aims to constitute its 'other'. It engages in a strategy of conquering outposts on the plain of civil society, but only in order to mobilize these in

---

9   Perry Anderson (1976) criticized these readings, not entirely unjustly, as a return of Kautskyanism under the cover of left rhetoric.
10 Ernesto Laclau and Chantal Mouffe are the chief representatives of this widely diffused reading. One could even say that their interpretation represents the image of Gramsci of the academic *senso comune*.

an assault upon the citadel-state; it is distinguished from the supposedly all-out confrontation urged by the war of manoeuvre not in terms of strategy, but in terms of tactics, tempo and logistics, rallying its forces before engaging the enemy in order to be all the more sure of a successful assault.

The novelty of such (implicit) propositions gives us reasons to pause, in order to consider their effects upon Poulantzas's own theory. In particular, they give rise to two questions concerning the fundamental differences between Poulantzas's and Gramsci's seemingly similar 'expanded' concepts of the state. First, was Poulantzas correct about the theoretical presuppositions of Gramsci's conception of the relation between the state and civil society? That is, did Gramsci posit a terrain outside the state on which a new political power could emerge, which could then go on to capture the state (apparatus) and replace it? Second, did Gramsci conceive of social and political power as a 'quantifiable substance' possessed by one particular class, which could therefore be opposed by another 'quantity' of power in the possession of another class? In other words, is Gramsci's war of position really merely a more sophisticated variant of the strategy of dual power, in its fundamental presuppositions still open to the same criticisms that Poulantzas directed at its Leninist, Third Internationalist and social democratic versions?

These questions are not merely of philological interest for Gramscian scholars. They go to the very heart of the question of the cogency of Poulantzas's final advice to the Western European workers' movement – and the actuality of this legacy for the central debates of our movement today. For the 'democratic road to socialism', the 'mature' Poulantzas's final contribution to the debate about the 'crisis of Marxism', was explicitly formulated as a superannuation, or more coherent version, of the Gramscian 'war of position'. Poulantzas argued that 'the long process of taking power essentially consists in the spreading, development, reinforcement, coordination and direction of those diffuse centres of resistance which the masses always possess with the state networks, in such a way that they become the real centres of power on the strategic terrain of the state' (258). The democratic road to socialism therefore proposed a 'war of position' conducted *within* the state itself. The state was thus redefined in relational and strategic terms; it encompassed the terrain that Gramsci had continued to identify as civil society. It was a strategy to be pursued by means of struggles at varying levels of intensity and depth, some closer to the centre of the state apparatus, others at a certain 'distance' from it. In this way, Poulantzas proposed to overcome the risk of 'traditional reformism' (ibid.). In short, the democratic road to socialism can be regarded as an attempted

Aufhebung of the lingering Leninist residues of Gramsci's state theory.

Poulantzas's reading of Gramsci thus raised themes that are, today, once more occupying the practical and theoretical energies of the Left. For the first time in 30 years, the Left, and the Marxist revolutionary Left in particular, is confronted with the need to clarify the question of its relationship to the state in concrete and institutional terms. Not only in Brazil and Venezuela, but also, in more complicated and varied forms, in Europe, the revival of electoral fortunes for the Left has seen a 'return of the political question'. Here, a rhetoric of 'Changing the world without taking power' is to be avoided, for social reality demands a responsible engagement with the difficult questions of state power and the possibilities for furthering the socialist project through different strategies in relation to it.

3. Road to democratic socialism or war of position?

Adjudicating between the conceptions of Gramsci and Poulantzas will be the task of the remainder of this essay. As we will see, Gramsci's 'integral state' and the Poulantzas's 'states as the material condensation of a power relation' are in fact much closer than Poulantzas was willing to concede. Indeed, in certain respects, Poulantzas's theory can be regarded as a reformulation of Gramsci's thesis of the indivisible unity and extensive efficacy of the capitalist state, expressed in the *linguaggio* of the debates of the 1970s. Nevertheless, Poulantzas was mistaken about the nature of the relation between the state and civil society in Gramsci's fully developed 'integral' notion of the state. As a consequence, he misunderstood Gramsci's notions of social and political power (or hegemony, grasped in the broadest sense) and inscribed the war of position in a tradition of dual power strategies that were distortions of the original Leninist thesis.

Properly understood, Gramsci's theory of hegemony describes how political power is *immanent* to the hegemonic projects in which it is elaborated. Gramsci's and Poulantzas's state theories and strategic proposals are thus located on the same terrain. The difference between them consists in Gramsci's historicist explanation of processes of modern state formation that Poulantzas, against his better intentions, was only able to describe in conjunctural terms. Poulantzas's analyses of Gramsci focused on the problematic and sometimes incompatible versions of the couplet 'state/civil society' that are found in the *Prison Notebooks*. Following the established uses of these terms in the Marxist tradition, he assumed that in Gramsci these concepts referred to two distinct terrains of a social formation, as the location of two different forms of power: coercion was a monopoly of the former, while consent pervaded the latter. Troubling formulations (such as

Gramsci's definition on a number of occasions of the state as encompassing both 'political society' and 'civil society') were either ignored or explained as residues of Gramsci's youthful influence by Italian neo-Hegelian idealism, in the figures of Croce and Gentile.[11]

It is a twofold irony that Poulantzas should have adopted this reading: first, because one of his close collaborators, Christine Buci-Glucksmann, was among the first to direct attention to the new articulation of the concepts of 'state' and 'civil society' in the *Prison Notebooks*; second, because, of all prior Marxist theoreticians, Gramsci perhaps goes the furthest towards breaking definitively with an exclusively instrumentalist conception of the state. More precisely: with the concept of the 'integral state', Gramsci describes the formation of the modern states in the West as – to adopt Poulantzas's own terms – a material and institutional condensation of power relations between and within classes. He formulated this concept in order to analyse the mutual interpenetration and reinforcement of 'political society' and 'civil society' within the state form. According to this concept, the state in its integral form was not to be limited to the state apparatus (the state understood in a limited or instrumental sense, 'political society', in opposition to 'civil society'). Rather, the concept of the integral state was intended as a dialectical unity of civil society and political society. According to Gramsci, civil society is the terrain upon which social classes compete for social and political leadership or hegemony. The continuance of such hegemony is only guaranteed, however, 'in the last instance', by capture of the legal monopoly of violence embodied in the institutions of political society, or the state understood in a limited sense, that is, the state apparatus (cf. Liguori 2004: 224). Understood in its integral sense, however, Gramsci argued, 'the state is the entire complex of practical and theoretical activities with which the ruling class not only justifies and maintains its dominance, but manages to win the active consent of those over whom it rules' (SPN: 243ff.). In the famous formulation previously alluded to in this essay, 'The general notion of the state includes elements which need to be referred back to the notion of civil society (in the sense that one might say that the state = political society + civil society, in other words hegemony armoured with coercion)' (SPN: 262f.; PN 3: 75f.).

Gramsci analysed the complex unity-in-distinction of consent and coercion throughout the 'long' 19th century that gave rise to this qualitatively new state form requiring a conceptual reorganization for its analysis. From the French Revolution to 1848 (and in a different sense,

---

11 Traces of this reading are already to be found in Bobbio's famous and highly contested reading; Anderson (1976) presented what became the canonical statement of this view.

until the defeat of the Paris Commune), he detected a period of expansion in which the hegemonic project of the victorious bourgeoisie undertook a programme of social and political 'education'. After the French Revolution, the bourgeoisie 'was able to present itself as an integral "state", with all the intellectual and moral forces necessary and sufficient for organizing a complete and perfect society'. (SPN: 270ff.; PN 3: 6ff.; cf. FS: 17f., PN 3: 74f. in relation to the Jacobin "attempt to create identity between state and civil society"). A hegemonic project on the terrain of civil society had progressed to the capture of state power, followed by the 'new' power then attempting to remake the state in its own image. The bourgeois state – or at least, the *idea* of the bourgeois state, theorized in its ethical dimensions most forcefully by Hegel (cf. PN 1: 153f.; SPN: 259f.; FS: 75f.; PN 3: 20f., 343f.) – was born.

4. Hegemony, coercion, passive revolution

However, the *Staatswerdung* of this hegemonic project fundamentally altered the terrains on which it had been formed, due to the internal logic of this project itself. It tended to make the borders between the state and civil society (which only now really began to become *Zivilgesellschaft*) more porous. As Burgio argues, the emerging state of the revolutionary bourgeoisie in the early 19th century 'is not longer so much a question of military power [...] as of the *capillary and permanent direction of an entire social fabric*' (Burgio 2002: 29). The bourgeois state was to be conceived no longer merely as an instrument of coercion, imposing the interests of the dominant class, and a sovereign instance 'above' civil society (as was arguably the case with pre-modern state apparatuses). Rather, it was also increasingly a social relation for the production of consent, for the integration of the subaltern classes into the project of the leading social group. Expressed in Poulantzas's terms, the state understood in this broader sense was the process of the condensation and transformation of these class relations into an institutional form.

On the other hand, the fact that the new type of state was ruled by the bourgeosie produced determinant effects. *Contra* interpretations claiming that Gramsci's 'cultural' emphasis displaces a more properly Marxist concern with the critique of political economy, it should be emphasized that Gramsci stressed, from the outset of his researches, that the specificity of the capitalist state in bourgeois societies consists in the dialectical interpenetration of the economic and political. He argued that 'for the productive classes (capitalist bourgeoisie and modern proletariat) the state is not thinkable other than as a concrete form of a determinate economic world, of a determinate system of production' (PN 1: 229). It was therefore not a question for Gramsci of the state as instrument of regulation imposed from outside the economic sphere, but rather as a regulative principle within it. In this sense, Gramsci recognized that the state as 'the regulating factor of [the capitalist mode of production's; P.T.] global equilibrium as a system' (PPSC: 45) is dialectically linked to the mode of production and does not impact upon it from the outside.

1848 and the Paris Commune, despite the defeat of both, ushered in a qualitatively new phase of historical development. The previous, fragile equilibrium of class forces and their superstructures became 'catastrophic' following the 'organic crisis' of the bourgeois hegemonic project, that is, the refusal of the working classes to be subsumed pacifically into the bourgeois integral state. It was only in this, the moment of its most profound crisis, that the new integral state really came into its own, as the institutionalized and solidified form of bourgeois political power or state domination. The bourgeoisie overcame these revolts by elaborating what Gramsci described as a 'passive revolution'.[12] Neither revolution nor counter-revolution, the category of passive revolution denotes 'the persistent capacity of [...] the bourgeoisie [...] to produce socio-political transformations', without being a revolutionary class (Losurdo 1997: 155). The purpose of passive revolution was to prevent the emergence of an organized working-class hegemonic project. The capacity to act of the subaltern classes was reduced by means of the absorption of their leading layers within the bourgeoisie's own programme of modernization, from the so-called 'private initiatives' of civil society right up to the representative mechanisms of the state apparatus.

5. A dialectical concept of the state and dual power

For Gramsci, therefore, civil society was not to be conceived topographically, as a terrain outside the state, but rather, as the 'social basis' of the integral state (SPN: 264f.; PN 3: 107f.). He thus refused to abolish the distinction between the state as state apparatus and civil society. Rather, he maintained both terms, in both their unity and distinction, even after his elaboration of the new concept of the integral state (PN 2: 177ff., written in October

---

12 'Passive Revolution' is one of Gramsci's central historiographical and political concepts. He appropriated it from Vincenzo Cuoco (in order to provide an analysis of the distinctive features of the Italian Risorgimento) (PN 1: 136ff.). However, it soon became clear to Gramsci that the concept could have a more general significance and be used to indicate the curiously unpeculiar *Sonderweg* to modernity taken also by other nation states lacking in the radical-popular 'Jacobin moment' which had distinguished the experience of the French revolution. In a third moment, he extended the concept to signify the pacifying and incorporating nature assumed by bourgeois hegemony in the epoch of imperialism, particularly in its Western European heartlands but with determinant effects upon the colonial periphery.

1930).[13] He explains that it is analytically useful to distinguish between them, even if in reality they progressively 'identify' with each other (SPN: 158ff.). Almost in a 'Spinozian' fashion, Gramsci comprehended 'political' and 'civil society' as 'attributes' of the 'substance' of the 'integral state': whereas 'political society' refers to this 'substance-state' after the consolidation of the political power of a class in (state) institutions on the basis of the degree of coercion, 'civil society' is associated with the constitution of such (potential) political power in the forces on the social terrain on the basis of consent.

Poulantzas was therefore incorrect to argue that Gramsci posits a terrain outside the state on which a new political power could emerge. Similar to Poulantzas, the *Prison Notebooks* attempted to grasp the specificity of the capitalist state as a condensation of power relations between classes, realized under the dominance of the bourgeoisie. The logic of the passive revolution, as an extension of the integrative dimensions of the integral state, therefore meant that the working-class movement did not enjoy the luxury of a terrain external to the state from which it could launch its bid for political power. He argued that 'war of movement [after 1870; P.T.] increasingly becomes war of position [...]. The massive structure of the modern democracies, both as statal organizations and also as a complex of associations in civil life forms for the art of politics something like the "trenches" and the permanent fortifications of the front in the war of position: they render the element of movement, which before was the "entire" war, only a "partial" element etc' (SPN: 243). Under the conditions of passive revolution, therefore, a war of position within the integral state was the only viable strategy for the working class movement. The concept of hegemony therefore functions for Gramsci as a sort of mobilizing antidote to the lethargy diffused by the passive revolution and results in a strategy on the basis of the emphasis on the hegemonic moments of the state.

The possible decisive break in this configuration would not come from the confrontations between the state and a second power 'lying wholly outside the state' (SPS: 258). It would come *within* the working-class movement itself, as a break with its economic-corporative constitution, when the masses could break with the stultifying integration of the passive revolution and elaborate their own hegemonic project as a class, reducing the capacity to act (or rather, the capacity to dominate) of the bourgeoisie

---

13 Giani Francioni (1984) defended Gramsci's dialectical conception of the state and its 'attributes' against very widespread misunderstandings (particularly those canonized by 'Antinomies of Antonio Gramsci') regarding Gramsci's supposed conceptual 'slippages'. Unfortunately, this aspect of Francioni's philological analysis has not often been attended to in international Gramscian scholarship.

by means of increasing their own capacity to act. The path to political power for the proletariat would involve, in the first instance, modifying the relation of forces within the integral state, dislocating the mutual reinforcement of coercion and consent exploited by the bourgeoisie in order to further its own class domination. The attempt to conquer the existing state with a u- or atopian power was not a viable strategy – Gramsci was well aware of the catastrophic failures of such strategies in Germany in the early 1920s. The state apparatus of the bourgeoisie could be neutralized only when the proletariat had deprived it of its 'social basis' through the elaboration of an alternative hegemonic project. Gramsci conceived this project in concrete terms, as 'hegemonic apparatuses' (cf. PN 1: 155; SPN: 264f.; PN 3: 107f.): i.e., the wide ranging series of 'institutions' and practices – from newspapers to educational organisations and cultural initiatives to political parties – by means of which a class could concentrate its forces – with Poulantzas one could say: institutionally and materially 'condense' – and by means of which a class and its allies could engage its opponent in a struggle for political power, or leadership over the society as a whole. Such a movement would eventually lead to a moment in which these forces would have to institutionalize themselves as power in the state apparatus – but as we will see, in a specific and distinctive way (cf. SPN: 260f.; PN 3: 108f.).

Political power is here conceived not as an instrument or 'quantifiable substance', but in relational terms: as the capacity, or incapacity, to act of one class in relation to another, but also as the ability of a class's initiatives in political society to relate adequately to its 'social basis' in civil society. In other words, for Gramsci, political power is immanent not simply to the state as a condensation of power relations (relations between classes), but rather, it is immanent to the hegemonic projects by means of which classes constitute themselves as classes capable of exercising political power (as opposed to an incoherent mass of 'corporative' interests). Only subsequently do such concrete social relations, in their relationships with other classes, take on the state form. The potential of a class for political power therefore depends upon its ability to find the institutional forms adequate to the *differentia specifica* of its own particular hegemonic project.

Poulantzas was therefore indeed correct to argue that Gramsci's notion of war of position presupposed a more sophisticated variant of the strategy of dual power – though not for the reasons that he thought. Highly over-determined by contemporary debates (e.g., the debate on the dictatorship of the proletariat in the PCF) and undoubtedly deeply influenced by the failure of the Chilean and Portuguese revolutions), Poulantzas focused on the absence in the strategy of dual power of a theory of 'a transformation of the state apparatus' (SPS: 255). The soviet apparatus seized the state apparatus, but only in order to destroy it and take its place, direct democracy immediately replaced representative democracy. The democratic road to socialism argued for an articulation rather than opposition of these forms, one that could eventually lead to the transformation of the state apparatus itself.[14] Precisely what such a transformation of the state apparatus would involve, however, and whether it could lead to the withering away [*Absterben*] of the state as the prior Marxist tradition had expected, remained enigmas that Poulantzas was never able to resolve.

6. Democratic road to socialism and war of position

Lenin's thesis of dual power described a conjuncture that had already (and unexpectedly) arrived.[15] Gramsci's theory, on the other hand, elaborated in a moment of defeat in a fascist prison cell, sought to regroup the forces that would make possible the return of such a dual power situation. Unlike the intransigent ultra-leftism of the years of the founding of the PCI, the Gramsci of the *Prison Notebooks* acknowledged that such a process may indeed need to pass through a phase of transformation within the existing state. His belated embracing of the strategy of the United Front and final advice to the Italian workers' movement on the necessity for a broad anti-fascist front to reconstitute representative institutions (against the lunacy of third-period dogma) explicitly argued for such transformations in the given conjuncture. That meant a tactical movement with the strategic goal

14 Poulantzas based himself here on Rosa Luxemburg's famous critique of the Bolshevik's over-reliance on the soviets and their disregard for the nourishing, dialectical relationship between representative and direct democracy for political life in general. Yet his reasoning was inductive and imprecise. First, the degeneration of direct democracy in the absence of parallel representative institutions *in that specific conjuncture* presumably does not mean that all attempts at social organization of a participatory type will perforce end in their negation, or that representative democracy could hinder such a degeneration. Poulantzas here skates dangerously close to the most banal of Arendtian platitudes. Second, the opposition between 'direct' and 'representative' democracy encourages analytic and strategic errors, because any process of political decision includes both direct and representative instances. Instead of the continuation of representative democracy as a social institution (i.e., making the masses absent, in order then to 're' present them once more), Poulantzas would have been better advised, in my opinion, to dedicate himself with greater attention to the question of the strengthening of the *participatory* dimensions of the mediating instances of political decision making processes.

15 Lenin elaborated the concept of dual power not as a potential political strategy, but as an analysis of the 'negative state of exception' in Russian in 1917 that was characterized by two interlocking 'dictatorships'. Lenin insisted on the exceptional nature of this bifurcation: 'There is not the slightest doubt that such an "interlocking" cannot last long. Two powers *cannot exist* in a state', he argued (1964c: 61). 'Dual power merely expresses a *transitional* phase in the revolution's development' (ibid.).

of empowering the subaltern classes, by means of the experience of dealing with the representative institutions of the state, to make the transition from a leading to a dominant group. The primary goal remained the foundation of a 'state of a new type'.

'It is therefore not a question', to modify one of Poulantzas's final formulations in *State, Power, Socialism*, 'of a straight choice between' the democratic road to socialism 'and war of position, because in Gramsci's use of the term, the latter always comprises' a tactical deployment of the former (SPS: 258). Gramsci could formulate this 'true' third way because he recognized the reality of the exisiting integral state (as the only location of political power and therefore the horizon within which the workers' movement must operate), as well as, simultaneously, the reality of the mode of existence of the state (as an immanent condensation of class forces under the hegemony of the forms of power of one class). The Gramscian war of position certainly implies a more sophisticated version of the strategy of dual power – but not in the sense of social democratic compromise or Stalinist depoliticization. Rather, in the sense of an actualization of the original insight of Lenin, that the workers' movement must develop its own form of political power and have faith in its ability to realize its institutional consequences. This democratic road to socialism necessarily transcends the capitalist state – and in this sense, a tactical deployment of Poulantzas's perspectives within the strategic horizon of Gramsci's war of position for a 'new type of state' may well turn out to be the most viable and actual form of Poulantzas's legacy today.

References

Anderson, P. (1976) 'Antinomies of Antonio Gramsci', *New Left Review*, vol. 17, no. I/100, 5-78.
Buci-Glucksmann, C. (1969) 'A propos de la théorie marxiste de l'Etat capitaliste: vers une conception nouvelle de la politique', *L'Homme et la Société*, vol. 4, no. 11, 199-207.
Burgio, A. (2002) *Gramsci storico: una lettura dei 'Quaderni del carcere'* (Roma: Laterza).
Demirović, A. (1987) *Nicos Poulantzas. Eine kritische Auseinandersetzung* (Hamburg: Argument-Verlag).
Francioni, G. (1984) *L'officina gramsciana* (Napoli: Bibliopolis).
Haug, W. F. (1996) *Philosophieren mit Brecht und Gramsci* (Hamburg: Argument-Verlag).
Jessop, B. (1985) *Nicos Poulantzas. Marxist Political Theory and Political Strategy* (Basingstoke: Macmillan).
Jessop, B. (1990) State Theory: *Putting capitalist states in their place* (Cambridge/

UK: Polity Press).
Lenin, V. (1964a) 'The Tasks of the Proletariat in the Present Revolution', in Lenin, V. *Collected Works*, vol. 24 (Moscow: Progr. Publ.) 21-29.
Lenin, V. (1964b) 'On Dual Power', in Lenin, V. *Collected Works*, vol. 24 (Moscow: Progr. Publ.) 38-41.
Lenin, V. (1964c) 'The Tasks of the Proletariat in our Revolution', in Lenin, V. *Collected Works*, vol. 24 (Moscow: Progr. Publ.) 55-91.
Ligurori, G. (2004) 'Stato-società civile', in Frosini, F. / Liguori, G. (eds.) *Le parole di Gramsci: per un lessico dei 'Quaderni del carcere'* (Roma: Carocci) 208-226.
Losurdo, D. (1997) *Antonio Gramsci dal liberalismo al 'comunismo critico'* (Roma: Gamberetti).
Thomas, P. (2004) 'Historizismus, absoluter', in Haug, W. F. (ed.) *Historisch-Kritisches Wörterbuch des Marxisimus*, vol. 6/I (Hamburg: Argument-Verlag) 411-422.
Tosel, A. (1995) 'In Francia', in Hobsbawn, E. (ed.) *Gramsci in Europa e in America* (Roma: Laterza). 5-26.

Abbreviated References

Louis Althusser/Étienne Balibar

FM   Althusser, L. (1965): *For Marx*, Penguin: Harmondsworth 1969.

IISA   Althusser, L. (1970): 'Ideology and Ideological State Apparatuses' in: *Lenin and Philosophy and other Essays*, 121-176, London: New Left Books 1971.

RC   Althusser, L. / Balibar, É. (1968): *Reading Capital*, London: New Left Books 1970.

Michel Foucault

BP   *The Birth of Biopolitics: Lectures at the Collège de France, 1978-1979*, ed. by Michel Senellart et al., Basingstoke: Palgrave 2008.

DP   *Discipline and Punish* (1975), Harmondsworth: Penguin 1979.

STP   *Security, Territory, Population: Lectures at the Collège de France, 1977-1978*, ed. by Michel Senellart et al., Basingstoke: Palgrave 2007.

WK   *The History of Sexuality, vol. 1: The will to knowledge* (1976), Harmondsworth: Penguin 1990.

Antonio Gramsci

FS   *Further Selections from the Prison Notebooks*, ed. by Derek Boothman, London: Lawrence & Wishart 1995.

PN   *Prison Notebooks*, ed. by Joseph A. Buttigieg, New York: Columbia University Press 1992ff.

SPN   *Selections from the Prison Notebooks*, ed. by Quintin Hoare and Geoffrey Nowell-Smith, London: Lawrence & Wishart 1971.

Karl Marx/Friedrich Engels

CI   Marx, K. (1867/1872), *Capital: A critique of political economy, volume I, book one: the process of production of capital*, MECW vol. 35, London: Lawrence & Wishart 1996.

CII   Marx, K. (1885), *Capital: A critique of political economy, volume II, book two: the process of circulation of capital*, MECW vol. 36, London: Lawrence & Wishart 1997.

CIII   Marx, K. (1894), *Capital: A critique of political economy, volume III, book three: The Process of capitalist production as a whole*, MECW vol. 37, London: Lawrence & Wishart 1998.

MECW   *Marx/Engels Collected Works*, London: Lawrence & Wishart 1975ff.

Nicos Poulantzas

CCC   *Classes in Contemporary Capitalism* (1974), London: New Left Books 1975.

CD   *The Crisis of the Dictatorships* (1975), 2nd ed., London: New Left Books 1976.

FD   *Fascism and Dictatorship* (1970), London: New Left Books 1974.

PPSC   *Political Power and Social Classes* (1968), London: New Left Books 1973.

SPS   *State, Power, Socialism* (1978), London: New Left Books 1978.

Name Index

Abendroth, Wolfgang 262-66, 268f.
Abercrombie, Nicholas 27
Abraham, David 15, 243
Adolphs, Stephan 19
Agnoli, Johannes 170f., 263f., 266, 268f.
Ahmad, Ajjaz 138 fn.
Allende, Salvador 235
Almond, Gabriel 31
Alnasseri, Sabah 220
Althusser, Louis 12f., 16f., 27-29, 33ff., 56f., 73f., 80, 93 fn., 108, 122f., 129, 138, 142, 144, 145, 151, 159 fn., 174, 183, 231, 236, 244, 267, 274, 277-79, 281
Altvater, Elmar 197 fn.
Anderson, Perry 282 fn., 285 fn.
Apeldoorn, Bastian van 203
Apter, David 31
Aronowitz, Stanley 29
Atatürk, Mustafa Kemal 192 fn.
Bachrach, Peter 82
Balibar, Etienne 29, 34-36, 38
Baratz, Morton 82
Barrow, Clyde 12, 20, 232 fn., 277 fn.
Bauer, Otto 264
Belina, Bernd 186 fn.
Benevolo, Leonardo 189
Bettelheim, Charles 181 fn.
Bieling, Hans-Jürgen 18 fn., 21
Bobbio, Norberto 285
Bonaparte, Louis 97, 108
Bonnett, Kevin 15
Böttcher, Herbert 186 fn.
Boukalas, Christos 18 fn.
Bourdieu, Pierre 107, 182 fn.
Brand, Ulrich 17, 21, 186 fn., 210, 249 fn., 273 fn.
Bratsis, Peter 29
Brenner, Robert 244
Bretthauer, Lars 9 fn., 18, 20, 72
Brodie, Janine 131f.
Bromley, Simon 15

Buci-Glucksman, Christine 160, 278 fn., 285
Buckel, Sonja 21, 63.
Burgio, Alberto 286
Bush, George W. 18
Castells, Manuel 38 fn., 196f.
Clarke, John 14
Coleman, James 31
Connell, Robert 129f.
Critcher, Chas 14
Croce, Benedetto 278, 285
Daly, Mary 130f.
Deleuze, Gilles 142
Demirović, Alex 14, 17, 19, 22, 242, 249, 281, 281 fn.
Desrosières, Alain 176 fn.
Deutsch, Karl 31
Dreier, Wiebke 186 fn.
Easton, David 31
Elsuni, Sarah 161 fn.
Engel, Antke 161 fn.
Engels, Friedrich 58, 97 fn., 108, 145 fn., 170-173, 186
Esping-Anderson, Gösta 130
Esser, Josef 162
Felder, Michael 210 fn.
Fischer, Anita 19
Flatow, Sibylle von 63 fn.
Freud, Sigmund 80 fn.
Foucault, Michel 21, 123, 126f., 138ff., 154, 156f., 159, 161f., 165f., 171-174, 176, 178f., 181-183, 187, 218 fn.
Francioni, Giani 288 fn.
Gallas, Alexander 9 fn., 18-20, 18 fn., 77fn., 89
Gaulle, Charles de 12, 53, 56
Gentile 285
Georgi, Fabian 18
Gill, Stephen 209
Gindin, Sam 203-207, 211, 227
Gold, David 32
Görg, Christoph 17, 210

Gossweiler, Kurt 243
Gottschalk, Karin 176 fn.
Gowan, Peter 206
Gramsci, Antonio 11, 14, 17, 22, 28, 33, 42, 44, 53, 56, 58, 68, 73, 81, 85f., 109, 115, 123, 129, 140-142, 156, 160, 194 fn., 235f, 244, 249, 258, 277-91
Habermas, Jürgen 163
Hack, Lothar 220 fn.
Hall, Peter 203
Hall, Stuart 14f.
Haney, Lynne 132
Hardt, Michael 222, 227
Hartmann, Michael 220 fn.
Harvey, David 186, 194 fn., 196
Haug, Wolfgang Fritz 101, 278 fn.
Hegel, G.W.F. 57, 63, 127 fn., 265, 286
Heigl, Miriam 22, 273 fn.
Heinrich, Michael 97fn.
Hirsch, Joachim 10 fn., 16f., 20, 154 fn., 163 fn., 218 fn., 249 fn.
Hobbes, Thomas 146
Holloway, John 10, 89-93, 96
Hudson, Michael 206
Huisken, Freerk 63 fn.
Huke, Nikolai 18
Ingrao, Pietro 253, 253 fn.
Jacques, Martin 15
Jefferson, Tony 14
Jessop, Bob 14f., 15 fn., 17f., 20, 27f., 32, 79 fn, 84, 101, 103 fn., 118 fn., 138f., 152, 154, 162, 165, 171, 187, 243, 249, 275 fn., 277, 278 fn., 281
John, Vincenz 176 fn.
Kannankulam, John 9 fn., 10 fn., 18, 20, 154 fn., 163 fn., 218 fn.
Karakayali, Serhat 19
Kautsky, Karl 204
Kelsen, Hans 158
Knapp, Gudrun-Alexi 161 fn.
Koch, Max 20, 107, 232 fn.
Kohl, Helmut 108
Korsch, Karl 33
Kostede, Norbert 77 fn.
Krätke, Michael 172
Kuhn, Thomas 180 fn.

Labriola, Antonio 33, 278
Lacan, Jacques 14, 80 fn., 146, 160
Laclau, Ernesto 15, 152, 242 fn., 282 fn.
Lapassade, George 11 fn.
Läpple, Dieter 188 fn.
Laski, Harold 50
Lefebvre, Henri 186-188, 190 fn., 199
Lenin, V.I. 15, 204, 271, 279 fn., 279f., 282, 290f., 290 fn.
Lewis, Jane 130
Liguori, Guido 285
Lindner, Urs T. 21, 89 fn., 138, 177 fn., 210 fn.
Ling, Tom 15
Lipietz, Alain 16
Lo, Clarence 32
Lockwood, David 115
Lorau, René 11 fn.
Losurdo, Domenico 287
Ludwig, Gundula 19
Lukács, Georg 33, 278
Luxemburg, Rosa 11, 247, 271, 290 fn.
Mahnkopf, Birgit 197 fn.
Mandel, Ernest 18, 201f.
Marx, Karl 10, 33, 43, 56f., 60, 62-66, 75, 89-92, 94, 96-105, 109-112, 116, 118, 139, 144, 145 fn., 151, 155, 159 fn., 163, 171f., 172f., 179, 182, 186, 232f.
Massey, Doreen 187
Miliband, Ralph 12, 16, 27-29, 27 fn., 32, 34, 277
Mouffe, Chantal 152, 160, 282 fn.
Müller, Wolfgang 11, 56 fn.
Naumann, Matthias 186 fn.
Negri, Atonio 222, 227
Neumann, Franz 155-159, 165
Neusüß, Christel 11, 56 fn.
Nietzsche, Friedrich 138, 139 fn.
Nowak, Jörg 18, 18 fn., 20f, 122.
Offe, Claus 82
Panitch, Leo 15, 203-207, 211
Parkin, Frank 119
Parsons, Talcott 32
Pashukanis, Evgeny 41, 56, 58, 61ff., 64, 69, 147, 155, 163

Piciotto, Sol 10
Pierce, Charles Sanders 98fn.
Pijl, Kees van der 205 fn.
Plato 193
Porter, Theodore M. 176 fn.
Postone, Moishe 89-93, 96, 105
Pühl, Katharina 19
Rake, Katharine 131
Rancière, Jacques 152
Roberts, Brian 14
Rousseau, Jean-Jacques 146
Sablowski, Thomas 14 fn., 15f., 21
Samuelson, Paul A. 170
Sartre, Jean-Paul 33, 277
Sauer, Birgit 19, 132f.
Sayer, Derek 99fn.
Schelsky, Helmut 107fn.
Schmitt, Carl 146
Servan-Schreiber, Jean Jacques 201
Shaw, Martin 206
Smith, Neil 186
Sohn-Rethel, Alfred 243
Soja, Edward 187
Soskice, David 203
Spinoza, Baruch de 288
Statz, Albert 208
Strange, Susan 206
Stützle, Ingo 9 fn., 18, 21
Therborn, Göran 29, 34, 38, 160
Thomas, Paul 28, 34
Thomas, Peter 22, 278 fn.
Tosel, André 279 fn.
Turner, Bryan 27
Urry, John 27
Weber, Max 32, 36 fn., 56, 107, 119 177
Wissel, Jens 18, 21, 167 fn., 217 fn., 218 fn., 225 fn.
Wissen, Markus 16 fn., 17, 21, 223 fn.
Wöhl, Stefanie 19
Wright, E.O. 16, 32, 107f., 117

Subject Index

Accumulation (see also capital) 32, 32 fn., 37, 42, 44, 47, 49, 53f., 67, 91, 94f., 98f., 103 fn., 113, 115, 149, 151, 175, 181f., 205 fn., 220f, 226, 233, 236, 244, 255, 274
  Primitive accumulation 112
Administration (see also bureaucracy) 32, 46, 48-52, 68, 75f., 83, 114, 143, 152, 159, 162, 176f., 177 fn., 211f., 252, 261, 268f., 275
Alter-globalization movement 228, 256f., 275
Army (see also military) 51, 74, 83, 114, 143, 177, 236, 266, 275
Anti-Semitism 228, 239 fn.
Authoritarian socialism 9, 12
Authoritarian statism 9, 13, 15, 18, 48ff., 79, 225, 244, 246f., 252, 263, 272, 275

Base-superstructure 35, 58f., 62, 66f., 79, 159 fn.
Bonapartism 48, 50, 97, 108, 237, 269
Bourgeoisie (see also capitalist class, power bloc) 11, 41, 46, 49, 52, 61, 80, 80 fn., 83, 109, 115, 149f., 155, 161f., 167, 171, 188, 203, 216ff., 244, 247, 249f., 254, 255, 261f., 265f., 271, 280f., 286-289
  Interior bourgeoisie 21, 70, 113, 205, 205 fn., 218-221, 227
  Petty bourgeoisie 49, 109-112, 117f., 232f., 238-243
Bureaucracy (see also administration) 10, 47, 50, 52, 69, 75f., 78, 81, 83, 86, 147, 177, 177 fn., 252, 271f.

Capital (see also accumulation, bourgeoisie, capitalist class) 89ff.

Fractions of capital 11, 45, 49, 84, 113, 116, 151, 175, 182, 204, 207, 254f., 267
Monopoly capital 51, 112, 239-241, 243, 263
Transnational capital 112, 203, 208, 212, 216ff., 220, 222, 274
Capitalist class (see also bourgeoisie, power bloc) 33, 42, 66, 94f., 102, 104, 109-113, 221
Capitalist mode of production 20f., 30f., 41, 57, 60, 76f., 90-92, 96-98, 102f., 105, 107f., 109 fn., 111f., 123, 141, 141fn., 148, 150f., 170-173, 176, 178f., 182, 188, 190-192, 197, 231f., 265, 268
Capitalist social formations 19f., 38, 41f., 80, 105, 109, 171, 173 fn., 195, 249, 282
Civil society 15, 18, 62, 85f., 123, 127 fn., 209f., 212, 225, 249, 270, 277, 278 fn., 280, 282-289
Class (see also bourgeoisie, capitalist class, class struggle, proletariat, working class) 107ff.
Class domination 19, 30, 42, 47, 54, 66f., 80f., 84, 114, 119, 162, 201, 237, 289
Class fractions 43, 46, 48, 67f., 73, 81, 82fn., 83f., 109, 111f., 114f., 117, 133, 149-151, 157-159, 174f., 182, 204, 207, 210, 217, 222 fn., 232f., 236, 243, 248, 254f., 264, 266f., 269f.
Class struggle 28-30, 33, 37, 42, 44, 46, 48, 62f., 65, 78, 80f., 89ff., 114, 122, 124, 126, 140f., 140 fn., 152, 162, 197 fn., 201, 204, 225, 234-238, 242 fn., 252, 264, 273
Coercion (see also state monopoly of violence) 47, 61, 66-68, 90, 104, 132, 249, 277, 284-288.
Cohesion 21, 31, 45, 47, 54, 80, 115f., 154ff., 161, 165-167, 195, 197, 202, 208f., 212, 238f., 265
Comintern (see also communism/ communist parties) 233, 238-240, 242

Commodification 49, 95, 134, 274
Communism/Communist Parties (see also Comintern) 56, 237, 242f., 247, 252, 253fn., 264
Euro-communism 11, 269, 272
Competition 62, 66, 68, 90, 99, 112, 133, 151, 203f., 209, 217, 226f., 255, 272
Condensation (see also materiality, relations of forces, state power, state theory) 72ff.
Consent (see also hegemony) 41, 46, 64, 68, 74, 158f., 161f., 166f., 172, 174, 249, 284-286, 288f.
Constitutionalized violence (see also state monopoly of violence) 46, 159
Crisis 231ff.
Crisis of Fordism 13, 129, 216, 243f., 255
Crisis of Marxism 159, 239, 283
Crisis tendencies 31, 49, 115, 202
Economic Crisis 49, 202, 231ff., 238, 244
Hegemonic Crisis 14, 45-47, 236, 238f.
Ideological Crisis 47, 49, 236, 238f.
Political Crisis 45f., 52f., 226, 231ff., 238 fn., 239, 244, 270
State Crisis 45, 49, 52, 234
Critique of political economy 10, 20, 57, 89ff., 109 fn., 151, 286

Democracy 46, 48, 130, 167, 242 fn., 261ff.
Direct/grassroots democracy 247, 251-253, 257, 271f., 290
Economic democracy 273
Liberal/bourgeois democracy 42, 45, 156, 271
Representative/parliamentary democracy 22, 48, 51f., 127 fn., 247, 251, 257, 261, 263, 268f., 271, 290
Theory of democracy 22, 272f.
Democratic socialism 11, 13, 19, 22, 250, 271, 284
Dependency (see also: interior

bourgeoisie) 190, 205 fn., 219
Dependency theory 223
Dictatorship of the proletariat 289
Discourse/discourses 12, 16ff, 73, 113, 115, 119, 131f., 139, 146, 167f., 174-176, 178-180, 180 fn., 182, 209, 225, 233 fn., 242 fn., 256
Division of labour 16, 19, 37, 42, 49, 62, 76f, 110f., 113-116, 123f., 126, 155-160, 173f., 173 fn., 174fn., 188, 190-192, 194, 196, 261, 268f., 273f.
Gendered division of labour 127, 131, 135, 145, 160
International division of labour 120, 220
Domination (see also: class/class domination, patriarchy, race, racism) 138ff.
Political domination 20, 41, 60, 66, 110, 124, 158, 173, 234, 236, 240, 244, 263, 265, 281
Relations of domination 10f., 16-18, 20, 65, 72, 75, 87, 109, 122, 126, 152, 159-161, 165, 181, 228
State domination 73-76, 86, 127f., 152, 177 fn., 261f., 274, 287

Economic state apparatuses 225, 236
Economism 28, 33f., 38, 58, 61f., 110, 123, 147, 233, 235, 238, 242
Empire 189f., 192, 203, 205-207, 211, 225-228
Empiricism 28
Epistemology 12, 14, 20, 27ff., 57f., 60 fn., 143, 193
Equilibrium of compromise 30f., 47, 50, 52, 104, 149, 239, 263f., 287
Essentialism 74, 128, 146, 218, 267
Eurocommunism 11
Europe 27, 33, 116 fn., 122, 201ff., 219, 221, 270, 272, 275, 284, 287 fn.
Eastern Europe 9, 198
European Integration 21, 198, 201ff.
Western Europe 10, 18, 109, 113, 189, 201, 205, 283
Exceptional state/exceptional regime 12, 14, 15, 22, 33, 42, 45-49, 51, 53, 192, 195, 237, 269
Exploitation 10, 18, 22, 31, 35, 42, 65f., 76, 110, 115, 120, 123, 133, 135, 139, 140, 180 fn., 201, 204, 239

Family 86 fn., 123, 125-128, 130f., 133, 144f., 176
Fascism 11f., 15, 22, 28, 33, 34, 42, 45f., 48, 53, 231, 234, 237-244, 269
Feminism (see also gender) 122ff., 128, 130, 132, 134
Feudalism 61, 114, 189, 191, 192
Finance 37, 225, 244, 267
Fordism 13, 16, 21, 39, 53f., 129, 167, 187, 194 fn., 216, 221, 224, 243f., 255, 258
Foreign direct investment 113, 202, 204f.
Form (see also law)
Form analysis 14, 20, 41-44, 53f., 56ff., 61, 63-67, 69, 77, 90, 96, 98f., 101-104, 154, 163, 165, 171, 218 fn., 249
Commodity form 61, 65, 96, 99f., 104, 111
Economic form 66, 90, 182
Institutional form 42, 198, 201, 219, 286, 289
Legal form 61, 64f., 75, 154-156, 162-167, 172 fn.
Political form 11, 57, 66-68, 171 fn., 172, 204, 222, 251, 273
Social form 61, 90f., 96, 163, 165, 251
State form 14f., 17, 22, 38f., 53, 79, 95, 131-133, 171f., 175, 212, 223, 262, 268, 275
Value form 57, 63, 99, 101, 155, 163
France 94, 95, 97, 107, 108, 218 fn., 231, 235, 255, 277
Frankfurt School 155, 239 fn.
Functionalism 32, 57, 127, 146, 162, 171, 197

Gender (see also division of labour, feminism, women's movement) 16,

18-20, 85, 122ff., 139, 142, 145, 151, 160f., 176, 192, 197 fn., 258
Germany 9, 12, 33, 53, 56, 58, 107f., 231, 235, 238f., 241-243, 262 fn., 267, 272, 289
Globalization 17, 38, 52, 70, 113, 115f., 186f., 197-199, 205, 216f., 224, 258
Governmentality 21, 138, 146, 150, 165, 166, 167, 182
Greece 13, 237, 243

Hegemony (see also consent, crisis) 11, 18f., 21, 44, 48-53, 58, 68f., 85f., 110, 116, 122f., 129, 140, 152, 156-162, 165-167, 172, 199, 203, 234f., 237, 239-241, 249f., 252, 264, 267, 277f., 282, 284-286, 288, 291
   Bourgeois hegemony 46, 52, 244, 248, 287
   Crisis of hegemony 14, 45-47, 236, 238
   US hegemony 198, 207, 221
History (see also time) 17, 31, 33, 35 fn., 37, 53, 78, 100, 102, 117, 159 fn., 186ff., 193-195, 197f., 198, 250. 267 fn.

Ideology (see also crisis) 12, 15, 31, 34f., 37, 47, 51, 58, 72-74, 80, 110, 112, 118f., 129, 144, 145, 159 fn., 173f., 178, 236-240, 242, 261, 264, 268, 278
International Monetary Fund 198
Imperialism 13, 15, 37, 39, 53f., 118 fn., 202-205, 219, 224-227, 287 fn.
Integral state (see also hegemony) 22, 85f., 277ff.
Intellectuals 57, 134, 162, 164, 173, 178, 221, 239
Internationalization 14, 17, 21, 49, 70, 113, 115f., 198, 201f., 204, 208, 216-221, 243, 256, 259
Interpellation 15, 73, 145, 242
Interventionist state (see also state intervention) 45, 52, 53, 195
Instrument 13, 19, 43, 56, 74, 86, 113f., 124, 126, 132, 144, 149, 155f., 162, 165f., 202, 210, 217, 246f., 254, 263, 271f., 277, 279, 281f., 285-287, 289
Isolation effect 144, 157, 161f.
Italy 12, 16, 33, 231, 238, 241-244

Knowledge 21, 54, 75, 97, 101, 111, 123, 140-144, 163, 170ff., 193, 196, 267

Labour movement (see also class, class struggle) 122, 167, 239, 262f.
Labour power 18, 37, 49, 60f., 61, 65f., 91f., 94f., 100f., 104, 112, 134f., 158, 161
Law (see also legal form, rule of law) 18, 21, 31, 37, 42, 44, 46, 48, 50, 52, 62, 64-66, 69, 72, 74-77, 81, 85f., 100, 112, 133, 154ff., 170, 172 fn., 174, 176-180, 204, 221, 233, 249, 257, 262f., 265, 278 fn.
Legitimacy/legitimation 41, 47, 49, 51f., 60, 68, 74 fn., 76, 143 fn., 152, 202, 226f., 236, 257, 267

Market 61, 64-66, 77, 92, 97f., 107, 113f., 117, 131, 133f., 144, 151, 158, 179f., 188, 191f., 202-204, 207-209, 220, 223f., 262f.
Marxism 11, 13, 33, 56-58, 62 fn., 90, 122, 129, 134, 145 fn., 154, 159, 180 fn., 187, 239, 242, 244, 279, 283
Marxism-Leninism 239, 242
Material concession 68, 244, 248
Materiality 20, 44, 68, 72ff., 123, 126f., 131, 141, 144, 149, 155, 158, 162f., 165f., 174 fn., 179, 222, 250, 255, 257-259, 281
Methodology 164
Micro-power (see also discourse) 166, 247
Military (see also army) 177f., 206, 227, 239, 267, 286
   military dictatorship 13, 45, 48, 237, 243, 269, 270

SUBJECT INDEX   301

Mode of production 14, 35-37, 39, 58, 104
  Capitalist mode of production (CMP) 20, 21, 30f., 33, 41, 49, 57, 59-62, 64, 66, 76f., 90-92, 96-98, 101-103, 105, 107-109, 111f., 123, 141, 148, 150f., 157, 170-173, 175, 178f., 182, 188, 190f., 197, 231f., 265, 268, 287
Monopoly capitalism 37, 53, 56, 238, 262

National state 18, 21, 53f., 54, 77, 116, 167, 192, 197-199, 201f., 205, 208f., 211f., 216-227, 258, 274f.
Nationalism 242
Neoliberalism 9, 12, 18, 21, 52f., 129, 132ff., 207, 209f., 212, 217, 221, 224, 244, 254ff., 258, 276
Networks 10, 32, 47, 54, 79, 84, 86, 133, 178, 208, 210, 212, 216ff., 239, 251, 270, 272, 275
Normal state 46ff.

Ontology 140
Over-determination 78, 80, 122, 125, 166, 265

Party 46, 49-52, 55, 68, 86, 237, 239ff., 247, 253, 267 fn., 269, 271f.
Passive revolution (see also hegemony) 286ff.
Patriarchy (see also domination) 120, 126ff., 130, 145, 160
People 22, 43, 50, 64, 76f., 85, 92, 94, 107, 110, 114, 126, 135, 139 fn., 155, 157, 158, 160f., 164, 167, 176, 189, 191, 195, 206, 211, 227, 236, 253f., 256f., 259, 261f., 266ff.
Periodization 45, 52
Police (see also coercion) 51, 74, 83, 85, 152, 178f., 236, 266f., 275
Political economy 10, 17, 20, 57, 89, 91, 102 fn., 109 fn., 151, 178ff., 182f., 203, 207, 258, 286
Political scene 269

Politicism 165, 278
Politics 9-12, 20f., 27, 38, 41, 43f., 50, 52, 58f., 63, 66, 70, 77, 80, 86, 110, 112, 117ff., 122f., 127ff., 131, 138, 140 fn., 141f., 145 f., 148-152, 159 fn., 162, 166, 172, 177, 179f., 182, 198f., 204, 208, 211ff., 222-226, 231, 235, 252, 261, 265, 269, 274, 281, 288
Popular struggles 25, 123, 126ff., 133, 270
Post-structuralism 138 fn., 142, 160
Power 16, 18-22, 32ff., 37ff., 41-54, 60f., 64ff., 68, 73f. 83-86, 91-95, 100f., 104, 109, 112, 114ff., 119, 122-135, 138-144, 146ff., 150, 152, 155-161, 164-167, 173-183, 190, 192, 203-208, 210f., 216-228, 232-235, 237-241, 243f., 247f., 250, 252, 258, 261-275, 278-291
Power bloc 18, 21, 41f., 45, 49-54, 68, 83, 109, 112, 114f., 133, 157ff., 161, 204, 211, 217-223, 225-228, 232-235, 238-241, 243, 252, 265-270, 274
Power/knowledge 142f., 170ff.
Private v. public 85, 127, 131, 133, 144, 189f., 252, 270, 275, 287
Privatization 22, 128, 132, 144, 246, 254-257
Proletariat (see also: working Class) 80, 109, 111, 241, 279, 286, 289
Property 18, 31, 32 fn., 36, 60ff., 81, 97 fn., 114, 145 fn., 150, 155, 163, 176, 209, 268

Race 85, 160f., 206
Racism 122, 228
Reductionism 16, 21, 57, 91ff., 98, 105, 119, 135, 138 fn., 140, 151f., 154, 160, 242 fn., 253
Reform 56, 89, 128, 138, 175, 204, 251, 258, 283
Regional theory 12, 38, 59, 232
Regulation approach 16, 244
Relations of production 19, 13, 21, 30f., 34f., 37f., 42, 44f., 53, 59-63, 65ff., 69, 73-79, 81, 83, 85f., 93f., 114, 117, 123,

125f., 128, 145, 156, 160, 173f., 179, 188-192, 194, 196f., 218f., 241, 265, 273

Relations of forces 11, 17f., 20, 67f., 77ff., 81ff., 85ff., 96, 104, 125f., 128, 141, 149ff., 154, 156-161, 163, 166, 170, 176, 182, 197, 199, 202, 207, 210, 212, 217f., 220ff., 224ff., 233, 247ff., 251, 255, 264, 270, 273, 277

Relative autonomy (see also form) 14, 31, 37, 57, 60, 66-69, 80f., 115, 150f., 158f., 162, 165f., 171, 205, 235, 240, 266

Representation (see also democracy) 11, 46, 50ff., 73, 76, 86, 157, 196, 208, 226, 234, 239, 249, 269

Repression (see also coercion) 31, 33f., 37, 44, 46f., 66f., 72, 74, 83, 132, 142, 146, 156f., 166, 174, 178, 201, 236, 242, 248, 250, 258, 267

Reproduction 10, 15, 20f., 30f., 35, 37, 44f., 49, 51, 54, 60f., 65-68, 73, 77f., 81, 84, 87, 91f., 94ff., 100-104, 110, 114, 126, 145, 161, 167, 173, 180, 193f., 198, 202f., 205ff., 212, 218f., 224, 233-237, 252, 254, 259, 265, 269

Resistance 31, 44, 47, 49, 64, 73, 78 fn., 81, 87, 92f., 100, 127 fn., 130, 139, 149, 197, 221, 228, 242, 251, 256f., 270, 275, 283

Revolution 27, 31, 39, 44, 91, 97, 152, 167, 197, 234, 249f., 258, 279, 284-290

Rule of law 42, 46, 48, 50, 52, 72, 85f., 155, 157, 165, 262

Selectivity 43, 82, 84, 149, 223, 228, 248, 255

Separation (see also form) 20, 41, 44, 47, 57, 59-63, 75, 77, 85, 111f., 128, 131, 143, 158, 162, 172f., 177 fn., 179-183, 218, 223f., 235, 251f., 261f., 265, 268-271, 275

Social democracy 130, 161, 240, 242, 247, 251f., 267 fn., 271, 281ff., 291

Social forces 42f., 46, 48, 84, 119, 156, 162, 166, 175, 220, 234, 247ff., 258, 262ff.

Socialism (see also democratic socialism) 9, 11-13, 19, 22, 39, 237, 242 fn., 246f., 250, 254, 263, 269, 271ff., 274, 283, 284ff., 290f.

Social movements (see also alter-globalization movement) 17f., 49, 85, 159 fn., 167, 246ff., 252f., 256, 258, 270, 272f., 275f.

Social transformation 252

Sovereignty 33, 44, 146-48, 155f., 173, 176, 179, 190, 194, 209, 211, 263, 286

Space 16, 21, 38, 76f., 167, 186ff., 210, 216f., 222, 224, 226, 235, 243, 250

Stalinism 279-81, 291

State apparatuses 13, 18, 21, 31-34, 37-39, 41, 43f., 46-51, 54, 61, 66-69, 72-87, 102, 113-15, 125-27, 132f., 139, 142f., 149, 151, 156, 158f., 161, 166f., 171-75, 178, 180-83, 197 fn., 198, 201, 205, 209, 212, 221f., 225, 232f., 235f., 241f., 244, 247-53, 255, 258, 263, 265f., 269-71, 274f., 282f., 285-87, 289f.

State derivation debate 10, 17, 20, 36 fn., 56-58, 61, 63-67, 77, 77 fn., 101f., 150f., 156, 172 fn.

State intervention (see also interventionist state) 10, 53, 58, 60, 155, 166, 236, 275

State monopoly of violence 46, 66, 147, 159, 164, 172 fn., 227, 284f.

State personnel 250, 256

State power 16, 32, 43f, 47, 52, 54, 122f., 127 fn., 130, 157, 174, 177, 203, 205, 206 fn., 211, 233, 235, 244, 247, 252, 261, 266, 271, 280, 282, 284, 286

State theory 10f., 14, 16f., 19-21, 27, 29, 30 fn. 36 fn. 56, 66, 69, 73, 75, 77-79, 81, 85-87, 119, 122, 124, 128f., 134, 146, 154, 157, 161, 165, 170f., 182f., 206 fn., 210-12, 232, 234, 280f., 284

State transformation 65, 139, 221

SUBJECT INDEX

Strategy 13-15, 19, 22, 44, 105, 128, 132, 139, 144, 148f., 165, 174f., 181f, 202f., 231, 243, 246, 250, 255, 258, 266, 270-71, 274, 276, 279-83, 288-90, 290f.
Structure 10, 20, 30-33, 35, 42, 45, 49, 50, 51, 58-62, 66f., 69, 77-81, 83, 86, 89, 90 fn., 91, 93, 93 fn., 98, 107-111, 114-16, 119, 123-30, 133, 140f., 144, 148, 158, 177f., 180, 189, 202f., 205f., 209f., 213, 217, 218, 222, 227, 235, 248, 249, 252, 254, 258, 263-67, 271f., 277, 288
Structuralism 13, 27ff., 29, 34, 36, 38, 108, 163
Surplus value 30, 32, 37, 45, 59, 63, 99, 100, 110, 116f., 233, 241, 241 fn.

Territory (see also space) 77, 150, 186ff., 211, 274
Totalitarianism (see also fascism) 192, 195
Tendency of the rate of profit to fall 233
Time 16, 21, 38 fn., 67, 76, 77, 91, 101, 186ff., 193-97, 199
Trade unions 123, 209, 256, 269
Transnational capital (see also globalization) 112f., 203, 208, 212, 216ff., 220-222, 226, 274

USA 33, 118, 219

Value/value form 57, 61, 63, 98f., 101, 105, 151, 155, 163, 176, 196, 197 fn., 199, 236
law of value: 62, 66

War of manoeuvre (see also hegemony) 47, 281ff., 288
War of position (see also hegemony) 280f., 281ff., 288f., 290f.
Welfare state 10f., 56, 115, 128-31, 133, 212
Women's movement (see also feminism, gender) 120, 128f., 134, 161, 167, 251
Working class (see also proletariat) 46, 49, 89f., 94, 100, 102, 104, 109-111, 116-18, 122, 130, 160, 197, 232, 238, 239, 241f., 244, 253, 263, 265, 274, 280-82, 287f.
World Trade Organisation 198, 221, 223
World view 73, 85, 122

www.ingramcontent.com/pod-product-compliance
Lightning Source LLC
Chambersburg PA
CBHW051420290426
44109CB00016B/1374